THE BULGARIAN ORTHODOX CHURCH:
A Socio-Historical Analysis of the Evolving Relationship Between Church, Nation and State in Bulgaria

JAMES LINDSAY HOPKINS

EAST EUROPEAN MONOGRAPHS, BOULDER, CO
DISTRIBUTED BY COLUMBIA UNIVERSITY PRESS, NEW YORK
2009

EAST EUROPEAN MONOGRAPHS, NO. DCCXXV

Printed in the United States of America

"Praise God from whom all blessings flow..."
(Christian doxology)

To my son
Adam James Iliya Samuel Hopkins

CONTENTS

ACKNOWLEDGMENTS

I want to acknowledge the help of the staff of New College, University of Edinburgh and particularly the staff and students who make up the family within the Centre for the Study of Christianity in the Non-Western World. Margaret and Liz were always an inspiration to a flagging student. To my supervisor and former director of the centre, Professor David Kerr, I profess my profound appreciation. Your friendship, enthusiasm and erudite knowledge of the subject motivated me to achieve more than I could ever imagine.

To Janice Broun, I express my thanks for her hospitality on the Black Isle and for opening her personal archive on the history of the Bulgarian Orthodox schism. To Spas Raikin, Professor Emeritus of History in East Stroudsburg University in Pennsylvania, I am grateful for his generosity in sending me his political and autobiographical accounts of life in Bulgaria during the early years of communism. To my dear friend Miroslav Rashev, thank you for your help in introducing me to the wonders of the National Library in Sofia. I also wish to thank Daniela Kalkandjieva and Ina Merdjanova who assisted me in detailed areas of my research and who together established the Centre for Inter-religious Dialogue and Conflict Prevention within Sofia University. I am also grateful to Bistra Nikolova, lecturer in Church History at Sofia University who helped guide me through the perils of Balkan history. I am eternally grateful to the people of Bulgaria and express my support for them as they struggle to express themselves as the nation is driven interminably towards European union. As the Bulgarian people are yet again being forced to accept an alien way of life, I am reminded of their strength, courage and sufferance in surviving the rule of despots, empires and political philosophies. I also wish to express gratitude to my readers Gary Griffith and Peggy MacPhee.

Simultaneous with this research process my wife and I adopted our son from Bulgaria. I am therefore thankful for the doctoral process itself because in the midst of some very difficult times dealing with international bureaucracy the act of research kept me focussed and sane. I am happy to say the adoption was finalised and now in my son a part of Bulgaria shall remain with me forever. Ultimately I could not have reached this moment without the love and support of my family and to Muriel and Adam I shall be forever grateful.

ABBREVIATIONS

AMAE CP	Archives du Ministere des Affaires Etrangeres, Correspondance Politique
AMAE MD	Archives du Ministere des Affaires Etrangeres, Memoires et documents
ANF	Archives Nationales de France
BANU	Bulgarian Agrarian National Union
BCP	Bulgarian Communist Party
BCRC	Bulgarian Central Revolutionary Committee
BHR	Bulgarian Historical Review
BOA	Basbakanlik Ottoman Archive
BOC	Bulgarian Orthodox Church
BRA	Board of Religious Affairs
BSCC	Bulgarian Secret Central Committee
BSP	Bulgarian Socialist Party
BWP	Bulgarian Workers Party
CSHB	Corpus Scriptorum Historiae Byzantinae
CUP	Committee for Union and Progress
DRA	Directorate of Religious Affairs
FF	Fatherland Front
GOTR	Greek Orthodox Theological Review
IMRO	Internal Macedonian Revolutionary Organisation
MGH	Monumenta Germaniae Historica

MPE	Ministry of People's Education
MSCC	Moscow Slavonic Charitable Committee
NMSII	National Movement for Simeon II
OSCE	Organisation for Security and Cooperation in Europe
PU	Priests' Union of Bulgaria
RFE	Radio Free Europe
RL	Radio Liberty
UDF	Union of Democratic Forces
USNA	United States National Archive
WCC	World Council of Churches
АВПР	Russian Federation Archive of Foreign Politics
АМВнР	Archive of the Ministry of Foreign Affairs
АЦИАИ	Church History Archive and Archival Institute
БИА НБКМ	Bulgarian Historical Archive of the National Library "Sts. Cyril & Methodius"
БРП(к)	Bulgarian Workers Party (communists)
ГАРФ	Gosudarstven Russian Federation Archive
ГСУ БФ	Annual of Sofia University "St. Kliment Ohridski" Theological Faculty
ДА-Пловдив	State Archive – Plovdiv
ДВ	State Gazette
ИАНГ	The Archive of Naiden Gerov
Изв. НБКМ	Reports of the National Library "Sts. Cyril & Methodius"
ИПр	Historical Review

МВнР	Ministry of Interior Affairs
НА БАН	Academic Archive of the Bulgarian Academy of Sciences
НБКМ Ор. отд.	National Library "Sts. Cyril & Methodius", Oriental Department
ОДА	Regional State Archive
ПС	Proceedings of the Holy Synod
РМС	Young Communists League
РЦХИДНИ	Russian Centre for Preservation and Study Documenting Modern History
Сб БАН	Collection of the Bulgarian Academy of Sciences
Сб НУНК (Сб НУ)	Collection for National Folklore, Science and Literature
СДС	Union of Democratic Forces
ЦА	Church Archive
ЦВА	Central Military Archive
ЦДА	Central State Archive
ЦДИА	Central State Historical Archive
ЦИАИ	Central Historical Archival Institute
ЦК	Central Committee
ЦПА	Central Party Archives

GLOSSARY

Archimandrite	An eminent priest/monk. The rank below a bishop
Archpriest	A title of honour given to a non-monastic priest
Autocephaly	Status of a local Orthodox Church with administrative independence
Ayan	An autonomous local leader
Bashibazouks	A group of irregular Turkish soldiers
Boyar	Bulgarian aristocracy
Cheta	Insurgent armed bands
Chorbadzhi	Well-to-do Bulgarian traders
Devshirme	Child levy – culling of Christian children to serve Ottoman bureaucracy
Exarch	Ecclesiastical position higher than a metropolitan but lower than a patriarch
Eyalet	Administrative province of the Ottoman Empire (reformed into vilayets)
Firman	Imperial Ottoman decree
Groschen	The Prussian 'groschen' became the widely accepted international monetary unit until the late 19th century: 1 Taler = 30 Groschen = 360 Pfennigs
Hadith	Body of tradition regarding Muhammed and his followers
Haidouks	Rebel brigands
Hieromonk	A priest-monk
Ilinden	Celebration of St. Elijah (literally Elijah's Day)
Janissaries	Personal sultanic guard

Jizie	Tax collected from non-Muslims
Kadi	Muslim judge
Kahn	Title borne by medieval Bulgarian rulers
Kurdzhali	Nomadic bandits
Medresse	Islamic school
Megali	'The Great Idea' – political programme to create Greater Greece
Metropolitan	Presiding bishop of a province or capital city
Millet	State recognised community defined by religion
Mount Athos	Autonomous island of the Greek Coast inhabited by Eastern Orthodox monasteries
Osmanlili	Ottoman citizenship
Patriarch	The head of an autocephalous Church
Phanariots	Members of influential Greek or Hellenized families (originally from the Phanar district of Constantinople)
Pomak	Indigenous Bulgarian Muslim population
Porte	The government of the Ottoman empire
Proselytism	The act of converting someone from one faith to another
Protosingel	Administrative assistant to a Metropolitan
Raya	The Sultan's Christian tax-paying subjects
Sanie	Leading position within Ottoman administrative hierarchy
Sanjak	Early Ottoman province, later a sub-province
Sharia	Islamic law
Sipahi	Ottoman landlords who provided troops in proportion to the size of their property (*timars*)

Tanzimat	The reformist 'reorganisation' of the Ottoman Empire
Timar	Land held in exchange for military service
Uniate	Eastern Churches that retain their own liturgy but submit to papal authority
Vakif	A tax-exempt pious foundation
Vali	Ottoman governor
Vilayet	Ottoman province
Vizier	Ottoman minister of State
Yataghan	Ottoman sword with a curved single edged blade
Zveno	Bulgarian pressure group set up in 1927

ILLUSTRATIONS

INTRODUCTION

Ignorance of Eastern Orthodoxy is the
scandal of Western Christianity.[1]

AIM OF THE RESEARCH

As a Western Christian who has worked in Bulgaria for over a decade, the researcher and author of this thesis agrees with the sentiment expressed in the words quoted above from Anthony Ugolnik. It is not only the general lack of knowledge displayed by the western public and their political leaders that is surprising, but the historical, cultural and spiritual ignorance exhibited by my missionary peers in Bulgaria is indeed a scandal. Without an understanding of Eastern Orthodoxy's history, culture and rich Christian heritage, how can western Christendom seek to minister in predominantly Orthodox societies without indulging in intra-Christian proselytism? If western Christians are to minister in the Balkans with any degree of cultural sensitivity and respect, it is imperative that they have an understanding of Eastern Orthodox life, history, thought and doctrine.

This missiological and cultural imperative prompts the research that has been undertaken in the preparation of this thesis. However, it was not Ugolnik's reference to the ignorance of Western Christendom that underlay the investigation. Anyone interested in the position of the church in Bulgaria is confronted by a seemingly contradictory reality: although a mere 0.5% of the population are actively involved in the church, over 85% of Bulgarians consider themselves to be Orthodox, or more precisely Bulgarian Orthodox. The connection between religious, societal and national identity is acutely felt at every level of Bulgarian society to the extent that it is believed that 'to be Bulgarian is to be Orthodox'. One could liken this bond to an umbilical cord transferring strength and security between mother and child, between church and nation. This raises important questions about the relationship between the church and the people, their history as a nation, and their identity as a state which it is the intention of this thesis to pursue. The question is not whether there should be a church-state relationship; this may be an issue

---

[1] A. Ugolnik, *The Illuminating Icon*, (Grand Rapids, 1989), p. 30.

1

for Western secular analysts of Balkan politics, but not for Bulgarians themselves for whom it is a given fact of history and modern national identity, the sole distinguishing factor separating Bulgarians from those powers that have dominated them in the past. The question, rather, is the nature of this relationship, and its import for the church.

In order to answer this question the thesis will examine aspects of Bulgarian history from the ninth century when King Boris introduced Christianity to the Kingdom of Bulgaria, establishing the Bulgarian Orthodox Church as an autocephalous entity, and inaugurating its relationship with the state. Against this background, more detailed attention will be given to the evolution of the church's relationship with political power when the latter exercised itself in the form of Byzantine and Ottoman imperial rule, Bulgarian nationalism, and Communist and post-Communist national governments. This thesis will demonstrate that the impact of the Bulgarian Orthodox Church (BOC) upon Bulgarian history and its relationship with state and society, has been built on a mixture of historical fact and fiction, myth and manipulation, especially during the Bulgarian national revival. The national myths depict the BOC as synonymous with national self-consciousness. Ugolnik's 'scandal of ignorance' applies therefore not only to Western neglect of Bulgarian history, but to historiographical trends within Bulgaria itself.

It is hoped that this thesis will contribute toward the remedying of both dimensions of ignorance by offering an account of the historical development of church-state relations in Bulgaria that recognises the power of myth while at the same time seeking to give a more dispassionate interpretation of the empirical history of the church in Bulgaria.

RESEARCH METHODOLOGY

Although covering a broad socio-historical spectrum, the research falls specifically within the discipline of ecclesiastical history and is intended to contribute to the fields of World Christianity and Balkan missiology. The research is based primarily on Bulgarian sources including unpublished archival, published literary and oral materials. These have been extensively consulted in a way that combines textual analysis and qualitative interpretation. The result is not an innovative account of the history of church-state relations in Bulgaria, for the contours of this history are quite well established in terms of periods, persons and problems, and they are broadly accepted as the framework within which this thesis has been written. It is hoped, however, that the research herein offers a re-interpretation of that history that is original, and contributes a new perspective to European, Balkan and Orthodox Church history.

The focus of the thesis centres on the Bulgarian national revival period, which commenced in the late eighteenth century and remains a historic, economic, social and cultural phenomenon in which Bulgaria takes great pride for, following five centuries of Ottoman domination, it led to Bulgaria reclaiming ecclesiastical autonomy in 1870 and national independence in 1878. Following this pivotal period in history the Bulgarian state raised the Bulgarian Orthodox Church to a pre-eminent position within Bulgarian society. Contemporary Bulgarian historiography claims that without the church the nation would not have survived the Ottoman era that is portrayed in terms of Islamic tyranny, and that the national revival would not have occurred. The BOC is therefore portrayed as the cultural and spiritual protector and liberator of the nation. The present hierarchy of the BOC not only accepts this honour, but actively advances its position as national saviour by maintaining that anything which is not 'orthodox' is to be identified as the antagonistic or hostile 'other'.

By subjecting this period of history to scientific scrutiny, based substantially on the evidence of the archival record itself, this thesis will reveal a number of discrepancies between verifiable history and modern interpretations of history. For example, against the received opinion that the BOC struggled to preserve the Bulgarian nation under the evil tyranny of Ottoman rule, the archival evidence proffers a picture of a religiously tolerant Ottoman society. This contradiction requires critical questions to be asked of key elements in Bulgaria's traditional historiography, subjecting it to socio-historical criticism, and distinguishing myth from verifiable history.

Following an extended discussion of the Byzantine and early Ottoman eras, the thesis will focus its investigation on the nineteenth and twentieth centuries, providing a detailed account of the evolution in church-state relationships during the later Ottoman, inter-war, Communist and Post-Communist periods. Comparative analysis will measure prevailing mythological assumptions against archival evidence, thereby offering a balanced interpretation of Bulgarian and South-Eastern European history.

Qualitative research was undertaken to comprehend contemporary attitudes of Bulgarian society toward the church. Between March and

June 2003 thirty-five research assistants, in ten centres (Sofia, Plovdiv, Veliko Turnovo, Varna, Burgas, Stara Zagora, Sliven, Blagoevgrad, Shumen, Ruse) asked a number of questions, listed in Appendix Four – 7,203 questionnaires were returned for analysis. A number of Group discussions were also organised to assist toward a further comprehension of Bulgarian relations with the Orthodox Church. The results from the returned questionnaires were used as a starting point for a discussion forum, which took the form of an introductory overview of the situation followed by a period of open debate directed by a chairperson. It was agreed that there was a distinction between Bulgarian 'Orthodox' religiousness and affiliation to the Church. The general conclusion was that this is because Orthodoxy is comprehended not as religion but as a national and cultural identifier.

The primary objective of this research is to advance an interpretative narrative of church-state relations in Bulgaria throughout this pivotal era in Bulgarian history that clarifies the evolution of political and societal thinking on the national role of the BOC based on verifiable sources and shorn of nationalistic bias. By doing so it will elucidate the influence of political, religious and national ideology on history.

SURVEY OF LITERARY SOURCES

Such claim as this thesis can make to originality amongst other western histories of the Bulgarian Orthodox Church is the priority it gives to Bulgarian sources, archival, published and oral. In this way full account is given of Bulgarian national self-understanding and its interpretation of the role of the Bulgarian Orthodox Church in the formation and development of the Bulgarian State. It is within this framework that critical analysis will be applied, on the basis of the archival record itself, in order to come to a scientific assessment of the Bulgarian Orthodox Church in its relations with the Bulgarian nation, state and society throughout the research period.

This investigation would have been impossible only few years ago, and even today remains a formidable task. Although national state and church archives are now officially open to the public they continue to remain beyond the reach of those without proper contacts. Even when one is granted admission, investigation remains a difficult exercise. For example, the archives of the Bulgarian Holy Synod, although in the process of reclassification, remain in great disarray; many of the most important documents having been lost, stolen or destroyed. The majority of the archives examined in the course of this research are housed, classified and well maintained within the Sts. Kiril and Methodius National Library in Sofia.

Recent bilateral agreements between Bulgarian and Turkish governments have resulted in the opening of archives relating to the Ottoman period that were previously closed. Amongst the disclosed Turkish archival sources that have been critical for the present research is the *Basbakanlik* Ottoman archive, which is now in the process of being translated into Bulgarian. This archive includes the Jizie (*джизие*) tax registers for Bulgaria that provide data on religious affiliation of the populace. These registers make it possible to trace religious demographic change during the Ottoman period, from the fourteenth to nineteenth centuries. The Ottoman archives held within Rila Monastery, which date from the early fifteenth to the late nineteenth centuries, also provide the researcher with a wealth of detailed material that evidences a surprisingly stable relationship between the Ottoman authorities and the Christian population of Bulgaria.

A vast array of published literature in the Bulgarian language is available for the study of the history of the Bulgarian Church. However, this literature needs to be handled selectively and with appropriate criticism. The first book of the Bulgarian National Revival, Paisii Hilendarski's *A Slavo-Bulgarian History* (1762), must take pride of place. This book marks the transition in Bulgarian cultural history from a state of stagnation to creative thought and action, leading to independence almost one hundred years later. However, it was to take a further sixty-seven years before Hilendarski's expectations received widespread public influence, due to another work, by the Russian author Yuri Venelin, entitled *The Ancient and Present Day Bulgarians* (1829). This fired the historical and national imagination of the Bulgarians, raising Bulgaria to a pre-eminent place amongst other Slavic nations by uncovering its Slavic origins, rather than its presupposed Turko-Tatar connections. Marin Drinov's *Historical Survey of the Bulgarian Church* (1869) can be described as the first modern history of the Bulgarian Church. However, it was a Czech, Constantin Jiracek, whose *Geschichte der Bulgaren* (1876) was the first to recognise the presence of a double yoke of tyranny upon the Bulgarians, in the form of Ottoman political, social and economic oppression combined with Greek religious, cultural and linguistic subjugation.

By the late nineteenth and early twentieth centuries a negative attitude towards the Ottoman authorities came to predominate in Bulgarian
literature. As the national independence movement strengthened, the
need to generate animosity toward the Ottomans became important.
Stefan Zakhariev's attempt to promote a faked seventeenth century
document entitled, *The Chronicle of Metodi Dragonov* (1870), is a
perfect example of this operation. The chronicle was for many years
accepted as the most striking evidence pointing to enforced Islamic conversion of Bulgaria's Christian population, and was intended ultimately
to create civil unrest in nineteenth century Bulgaria. Histories written
during the communist era such as Petur Nikov's *Revival of the Bulgarian
Nation* (1929) and particularly Petur Petrov's *The Fateful Centuries of
the Bulgarian Nation* (1975) and *More Traces of Violence Regarding the
Imposition of Islam* (1987), continued to emphasise the enforced conversion of innocent Bulgarian Christians to Islam. A similar anti-Islamic
sentiment pervades Bulgarian history to the present day as Ottoman
oppression continues to be included in Bulgarian educational textbooks
as historical fact.

If few Bulgarian scholars have challenged this reading of history, it
must be due in part to the strength of the traditional relationship between
church and nation. Only three contemporary Bulgarian authors have
braved the animosity of popular opinion by questioning the role of the
church as national saviour: Ina Merdjanova in *Religion, Nationalism and
Civil Society in Eastern Europe* (2002); Daniella Kalkandjieva in *The
Bulgarian Orthodox Church and National Democracy* (2002) and Maria
Todorova in *Balkan Identities* (2004).

Within English language literary sources the starting point for any
information on Bulgaria has been Mercia MacDermott's *History of
Bulgaria* (1982) and Professor Richard Crampton's *A Concise History of
Bulgaria* (1997). However, their interpretation of the role of the Orthodox Church is concise in the extreme. Although dealing with the Balkans
in general, Misha Glenny's *The Balkans* (1999), gives a clear perspective of Bulgaria's political progression during the period 1804-1999,
particularly in comparison to the other Balkan states. One of the most
significant authors writing on Bulgarian affairs over the last decade has
been Janice Broun, particularly her journalistic investigations into the
Bulgarian Church schism. Nevertheless, the book that challenges the
traditional Bulgarian historical perspective to the greatest degree is
Carsten Riis's *Religion, Politics, and Historiography in Bulgaria* (2002).

CHAPTER OUTLINE

The thesis is organised in eight chapters covering the lengthy period from the inception of the Bulgarian Church in the ninth century to the present day. Although the historical focus of the thesis centres on the activities of the Church during the national revival period it is necessary, to fully appreciate the historical depth and intricate development of relations, to investigate an earlier period in Bulgarian history. Chapter One fulfils this requirement by providing a brief historical evaluation, covering the period 865-1396, of four critical moments which influenced the formation of modern Bulgarian Orthodox identity. The chapter will demonstrate that 'nationalism' has been an integral part of the Bulgarian Church from its inception and has helped create the unifying link between church and nation throughout the centuries.

Chapter Two investigates the early Ottoman period of Bulgarian history, covering the four centuries from the Ottoman conquest to the onset of the Bulgarian National Revival process (1396-1812). It examines the socio-historical factors that shaped Christian-Muslim relations during the era, and challenges the widely accepted *catastrophe theory* which argues that during the period of Ottoman domination Bulgaria suffered under a relentless process of Islamicization, at the hand of the Ottoman authorities. Progressing from this argument, the chapter emphasises the significance of two Bulgarian clergymen, Paisii of Hilendar and Sofroni of Vratsa, as the first promoters of the national revival. By comparing their activities with the Ottoman evidence the chapter will ask whether the *catastrophe theory* is national myth or a verifiable fact of Bulgarian history.

Chapter Three examines the cultural regeneration of the Bulgarian National Revival that grew in intensity during the nineteenth century. By investigating the political, economic and social circumstances that made renaissance possible, the chapter provides a framework in which the role of the Bulgarian Orthodox Church during this period of cultural awakening can be assessed. Whereas the Church claims to have kept alive Bulgarian cultural, educational and linguistic traditions, it will be argued that the journey towards cultural revival, although influenced by the Church, was driven more by foreign and secular forces.

Chapter Four focuses specifically on the struggle to re-establish Bulgarian ecclesiastical independence after its abolition by the Ottomans in 1393. It investigates the development of the National Church movement, and seeks to explain why independence was not achieved until

1870. The chapter will offer a critical analysis of the Bulgarian Orthodox Church's claim that its endeavours were central to the National Revival movement, providing a model for liberation from Ottoman domination. It will demonstrate that the concept of Bulgarian ecclesiastical independence germinated not from national sentiment, but as a result of foreign national intrigue. It will be argued that it was the involvement of foreign political agents from Poland, France and Russia that steered the Bulgarian Church toward independence.

Chapter Five investigates the period between the establishment of the independent Bulgarian State and the end of the Second World War (1878-1945). Church-state relations are analysed in relation to the struggle for national independence, and it will be shown that, far from being raised on a pedestal and praised for its role during the national revival period, the church was actually marginalised from the political arena and denied a political voice in the new state. It will be argued that the church forged a role for itself in Bulgarian foreign and national affairs by willingly becoming an instrument in Bulgarian geopoliticism, allowing itself to get used by the government, as a necessary medium toward the realisation of its goal of national unification.

Chapter Six investigates the effects of almost fifty years of communism in Bulgaria from 1944-1989. It seeks to clarify the church's position as a national institution under socialism, by examining the development of Orthodox church-state relations under the communist regime, which stood in sharp contrast to the atheistic rhetoric of the government. The church's involvement in the Process of National Rebirth – the term for the policy of socialist self-legitimisation by appealing to Bulgarian history in ways that suited its purposes – will be examined, with critical appraisal of the so-called *catastrophe theory*. In light of new evidence allegations of church collaboration in these events will be considered.

Chapter Seven moves forward in time to research church-state relations in post-communist Bulgaria (1989-2005). It examines this period through the perspective of the struggles between the church's pro-socialist and anti-democratic political forces, a clash that culminated in schism. In its efforts to survive, the BOC emphasised its historical/cultural role as saviour of the Bulgarian nation. Nevertheless, the church failed to reassert itself as a dominant force in contemporary Bulgarian society. A number of qualitative research techniques will be applied in an attempt to assess contemporary society's attitude to the Bulgarian Orthodox Church.

Finally, Chapter Eight collates all the evidence to construct a historical interpretation of church-state relations in Bulgaria in relation to modern debates about the genesis and nature of nationalism. Against the historical analysis of previous chapters, it rejects the modernist hypothesis that nationalism only developed as a concept in relation to the emergence of nation-states in the nineteenth century, and argues instead for a direct connection between modern Bulgarian nationalism and pre-nineteenth century pro-Bulgar sentiment. In a concluding reflection on the nature of the relationship between church and nation in Bulgaria, the chapter seeks to relate the particularities of the Bulgarian case to contemporary research in the area of religion, nation and nationalism.

1

THE BULGARIAN CHURCH: AN HISTORICAL ANALYSIS OF THE CRITICAL MOMENTS IN THE FORMATION OF BULGARIAN ORTHODOX IDENTITY (865-1396)

The historical focus of this thesis centres on the period dating from the onset of the Bulgarian National Revival in the late eighteenth century through to the present status of the Bulgarian Orthodox Church (BOC). However, in order to respect the sacred historical tradition of Orthodoxy, to fully appreciate the development of relations between church, nation, and state in Bulgaria and to provide a significant comprehension of Bulgarian national and ecclesiastical self-understanding, it is important to investigate an earlier era in Bulgarian history. This chapter aims to provide a brief historical synopsis covering five centuries from the introduction of Christianity into Bulgaria (865) to the period of the Ottoman conquest (1396). Thereby the investigation will be enabled to identify and analyse the critical processes that have formed modern Bulgarian Orthodox identity.

The chapter will demonstrate that when Bulgaria's Khan Boris opted for Byzantine rather than Latin Christianity, he determined the destiny of Bulgaria residing in the framework of Eastern Orthodoxy. It will also show that the church not only influenced the Bulgarian nation, but was itself considerably affected by forces both secular and nationalist, which help to explain the formation of modern Bulgarian Orthodox identity. The evolution of terms such as nation and nationalism, particularly in the Balkans, are commonly considered to have originated in the nineteenth century during the birth of nation states. This chapter will argue, however, that such concepts germinated within Bulgaria and her Church at a much earlier stage in her history.

This chapter includes an historical examination of four significant events that have contributed to the formation of Bulgarian Orthodox identity and shaped the trends of modern Bulgarian history: the introduction of Christianity into Bulgaria, Byzantine and Latin ecclesiastical disputes over jurisdiction of Bulgaria, the importance of vernacular translation and the influence of Bogomilism. The critical episodes chosen for investigation have been widely accepted by secular and ecclesiastical historiographers as being important markers in Bulgarian history, without suggestion that they were crucial in the formation of the Bulgarian Church.[1] Other Eastern scholars such as D. Obolensky, L. Simeonova and F. Dvornik have produced detailed historical studies of particular 'critical' events such as the Bogomil movement, the Latin and Byzantine disputes, and the Cyrillo-Methodian tradition, but again have not analysed them as significant in Bulgaria's ecclesiastical formation. The highlighting of these particular issues as pivotal in the construction of Bulgarian ecclesiastical organisation has arisen solely as the result of this research. The findings of this research will advance the argument that Eastern Orthodox religion, Slavic vernacular translation and Bulgarian nationalist sentiment cohered as an indigenised national characteristic only after the Bulgarian Church transformed itself by accepting and promoting the popular dissenting traits of the Bogomil movement.

KHAN BORIS AND THE CONVERSION OF BULGARIA

This section will investigate the intimate involvement of Khan Boris (852-888) in Bulgaria's Christianisation process. It will look briefly at Bulgaria's history before Christian conversion and will explore some of the diplomatic, political and spiritual problems that faced the khan during Bulgaria's transition from a system of traditional religious belief. It will plot Boris' participation through the institution and development of ecclesiastical organisation and will seek to determine whether the progress of the Church under his reign mirrored his own nationalistic desire.

Bulgaria Before Christianity

The Bulgarian State was initially established in AD 681 within the former Roman imperial provinces to the south of the River Danube. Under the command of Khan Asparuch (681-700) the Bulgars crossed the Danube and established themselves in the provinces of Moesia and Thrace. Asparuch and his successors were imposing figures whose warlike tendencies and territorial gains led quickly to Bulgaria's southeastward expansion to the Byzantine capital of Constantinople. The Bulgars were not the only people to inhabit the region at this time. Slav raiding parties had been settling in the provinces since the early sixth century, while Emperor Justinian I (527-565) had been trying to restore Roman imperial authority in Africa and Europe. Nevertheless, the Slavs proved no match for the aggressive Bulgars and although in the majority soon acquiesced to the new invaders.

The Byzantine Empire was also compelled to acknowledge the marauding Bulgars in a humiliating peace treaty agreed with Khan Asparuch in 681. From this firm foothold the Bulgars increased in power and territory over the following centuries. In 811 Khan Krum (803-814) defeated and killed Byzantine Emperor Nicephorus I (802-811) as the Byzantine Empire sought to vanquish its Bulgar problem.[2] Two years later Krum defeated Nicephorus' successor, Michael I, sacked the city of Adrianople and reached the walls of Constantinople. Only Krum's sudden death in 814 spared the Empire further humiliation. Krum's successors, Omurtag (814-831) and Malamir (831-852), agreed terms with the Byzantine Empire halting the eastward expansion of the Bulgar State which instead continued westward into Macedonia. Thus by the early ninth century Bulgaria's population comprised the proto-Bulgars and majority Slav inhabitants.[3]

Little is known about the religious beliefs and practices that the proto-Bulgarians brought with them from the Central Asian plains. It appears to have been a highly syncretistic faith influenced by Iranian traditional beliefs. They preserved certain traits from the traditional religion of their Turkic forefathers. An inscription from the reign of Omurtag records a sacrifice to Tangra, who has been linked to the Turkic sky-god Tengri.[4] The cult site at Madara, near Shumen, preserves the most celebrated symbol of the proto-Bulgarians traditional religion in the rock face relief known as the 'Horseman of Madara' which is accompanied by an inscription to the god Tengri. Byzantine sources also describe sacrifices of human beings and animals offered by Khan Krum outside the walls of Constantinople before the horrified eyes of the Christian defenders of the city.[5]

The traditional religion of the Bulgars quickly came into contact with Christianity which had survived within the inherited Romano-Byzantine society. Add to this original Christian presence the many thousands of Christian prisoners taken during Bulgaria's wars of expansion and the Christian population constituted a significant number.[6] This Christian element was constantly suspected of owing allegiance to the Byzantine emperor and patriarch in Constantinople and therefore faced intermittent persecution. The hostile attitude toward Christianity was linked to a fear of Byzantine imperialism, the perception being that the Christians would make converts from among the Bulgars, weakening traditional religious beliefs and strengthening Byzantine authority among the majority Slav population. This perception was so pervasive that when Khan Omurtag's son, Enravotas, converted to Christianity, it is recorded that he was executed as part of the Christian repression of 833.[7]

By the ninth century the tension between the Bulgarian State and the Christian religion had become acute. The number of Christians among the khan's subjects had grown alarmingly, and now included members of the Bulgar elite. Moreover, diplomatic relations with neighbouring states were becoming increasingly complicated as surrounding Christian nations refused to cooperate with Bulgaria's 'pagan' state. Lastly, Bulgaria's traditional religious beliefs were becoming internally divisive, in so far as they distinguished between Bulgar and Slav, at a time when her rulers were attempting to replace tribal polycentrism with a centralised government.

Fig. 1 The 'Horseman of Madara'

The Conversion of Bulgaria

Historians identify the baptism of Khan Boris in 865 as the moment of Bulgaria's conversion to Christianity. However, Bulgaria's process of Christianisation commenced long before the reign of Boris. Indeed, as soon as the Bulgar invaders set foot south of the Danube they began to feel the impact of Byzantine Christian civilisation. Tens of thousands of Christian prisoners of war continued to practice their religion among the non-Christian Bulgar population. We know Christian influence was strong as it had reached within the Bulgarian royal family. Nevertheless, the fear of Byzantinisation through Christianisation set Bulgaria in an anti-Byzantine orbit. The problem facing Boris was that adopting Byzantine Christianity as the religion of State would have implied becoming a small cog in a larger ecclesiastical and political wheel. How would it be possible for Bulgaria to enjoy the advantages of Christianity without falling under the political sway of the Byzantine empire? It was this religious and political dilemma which had forced the Bulgars to look westwards and which motivated Khan Omurtag to form an alliance with the Frankish empire against Byzantium.[8] Thus, by the time Boris became ruler the pro-Frankish partnership dominated Bulgarian foreign policy.[9] At this point South-Eastern Europe divided into two main coalitions: the Bulgarian and Frankish kingdoms on one side, and Byzantium, Moravia, and the Slav tribes of Serbia and Croatia on the other.

In 862 Boris met with Louis, King of the Franks, to discuss military and religious collaboration, inviting him to send clergy to teach and convert the Bulgarian nation to Christianity.[10] As a result, the following year Byzantium encouraged its coalition partners to attack Bulgaria, alarmed by the rumour that Boris was planning to accept Latin Christianity. Besieged on three fronts and simultaneously stricken by natural disaster, earthquake, plague and disastrous harvest, Boris was forced to sue for peace.[11] The main conditions of the treaty were that the alliance with the Franks had to be terminated and Bulgaria would accept Christianity via Constantinople.

Boris' worst fears materialised as his infant Christian nation fell completely under the control of the Patriarchate of Constantinople, which acted as an agent of the Byzantine government. The Bulgarian ruler, having accepted the faith of the Byzantines, was compelled to acknowledge the sovereignty of the Byzantine emperor, much to the consternation of Pope Nicholas I.[12] Despite western concerns Boris showed no signs of willingly subjecting himself to Constantinople's demands. Indeed, to counter Byzantine influence he immediately appealed to the West for help. Thus, as the Christianisation process advanced, a ruthless competition arose between Rome and Constantinople for ecclesiastical jurisdiction over Bulgaria.

Problems Facing Boris During the Conversion Process
<u>Diplomatic, Political and Spiritual Reasons for Conversion</u>

By the ninth century Christian presence in Bulgaria could no longer be ignored. Even Boris' own family had been influenced by the religion: his sister was a Christian as was his cousin Khavkan Petur, later to be sent as an envoy to Rome and Constantinople.[13] Boris himself may already have been personally convinced of the truth of Christianity and his later abdication to enter a monastery in 889 suggests that he had become a deeply religious man. However, apart from personal matters of faith, other factors emerged to drive the khan towards a decision in favour of converting his nation to Christianity.

Amongst these factors was the continuing struggle to unite the cultural division between the Bulgar and Slav inhabitants and fully integrate the population into a single nation. Boris, the diplomat, comprehended the delicate situation that existed and the divergent possibilities for his nation's domestic and international future. He needed to consolidate the ethnically divided population and a common religion offered a means to this end. Boris understood that the only way to persuade the majority Slav population to accept his reign and Bulgar authority would be to create a Christian dominion. He also needed to transform Bulgaria into a legitimate international power and by adopting Christianity he would gain wider diplomatic acceptance for Bulgaria.

These factors drove Boris toward the establishment of Christianity in Bulgaria. Despite constant Byzantine pressure to accept their ecclesiastical rule, Boris struggled to maintain his freedom to choose the direction of conversion that would allow him to reap the most benefit for his nation. Thus, Boris attempted to ally with the Franks rather than Byzantium. However, Boris' attempt to capitalise on his conversion by exacting diplomatic advantage for the Bulgarians came to nothing. Christianity, rather than being invited in, was imposed on Bulgaria by her most menacing foe. The Bulgarian ruler had miscalculated the international implications of Bulgaria's conversion. Despite recognising the internal pressures pushing Bulgaria towards Christianity, he failed to comprehend the significance that the Christian world would attach to the conversion of his nation, therefore underestimating the extent to which outsiders would insist on being involved in Bulgarian affairs in the name of the Christianising process.

Dealing with Dissenters

Byzantium's aggressive entry into Bulgaria, justified in the name of assisting its conversion, introduced elements into the Bulgarian social context that significantly compromised Boris' authority. Confusion circulated throughout the country, centred around the conviction that the acceptance of Christianity and repudiation of traditional religion would have drastic consequences on Bulgaria. This fear and resentment led the boyars to organise a nation-wide revolt in 865.[14] For the Bulgarian aristocracy Boris' acceptance of Christianity was not only a denial of ancient tradition but a symbol of betrayal, gifting the nation into the hands of its fiercest enemy. Furthermore, with the introduction of this new religion, the khan no longer claimed to be *primus inter pares* among the boyars, but accepted the Byzantine title of prince established by the grace of God.[15]

This situation made it difficult for Boris to maintain his authority. Coupled with the onslaught of foreign influences, prevailing domestic unrest undermined, at least temporarily, Boris' control over the nation. He re-established order by brutally crushing the rebellion in a crucial battle near the capital of Pliska. Fifty-two of Bulgaria's aristocracy, the leaders of the revolt, were put to death, along with their families and servants.

The Institution of the New Religion

Boris survived the social and political disturbances that had gripped the nation immediately after his decision to Christianise Bulgaria, but other problems awaited him. After consolidating his authority in Bulgaria Patriarch Photius of Constantinople (r. 858-867, 877-886) wrote Boris a letter painting the ideal portrait of a Christian leader. He hailed Boris as the new Constantine and reminded him of his duties to Christianise the nation, he alone being responsible to direct his realm from "darkness to light." [16] In order to live up to Byzantine expectations Boris ought to accomplish for his own people what Constantine the Great had achieved for the Romans: to convert his subjects to the true faith whose one and only source was the Patriarchate of Constantinople. For Boris, only recently relieved of the crisis accompanying his conversion, Photius' letter laid upon him the terrible burden of teaching his subjects the outward forms and basic tenets of the Christian faith. Boris did not shirk his responsibility. From the time of his baptism to the end of his reign he absorbed himself in the establishment of Christianity among his subjects.

The first major task Boris faced in instituting Christianity within Bulgaria was to provide for the baptism of his subjects. Understanding that it was his personal duty to undertake this fundamental step in the Christianisation of Bulgaria, Boris supervised this mission for the remainder of his reign. During the time between his conversion in 864 and his appeal for Latin assistance in 866, Byzantine priests undertook the task of baptising the nation.[17] Latin priests took up the baptismal role after replacing the Byzantines, but Boris remained unhappy with the progress being made and asked for additional clergy to accomplish the task. Some twenty years later the baptism of the nation had still not been completed, particularly in the remote regions of the country. Therefore in 885 when the disciples of Cyril and Methodius arrived after their expulsion from Moravia, they were welcomed and put immediately to the work of baptising the Macedonian Slavs.[18]

Boris was also faced with the problem of educating his subjects in the basic concepts of Christian doctrine. However, this process did not occupy Boris' attention, his efforts were almost exclusively directed towards baptising the nation. This lack of attention stemmed from the khan's inadequate grasp of the doctrinal side of the new faith and from his inclination to perceive Christianity purely as a ritualistic discipline. By the year 866 Boris had already revealed that he was confused by the various strands of the Christian faith which were present in Bulgaria: "should we obey all of these according to the various meanings or what should we do?"[19] It would seem likely that his confusion about the source and the content of Christian doctrine had some bearing on his decisions to abandon Byzantium and Rome during his reign.

Whilst investigating the range of activities involved in establishing the Christian religion in Bulgaria one is struck by how often the crucial issues seem to have rested on relatively minor matters. Boris' concern with these minor issues and Pope Nicholas' meticulous care in providing explanations for what seem to be petty technicalities, as opposed to

Patriarch Photius' total neglect of practical consideration, may well provide the secret to the Christianisation process in Bulgaria. These 'minor
issues' were dealt with superbly by Nicholas in his *Responsa Nicolai
Papae ad Consulta Bulgarorum*. The issues dealt with ranged from the
treatment of rebel boyars, to the permissibility of sexual intercourse
during lent, from the organisation of the church in Bulgaria, to the
procedure for dealing with Islamic books which had played a part in
Bulgarian traditional beliefs, from the use of jokes and spells to the
function of Christian prayers. The *Consulta* was above all concerned
with behaviour rather than doctrine. It dealt not with trivialities but with
matters that vitally concerned the lives of every Bulgarian. What was
Christianity going to mean for the way Bulgarians dressed, washed, ate,
made love or war, and how offensive would the new faith be to their
ancestral gods?[20] One is thus drawn to the conclusion that the decisive
elements in the process of instituting Christian practice in Bulgaria were
the ability of both the khan and the church to provide two things: the
substitution of Christian practices for everyday traditional usages not
acceptable to the Church and meaningful rationales for abandoning
practices which were less clearly religious but which ran counter to
Christian tradition. Conversion, therefore, did not involve the glorious
rebirth which Photius and Nicholas eloquently described; rather it
entailed the tortuous process of substituting Christian practices as recog-
nisable equivalents for time honoured traditional usages. The burden
upon Boris was to make evident the equivalence and acceptability of the
new ways.

The Development of Formal Ecclesiastical Organisation

While contending with the numerous complications associated with
the teaching of Christian doctrine and practice in Bulgaria, Boris
engrossed himself in the development of formal organisation within the
emerging Bulgarian ecclesiastical community. This problem was complicated not only by the novelty of Christianity in Bulgaria but also by
the involvement of external foreign elements, which had to be respected
whilst establishing a specifically Bulgarian ecclesiastical organisation.

There is no clear evidence to indicate what organisational pattern
the first Byzantine clergy followed after their arrival in 864/5. We can,
however, compare the procedures employed by the Byzantine mission to
Moravia in 863 when Patriarch Photius commissioned Constantine-Cyril

and Methodius to lead a missionary expedition. If the same procedures were used in Bulgaria, we can assume that the original Bulgarian mission would have been led by one or two figures whose authority rested primarily on their reputation as pious, learned men of exemplary Christian life and their designation as missionary and spiritual leaders by the imperial government and patriarch. Photius made it abundantly clear from the outset that the leadership and head of the emergent Bulgarian Church would come from Constantinople. Indeed, nowhere in his pastoral letter to Boris did he indicate the need to establish indigenous ecclesiastical organisation in Bulgaria: the Greek leadership of the Patriarchate would suffice.

Khan Boris was clearly not satisfied with this declaration. In order to preserve the independence of his country, whilst continuing to reap the benefits of his new association with the Byzantine Empire, it was essential to construct an autonomous ecclesiastical organisation in Bulgaria. Boris must have been deliberating the idea of creating a separate patriarchy, as in 866 he asked Pope Nicholas I if it would be possible for Bulgaria to have its own patriarch and if so, how would he be ordained, and interestingly, could a khan hold the position of patriarch?[21] In these questions we can observe the political manoeuvrings of Boris' mind. He had begun to envisage a hierarchical arrangement of the most ambitious kind. However, as Photius before him, Nicholas promptly dismissed these possibilities. Instead he laid out a plan for the Roman organisation of the Bulgarian Church: a bishop would be appointed to Bulgaria, who in time would be granted the title of archbishop, who would then consecrate other bishops, who in turn would be able to elect future successors to the archbishop's position. Both schemes left the khan in no doubt that Bulgaria would always remain subordinate to external control from either Constantinople or Rome.

This ecclesiastical dilemma will not be covered in detail here, as the Latin-Byzantine struggle for Bulgarian ecclesiastical jurisdiction will be dealt with in the next section. However, it is important to recognise that, disappointed by both Rome and Constantinople, Boris exposed his intense desire to establish autonomous Bulgarian Church authority. He dispatched a diplomatic delegation to the Ecumenical Council of Constantinople in 870 to establish whether Bulgaria belonged under Byzantine or Latin jurisdiction. In doing so the khan created an auction for the ecclesiastical jurisdiction of Bulgaria where the winner would be the one offering the best incentive. The synod of the council granted jurisdiction to the Patriarchate of Constantinople.

In a letter written in 872/3, Pope John VIII indicated that Patriarch Ignatius (867-877) had appointed an archbishop in Bulgaria, contravening previous Byzantine rulings, and suggested that this concession was made by the Patriarchate to gain jurisdiction in Bulgaria in 870.[22] The evidence suggests that following a tenuous start Boris was now satisfied with the organisational progress of the Bulgarian Church. Indeed, by the 880's the ecclesiastical hierarchy of Bulgaria was so pliable to his will and so oriented to Bulgarian problems that it no longer felt any particular interest in the continuing jurisdictional battles between Constantinople and Rome. Toward the end of his reign Boris took steps to increase the number of indigenous clergy by sending large numbers of Bulgarians to Constantinople for monastic training. It is particularly significant that he sent his son, Simeon, to become a monk in 878. One might suspect that Boris planned for Simeon ultimately to return to Bulgaria and assume the role as its first patriarch.

The Introduction of Indigenous Clergy[23]

In 885 an unexpected opportunity arose which permitted Boris to progress toward his goal of introducing indigenous clergy sooner than expected. After the deaths of both Cyril and Methodius, the Germanic clergy forced their Slavic speaking disciples to flee Moravia abandoning their efforts to develop a Slavonic liturgical tradition in the region.[24] A number of these clergy found their way to Bulgaria where Boris welcomed them. The biographies of two of those Slavic missionaries, Kliment and Naum, provide insight into Boris' use of their talents and illuminate further his plans for Bulgaria.[25]

In the Macedonian region of his realm, where the population was predominantly Slav, Boris commissioned Kliment to be a missionary leader and teacher to the Slavs. The description of his task indicates that he enjoyed considerably greater authority than his title suggested as he worked independently of the Byzantine archbishop in Bulgaria. He was used specifically to convert Slavs to the new religion and to represent the khanate where Bulgarian lordship had not been popular. We know that he established schools where the best students were singled out to be ordained as presbyters, deacons and priests. This would prove to be a successful strategy in bridging the gap between Bulgar and Slav communities. The continuation of the Cyrillo-Methodian tradition began to produce solid Bulgarian ecclesiastical figures erudite in Byzantine theology but with Slavic linguistic skills. As indigenous clergy increased, Bulgaria's dependence on Greek and Latin clergy decreased. By 893 the Bulgarian State had approved the Slavonic alphabet and liturgy as the official language of church and state.

The Impact of Boris on Bulgaria's Conversion

When Boris died in 907 the Bulgarian Church had developed substantially from its inception some forty years earlier. This progress reflected Boris' own nationalistic desires for an autocephalous church within an independent and unified nation. His initial reasons for accepting Christianity had not been purely spiritual, but were also politically motivated, hoping that the new religion would be the unifying factor to bring the Slav and Bulgar elements of his population together as one nation. There was also the factor of power. Boris foresaw that his own authority would be internationally enhanced as a result of accepting Christianity and hence modelled his leadership style on the Byzantine emperor. However, many problems hindered his progress, particularly whilst the establishment of Christian organisation was dependent on external foreign involvement, reluctant to permit the growth of an independent Bulgarian ecclesiastical hierarchy. These anti-Bulgarian attitudes prevented the khan from promoting the organisational structure he so desired, especially since the two sources of missionary aid were engaged in bitter competition for jurisdiction in Bulgaria. However, the arrival of the missionary fugitives from Moravia put at the khan's disposal clergy prepared to teach, organise and establish an independent Slavic speaking church without Byzantine or Latin assistance.

Boris was the driving force behind every aspect of the Christianisation process in Bulgaria. He chose the moment of Bulgaria's conversion, he defined the rules that would govern his nation, he punished those who opposed the introduction of the new religion in Bulgaria, he decided which missionaries could enter the country and when their practice did not concur with his desires he expelled them in pursuit of his nationalistic goal. He eventually gained control of the ecclesiastical personnel who worked in Bulgaria and in doing so made the decisive move that resulted in the eventual adoption of the Slavonic rite within Bulgaria.

BYZANTINE AND LATIN ECCLESIASTICAL DISPUTES
OVER BULGARIAN JURISDICTION

The competition between Constantinople and Rome for ecclesiastical authority in Bulgaria took place prior to the Great Schism of 1054. Nevertheless, the tension between East and West was already apparent, the issue in Bulgaria being essentially one of canonical influence and territorial jurisdiction. The section will investigate the various periods of Latin and Byzantine ecclesiastical control in Bulgaria, revealing that in order to gain outright dominance one of the Churches eventually conceded to Bulgaria's nationalistic desire.

Bulgaria and Byzantium

By the mid-ninth century, Bulgaria, then the third largest kingdom in Europe, had indicated its readiness to adopt Christianity. This interested the Latin, Frankish and Byzantine Empires. The Bulgarians and the East-Franks had been on diplomatic terms since the late eighth century when the expansion of their respective kingdoms established a common border. Connected by the menacing threat of Byzantium and Moravia they renewed their treaty sometime in the early 860's. For this reason the Frankish clergy were the natural candidates to undertake the first missionary work amongst the Bulgarian population.

However, neither Constantinople nor Rome could afford to tolerate a strengthening of the Bulgar-Frankish alliance. For reasons of their own each empire wanted to bring Bulgaria under its jurisdiction, as a huge eastern territory would be a powerful ally in the field of continental diplomacy. Bulgaria's conversion to Byzantine Christianity would eliminate the constant military threat that Bulgaria presented to the empire and would create a missionary stepping stone for the proliferation of Eastern Christianity into Eastern and Central Europe. Equally, Bulgaria's conversion to Latin Christianity would open a route for the advance of papal influence among the Slavs, creating a Latin stronghold adjacent to Byzantium's capital and spiritual heart. A fierce rivalry developed over this mission field between the Christian powers of the day, leading Boris to ponder which of these Churches would best benefit Bulgaria.

Renewal of Byzantine Missionary Enterprise

The seventh and eighth centuries had been the unhappiest experienced by the Byzantine Empire in its long history. Its eastern and western territories had both been steadily eroded; the Mediterranean had been lost to the Lombards; the Avars had overrun its Danubian provinces and the eruption of Islam in the Middle East had wiped out the empire's oldest and holiest provinces; Slav and Bulgar infiltration of the Balkans further weakened this once great empire. Nonetheless, Byzantium survived this turbulent period. The Islamic threat temporarily abated after the displacement of the Umayyad caliphate of Damascus by the Abbasid caliphate of Baghdad in the middle of the eighth century. New administrative structures, or 'themes', were established within the slimmed down empire, enabling the tempo of diplomatic and economic life to quicken once again. One can point to the re-opening of the University of Constantinople in the 830's as a major reason for the resurgence of self-confidence and self-assurance within the empire.[26] The university in turn gave birth to a new body of scholars, ecclesiastics and politicians, from whom a revived sense of mission developed within Church and State. The key to understanding the Byzantine Empire's sense of mission is the notion that the emperor was the divinely appointed instrument of God for the achievement of His purposes on earth through the diffusion of the Orthodox Christian faith. Thus, the re-conquering of the Balkans meant both the Christianisation of the Slavs and their submission to imperial authority. Of this process Emperor Constantine Porphyrogenitus commented:

> The nations of those parts [the Balkans]...shook off the reigns of the empire of the Romans and became self-governing and independent, subject to none.... But in the time of Basil, the Christ loving emperor (867-886), they sent diplomatic agents, begging and praying him that those of them who were unbaptised might receive baptism and that they might be subject to the empire of the Romans, and the glorious emperor, of blessed memory, gave ear to them and sent out an imperial agent and priests with him and baptised all of them...and after baptising them he appointed for them princes whom they themselves approved and chose, from the family which they themselves loved and favoured.[27]

Unfortunately the conversion of Bulgaria was not so serene, but the quotation does reveal how the governing circles in Constantinople looked upon their world. Their words also help us understand the Bulgarian khan's reluctance to accept Christianity from Byzantium, for this would have been tantamount to acknowledging the suzerainty of its emperor.

The Byzantine Mission

Two events in the early 860's marked the beginning of a new asser-
tive phase in the Constantinople Patriarchate's ecclesiastical policy. The
first was a request for Byzantine missionaries received from Prince
Rastislav of Moravia; the second was the Bulgarian announcement that
the nation was preparing to adopt Christianity. The Byzantine Church
willingly dispatched clergy to Moravia with the goal of extending the
empire's sphere of influence in Central Europe. However, an alliance
with Moravia also provided the empire with a means of exerting pressure
upon Bulgaria, which lay between Byzantium and Moravia. This mission
was entrusted by Patriarch Photius to his friend Constantine-Cyril and
his brother Methodius, who according to their Slavic vitae were chosen
because of their profound knowledge of the Slavonic tongue.[28]

No sooner had the Byzantine mission left for Moravia than Photius
found himself with another challenge: Bulgaria's readiness to accept
Christianity. However, Bulgaria's final adoption of Byzantine Christianity was the result of a military operation planned with the utmost
precision by Caesar Bardas.[29] Photius was surprised by the Bulgarian
decision, admitting in an encyclical letter that he thought it strange that
the "barbaric and Christ-hating Bulgarian people" should have turned to
the Christian faith so suddenly.[30] The two Byzantine missions were
therefore undertaken in response to unexpected challenges, rather than as
the result of careful planning. Patriarch Photius was clearly a man of
quick and sober mind, capable of rapid assessment and action. Ostrogorsky rightly points out that "the greatness of Photius lies in his appreciation, clearer than anyone else at that time, of the near approach of this
era of new tasks and possibilities, for which he, more than anybody,
helped to prepare the way."[31]

After the baptism of Khan Boris, Patriarch Photius sent him a long
letter providing him with not only religious instruction but also advice
on leadership. The contents of the letter included most of the patriarch's
published papers including his, *Biblioteka, Questions to Amphilochios*,
and *Mystagogia*. However, the way in which the letter was received by
the Bulgarian court must also be considered. Modern scholarship has
suggested that the patriarch's letter was ignored in Bulgaria for two reasons: it was too difficult to translate the classical Greek text into the
Bulgarian vernacular, it being almost impossible to find Bulgarian
equivalents for the abundance of Christian terminology,[32] and secondly,

Boris had no time to take interest in the patriarch's copious admonitions because of the turmoil caused by Bulgaria's recent conversion.[33] While there is a certain legitimacy in these opinions, this research would suggest that they are overly simplistic. Could Photius, one of the most erudite men of his age, have been so naïve as to send a sophisticated document into the hands of an unintelligent barbarian? Surely a man who had spent many years in the imperial foreign office would not send an important diplomatic message that could not be interpreted. Moreover, Greek had been the official language of diplomacy between Byzantine and Bulgarian governments over the two centuries prior to Bulgaria's conversion. Also, the argument regarding the difficulty in translating Christian terminology is specious. Apart from having Christians among his own family, government and subjects, Boris employed aides whose sole task it was to guide Bulgaria through the Christianisation process. Therefore one must consider that Photius' letter was ignored not because of failure to comprehend it, but because the khan had already decided to abandon Constantinople and turn again to the West.

Bulgaria and the Papacy

The situation in which Pope Nicholas I found himself in the mid-ninth century with regard to Latin Christian expansion in eastern and south-eastern Europe was rather depressing. Byzantine Emperor Michael III had repeatedly refused to transfer Illyricum (the former Roman province that included the Balkans) back to the Papal See. Moravia's relationship with Rome was practically cut off due to the Byzantine mission operating in that region, and Bulgaria's union with the Patriarchate further blocked any papal initiative to expand its influence eastwards. Finally, gaining confidence Byzantium had begun to adopt an attitude towards the papacy that could only be characterised as denying papal claims to primacy in the Church. However, by the end of 866, this discouraging scenario took a fortuitous turn, with Bulgaria becoming the missionary battleground in which the pope would go on to challenge the patriarch not only for control of the Balkans but also for the primacy of the Church. Indeed, the dispute over Bulgaria was to mark a turning point in the east-west ecclesiastical conflict, transforming the existing rivalry over spheres of jurisdiction into a doctrinal controversy with calamitous consequences for Christendom as a whole.

A Fortuitous Turn

Although the situation in the east appeared dire Nicholas I adopted an uncompromising attitude. In a letter to the Byzantine emperor, he elaborated on the theme of the pope being divinely instituted as ruler over the whole of Christendom, *princeps omnem terram*.[34] Dvornik rightly points out that this document, proclaiming papal primacy, is one of the most important documents in the evolution of the papacy.[35] The arrival of a Bulgarian delegation in Rome in August 866, formally asking for Latin assistance to replace the Byzantine clergy was heralded as a godsend. The papal secretary describes the reaction to this news in the following manner: "Upon hearing this, the most blessed pope, filled with great joy, rendered ample praise to Christ and, rejoicing together with the entire Church which was divinely entrusted to him, he with devoted heart and humble voice released endless praise of our Lord, who had done such a miracle...."[36] The pope immediately dispatched clergy to Bulgaria under the leadership of two bishops, Formosus, bishop of Porto and Paul, bishop of Populonia. On their arrival in Bulgaria Boris gave them full authority within his kingdom, and with this they set about dismissing all Byzantine clergy from Bulgaria, replacing the Greek with Latin liturgy and re-baptising all the people into the Latin Church.

In response Patriarch Photius composed a letter alerting Boris to the dangers of the erroneous practices of the Latin Church, for the first time accusing them of doctrinal aberration. A copy of this letter was sent to the eastern patriarchates in an effort to obtain support for the Bulgarian cause, stating that Rome was trespassing onto Constantinople's missionary field, diffusing erroneous doctrine and ritual and demanded that papal policy regarding Bulgaria be decided by the arbitration of an ecumenical synod.[37] Thus, by the spring of 867 the East-West conflict was further aggravated by the dispute over Bulgaria. Photius poured oil onto the fire by accusing the Latin Church of doctrinal error, thereby involving Bulgaria circumstantially in the argument that would later culminate in the Photian schism.[38]

Photius' irritated response did not hinder the success of the papal mission in Bulgaria. This was due to the tact of one man, Formosus, the bishop of Porto, who won the khan's affections and trust, so much so that Boris destined him for the post of patriarch. After only twelve months of the Latin mission Boris wrote to the pope suggesting that Formosus be appointed patriarch. Boris' predisposition toward having a patriarch has already been mentioned. However, in this instance it was the ambition of Formosus that came to the fore using Boris' predilection to prompt the khan to propose his promotion to the pope. Nicholas refused to endorse his appointment under the pretext that canon law could not permit Episcopal translations between dioceses. Behind this decision lay another surreptitious reason. It was claimed that Boris had fallen under the spell of Formosus and the pope was aware that the bishop might use this power over the khan to direct the affairs of his diocese without papal control.[39] For this reason Formosus was removed from the Bulgarian mission by papal order. That such fears existed is confirmed by the charges raised against Formosus in Rome in 876, amongst which he was accused of having sought to usurp the Bulgarian archdiocese and having by means of "most terrible promises" attempted to corrupt the Bulgarian khan.[40]

Bulgarian Exasperation

In June 868 another Bulgarian delegation arrived in Rome to enquire about the possibility of appointing an archbishop of the pope's choice. However, the new pope, Hadrian II (consecrated on 14 December 867) steadfastly ignored the khan's requests. The following year Boris sent a letter to Hadrian demanding that Formosus be returned to Bulgaria as their archbishop immediately. Hadrian, an adversary of Formosus, refused Bulgarian demands again. Almost four years had passed since Bulgaria had turned to the pope in Rome, who consistently failed to recognise the increasing exasperation of Boris, even though a source close to the pope admitted that Khan Boris was "unable to endure the pope's unwillingness to meet his expectations."[41]

Meanwhile Byzantium had not remained idle. The patriarchate continued its ferocious denunciation of the Latin mission and behind its rhetoric the machinery of Byzantine diplomacy moved stealthily. Witnessing Boris' exasperation with Rome, it was put to the khan that Constantinople's position could be more accommodating than it had previously been. Boris therefore decided to raise the question of Bulgaria's ecclesiastical allegiance at the Eighth Ecumenical Council (869/70). The Bulgarian question was not on the main agenda, but a carefully prepared action by delegates of the khan determined the final session. They requested an authoritative and binding ruling on the issue of to which Christian see, Rome or Constantinople, Bulgaria would belong. The council re-convened for an extraordinary session on 4 March 870 with only one issue to debate, the future of the Bulgarian church. When asked what clergy, if any, the Bulgarians had encountered when they first settled in the disputed territory, the Bulgarian delegation stated that they had found Greek speaking clergy. This tipped the balance in favour of the Patriarchate of Constantinople and the council ruled that the Church of Rome had no jurisdictional rights in Bulgaria.[42]

Bulgarian Satisfaction

With the decision of the Ecumenical Council Boris achieved his heartfelt desire. Bulgaria was granted an archbishop and was given maximum autonomy over its internal affairs. Although remaining under the Patriarchate of Constantinople its dependence on Constantinople was limited to dogmatic issues while disciplinary matters were to be solved by the Bulgarians themselves. Indeed the *notitiae episcopatuum* compiled under Emperor Leo VI reveal that by the end of the century the Bulgarian bishoprics were no longer viewed by the Patriarchate as being under its ecclesiastical jurisdiction.[43] Khan Boris must have been satisfied with the progress the Bulgarian Church had made thus far. The great Christian Sees of Rome and Constantinople recognised that they could not take Bulgarian compliance for granted and therefore had to compromise and negotiate on matters of internal jurisdiction, as Bulgaria progressed on its path toward its goal of establishing an autocephalous church.

Today the Church in Bulgaria propagates the myth of a pure unbroken Orthodox lineage, from the moment of the nation's conversion to the present. However, historical sources reveal an ecclesiastical struggle taking place during the ninth century between Rome and Constantinople for control of Bulgaria. The ultimate beneficiary in this dispute was Bulgaria, emerging initially with an archbishopric and eventually an autocephalous church. Under the leadership of Khan Boris Bulgaria played a strategic game with the leading Christian powers of the day, at one moment accepting their authority and then playing them in opposition to one another, in order to achieve a greater aim. The contest between these competing Christian Sees only succeeded in promoting increased nationalistic desire for a separate church within Bulgaria.

CYRILLO-METHODIAN VERNACULAR TRADITION

The role and legacy of Constantine-Cyril and Methodius in the development of Slavic linguistics, whether reflected in their own actions in connection with the Byzantine mission to Moravia, or in the activities of their disciples in Bulgaria, has come to be known as the Cyrillo-Methodian tradition. The role of these missionary brothers, and of their disciples, in the Slavicisation of ecclesiastical organisation in Bulgaria and indeed throughout the Slavic world is legendary. To appreciate this tradition and gauge its influence on Bulgaria it is necessary to consider briefly the life and work of Cyril and Methodius, the introduction of the Slavic vernacular tradition and the establishment of the cult of Cyril and Methodius within Bulgaria.

Our knowledge of the tradition comes from a variety of sources. Particularly informative are the brothers' extensive *vitae*, known collectively as the *Pannonian Legend*, but usually referred to as *Vita Constantini* and *Vita Methodii*.[44] There is also an *Italian Legend*, which is a Latin version of the *vita* of Constantine. This was composed by Gauderich, bishop of Velletri, who participated in the Latin ordination of the brothers in Rome.[45] Yet another document bearing directly on the careers of Cyril and Methodius, particularly on the Bulgarian chapter of their mission, is the so called *Bulgarian Legend*, which includes the *vitae* of their disciples Kliment and Naum, composed at the beginning of the twelfth century by the Metropolitan of Ohrid, Theophylact.[46]

Constantine-Cyril (826-69) and Methodius (815-85):
A Brief History

The brothers were born in Thessalonica into a family with a strong tradition in the imperial civil service. By birth and later by education and profession they were part of the Byzantine elite. Methodius, the elder brother, held the high administrative post of *archon* in one of the Slav provinces before becoming a monk and then abbot on Mount Olympus. Constantine, a scholar of outstanding ability, held the chair of philosophy at the University of Constantinople during the 850's, earning himself the epithet 'Constantine the Philosopher'. However, as a result of political upheaval in Constantinople, he relinquished his academic position and was ordained as a deacon before joining his brother on Mount Olympus. Their joint ability and experience were highly valued in

Constantinople which resulted in the brothers serving on a number of imperial missions.

Fig. 2 Cyril and Methodius

On diplomatic, linguistic and ecclesiastic grounds the brothers were well equipped not only to serve but to lead these imperial missions, particularly in respect to their missionary enterprise in Moravia. This event, which was to dictate the rest of their lives, was initiated at the request of Prince Rastislav of Moravia to send his people "a bishop and teacher... able to explain to them the true Christian faith in their own language [Slavonic]."[47] Thessalonica, the brother's hometown, was at that time a bilingual city which explains their knowledge of the Slav language. Methodius' biographer explains that the Byzantine emperor, in urging the brothers to go to Moravia, induced them by saying "you are both natives of Thessalonica and all Thessalonians speak pure Slav."[48] Nevertheless, the success of their mission, and future Slavic missions, depended not only on the ability of its members to preach and teach in the Slavonic dialect, but on the provision of written Slavonic translations of the Scriptures and Liturgy. Before departing for Moravia it was the brothers who first devised an alphabet for the writing of Slavonic.

In the autumn of 863 the Byzantine mission arrived in Moravia bearing with them the new Slavic alphabet and various translated liturgical texts. The mission immediately had two tasks: the first religious and cultural, the establishment of a Slavonic church through the translating of liturgical and biblical documents and the training of a Moravian indigenous clergy; secondly, political and diplomatic, establishing a working relationship with Rastislav and the resident Frankish clergy. In the first of these tasks the mission achieved noticeable success, particularly as the liturgy had so far been celebrated in Latin, a language unknown to most Moravians. However, in the second task they met with opposition from the Frankish clergy who regarded the Byzantines as unauthorised intruders competing for the religious loyalty of the Slavs. From a legalistic point of view, the brothers were working in a region that was traditionally part of the sphere of influence of the Latin Church. The introduction of Slavonic liturgy was especially criticised by the Latin Church which claimed that only three languages were worthy of expressing the Word of God: Hebrew, Greek and Latin. It became obvious that if the Slav mission was to survive it would require securing the support of Rome.

Thus, in the winter of 867/8 Constantine and Methodius arrived in Rome to defend, and seek blessing for, the Slavonic ministry. They met with the pope at an advantageous moment in history: Rome had just gained the spiritual allegiance of Bulgaria, bordering Moravia, and dreams of a Slavonic world under the Holy See were becoming a real possibility. Hadrian II therefore gave the brothers his full support and issued a papal bull authorising the use of the Slavonic liturgy. The pope also ordained Constantine giving him the name Cyril and appointed Methodius as Archbishop of Pannonia. In doing so Rome endeavoured to use the brothers and their Slav ministry to bring the Slavs in central and Eastern Europe closer to itself. Unfortunately a few weeks after his ordination Cyril died and according to his wishes was buried in Rome. Methodius returned to Moravia, this time with the blessing of the pope and the Latin Church. Over the next twelve years his mission worked to establish a Slavonic church but faced increasing opposition: the Frankish clergy continued to do everything to undermine their position; Svatopluk, the new Moravian ruler began to favour the Frankish clergy rather than Methodius; and finally Rome itself began to lose interest in the Slavonic liturgy eventually leading to papal proscription against the use of the Slavonic vernacular.[49] In 885 Methodius died, tired of relentless Frankish opposition and the indifference of Rome. With the death of both of its leaders the mission edged toward disaster. The work that the missionary brothers had devoted so much of their life to accomplish was frustrated and their disciples were eventually driven out of Moravia altogether. Nevertheless, the brothers had not completely failed in their task. So influential were their Slavonic translations that by the following century the use of the Slavonic liturgy was universally accepted among the Slavic peoples of central and Eastern Europe, progressing to become one of the great ecclesiastical traditions within Eastern Christendom.

The Slavonic Mission in Bulgaria

From the ashes of the Moravian mission arose a phoenix that was to have momentous consequences for Bulgarian Christianity and culture. After their expulsion from Moravia, three of the missionary brothers' closest disciples, Kliment, Naum and Angelarius, managed to flee by sailing down the Danube to Belgrade, which was then a Bulgarian frontier town. Khan Boris enthusiastically welcomed the Slavonic missionaries. He understood the implications and advantages to be had in using these clergymen in the continuing Christianisation of Bulgaria. If they could achieve the same level of success in Bulgaria as had been achieved in Moravia, the stranglehold of Byzantine culture on Bulgaria might be broken. It is significant that while Boris' delight has been recorded, there is no mention in any Greek source about the arrival of the Slav missionaries in Bulgaria. This reveals a certain coldness on the part of the Byzantines towards the use of Slavonic in Bulgaria. It appears that for the Byzantines, what had been permissible in distant Moravia would not be tolerated in neighbouring Bulgaria, as they considered that the khan would use it to increase Bulgarian independence. The Byzantine authorities were correct in their assumption as Boris placed the weight of his royal patronage behind the work of the Slav clergy. He made the decision to send the missionaries to evangelise his Macedonian provinces. The Macedonian Slavs as well as being Boris' most recent Christian converts were also the most difficult of his inhabitants to govern. He therefore sought to endear them to his rule by means of Slavonic Christianity, bidding for their heart and soul against the Byzantine Empire by offering them a faith, culture and government that they could understand and accept. Bulgaria would then be bound by two strong bonds – a common Christian faith and Slavonic language.

The first task for the missionaries was exactly the same as it had been in Moravia: to train an indigenous clergy and multiply the number of Slavonic liturgical and literary materials. Kliment was commissioned by Khan Boris to be the mission leader and teacher of the Slavs, and was dispatched to Macedonia where he spent the remainder of his life teaching, preaching and writing. It is said of his ministry that he taught no less than 3,500 students, many of whom went on to become priests.[50] Naum initially remained at the royal court where he busied himself with the Christianisation of the khan and his royal household before joining Kliment in Macedonia. It should be noted that, at the same time as taking Christianity to the Slavic population of Bulgaria, the Slav mission also contributed to an intensification of the Slavicisation of the Bulgars.

In 894 Boris convened a national congress to announce his abdication and to name his son Simeon as his successor. During his reign the Bulgarian church had become firmly established under the Slavic mission of Kliment, many Slavonic books had been translated, indigenous clergy had been trained, so much so that reliance on Greek clergy was no longer required. Therefore, during the congress, Boris took the opportunity to complete his last great reform. The Greek language of Church and State was officially replaced by the Slavonic and Bulgaria was divided into seven dioceses: Drista, Philippopolis, Serdica, Provadia, Margum, Bergalnitsa and Ohrid. Simeon's first act as Bulgarian ruler was to promote Kliment to the rank of Metropolitan of the new Ohrid diocese. The Bulgarian acceptance of Slavonic Christianity had been eager and rapid. Indeed, it was so spectacular that it has been called a cultural revolution. In the words of Kliment of Ohrid, "the rain of divine understanding came down upon my people."[51]

The Bulgarian Cult of Cyril and Methodius

That Bulgaria eventually became the repository of the Slavonic legacy of Cyril and Methodius was the result of a series of circumstances, some of them fortuitous. Its value within Bulgaria cannot be underestimated. However, a Bulgarian myth surrounding the creation of the Slavonic vernacular, and the place Bulgaria played in its creation, has somewhat distorted reality. The onset of this distortion can be traced to the period of Ottoman political domination over Bulgaria and Greek hegemony of the Bulgarian church, when the championing of the rights of the Slavonic vernacular became a medium of Bulgarian political and ecclesiastical independence and nationalism. The promotion of these distortions can clearly be seen in modern Bulgarian authorship, particularly in the writing of Professor Emil Georgiev of the Department of Slavonic Literature in Kilment Ohridski University.

Prof. Georgiev included in the symposium 'Bulgaria's Share in Human Culture' an essay entitled 'Creation of the Slav Script'. He argued that Cyril and Methodius "laid the foundations of Bulgarian and Slavonic letters which evolved into the Slavonic or more precisely Old Bulgarian language."[52] He suggests that the beginnings of the missionary brothers' work can be traced back to Bulgaria and that they were in fact Bulgarian by birth. Therefore, the Slavonic heritage is not Byzantine but more correctly Bulgarian.[53] However, historical sources clearly state that the brothers were born in Salonica (Thessalonica); although they lived in and had an aptitude for Slavonic culture and language they cannot by any means be classed as Bulgarian.

Modern scholarship has raised the query whether the Slavonic mission can even be classed as Byzantine, suggesting that it was in fact Latin. This quandary arises as a result of the evidence that from the moment of Cyril and Methodius' arrival in Moravia until their deaths, their eyes were turned towards Rome rather than Constantinople: it was to Rome that the brothers travelled to receive support for their work, Methodius visiting the city three times. Cyril insisted on being buried in Rome against his family's wishes. It was Rome and not Byzantium that defended the Slavonic work in Moravia, and today Rome continues to revere the brothers as blessed saints.[54] Both brothers were ordained into the Latin Church, Cyril as a monk and Methodius as Archbishop of Pannonia. Whatever correspondence we have concerning the brothers comes from Rome, while contemporary Byzantine sources remain silent about their activities. Indeed, according to Methodius' biographer the Byzantine emperor was so angry with them that if he [the emperor] had laid hands upon them, they would not have escaped alive.[55] Why then is their mission traditionally associated with Byzantium? The brothers were of course born as Byzantine citizens and were sent to Moravia with the emperor's blessing. However, all evidence suggests that during the lives of the brothers their mission leaned towards Rome rather than Byzantium. It is only from later perspective, particularly after the adoption of the legend by the Bulgarians, that the mission's work can be viewed as Byzantine.

This research would argue that from the moment the Slavonic mission was ejected from Moravia it ceased to be either Latin or Byzantine, becoming solely Bulgarian. Indeed, from that moment, the promotion of Cyril and Methodius as Holy Saints and the introduction of their cult in Bulgaria had a dual purpose. On one hand the aim was to establish the Slavonic alphabet as an acceptable script but more importantly, Slavonic vernacular as a holy language blessed by God. Therefore the myth was accentuated that the brothers were sent to the Slavs by God, giving the Slavs and the Slavonic vernacular divine significance. In this respect it was important to raise the relevance of Bulgaria, proclaiming Cyril and Methodius, not only to be Slavs, but especially as being born Bulgarian Slavs writing specifically for their nation, who with divine approval continued to spread God's gift amongst the Slavonic world.[56] This instilled in the Bulgarian people a cultural and vernacular nationalism, an increasingly pro-Bulgar and anti-Byzantine spirit, but it did not stop the Byzantinisation of the Bulgarian church. Despite the introduction of the Slavonic language it actually preserved the Byzantine character of Christianity which indwelt the Slavonic liturgy. Not even wars with Byzantium conducted by Simeon, and later by Samuel, could change this. Bulgaria was, despite her unwillingness, a Slavic component of Byzantium.

This section has brought to the fore the elevated and even 'sacred' position that the Cyrillo-Methodian tradition has established for itself within Bulgarian culture. The development of the vernacular tradition had several significant outcomes: It enabled Bulgaria to develop an indigenous clergy, speaking the language of the people and sharing their same nationalistic desire; a Slavic Church rather than Greek Church in Bulgaria; a Bulgarian Church no longer reliant on Greek clergy or Greek hierarchy in Constantinople; and finally a Slavic language and a Slavic Christian culture which would become the medium for Bulgarian political and ecclesiastical independence and nationalism. The tradition has become so important to the people of Bulgaria that myth has developed around it, elevating its cultural and spiritual importance over and against the Greek forces that were threatening to subjugate Bulgaria.

BOGOMILISM – A DISSENTING TRADITION

Generally speaking, the Bogomil movement is considered to have been inconsequential in the history of Byzantine Christianity. However, this research would advance the theory that aspects of Bogomilism greatly influenced the Bulgarian church, enabling it to develop as a popular nationalist body. It is necessary then to briefly examine the history of Bogomilism, a dualistic Christian movement, and analyse its effect on the development of the Bulgarian church. This heterodox movement arose in Bulgaria during the tenth century through the transmission of Zoroastrian and Paulician beliefs, originally from Sassanid Persia, via the Russian Steppes and Armenia. The Bogomil movement gained popularity as it responded to economic, political and religious circumstances in Bulgaria, particularly its resistance to the Byzantinisation of Bulgarian culture, law and religion. For this reason Bogomilism has come to be recognised as one of the major 'problems' of Byzantine history.[57] The influence it has exerted on the history of all Balkan peoples, especially on Bulgarian Church and State, on their society and literature, on their religion and folklore, make a study of Bogomilism essential to this research.

The Rise of Balkan Dualism

During the eighth and ninth century Byzantine foreign policy was aimed above all at defending the empire from the incessant threats to its eastern borders. As the Byzantine armies defended these borders, groups of heterodox Armenian believers, calling themselves Paulicians, came under their control. Several Byzantine emperors pursued a policy of transporting groups of these Paulicians into Thrace and Macedonia, assuming this to be an effective way of breaking up troublesome heretical communities. By settling them in a region largely inhabited by Byzantine Christians they hoped to render them accessible to Orthodox Christian influence. However, Constantine V Copronymus (741-775) records his reasons for Armenian transportation differently: to re-populate Thrace after the effects of plague and to create a defensive buffer zone against Bulgar attacks. Constantine's biographer also comments that these Armenian refugees were beginning to diffuse their dualistic heresy in the Balkan region.[58]

Although the Paulicians were originally settled in towns within the Byzantine Empire, they were soon incorporated into Bulgarian territory. Any Bulgar attack on the empire pre-supposed an invasion of Thrace. Thus records of Bulgar invasions by Khan Telets in 763 and Khan Krum in 796 tell us that many prisoners were taken from these border towns to be resettled in the Bulgarian provinces. It appears highly likely that among those taken prisoner would be large numbers of Paulicians who were placed in these defensive zones and whose missionary zeal would now be exerted in Bulgarian territory. The policy of Byzantine colonization therefore proved to be a failure in regard to its intended purpose: as a military defensive force the Armenian refugees in Thrace did not justify the hope placed in them by the Byzantine authorities. Moreover, far from abandoning their heterodox beliefs as a result of contact with Orthodox Christians, the colonists indulged in vigorous proselytism spreading their convictions throughout Thrace. In one respect they did contribute to the weakening of Bulgaria, the gradual penetration of the Paulicians into Bulgaria and the consequent spread of their heterodox doctrines became a serious menace to the evolving Bulgarian church. They paved the way for several anti-ecclesiastical movements, the most important of which was the Bogomil movement.

Bogomilism in Bulgaria

According to its religious content, Bogomilism was simply a dualistic Christian heterodox movement, but in its Bulgarian context it was a popular social movement conditioned by the economic, religious and political circumstances of the tenth century. Bogomilism rejected established Christian institutions and preached the value of poverty, simplicity, and asceticism. It espoused antiestablishment concepts condemning existing political and social institutions.

This was a very different time in comparison to those heady days under Boris and Simeon's rule. The reign of Tsar Petur (927-969) reflected a new relationship with the Byzantine Empire. In the first year of his reign an alliance between Bulgaria and Byzantium was cemented by a treaty, in which Emperor Romanus I Lecapenus (920-944) recognised Petur's title as *Basileus*, granted the Bulgarian church autocephality in 925, and through Petur's marriage with Maria Lecapena, the emperor's granddaughter, Byzantium gained a foothold in the Bulgarian royal court. Intense Byzantinisation of Bulgaria ensued.

There are important internal explanations for the Byzantinisation of Bulgaria during Petur's reign. The presence of a Byzantine tsarina increased Byzantine influence at Petur's court. Bulgarian officials began using Byzantine court titles. Byzantine influence also affected religious and cultural activities: church architecture, decoration, literature and music. The hope that Petur's reign would continue the age of Bulgarian independence and prosperity was shattered by the rapid Byzantinisation of Bulgar society. Evidence of this Byzantinisation can also be witnessed in the economic changes of the tenth century, particularly in the growth of large land estates which saw a steady increase in the economic and social power of the landowner, the Church being one of the most powerful. As the Church rapidly grew in property and wealth, life became increasingly difficult for those living on church land, and resulted in their alienation from the Church. This new pattern in social structure and distribution of wealth caused widespread misery amongst the Bulgarian peasantry, which by the middle of the tenth century erupted in revolt against the authorities of Church and State, in which anti-Byzantine overtones were apparent.

The very suddenness of Bulgaria's conversion in the previous century had left many in Bulgaria Christian, but in name only. The mass of the population were insufficiently educated in, and therefore insecurely committed to, their new church. Therefore, during this period of increasing animosity towards the church it was natural for the population to seek something else in which to put their faith and hope. If they could not trust the church they would escape into heterodoxy, especially toward a belief system which offered sensible explanations and practical answers to their present sufferings. The Bogomil teachings achieved this, satisfying both spiritual hunger and offering practical advice on life in the present situation. As Bogomilism appeased mounting social pressure its popularity increased in times of hardship.

It has been suggested that the Bogomils were little more than a nuisance to the authorities of Church and State.[59] However, aware of growing discontent among his population and equally aware of the emerging religious/social movement which was gaining popularity around it, Tsar Petur wrote to the Patriarch of Constantinople, Theophylact Lecapenus (933-956), seeking guidance on how to deal with this heresy. This would appear to be a response to something more than a mere nuisance within general society. In Theophylact's reply, which provides us with the earliest evidence for the existence of Bogomilism in Bulgaria, the patriarch describes the heresy as both "ancient" and "newly appeared" and defines it as "Manichaeism mixed with Paulicianism."[60] It is unlikely that Petur found the patriarch's comments enlightening; its abstract terminology, its tendency to describe heresy in terms of its doctrinal ancestry, and its almost total lack of practical advice were not very helpful to the predicament that faced the Bulgarian ruler. This lack of appreciation was typical of an Orthodox hierarchy who regarded Bogomilism simply as a delusion. In fact, there is only one example of an Orthodox writer, the Bulgarian priest Cosmas, who, despite his antipathy toward the Bogomils, was aware that behind their teachings lay a problem of singular poignancy to which the Church in Bulgaria was not able to respond. This was the Church's teaching that God was the source of all perfection and that the whole world, visible and invisible, was his creation, yet in this world moral and physical evil, suffering, cruelty, decay and death were clearly present. How then, the people begged, could God, the supreme good, be the cause of all suffering and evil? The Bogomils responded with an answer that was at least logical and consistent: evil and suffering were inherent in the world because this world was the creation of the Evil One.[61] In pitting metaphysical 'good' against a material 'bad' they rejected orthodox Christian doctrine but attracted troubled Bulgar society.

Superficially Bogomilism appears to have had much in common with Paulicianism. Both were Christian dualist movements whose adherents denied that a good God could have made the visible evil world; both rejected that Christ had taken real humanity upon himself. They also rejected the Old Testament, and both renounced the Byzantine Church, its authority, hierarchy and sacraments. However, the view of spiritual reality which lay at the heart of Bogomil belief was quite separate from that of the Paulicians. The Bogomils believed in one God, the source of all being, who had two sons, Christ and Satan. This view has its parallels in the Near Eastern religious ideas of Zurvanism, which postulated the existence of a High God, Zurvan, who was father to Ohrmazd, the God of Light, and of Ahriman, the God of Darkness.[62] Ivan the Exarch comments that this belief was present in Bulgaria before the rise of Bogomilism and may therefore date from a period when the Bulgars lived on the Russian Steppes and had direct contact with Sassanid Persia.[63]

However, there is no need to postulate such a singularly exotic origin for Bogomil dogma. The Bulgarian priest, Father Bogomil, is considered to be the founding father of the Bogomil movement. He encouraged his disciples to live as monks, to meet together for prayer at regular times of the day and night, to remain celibate, and abstain from eating meat and drinking alcohol. He believed monasticism to approximate most closely the life of Christian perfection. However, the Christian tradition stated that the monastic life involved giving up things which were of their nature God given, in order to respond better to Christ's invitation to self-denial, whereas the Bogomils gave up these things because they believed them to be inherently evil and therefore incompatible with Christian living. Bogomilism was indebted to the Bulgarian church in another way, owing much of its success to the introduction of vernacular translation. It was the Old Slavonic text of the New Testament which Father Bogomil used as the foundation of his teachings. Yuri Stoyanov rightly observes that the materials used in Bogomil development came to hand because of the Ohrid School of translation founded by Kliment and Naum: "What remains undisputed is the link of a rich and diverse apocryphal literature in tenth century Bulgaria, some of which came to be adopted for the purpose of Bogomil propaganda."[64] These considerations suggest that Father Bogomil's movement was deeply indebted to the Christian Church, from which it derived its monastic concept of holiness and desire for the New Testament scriptures. His dualism owed much to the Paulicians and had close resemblance to the beliefs of the Zurvanite Zoroastrians with whom the Bulgars had contact before settling in the Balkans. Bogomilism therefore revealed itself to be a highly syncretistic religion.

In 969 the reign of Tsar Petur was cut short by an unprovoked Russian invasion. Svyatoslav of Kiev, prompted by Constantinople, invaded the Bulgarian Empire as part of Byzantium's decision to reconquer the Balkans. Despite the initial success of the invasion the advance was stopped in western Bulgaria (modern day Macedonia) by an army commanded by a group of brothers, known as the *Cometopuli* (sons of the count). The youngest of the brothers, Samuel, was crowned tsar of a new independent Bulgarian State in 997. Within his kingdom, due to the strong anti-Byzantine persuasion, Samuel was obliged to pursue an essentially pro-Bulgar nationalistic policy, both ecclesiastically and politically. To be successful this policy required the collaboration of all the people in the pursuit of one end – the destruction of Byzantine power and its dominion over Bulgaria. Consequently, during this period Bogomilism was able to expand unchecked. The explanation for Tsar Samuel's leniency toward the Bogomil movement is simple: it was the only anti-Byzantine movement with clear Slavonic orientation. How-

ever, the Byzantine Empire continued its offensive against Bulgaria and
under Emperor Basil II (976-1025) the First Bulgarian Empire eventually collapsed and became a Byzantine province, remaining so for the
following one hundred and sixty-eight years.

Bulgaria remained an integral part of the Byzantine Empire until
1185 when she secured her independence once more. During this period
of Byzantine domination there had been numerous outbreaks of social
unrest making it clear that a sense of Bulgarian cultural identity and
separateness had survived. This was due in part to Bogomil influence,
particularly because of its pro-Slavic, anti-Byzantine tendencies. Bogomilism had also assisted in preventing any commitment to the ruling
Byzantine State or Church. However, in 1202 Tsar Kaloyan, wishing to
secure Bulgaria's independence, during the period of the fourth Crusade
and the Latin rule of Constantinople, opened negotiations with Pope
Innocent III, leading to a reunion of the Bulgarian church with Rome. In
1206 Innocent sent his legate to Bulgaria to persuade the new ruler, Tsar
Boril, to prosecute the Bogomils.[65] This resulted in Boril presiding over
the Council of Turnovo (1211) which finally legislated against Bogomilism in Bulgaria.

The Success of Bogomilism

The success of the Bogomil movement in medieval Bulgaria indicates that the impact of Byzantine Christian culture could be withstood
and repelled, not by the Bulgarian Church, but by a strong heterodox
dissenting tradition. The most effective carrier of Byzantine influence to
the Bulgarian population was the Christian clergy who instilled in their
flocks a loyalty to the mother church in Constantinople. However, the
Bulgarian priest Cosmas in his discourse *Against the Bogomils* paints a
gloomy picture of the state of his country's clergy. He described them as
greedy, wealthy landowners who had lost contact with their flocks and
alienated the people from the church. He charged the parish priests with
sloth, drunkenness and peculation, going so far as to place the main responsibility for the spread of Bogomilism on the depravity of Bulgaria's
ecclesiastical personnel. By the same token the Bogomils, by the auster-
ity of their lives, their intimate knowledge of the New Testament scriptures, their bold proselytism, and their courage in the face of persecution,
appeared to the Bulgarian people to be the true bearers of Christianity.

Monasticism, which developed rapidly in tenth century Bulgaria, also proved to be a two-edged sword in Byzantine hands. Undoubtedly the monks made a notable contribution to the cultural life of Bulgaria. Nevertheless, the overall picture of contemporary Bulgarian monasticism was not an edifying one. Cosmas writes of monks who ignored their vows, lived worldly lives, engaged in business, indulged in gossip, and simply wandered the country on the excuse of pilgrimage. Cosmas explains that the Bogomil doctrine, that the human body was intrinsically evil, had gained wide acceptance within monasticism. This led to a contamination of Orthodoxy by dualist doctrine; it is therefore significant that Cosmas' apologetic was written against both the Bogomils and the abuses of contemporary Bulgarian monasticism and Church personnel.[66]

For four centuries the Bogomils revealed themselves not only to be anti-Byzantine but also ardently pro-Bulgarian, the relationship of the Bulgarian church to Constantinople was never so apparent. The mass popularity of Bogomilism led to the movement being anathematised by both the Byzantine and Latin Churches, but only after four centuries of existence. The evidence suggests that the success of the Bogomil movement only accentuated the unpopularity of Byzantine Church and State, especially their policy of Byzantinisation in Bulgaria. The Bulgarian Church appears to have failed to meet the spiritual and practical needs of the Bulgarian people and this resulted in increasing alienation. After the demise of Bogomilism, during the period of Ottoman domination, we witness the Bulgarian Orthodox Church actually taking on many of the popular characteristics of Bogomilism, becoming the main advocate of Bulgarian nationalism and the chief motivator of anti-Greek sentiment. In doing so the BOC sought to meet the spiritual, political and practical desires of the Bulgarian people. It was with these dissenting characteristics, fully adopted from Bogomilism, that the BOC reached its apogee during the period of the National Revival.

CONCLUSION

As a historical introduction this chapter has provided only a preliminary sketch of five centuries of Bulgarian Church history. However, respecting the sacred position of tradition and history within Eastern Orthodoxy, it has been essential to place this research in a correct historical framework. This was achieved by selecting widely acclaimed elements from Bulgarian history that this research deemed elemental to the formation of Bulgarian Orthodox identity. From the outset the chapter had two goals: to increase the reader's awareness of the preliminary processes that helped create Bulgarian Orthodox and national identity; and to facilitate appreciation of how initial relationships developed between the BOC and the Bulgarian nation, state and society. In achieving these goals the chapter assists the reader to comprehend fully the syncretistic and nationalistic nature of Bulgarian Orthodoxy. This chapter establishes that the Bulgarian Church developed as a result of a series of contacts with historical issues, which were not necessarily ecclesiastical, but rather secular and nationalist, which it then adopted and absorbed within its own characteristics.

In the section entitled 'Khan Boris and the Conversion of Bulgaria' we witnessed the Bulgarian Christianisation process being defined by a series of non-ecclesiastical issues, dictated from the outset by the nationalistic desires of Khan Boris. These issues included the need to cement a union between the proto-Bulgar and Slav inhabitants of his kingdom and his desire to establish an autocephalous church within a strongly independent nation. This first stage in the development of state nationalism helped to define the independent nature of the Bulgarian Church. In the second section we witnessed what can only be called 'ecclesiastical nationalism'. In the international struggle for jurisdictional authority over Bulgaria we observed how three Christian power centres – Constantinople, Rome and the East Franks – attempted to enforce their model of Christian doctrine and practice as well as the political might of their nations upon Bulgaria. The ultimate beneficiary in these ecclesiastical disputes was Bulgaria who eventually gained an independent and then autocephalous Church. Through a series of fortuitous events we observed how the birth of the Slavonic vernacular tradition taking place in Bulgaria, creating a form of 'linguistic nationalism'. This tradition enabled the Bulgarians to rid themselves of Greek language and liturgy and replace it with Slavonic as the official language of the Bulgarian church and state. The Cyrillo-Methodian tradition therefore united Bulgaria as one nation speaking one language. However, following an intense period of Byzantinisation, the Bulgarian Church became the enemy of the people, alienating itself from the nation, losing its original independent focus. Through the pro-Bulgar/anti-Byzantine tendencies of the Bogomil movement 'popular nationalism' arose. The Bulgarian

Church had lost sight of the very thing that had helped define it in the first place. Consequently, after the demise of Bogomilism, we witness the Church taking on many of the popular nationalistic characteristics of Bogomilism.

By observing and analysing these different historical factors, some endowed with mythic value, this research has been able to make appropriate judgements on Bulgaria's early ecclesiastical development. In light of the evidence this research would argue that Bogomilism helped to indigenise Bulgarian Orthodoxy, thus securing the church's future role as popular national saviour. The Bulgarian church had been struggling to equate local and universal aspects of the Church. However, by connecting Orthodox faith, vernacular language and Bulgarian culture, the Bulgarian church used popular heterodox traits to find a balance between those local and universal aspects of church authority. Thus religion and nationalism became inseparable, a fact one cannot fully comprehend without looking closely at the Bogomil tradition in Bulgaria.

The evidence provided in this chapter would suggest that from its inception, nationalism has been an integral part of the Bulgarian Church. Throughout the transitional period of Bulgarian Church history covered in this chapter nationalism directed ecclesiastical development. From its establishment the Bulgarian Church has been indelibly linked with the Bulgarian nation by a unique relationship in which nationalism was an elemental factor.

2

RELIGIO-HISTORICAL CONTEXT PRIOR TO THE BULGARIAN NATIONAL REVIVAL

This chapter will explore the religio-historical situation in Bulgaria prior to the National Revival period. It will accomplish this by exploring the socio-historical factors that moulded Christian-Muslim relationships during the period. It will concentrate on the widely held *catastrophe theory*, which argues that during the Ottoman period Bulgaria suffered destruction of her economic, cultural and spiritual development due to the relentless Islamisation process of the Ottoman authorities. This *theory* has established itself at the core of Bulgarian national history but is at variance with modern Islamic research that speaks of religious toleration within Islamic society. This chapter will seek to offer an alternative theory through its investigation of contemporary source materials from Ottoman and Bulgarian archives. The chapter continues its religio-historical investigation with a study of two Bulgarian clergymen who were influential in the period prior to the national revival, Paisii of Hilendar and Sofroni of Vratsa. A literary investigation of Paisii's *Slavo-Bulgarian History* predominates as it is claimed to have been a main motivating textbook of the Bulgarian National Revival.

THE SOCIO-HISTORICAL CONTEXT

Bulgaria, during the reign of Tsar Ivan Alexander (1331-1371), experienced one of her richest cultural periods. Many churches and monasteries were erected, numerous literary works were produced and religious art flourished in the painting of frescoes, icons and the illumination of manuscripts. However, due to internal fragmentation the kingdom devolved into three regional states governed by Tsar Ivan Shishman (1371-1393), Ivan Stratismir the tsar's half brother, and Ivanko a rebel boyar. This political disunity made Bulgaria easy prey for conquest.

The lack of harmony within Bulgaria was mirrored by a similar lack of unity amongst the other Balkan states resulting in their inability to join in combined defensive action against Ottoman expansion. The

Bulgarian military attempted to check the Ottoman advance, failing at the battle of Chernomen, near Adrianople in 1371. Shishman attempted to remain in power by becoming a vassal of Sultan Murat I (1362-1389) but to no avail. The Ottoman military advanced along the Maritsa Valley, seizing Stara Zagora, Plovdiv, Samokov and Sofia, before proceeding toward the capital city of Turnovo. Tsar Ivan Shishman fled the city leaving it in the hands of Evtimi the Bulgarian patriarch. Under the patriarch's leadership Turnovo resisted the Ottoman onslaught for three months, surrendering on 17 July 1393. The conquerors entered the city and destroyed the royal palace, the palace Church of 'St. Petka', the Patriarchal Church of 'St. Ascension', and the Boyar Church. They condemned the resistance leaders to death but Patriarch Evtimi was exiled to Bachkovo Monastery in the Rhodope Mountains. This marked the cessation of Bulgarian church independence simultaneous with the political collapse of the kingdom.[1] A year later Patriarch Anthony IV (1391-1397) of Constantinople named Metropolitan Jeremias of Moldavia Exarch over Turnovo, taking the first step towards the dissolution of the Turnovo Patriarchate.[2] By 1396 Bulgaria had completely succumbed to Ottoman rule. It would be another five centuries before Bulgaria would claim her independence once again.

Bulgarian historiography depicts the years under Ottoman control as the 'dark centuries', in which Bulgaria was reduced to slavery under the Ottoman yoke.[3] It is characterised as a time of Islamic despotism in which the Ottomans allegedly committed genocide and destroyed the economic and cultural life of the nation, persecuting Christians and forcing their conversion to Islam.[4] These hardships constitute part of the catastrophe theory that established itself in Bulgarian national mythology during the nineteenth century struggle for national independence, later to be enhanced during the communist regime as Bulgarian national-socialists sought religio-historical legitimation for a number of their political campaigns.[5] Ottoman and Islamic research, however, has brought to our attention a number of incongruities within the catastrophe theory. On the basis of detailed analysis of Bulgarian and Ottoman archival materials, including Ottoman tax registers and other documentation from Rila Monastery in Bulgaria, this chapter will evaluate the Islamic perspective, and offer a critique of the Bulgarian mythological paradigm.

Islamisation Under Ottoman Control

The Ottoman conquest of Bulgaria undeniably affected the religious demography of the country. At the outset of the conquest, midway through the fourteenth century, the number of Muslims in Bulgaria was insignificant, whereas, by mid nineteenth century, Muslims constituted almost a third of the population.[6] This fact is a major component in the popular notion that the conquest was succeeded by five centuries of continual repression and enforced conversion to Islam.

Bulgarian historians argue that coercion, as a method of Islamisation was an integral part of Islamic law. In support of this argument they cite an Ottoman collation of rulings on religious and legal matters by various Sheikh-s al-Islam. For example in this collation the question is raised: "If an unbeliever, after accepting Islam, refuses to give up the Christian God, becoming apostate, what should be done with him?" The answer follows, "The law of the apostate is to be applied (that is he is to be killed)." The same question asked of a female convert produces the advice, "Place her in prison until she is ready to accept the will of Allah."[7] A similar question is then asked of a person who converts while drunk but later recants: "Place him in prison and beat him until he returns to Islam."[8] Bulgarian historians also refer to the loathsome *devshirme*, or child-tax, whereby boys aged between seven and fourteen were taken from their Christian families and converted to Islam. They would be given a rigorous education, learning the Turkish language, customs and military training under the sultan's administration, after which they would enter the ranks of his elite janissary corps.

It is beyond doubt that the Ottoman era in Bulgaria, particularly the years immediately after the conquest, were marked by moments of violence, which included subjecting towns and villages to the sword, mass killings, torture, rape, mutilation, and an element of enforced conversion.[9] It is also true, however, that in the context of official Ottoman politics Islamic laws were normally applied with some discretion within a complicated system of social relationships that questions an uncritical assumption of bipolar contrasts between the Muslim rulers and their Christian subjects. This complex relationship reflects the ambiguity between Qur'an and *hadith* literature, which creates both a basis for repressive Muslim policy towards *ahl al-kitab*, 'the people of the Book', but also provides justification for their co-existence; whereas the Qur'an spells out a basis for co-existence and respect for *ahl al-kitab* the *hadith* tends to have a more negative attitude towards 'the people of the Book' stating they have to be 'humbled' or equally 'humiliated'.

In the face of such contradictions we shall attempt to demythologise the early Ottoman period in Bulgaria, offering an alternative to the distorted and selective view of the Bulgarian national myth. Among preserved Ottoman archives one of the most important sources for studying this period are the Ottoman land and tax registers, particularly the jizie (*джизие*) registers.[10] The Bulgarian jizie registers indicate that this was not an individual poll tax but rather a tax imposed on every non-Muslim household.[11] Thus, as the Ottoman administrative system distinguished between Muslims and non-Muslims in terms of juridical status and taxation these registers allow us to follow any changes in religious affiliation.

This research focussed on the jizie registers from the Rhodope region, as this district became one of the most densely populated Muslim areas, and remains so today. At the end of the fifteenth century, in the village of Zurnevo, the register records that there were 241 Christian households and only 1 Muslim home, but by the beginning of the seventeenth century there were only 120 Christian families.[12] Bulgarian historian Petur Petrov submits this as proof of Islamic conversion in this region.[13] However, while this demonstrates a decrease in the number of Christian inhabitants, it does not prove that Islamisation was coerced, it simply means there were fewer Christian families living there. During the same period the village of Belotnitsi records only 36 of 129 Christian families remaining. But the 1723 jizie register for this village may help us, as it records not only that a meagre 30 Christian families remained but also one solitary Muslim family, emphasising the fact that a decrease in the Christian population was not necessarily accompanied by an equivalent increase in Muslim numbers. In a contemporary report the region's judicial representative explains that the Rhodope region had suffered two epidemics of bubonic plague. From another source we find that Zurnevo and Belotnitsi, along with a number of neighbouring settlements (all of which were predominantly Christian), were centres of iron production, but that many families were forced to migrate to the developing cities when iron production decreased due to the purchase of cheap foreign imports.[14] This evidence shows that the decline in the Christian population was the result of various factors and cannot be attributed to the single cause of enforced conversion.

Another approach to Islamisation must therefore be taken into consideration, the socio-economic view. This approach attempts to understand the role that socio-economic factors played in the Islamisation process. This has raised disagreement and confusion amongst Bulgarian scholars as it reveals evidence of voluntary conversion to Islam, determined not by coercion but through economic motivation. The common hypothesis is that Islamic manifestation of the Imperial regime was influential in Bulgaria on account of its immediate proximity to the Ottoman capital. From here Bulgarian historiography constructs the theory of ruthless Ottoman rule, leaping to the conclusion that large groups of the Christian population converted under duress.[15]Although this investigation of the Rhodope jizie registers revealed no evidence of conversion under duress it does confirm that many Bulgarian Christians converted to Islam.

Of utmost importance in the construction of any new Ottoman state, before everything, was to master the newly conquered territory. Thus, in the Ottoman territorial plan for the Balkans we read of a period described as '*the Islamising of the new lands*' when Islamic character would be introduced upon the lives of the conquered community.[16] This raises the problematic question of priority – Islamisation through regional colonization or conversion. This issue relates directly to the legal concept of *Dar al-Islam*, i.e. the Islamising of a territory, not by the conversion of individual inhabitants, but by the implementation of Islamic law.

According to one of the earliest tax registers from 1445 not one Muslim was recorded in the Rhodope region. By the late fifteenth and early sixteenth centuries the jizie registers document a small rise in Muslim households throughout the region, with many villages having no more than twelve Muslim families.[17] This would suggest that the initial introduction of Islam among the Bulgarian Christians was through colonization – Ottoman mastery upon the territory was a gradual process. By 1723 we find the following situation in the 108 villages of the Nevrokop region: ten villages with only Christian residents; twenty four with mixed populations, and seventy four exclusively Muslim.[18] The Ottoman jizie registers record the chronology of the Islamisation process exceptionally well and the gradual increment in Islamic numbers suggests the absence of extreme activities in the region.

The reason for conversion most frequently proffered in Ottoman documentation is 'economic factors'. It is indisputable that fiscal relief was a major stimulus, as we know from available information that new Islamic converts were exempt from paying not only the jizie, but also land tax.[19] In this way a Christian's economic status could be improved by converting to Islam. This establishes a motive for conversion and explains the slow pace and process of Islamisation. However, the Ottoman authorities had nothing to gain by enforcing conversion upon their Christian subjects as the loss in tax revenue would have impoverished the empire, hence a seventeenth century traveller comments: "very many unable to bear any longer this cruel tyranny, wish to turn Turk; but many are rejected, because say their lords, in receiving them into the Moslem faith, their tribute would be much reduced."[20] Thus there was valid rationale for conversion to Islam deriving from Christianity's subordinate position within the Ottoman Empire. Social equality and access to a higher social standing could only be obtained by converting to Islam; it was for this reason that immediately after the Ottoman conquest Bulgaria's Christian nobility converted enabling them to maintain their social position.[21]

Despite these evidences of the nature and reasons for the gradual Islamisation of Bulgaria under the Ottomans, the national mythological view continues to predominate as it provides an account that responds to the interests of Bulgarian folklore and national revival histories. The fact remains that the majority of Christians within Ottoman society enjoyed relative peace, some even prosperity. A number of Muslim religious leaders actively advocated interfaith tolerance in Bulgaria. Sheikh Bedreddin Simawi (1364-1420), for example, emphasised the unity of human society and the equality of all people, regardless of their ethnic and confessional identity. He exhorted Muslims to overcome their differences with Christians and to co-operate across the religious divide.[22] However, "the myth of an interfaith, interracial utopia in which Muslims, Christians, and Jews worked together in equality and harmony in a golden age of free intellectual endeavour" has little justification.[23] For many Bulgarian Christians Ottoman domination caused a discontinuity in the course of their previous cultural and historical development. Islam was regarded by the local population as the "invaders" religion and hence an instrument of subjugation. This predetermined a general attitude towards the Islamic faith as alien, hostile and militant.

The death of two Christian men in 16th century Sofia highlights this conflicting relationship. In 1515, Georgi a young Christian gold-smith, was burned at the stake in Sofia for having publicly disparaged Islam. Father Pejo, who penned this 'martyr's' life, describes Georgi as a God-fearing Christian lured into a trap by Muslim scholars. After unsuc-cessfully seeking to convince Georgi of Islam's advantages the scholars demanded that he be burned. Although the Christians requested his release they were ignored by the Muslims who, supported by Islamic legal institutions, enjoyed superiority over the Christians.[24] A similar fate befell Nikola, a Christian shoemaker who claimed to have converted to Islam after being misled by a Muslim. On Easter of 1555 he recanted and returned to Christianity but under the *sharia* was charged with apostasy and stoned to death.[25] These examples display a troubled relationship between the two religious communities during this period but importantly they also provide evidence of a still vibrant Christian community surviving in a sixteenth century Ottoman administrative centre. A German priest, Stefan Gerlach, who visited Sofia in the sum-mer of 1578, confirms the presence of this active Christian community. According to Gerlach the district of Sofia contained three hundred active churches and he comments in his diary that the main church in Sofia had recently been restored with wonderfully painted murals. His words dis-close that Bulgaria's Christians were not exposed to debilitating oppres-sion.[26]

Although the catastrophe theory paints a picture of an oppressed Church, Bulgaria's Church and Christians were not generally victims of Islamic violence. Indeed a number of Ottoman documents actually guar-anteed protection for the Orthodox Church. The earliest evidence of protection being offered to Bulgarian Christians was to the monks of Rila Monastery in a *firman* dated October 1402. This was granted by Suleyman, the eldest son of Bayezit I, following the Battle of Ankara (28 July 1402), in answer to a request from the monks to prohibit any aggression or legal challenge upon their estates:

> We the monks, who live in Rila monastery and who have possessed until now the royal act for our right of free life, declare and mourn thus: our property and estates, which we have held for a long time, are gradually being taken away from our hands and are being destroyed. Foreigners/Bandits have violently forced their way onto our proper-

ties, invading our estates, not only against our will but against the will
of the *sharia* and the Canon.[27]

The *firman* confirmed the privileges granted by Tsar Ivan Shishman to
the monks in the Rila Charter of 1378.[28] The archives of Rila Monastery
include many such documents from the Ottoman era that testify to a surprising stability over this prolonged period.[29] In total there are 325
documents in Rila's archives, dating from 1402 to the 19th century,
which make it possible to follow the relationship of the monastery with
Ottoman state and society. Of these fifty are *firmans*, granted for various
provisions by the office of every Ottoman Sultan relating to the rights of
the monastery and the monks. Forty of the documents are entitled,
hudutnameta [худутнамета] (law of frontiers), that defined the borders
of the monastery's estates and another forty, *hujeti* [худжети] (legal
proofs), granting ownership of real estate in Thrace and Macedonia. In
so doing the Ottoman authorities not only protected a Christian monastic
institution but also the monks' trading activities and property rights.
Machiel Kiel confirms this from other sources claiming that the sultan
protected the monastery's estates and granted them extensive tax
exemptions.[30]

Contrary to this evidence, however, the Bulgarian mythological
view claims that the Ottomans destroyed Rila Monastery and drove the
monks away, and the fifteenth century Bulgarian author Vladislav
Gramatik blames Rila's destruction on the Ottomans.[31] The archives in
Rila speak of groups of *haidouks* repeatedly pillaging and burning the
monastery and one document speaks of an attack by 100 Samokov caval-
rymen who kidnapped eight of the monks, returning them once a ransom
had been paid. But there is no mention of specifically Islamic violence
against the monastery. Nevertheless, Rila Monastery seems to have been
destroyed by fire at least twice, once in the fifteenth century and again in
the eighteenth century. After the first fire we know that the reconstruction in 1466 was only made possible with financial help from the Russian monastery of 'St. Pantelemon' on Mount Athos, but this in turn was
only made possible when the Ottoman administration granted permission
for the Russian monastery to work in the region.[32] Also after the monastery was completely devastated by a second fire, Sultan Mustafa III
(1757-1774) gave permission for the construction of a new monastery
and provided an element of financial support towards this project.

Gramatik's negative impression of Ottoman rule is further eroded by his own words in *The Carrying of the Relics of St. Ivan Rilski from Turnovo to Rila Monastery.* Through this text we gain insight to Bulgarian Christian relationship with Ottoman society. When Ivan Rilski died in 946 he was buried in the Rila valley southwest of Sofia. After his canonization Tsar Petur I (927-969) exhumed Rilski's body and brought it to Sofia. At the creation of the Second Bulgarian Kingdom Tsar Ivan Assen I (1186-1196) had the relics transferred to his new capital of Turnovo. However, after the restoration of Rila Monastery in 1469 the monks ask Sultan Mehmet II (1451-1481) for permission to return the relics of St. Ivan to Rila. Not only was permission granted but they were also allowed to carry the relics in holy procession from Turnovo to Rila Monastery. It is interesting that the only recorded disturbance the monks faced on their journey was from the Christians of Turnovo who refused to release the relics. Gramatik's account of the procession gives us precious insight into Christian society at this moment. He tells us that the monks travelled to Nikopol where the relics were received with great honour by the town's population, and in Sofia St. Ivan's relics lay in state for six days. As the monks left Sofia for Rila the Christian inhabitants followed in procession burning torches and incense.

This account yet again portrays a very different picture than that of general Bulgarian history. It shows that Christian life was active and visible, rather than hidden away in remote monasteries. Christian clergy could freely travel and be received openly by their fellow Christians. This leads us to conclude that the initial phase of Ottoman conquest in Bulgaria was marked by violence as the conqueror's sought to Islamise the new lands, but after this initial phase passed the Christians as '*ahl alkitab*' were treated with toleration and permitted to practise their religion.

Hellenisation Under Ottoman Control

For many years the most striking evidence of enforced Islamic conversion upon Bulgaria's Christian population came from a seventeenth century manuscript entitled the *Chronicle of Metodi Draginov.* This was a brief account, supposedly written by a local priest from the village of Korova in the western Rhodopes of enforced mass Islamisation in his parish. It is set during the reign of Sultan Mehmed IV when Gavril, the Greek Metropolitan of Plovdiv, reported the local Bulgarian population to the Ottoman authorities for refusing to pay their taxes, suggesting that by doing so they were usurping the sultan's authority. As a result Turkish troops were sent to the village who forcibly converted the population to Islam. In general surveys of Bulgarian literature the *Chronicle* had been accepted as one of the few original texts from the seventeenth century and therefore considered trustworthy.[33] The *Chronicle* was published in 1870 by the patriotic Bulgarian writer Stefan Zakhariev.[34] However, modern scholarship revealed similarities between Zakhariev's find and two other chronicles which described the same events: the *Bakunski Chronicle* (1893) and the *Belovski letopis* (dated to the beginning of the nineteenth century). In 1984 the literary historian Iliya Todorov, after years of academic debate, published the definitive verdict on all three chronicles.[35] Apart from factual discrepancies he noted that the texts were modern and remote from the language of seventeenth century documentation, indeed, they reflected nineteenth century forms and conventions. This pointed to another inconsistency, that being the clear anti-Greek sentiment which resounded from the texts. This presented an anachronism as the Bulgarian-Greek ecclesiastical conflict only became widespread during the nineteenth century. However the most important contribution of Todorov was his critical and historical placing of the *Chronicle of Metodi Draginov* clearly within the genre of Stefan Zakhariev. The Chronicles had been forged. The invalidity of the Chronicles means that they cannot be used as proof of seventeenth century mass Islamic conversion. However, analysis of the manuscripts actually puts the emphasis of the Chronicles not on conversion at all but on the act of betrayal on the part of the Greek clergy. They are therefore historical proof of a nineteenth century ecclesiastical struggle. Konstantin Jirecek's *Geschichte der Bulgaren* draws attention to the fact that Bulgaria was subject to what he called "the double yoke", that is Ottoman political, social and economic oppression combined with Greek religious and linguistic subjugation.[36]

The Ottoman conquest of Constantinople in 1453 may have brought about the end of the Byzantine era, but for the Greek Church it brought the fulfilment of one of its most cherished aims – the subjugation of the Bulgarian Church. As has been previously mentioned, the Bulgarian Church had fallen with the Bulgarian monarchy, its Patriarchate being dissolved in 1394, where after it fell subject to the authority of the Patriarch of Constantinople. With the implementation of the *millet* system in

1454 the Patriarchate of Constantinople gained even greater authority, both secular and spiritual when Sultan Mehmet II (1451-1481) granted a *berat* recognising the patriarch as the official representative of all the empire's Christians.

Sultan Mehmet II quickly realised that supporting the Orthodox Church would prove to be an ideal weapon against the West, at the same time ensuring the loyalty of his Christian subjects. Indeed, many Orthodox clergy believed that the alternative, union with the Latin Church, would have been a greater heresy than submission to the Ottoman sultan. Thus, Grand Duke Notaras asserted that he would rather see, "the turban of the sultan than the tiara of the Pope in Constantinople."[37] Mehmet assumed the role of defender of the Orthodox faith and in so doing redefined himself and the sultanate, as the successor of Byzantium and undertook to re-establish the Church on a solid foundation by institutionalising its position within his empire.[38] In doing so he granted the Church greater powers than it had ever held under Byzantine rule. As well as authority in all spiritual matters the *berat* invested the Patriarch with considerable civil authority, making him head of not only the Orthodox Church, but also the supreme leader of the sultan's Orthodox subjects. In effect the Patriarch assumed a status equivalent to that of an Ottoman vizier.[39]

The *millet* was an administrative system for controlling the recognised religious confessions within the Ottoman empire. It followed the Islamic tradition of allowing *ahl al-kitab* a degree of internal autonomy under its own religious leadership. Thus, the 'people of the Book' were absorbed into the Ottoman empire and granted protection and toleration in their forms of worship, provided they accepted the dominion of the sultan. Hence in 1454, the year after the fall of Constantinople the population of Bulgaria was divided according to religious creed each group being governed by its own religious leaders.[40] The word *millet* literally means 'community' – often rendered 'mini-nation' – and for the Ottomans nationhood meant religious affiliation. Turkish, Bulgarian or Albanian Muslims, for example, spoke different languages and enjoyed widely different cultural traditions but were still be part of the same 'nation'. As far as the Ottoman state was concerned, religion took precedence over culture, language and race in defining identity. Consequently, Orthodox Greeks, Serbs, Bulgarians and Romanians were all gathered

together in one 'Roman' *millet* and subordinated to the Ecumenical
Patriarchate of Constantinople.[41]

The Patriarchate in Constantinople, and the ambitious Greeks
within it, the most powerful of whom were the Phanariots, gained
increasing power under Ottoman administration. They grew rich and
acquired enormous influence, both in ecclesiastical and secular matters,
by purchasing various offices from the sultan. It has been recorded that a
man could buy the patriarchal title for as little as a thousand gold pieces
in the fifteenth century rising to the highest recorded purchase of one
hundred and fifty thousand gold pieces. This enabled the buyer of patriarchal office to sell ecclesiastical districts to the highest bidder, who in
turn obtained a percentage of the taxes collected by the local clergy.[42]
This meant that the Bulgarian peasant was subject to a regime of double
taxation, from the Ottoman state on the one hand, and the Greek clergy
on the other. Commenting on this extortion a British representative at the
Sublime Porte commented: "Here, as everywhere else in Turkey every
sort of injustice, malversation of funds, bribery and corruption is openly
attributed by the Christians to their clergy."[43] It is therefore highly probable that those who entered the Church, as result of a purchasing a clerical title, would not be ideal for the spiritual task set before them. Rather,
their position was a financial investment from which they grew rich by
levying fees for all sorts of religious services. While Greek clergy
replaced the ecclesiastical hierarchy of the Bulgarian Church, at a local
level Bulgarian priests continued in their parish positions, a situation
which endured until the seventeenth century when the Greeks began to
control every aspect of Bulgarian Church organisation, being the only
ones who could afford to pay the bribes required to secure parish
appointments. Thus, what the Ottomans did not take from the Bulgarians
in the form of land, taxes and slaves, the Greek clergy appropriated by
unscrupulous means.

For many Bulgarians the Greek yoke became heavier to bear than
the Ottoman rule of their nation. For the Greek clergy the opportunity of
ridding themselves once and for all of these troublesome Bulgars was a
possibility too fortuitous to miss. This situation led to charges that the
Greek Patriarchate set out to conduct a systematic campaign of Hellenization to destroy Bulgarian national consciousness and culture. The consequence of their actions is evident in the words of an English traveller
who wrote of his experience in a Bulgarian village:

Danil was a Bulgarian, a patriot, vexed by the villagers' apathy. He tried to explain to them that by being forced to listen to the Church service in Greek rather than in their own Slavic tongue, they were being exploited by an anti-Bulgarian clergy. But they bolted raw cabbage and washed it down with *rakiya* and only said it did not matter; many of them spoke Greek. The priest took a suck on the bottle and was of the same opinion. He spoke the local Slavic dialect for ordinary purposes, but he had learned all the services in Greek. It was a good service so what did it matter? Danil was very annoyed, and told me that they were very ignorant; really they were all Bulgarians, and ought to have Bulgarian priests, but they did not know. Nor as far as I could see, did they care.[44]

The epoch of Ottoman rule and ecclesiastical Hellenization in Bulgaria had such a profound effect upon the pattern of life and was so enduring that even the Bulgarians themselves began to forget their national identity. The most damaging aspect of Patriarchal rule was its success in subverting large sections of the Bulgarian population, making them believe that both Bulgarian language and culture were vulgar and barbarous, only fit for the uneducated of society. However, it cannot be claimed that Bulgarian culture and desire for national and ecclesiastical independence abated completely. It would perhaps be fitting to claim that Bulgaria went into a literary and cultural period of hibernation.

Immediately after the fall of Turnovo (1393) many of Bulgaria's leading clergy and educated people fled for refuge to the monasteries. The Mount Athos monasteries of Hilander and Zograf, and particularly Rila, one of the more remote Bulgarian monasteries, played important roles in keeping Bulgarian culture and language alive during the Ottoman period. In these havens of 'Bulgarianness' the Old Slavonic manuscripts were preserved and copied, the arts of iconography and fresco painting were kept alive. They also became centres of education and literary activity, where Bulgarian culture was not only commemorated but restored. Responsibility fell on the Bulgarian clergy to keep alive a vestige of indigenous culture, art, language, education and religion.

A number of Bulgarian monasteries were able to survive these turbulent years by transforming their property into *vakif* lands whereby they secured their own income. Those monasteries able to retain their property sent out monks to collect revenue in the form of alms or taxes. These itinerant monks were to play an essential role in linking the Bulgarian people to the Bulgarian Church and therefore to what remained of Bulgaria's fading culture. As this work grew in stature the monasteries developed 'cell schools' in which small numbers of young men could be trained for service in the Bulgarian church or for monastic orders. However, we must not be tempted into making this painfully slow process into anything approaching a modern national revival. What the monasteries achieved was the preservation of a sense of ethnic separateness without which the Bulgarian national revival would have been impossible. This in itself was a remarkable achievement in view of the Patriarchate's general hostility to nationalistic sentiment.

The most detailed exposition of antinational attitude within the Patriarchate during this pre-revival period in Bulgaria can be found in the booklet entitled *Paternal Instruction*, published in Constantinople in 1798 by Patriarch Gregory V. This advanced the thesis that the Ottoman Empire was a divinely sanctioned institution established to ensure the religious liberty of Orthodox Christian believers and to protect them from the heretical west:

> Behold, how our merciful and omniscient Lord has arranged things, to preserve again the integrity of the holy and orthodox faith of us, the pious, and to redeem everybody; He raised from nothing this powerful kingdom of the Ottomans instead of our Roman kingdom, which had somehow started to deviate in matters of our Christian orthodox spirit. And He raised that Ottoman kingdom above any other kingdom, to prove beyond doubt that this was according to His divine will…. The Devil devised another evil trick in the current century, that is, the now much talked of system of liberty, which on the surface seems as if it were good. But there is an enticement of the Devil and a destructive poison destined to cast people down into catastrophe and disorder. Everywhere this illusory system of liberty has caused poverty, murders, losses, plunder. Deceitful, Christian brethren, are the teachings of those new apostles, be careful.
>
> He [the Sultan] is, after God, the Lord,
> The depository of the goods and guardian of life.
> Both divine and human laws command strongly,
> Call both young and old to submission.
> And above all, the Scripture says, that we should pray for our leader constantly…
> And that he who opposes such authority opposes God Himself.
> As we are indebted to the Sultan for all the charities
> We enjoy, both old and young of us,

Not only should we surrender every possession of ours
But also detest every anarchy.[45]

The Greek Patriarchate was therefore a strong supporter of Ottoman administration and an equally militant obstructer of nationalistic sentiment.
Such tenets would prove to be somewhat troublesome when the national
consciousness of the Bulgarian people was aroused during the period of
Bulgaria's National Revival.

Protests Against Ottoman Dominion

The seventeenth and eighteenth centuries were undoubtedly the nadir of Bulgarian social, spiritual and cultural history. However, contrary
to the tendency of many Bulgarian historians, we should not assume that
under these circumstances the Bulgarians were unconscious of their condition under Ottoman rule. On the contrary they were still aware that
they belonged to a community under Turkish feudal oppression and
Greek ecclesiastical hegemony, restricted in their opportunities to progress and prosper, but determined to resist and engage in various forms
of feudal struggle.

During this pre-liberation period it was the Bulgarian peasant class
who took a stand against the status quo. Due to Ottoman land reforms
Bulgarians' financial burden to their *vali's* increased. As armed conflicts
between Ottoman and European states broke out in the eighteenth
century, Bulgarian taxes and their obligation to give provisions to the
Turkish military and arbitrary acts of plundering increased.

Thus in the eighteenth century it was the rural population of Bulgaria, the peasant class, who were the first to take up the struggle against
their oppressors. It was they who appealed against the seizure of their
lands; it was they who opposed the interminable forms of taxation that
impoverished them. However, they held no hope of obtaining Ottoman
justice, as an eighteenth century Bulgarian commented: "Muslim justice
has gone so far in its unfairness that if devils were appointed as judges,
with full authority to make whatever use they pleased of their powers, I
believe they would be ashamed to do what the Turks are doing."[46] Their
struggle was expressed firstly in the simple refusal to pay taxes. During
poll-tax collections people would go into hiding, while others would flee
to safety, many emigrating to Romania, Serbia and Russia. It was from
Bulgaria's peasant population that the *haidouks* emerged, outlaws who

engaged in armed resistance against their feudal landlords. A Turkish document from the end of the seventeenth century testifies to the activities of a *haidouk* detachment of one hundred men under the leadership of a Bulgarian Orthodox priest from Cherna Reka.[47] Another Turkish document from the seventeenth century points particularly to the Bulgarian clergy as the chief supporters of the *haidouk* movement and mentions the monasteries of Lesnovo, Turnovo and Kriva Reka as refuges for these outlaws: "priestly brigands of the region have joined the outlaws and monks bind up the outlaws wounds and offer them shelter and food."[48]

It was the peasants who rose up in revolt, regularly under the leadership and with the support of Bulgarian clergy. Trouble flared up wherever and whenever circumstances were favourable, particularly during the Turkish wars with the European states and mostly in the districts close to the theatre of military operations. For example, the 'Long War' fought by the Habsburg Empire against the Ottomans at the turn of the sixteenth century created the belief in Bulgaria that a military campaign south of the Danube was imminent. This resulted in a civil uprising in the Turnovo region in 1598, which was suppressed with great brutality. Almost a century later, in 1686, there was another people's revolt around Veliko Turnovo, this time prompted by Russian intrusion into the Balkans after the failure of the Ottoman armies to take Vienna in 1683. Two years later another protest occurred in the Chiprovets region; the town was destroyed and two-thirds of the population killed in government reprisals.[49]

These random peasant struggles are all we really know about national and cultural consciousness in pre-revival Bulgaria. Nevertheless, there were vestiges of intellectual political activity that have been lost to the western historian because of their lack of a Bulgarian label. This in large part has been caused by the confusion between religion and nationality under the *millet* system. For example, thousands of Bulgarians joined Greek and Serbian armed units involved in their own political struggles, in the conviction that they were participating in a wider 'Greek' or 'Orthodox Christian' rebellion against imperial oppression, of which their own sense of a Bulgarian national struggle was a part. The Roman Catholic Church was also active in seventeenth century Bulgaria in stirring up political and religious unrest. A number of Bulgarians came to prominence in this Catholic movement. However, its essentially foreign nature deprived them of gaining lasting significance. For example Petur Bogdan Bakshish who became Archbishop of Antivari in Montenegro is commonly ignored as a Bulgarian because all his works were written in Latin. Archbishop Petur Parchevich, urged the Bulgarians to revolt on behalf of Catholic Austria but was ejected from the country. The Jesuit missionary Christophorus Peichich Bulgarus, again stirred agitation claiming Roman superiority over the Orthodox Church.[50]

Nevertheless, three documented peasant revolts, involvement in a number of foreign skirmishes, and Roman Catholic agitation, after almost three hundred years of Ottoman dominion does not represent a maelstrom of rebellious activity pointing towards a future national revival. Indeed, it took almost another century before a Bulgarian monk articulated the dire situation of the Bulgarian people and yet another century before the Bulgarian people were in a position to actively respond to his call. However, in the course of these centuries it would be the Bulgarian clergy who would coalesce these uncoordinated but defiant strands into a unified and nationalistic call for an independent Church.

FIRST AWAKENINGS: FATHER PAISII OF HILENDAR (1722-1798)

In 1761 Blasius Kleiner, a Franciscan monk from the Alvinic Monastery (situated in modern Romania, then part of the Bulgarian Franciscan province), prepared a history of Bulgarian Catholicism, the first part of which he devoted to a general history of the Bulgarians. Kleiner, after encountering difficulties with this history, laid stress on how little was actually known about the Bulgarians and their ancient state commenting, "this extremely belligerent nation…has been more prone to doing glorious deeds worthy of mention than to describing them."[51]

This is how an eighteenth century Franciscan monk conceived the journey of the Bulgarian nation through history. For Kleiner Bulgaria's past was unknown and obscure. However, when he comments that the deeds of the Bulgarians were neither 'described' nor 'understood' his words conceal the unfortunate truth of the deleted memory of a nation, of the absence of a literary heritage – a heritage that had either disappeared or been destroyed by centuries of domination. This was the view of a benevolent, tolerant and educated foreigner whose audience consisted of the literate readers of his own faith and language. However, only a year later in 1762, a very different Bulgarian history appeared compiled by a Bulgarian for Bulgarians.

By the time the Mount Athos monk Paisii of Hilendar completed his *Slavo-Bulgarian History* centuries of Islamisation and Hellenization had not only eradicated the Bulgarian state from memory, but had also destroyed or banished its aristocracy, its literary heritage, and its church. In the time that elapsed since 1369 servitude sank into the people's consciousness and obliterated all memories of Bulgaria's past. Thus in 1871 the Bulgarian historian Marin Drinov could write that the middle of the eighteenth century had been the most terrible time under the Ottoman yoke: "a time when all hope was utterly lost."[52] Yet it was from this despair that Paisii's voice arose urging his fellow Bulgarians to remember their nation, to have pride in her history, culture and language, warning them of the threat of national extinction. For that reason Paisii wrote his history so the past could be preserved within one book and easily read by future generations. He wrote to enable his compatriots know their history, so they might know themselves and dare be themselves.

Through his narrative Paisii recalls the major events of Bulgarian history. Of special significance for him was the fact that among all Slavs it was the Bulgarians who were the 'most glorious', for it was they who adopted Christianity first, as they were the first to have their own patriarch and hold sway over the largest territory. He remembers these moments of historical grandeur and suggests that what had happened once could happen again. Paisii's *Slavo-Bulgarian History* could therefore be described as a beacon in the darkness, giving warning of present danger and suggesting a strategy for survival, an exit from servitude under Turkish political and Greek ecclesiastical dominion, offering a hope of an independent future. By knowing their history, Paisii hoped that the Bulgarian people would realise that in losing their past they had also lost their identity. It was on the basis of this realisation that Paisii sought to cultivate a desire for knowledge and freedom among his fellow Bulgarians, with his *History* providing the basis for the necessary changes in both the Bulgarians' outlook and their self-esteem. His *Slavo-Bulgarian History* created the energy, knowledge and the myths necessary to transform Bulgarian hopelessness into a hope and desire for freedom.

In can be no surprise then that Paisii of Hilendar is credited with being the 'Father of the Bulgarian National Revival'. He also enjoys reputation as a brilliant historian: "Father Paisii stands much higher than many first historians of other nations whose attempts to write the histories of their people stand beneath all manner of criticism on the score of invention, credulity, and ignorance."[53] However, his *Slavo-Bulgarian History* may not have been as influential in his own times as modern Bulgarian history presumes. By 1862, one hundred years after Paisii's *History* was completed, and only fifteen years away from Bulgaria's liberation, there was no published edition available in Bulgaria. Paisii himself may have contributed to this anonymity. That he was intensely patriotic, there can be no doubt, but it is also abundantly clear from examining his work that he was a deeply humble man. Circulating the patriotic message of the book was more important to him than that attention be drawn to his name. Thus in his original draft he gave these instructions: "Copy this little history and pay those who can write so that you can have it copied, and keep it lest it should disappear."[54] Accordingly his work was widely and repeatedly copied, which unfortunately led to copyists ignoring its original authorship substituting their own name.

The absence of printing facilities for Cyrillic publications in Bulgaria also contributed to Paisii's obscurity. Indeed, until the late eighteenth century the only source for printing Cyrillic text was in Moscow. The first accessible Cyrillic press, in Vienna, did not become available until 1770, almost ten years after Paisii finished his *History*.[55] The first book published in Bulgarian did not appear until 1806, its author being Paisii's first known copyist, Sofroni of Vratsa. Paisii's original handwritten draft of *Slavo-Bulgarian History* is therefore one of the few authentic documents in Bulgarian literary history that have been preserved, being stored in the Bulgarian Monastery of St. Georgi-Zograph on Mount Athos. This draft is in fact the history of the first Bulgarian book of the National Revival period inspired by the idea of spiritual and national renewal of the Bulgarians.[56]

Apart from the few autobiographical details, with which Paisii provides his readers within his *History*, we know very little about the man. He was born in Bansko in 1722, and was buried in Samokov in 1798. He entered Hilendar Monastery in 1745, when he was 23 years old, remaining there until 1761. In that year he moved to the Bulgarian Zograph Monastery, also on Mount Athos, where he resided until 1791, and then returned to Hilendar where he remained until his death. It is likely that he began writing his *History* around 1760 when he became deputy-abbot of Hilendar Monastery. In this ecclesiastical post he was given opportunity to travel in search of materials. Undoubtedly, his desire for knowledge came much earlier – probably soon after 1745, when he arrived on Mount Athos. Within this monastic setting Paisii found himself in a novel social and cultural environment; not only was Mount Athos a centre of Balkan Christian spirituality but also a repository for new western cultural and educational ideas. In 1753, the Greek reformer Eugenius Bulgaris established his Athonite Academy where his students studied a secular gospel of philosophy and modern sciences. As a result new and pervasive ideas permeated the monastic environment rousing national sentiments. In his role as an alms-collector for the monastery Paisii travelled around Bulgaria witnessing at close quarters the dire situation of the Bulgarians who remained spiritually and culturally undeveloped. He connected closely with his fellow Bulgars who were suffering from a decaying feudal system and the slow redevelopment of the Ottoman empire.

Paisii was keenly aware of the autonomous nature of Bulgarian Christianity. He reveals this by explaining the significance of Rila Monastery to his fellow Bulgarians: "It is of great use to all Bulgarians, which is why all Bulgarians ought to keep it and make donations to the holy Rila Monastery, so that the great benefit and praise they derive from it should not become extinct."[57] He regarded Rila as a repository of Bulgarian Christian piety, a place where Bulgarian national spirituality and nationality were preserved. The monastery was a stronghold of the Bulgarian spirit, a positive sign that Bulgaria had not been totally eradicated by Islamic and Greek influence. It was, therefore, from his direct experience with the Bulgarian people, infused with western renaissance thinking and roused by Balkan rivalry and patriotic fervour, brought on by reviving Greek nationalism and with a keen understanding of Bulgaria's autonomous national and spiritual character that Paisii perceived the need for a modern Bulgarian history, the lack of which he linked to the low self-esteem of Bulgarians.

He finished his draft version of *Slavo-Bulgarian History* in 1762. However, a little before its completion he moved from Hilendar to Zograph Monastery. It appears that 1762 was a troublesome year in Hilendar, the result of a number of unpleasant disagreements amongst the Serbs, Greeks and Bulgarians about the glories and greatness of their respective nationalities and cultures. During these disputes the various histories of the nations involved were discussed, and Paisii found that Bulgaria was regularly disregarded since it had no history to speak of. Evidence of these quarrels can be found in the autobiography of the Serbian enlightener Dositei Obradovic, a contemporary of Paisii, who resided in Hilendar from 1765 where he mentions that, "Serbs and Bulgarians quarrelled and behaved obstinately because they could not come to an agreement on whose Hilendar was."[58] However, in the serenity of Zograph Paisii was able to complete his history.

It is beyond any doubt that, along with the numerous historical characters appearing in the pages of Paisii's *Slavo-Bulgarian History*, it is Paisii's personality that reaches out to us from the past most vividly: Paisii the monk, the enlightener, the patriot working for the benefit of the Bulgarian people. He personified most effectively amongst his contemporaries the qualities of the New Balkan Renaissance, illustrating the power of knowledge that would become the most important condition for the development of human society. Realising that ignorance and a lack of historical memory led to Bulgaria's spiritual death and slavery, he set upon himself the task of rebuilding the foundations of Bulgarian national culture, giving his fellow Bulgars historical knowledge – the first and most decisive prerequisite for recreating national identity.

The political incisiveness of this new Renaissance figure, however, suggested one more important task, developing in the minds of the Bulgarian people the idea of the actual geographical territory inhabited by the Bulgarian national community. Thus by mentioning throughout his *History* many different towns such as Sofia, Preslav, Turnovo, Plovdiv, Vidin, Samakov, Ohrid, Skopje etc., he sketches within the mentality of the Bulgarian an image of an actual geographical nation. Paisii understood clearly that establishing an awareness of belonging to a national community was an important prerequisite for creating patriotic pride and creative energy for the formation of national consciousness and the future development of the nation itself.

Led by his convictions, Paisii pinned his hopes for national revival on those who had been involved in the first social uprisings, the "ploughmen, diggers, shepherds and simple craftsmen."[59] He departs from medieval historiographic traditions by combining the stories of Bulgaria's rulers and saints with those of their subjects, celebrating the fact that the latter were ready to dethrone usurpers and weak rulers in the interests of the nation itself. Contrary to medieval religious norms, he rejects the dogma of the eternity of established order, and identifies the Greek Patriarchate and the Turkish government as enemies of the Bulgarian national idea. It is here that the concept of "Church freedom" figures for the first time in Bulgarian National Revival thinking. He speaks of Turkish slavery and Greek priests as the common face of evil oppressing the Bulgarian nation. His history does not preach Christian reconciliation; rather, it sows the seeds for future struggle to overthrow ecclesiastic and political domination. Therefore, one may say that Paisii's ideas rest in the very foundations of the Bulgarian revolutionary ideology, paving the way for the deeds of people such as Bozveli, Slaveikov, Karavelov, Rakovski, Levski and Botev.

Design and Execution

The full title of Paisii's work is *Slavo-Bulgarian History of the Bulgarian People and Kings and Saints and of all the Bulgarians Acts and Events. Collected and Arranged by the Ordained Monk Paisii, who lived on Athos and had come there from the Diocese of Samokov in 1745 finishing this History in 1762 for the Benefit of the Bulgarian People.* Its very length suggests the scope of the historical material it includes. It begins with a preface entitled 'The Benefit of History' which is almost in its entirety taken from the foreword of Cesar Baronius' *Annales Ecclesiastici.* This fitted neatly into the author's own designs as Baronius' preface was a dissertation on the significance and benefit of historical knowledge:

> History gives wisdom not only to every person on how to conduct himself or his home, but also to great rulers on how to exercise their power well: how to keep their God-given subjects in fear of the Lord, in obedience, serenity, truth and righteousness, how to subdue and eliminate rebels, how to rise in arms against foreign foes in wars, how to defeat them and how to conclude peace.[60]

Paisii's message begins with a secondary introduction, entitled 'A Foreword to Those Who Wish to Read and Hear What Was Written in This History'. The one who speaks here is not so much the monk and teacher but an enlightener and apostle to Bulgaria. From the style of writing it is clear that Paisii's intent was not simply to instruct his reader, but to press his opinions on them, not by coercion, but by reminding them of Bulgaria's noble history. His tone of intimate conversation changes to rebuke when he sees this history being ignored:

> But some people would not wish to know about their Bulgarian ancestors, and they turn to a foreign culture and a foreign language, and they neglect their Bulgarian language.... You unreasonable and foolish men! Why are you ashamed to call yourselves Bulgarians, why do you not read and speak your own language?[61]

Paisii was clearly an experienced wordsmith making frequent use of the impact of figurative expression to instil feelings of guilt and shame within his readers: "Why are you silly fellow ashamed of your race and favour a foreign language?"[62] He follows these personal arguments by giving beneficial examples to stimulate his readers: "But see here, you foolish fellow, there are many nations wiser and more glorious than the Greeks. Yet, does any Greek abandon his language and knowledge and race as you do, o senseless man!"[63] The anger and occasional sarcasm gradually subside and turn into encouragement, but not without a residual note of reprimand: "You, Bulgarian, do not fool yourself, know your ancestry and language and study in your own tongue! Bulgarian simplicity and innocence are much to be preferred."[64]

In support of his nationalist thesis, Paisii put forward his most compelling arguments in three particular areas:

1. **That of contemporary life**: Unlike others, Bulgarians "will invite in their home anyone and feed him" and will gladly "give alms to those who beg from them."[65]

2. **The biblical**: From Adam to David and Joseph whoever "was righteous or a holy prophet or a patriarch" was not "a merchant or an overly clever or haughty man" but "the uncouth and humble on earth, farmers and shepherds."[66]

3. **The historical**: "Did the Bulgarians not have their own kingdom and state? So many long years did they reign and they were glorious and famed the world over... Throughout the Slavic world, the Bulgarians were the most glorious, they were the first to call themselves tsars, the first to have a patriarch, the first to be Christianised, they conquered the largest domain. Thus among all the Slavs they were the mightiest and the most revered, and it was out of the Bulgarian race and language that the first Slavic saints arose...."[67]

As early as the Introduction, Paisii puts forward an important idea that will find fuller expression throughout his *History*: that the dignity of a nation is gained and judged through its political as well as spiritual and cultural achievements. In the main body of his work he offers an overview of the political, spiritual and cultural history of the Bulgarians from the time of the biblical flood to the fall of Bulgaria under Ottoman rule.

From here we enter into the main exposition with Paisii's historical material grouped in seven chapters. The first chapter entitled 'Historical Texts on the Bulgarian People' sets forth Paisii's view of the biblical origins of the Bulgarian people, tracing their roots to Japheth, the third son of Noah. He thus classifies the Bulgarian nation among God's elect. However, he lays special emphasis on the Slavic character of the Bulgarians and takes pride in distinguishing them among the Slavic peoples for their number and strength. He outlines the arrival and settlement of the Bulgarians in the Balkan Peninsula, their numerous wars with Byzantium for the consolidation of their state, and their international recognition up to the reign of Tsar Mihail Shishman (1323-30).

Paisii not only relates particular historical events but also takes every chance to point out the might and the valour of the Bulgarians in these events. His use of extra-Bulgarian sources is of importance here as evidence to support his nationalistic theories. Of special value are the opinions of Bulgaria's enemies, particularly the Greeks, when they comment on the merits of the Bulgarians: "The Bulgarians are wild and invincible in war.... Fierce are the Bulgarians and invincible in combat...."[68]

Challenged by the arguments of his fellow Slavic monks in Hilendar that Bulgaria had no history, Paisii entitled his second chapter, 'Here Reader, Take note, We Will Tell you Briefly about the Serbian Kings'. In this section he offers analysis of the successes and failures of the Serbian state and voices his dissatisfaction at Serb misrepresentation of historical truth:

> Their kingdom was small, very narrow, and existed for a short time.... Out of folly they consider themselves from the beginning to have been more glorious than the Bulgarians with their kingdom, army and land. But this is not true. All peoples on earth know the Bulgarians and in all histories this is recorded and found in writing. About the Serbs there is nothing written....[69]

Along with his history of the Serbian people the chapter covers Bulgarian events up to the eve of the Ottoman conquest during the reign of Tsar Ivan Shishman (1371-95). He warns against chauvinistic arrogance that leads to an unjust and dangerous overestimation of one's nation at the expense of other peoples. He repeatedly relies on the evidence of historical sources in Greek and Latin to back up his claims. In this chapter he also reproaches the Byzantine policy of conciliation with the Turks at the expense of the Bulgarian state but includes a bold statement concerning the common blame of both nations: "If there had been love and concord between the Greeks and the Bulgarians, the Turks would never have defeated them...."[70]

He continues by giving an apocalyptic description of the misfortunes that struck the Bulgarians after the invasion of the Ottomans: the violent abduction of "young and handsome lads" during the raising of the *devshirme*, the turning of the best Bulgarian churches into mosques, the plundering of houses, crops and vineyards, the slaughter of those who were rich and educated. "Thus" he utters tragically, "the people of that first generation after the Bulgarian Tsardom was conquered, had great sorrow and grief and they shed many tears until that first generation passed."[71]

However, to rekindle a positive knowledge of Bulgaria's 'glorious' past he includes two short chapters entitled, 'It is Necessary Here to put together the Names of the Bulgarian Kings and Tsars' and 'A Short Collection about how Renowned the Bulgarian Kings and Tsars Were'. He lists the names and records the deeds of all Bulgaria's rulers in chronological order. The enumeration of the royal names, almost biblical in style, creates the impression of an impregnable and steadfast dynasty throughout Bulgaria's history. The second of the chapters in this section continues the royal tradition, aiming at awakening national pride and a sense of honour and dignity in the Bulgarian people by describing the deeds of the more eminent and successful Bulgarian rulers.

In the following chapter, 'About the Slavic Apostles', Paisii explains how other Slavic nations boast about their pious men and defenders of the Orthodox faith. However, when doing the same in Bulgaria, he pronounces that we deal with something of a higher order. Here he establishes the Bulgarian character of the work of Cyril and Methodius and their disciples; it was they who created the Bulgarian alphabet, who translated into Bulgarian the Scriptures that would bring the light of knowledge and of the Christian faith to the Bulgarian people, and only thereafter to other Slav nations:

> Thus of the whole Slavic race it was the Bulgarians who received Slavic letters, books and Christianity. Although the Muscovites, the Russians, the Serbs and others boast that they adopted the Slavic letters and adopted Christianity earlier, that is untrue. They are unable to present any evidence for this. [72]

Apart from Sts. Cyril and Methodius, Paisii devotes a special chapter to other Bulgarian saints entitled, 'Here we Gather in Short the Names of the Bulgarian Saints who Shone out of the Bulgarian People in Latter Times'. He elaborates the significance of these saints in spiritual, cultural and political terms. He lays particular stress on their interests in the field of literature and education and also their concern for the establishment and consolidation of Bulgarian culture and state.

Finally, in the 'Epilogue' Paisii concludes his *History* as he introduced it, as though conversing with friends, with whom he has been sharing intimate thoughts. He talks again about his motives for writing this history and shares some of the conditions under which he had worked, concluding with the remark, that he had become, "gradually eaten up with zealousness and pity for my Bulgarian kin for there had been no history put together of the glorious exploits since the early ages of our ancestry, our saints and tsars."[73]

In many ways the introduction and epilogue of the *Slavo-Bulgarian History* are the most important chapters of the book presenting us with personal insight into the character of Paisii of Hilendar. He corresponds with his readers in conversational style, clearly explaining his motives, describing who he is and the conditions under which he was working at the time. Although his method of recalling history contains evidence of the medieval traditionalist it also demonstrates that he was a creative writer in the contemporary renaissance style, writing his history with his own patriotic motives in mind but not to flatter his own literary vanity. It was written, he comments, "for the benefit of the Bulgarian people."[74]

It has been generally assumed that Paisii was prompted to write a Bulgarian history by the disputes between the Slavic monks of Hilendar over which Balkan nation was the greatest. He himself acknowledges, "The Serbs and the Greeks reproached us many times for not having our own history."[75] His bruised nationalistic pride cannot be overlooked as a motivation of his endeavour. Equally as important, we argue, was his desire to promote the development of Bulgarian society. In his role as alms-collector, his travels throughout Bulgaria left a deep impression on him, notably with regards to the trials and tribulations of the Bulgarian peasantry. He was distressed to witness the social inferiority of his fellow Bulgarians to the Greeks and was angered by their willingness to adopt Greek language and culture:

> They neglect their Bulgarian language and learn and speak Greek instead and they deem it shameful to call themselves Bulgarians.... I saw many Bulgarians behave in that manner, take up a foreign language and customs, and scorn their own.[76]

It was above all his relationship with the Bulgarian people that ignited Paisii's desire to infuse them with a renewed sense of national consciousness and common cultural identity. He acknowledges this himself when he comments: "I was gradually eaten up with zealousness and pity for my Bulgarian kin for there had been no history put together of the glorious exploits since the early ages of our ancestry, our saints and tsars."[77] These were the words of a man who had observed and understood the material and spiritual plight of the Bulgarian people under Ottoman and Greek dominion. However, through his writing we can also sense the hope that he has in his fellow Bulgars, his faith in their potential to recover their esteem in Bulgaria's history, and to grow as a nation asserting their rights for spiritual and political independence. It was this belief in the virtues of his people, in the constructive forces inherent within them that inspired Paisii not only to write his *History*, but also to disseminate its message throughout Bulgaria.

Conclusion

The arrival of Paisii's *Slavo-Bulgarian History* was an epochal event in Bulgarian history marking the transition from a nation's cultural and spiritual stagnation to creative and independent thought and action. Although concise it was nonetheless a remarkably significant work. Though written in a medieval traditional style it contained the influence of renaissance thinking. Having comprehended the historical fate of his compatriots, knowing their present and foreseeing their future, Paisii cast the first spark into the people's minds that would give birth to national, spiritual and political awareness. He achieved this by establishing a goal, which would be advanced by future generations, calling for the education of his people in the Bulgarian vernacular, for Church independence and for the restoration of the Bulgarian state. Those who would follow Paisii during the National Revival period turned the goals expressed within *Slavo-Bulgarian History* into their own political manifesto, pointing to a new age of independence, an age where the love of nation and race would become the highest virtue. Paisii thus defined the goals which Bulgarian society would aspire to at the outset of the National Revival.

To assess the real value of Paisii's *History*, one ought to ask the critical question of what the Bulgarians really knew about their history in the era under Ottoman rule before its dissemination. This question is important because memory of the past shapes the present and the future of both the individual and the nation. Bulgarian histories could be found in European libraries; however, barring certain exceptions this evidence would have been unknown and inaccessible to the vast majority of Bulgarians. Moreover, historical records were kept in the libraries of a large number of churches and monasteries, but were known only to a limited number of literate priests and monks. Certain historical moments also found reflection in folklore but they took on legendary and mythical character. Thus, leaving aside a small number of exceptions, the majority of Bulgarians in their life under Ottoman rule, in the course of four centuries, had lost all understanding of their nation's historical significance and cultural identity, believing that their people had been living since time immemorial a life subordinated to the will of an alien ruler.

By evoking the memory and reviving the knowledge of an independent and mighty Bulgarian empire, Paisii instigated the slow process of awakening and developing Bulgarian national consciousness, associated with a feeling of pride of belonging to a national whole, unified by language, territory, historical fate, spiritual and material culture. It can be no coincidence that Paisii's *History*, which had been borne out of the need of the Bulgarian people, proved to be in harmony with their expectations and requirements. That is why Bulgarians look on Paisii of Hilendar as an outstanding figure of the Revival period, as a revolutionary enlightener and as the initiator of the Bulgarian liberation. His message continues to be relevant to his people, traversing the centuries of Bulgarian history. The Bulgarian poet Hristo Radevski could thus writes during the Second World War:

Hear Paisii's words resound
in the dark and hollow rumble!
Remember your people and your country!
Remember Levski's legacy profound
and the song of Granny Tonka, wise and humble.

The call of our fathers is in us today
and in the solemn hymns of our sons.
Be ready! Is that what they say?
You must finish what we have begun![78]

FIRST AWAKENINGS: SOFRONI, BISHOP OF VRATSA (1739-1814)

Somewhat neglected and generally underrated by modern Bulgarian history, Stoiko Vladislavov of Kotel, a contemporary of Paisii of Hilendar, was a man who advanced the development of Bulgaria's cultural awakening. He was born into a family of successful cattle-dealers before being ordained as a priest in 1762. The genesis of his personal cultural awakening came some three years later, in 1765, when Father Paisii visited Kotel complete with his *Slavo-Bulgarian History*. Paisii's *History* made such an impression on the young priest that he copied it and placed it in the local church with the following warning attached: "May he who appropriates or steals this book be anathematised and cursed by the Lord God and by the twelve apostles, by the holy fathers and the four evangelists. May hail, iron and stone fall on him and may he perish forever."[79] He was so influenced by Paisii's ideas that he decided, during 1775, to spend six months on Mount Athos enveloping himself in the atmosphere that had inspired Paisii's patriotic zeal.

Stoiko's own patriotic thoughts evolved in the midst of turbulent times. During the first Russo-Turkish War (1768-74), Russia sent agents into Bulgaria in an attempt to rouse the people to revolt, encouraging them to believe that their liberation from Ottoman domination was imminent if they rose in support of the Russian cause. When Russian troops entered Bulgaria via the Dobrudzha in 1773, the promise of liberation became tangible. Many Bulgarians, including men from Stoiko's parish, fought beside the Russians in volunteer partisan units. However, after the surrender of the Ottomans in 1774, Russia withdrew her troops from Bulgarian territory leaving the population at the mercy of the Ottoman military. Stoiko and the inhabitants of the Kotel area suffered greatly during the retribution of the Ottoman troops. Infuriated by Bulgaria's participation in the war, the Turks wreaked vengeance devastating the town and surrounding villages murdering at will.[80] It was in the midst of these repercussions that Stoiko left for Mount Athos. Thus, while the claim of Bulgarian historians that his stay on Mount Athos was inspired by Paisii's *History* may be partly true, his timing would suggest that recuperation and escape from Ottoman recrimination was an equally valid possibility.

His stay on Mount Athos affected him profoundly, igniting in him the spirit of enlightenment that had stimulated Paisii. On his return to Kotel, as well as acting as priest, he initiated an educational work, teaching the children to speak, to read and to write in vernacular Bulgarian rather than the standard Greek. He also willingly adopted the role of local politician, interceding on behalf of his parishioners over the crippling taxations placed on them by the Porte, the landowners and the Patriarchate. His patriotic preaching, social work and educational activities brought him to the attention of the local Ottoman officials and Greek clergy who decided to punish his insubordination. According to Stoiko's own biography, *The Life and Sufferings of the Sinful Sofroni*, he was sentenced to a period of imprisonment where he was ill-treated and fed rotting food, resulting in the loss of his hair.[81] On his release and return to Kotel he fell foul of the local *chorbadzhi* who disliked his patriotic methods and forced him to leave town. He then became the priest in Karnobat, but there fell foul of the Ottoman authorities: knowing that a local Christian girl had been chosen by the regional Pasha to be one of his wives, Stoiko disregarded this official arrangement and married her to a local Christian man whom she loved. Once more he had to flee, now in fear of his life, re-settling as priest in Karabounar, where he continued preaching and teaching in Bulgarian. In 1794 he was ordained as Bishop in the Diocese of Vratsa, taking the name Sofroni. That such an honour should be placed on this man is somewhat incomprehensible, considering the trouble he had caused the political and ecclesiastical authorities, and the anti-Bulgarian bias of the Greek Patriarchate. However, as Greek clergy were unwilling to officiate in this diocese, because of the mortal danger involved, the choice of a Bulgarian becomes understandable.

The area of Bulgaria where Sofroni's new diocese was situated had been terrorised from 1792 until 1815 by armed bandits known as *kurdzhali*, a movement composed of brigands, disaffected imperial troops and discontented Janissaries who saw in the Porte's proposed army reforms the end of their power. The leaders of these *kurdzhali* took control of large areas of Ottoman territory causing a virtual breakdown in the Porte's central governmental structure. This unstable period known in Bulgaria as the *kurdzhaliistvo* was a time of hardship causing much distress. English traveller E. D. Clark described its effects on the Bulgarian people:

> They are at present in a most wretched condition, owing to the extortions of the *kurdzhali*. In a short space of six months, they have paid their tax gatherers eighty purses, a sum equivalent to forty thousand piastres. Poverty is very apparent in their dwellings... nor can it be otherwise, where the wretched inhabitants are so oppressed by their lords. The whole of the earnings of the peasant is taken from him; he is scarcely allowed any means of subsistence.[82]

Further depredations of the *kurdzhali* are graphically depicted in Sofroni's biography where he reports: "Conditions defy description when these ferocious and cruel infidels went to war. How many evils do they do to the Christians! They do everything that came to their minds. The number of people they murdered! The many times they seized me and beat me up and cracked my head. They almost killed me, but God preserved me." [83] Sultan Selim III (1789-1807) was revolted by the activities of the *kurdzhali* of whom he said in 1795:

> These villains like parasites and reptiles have invaded many villages, towns and cities of our state, and the population, especially the raya's, have cried out to heaven for relief from the unheard of plunder and torture.... Law and order in the land is compromised, the state laws are disregarded, complete anarchy reigns within the Empire... The impetuous torrent of those barbarous hordes is sweeping all over Rumelia [South Eastern Bulgaria].[84]

As terrible as this period was for the Bulgarian people the rise of the *kurdzhaliistvo* merely reflected the extent of the Ottoman Empire's decaying structures. One of the most notorious *kurdzhali* leaders was the *ayan* Osman Pasvangolu (1758-1807). His father had been the *Pasha* of Vidin before being executed on suspicion of sedition against the sultan. From 1792 he determined to avenge his father's death. He attracted rebels against the empire, devastated villages and generally opposed the reforms of Sultan Selim III. In 1794 he captured his native town of Vidin (at the centre of Sofroni's diocese) and proclaimed himself as the independent ruler of the autonomous province.[85] Up to the year 1800 the Porte sent armies against Pasvangolu but they failed to remove him from power and in the end were forced to recognise his authority. During this violent period Sofroni's diocese was besieged not only by Pasvanoglu's marauding *kurdzhali*, but also by the sultan's troops.

Although Bishop Sofroni mentions the violent struggles that took place during the period of the *kurdzhaliistvo*, the Greek historian Stavrianos claims that Pasvanoglu was only able to retain his position of authority for such an extended period by satisfying the needs and winning the support and respect of the local population. He argues that Pasvanoglu is remembered not because of his violent practices but rather because he restored order, protected the poor from the extortions of the tax collectors, and provided security for his Christian subjects.[86] The testimony of a contemporary English traveller reporting from Pasvanoglu's capital, Vidin, agrees with Stavrianos in this respect: "Vidin owes its rise chiefly to the emigration of poor families from Wallachia and Moldavia, who pass over the Danube, and take refuge in Bulgaria, to avoid the tyranny and extortion practised by Greek and Turkish tax-gatherers...."[87] Neale is suggesting here that people migrated to Vidin both for their safety and because of its fair conditions. However, a study of the demographic composition, distribution and movement of Bulgarian peoples during this particular period disagrees with these reports and arguments. The effects of the *kurdzhaliistvo* period and especially the Russo-Turkish Wars had a profound effect on the peoples of Bulgaria. Indeed, a tidal wave of emigration is recorded between the 1790's and the 1820's when almost half a million people left Bulgaria to settle in Romania, southern Ukraine and Russia.

Undaunted by these precarious circumstances Bishop Sofroni set out for his new diocese. Unfortunately, from 1795 the violent disorders worsened as villages were plundered and burned by both the *kurdzhali* and the sultan's troops. However, it is important to note that this was not Islamic violence directed specifically at Christians, but rather the result of war in which innocents suffered. On many occasions Sofroni himself was forced into hiding fleeing from village to village, he hid in caves, forests and once in a harem. Although in continual fear for his life Sofroni never stopped preaching and teaching the people in vernacular Bulgarian; his patriotic teaching excited the eager ear of Bulgarians who suffered at the hands of bandits and government troops alike. Sofroni was able to persist in his patriotic ministry for six years within his Vratsa diocese before being tricked, apprehended and imprisoned for three years in Vidin. On his release in 1803, due to the continued activities of the *kurdzhali*, he was unable to continue his ministry in Bulgaria and was obliged to leave for the safety of Bucharest.[88]

In Bucharest the sufferings of Sofroni finally came to an end. He was welcomed and treated as a hero by the Bulgarian émigrés. However, the guilt of abandoning his flock led Sofroni to commence on a new literary career with an autobiographical work entitled *The Life and Sufferings of the Sinful Sofroni: Therefore, I am working day and night to write a few books in our Bulgarian language, so that if I, a sinner, cannot speak to them verbally for them to learn from me, then they can read my writings and benefit from them and pray to God for me, unworthy one, that He should correct my ignorance.*[89] In it he paints an extensive picture of Bulgarian life in the second half of the 18th century. He writes in the religious style of the day but uses a Bulgarian vernacular form mixed with Old Church Slavonic. His work also diverges from the traditional style by imbuing itself with the secular concepts of the European Enlightenment. Indeed, one might suggest that Sofroni's *Life*, although marking an incipient development in the Bulgarian National Revival movement, was his homage to Paisii's *History*.

With financial support from the Bulgarian merchants of Bucharest Sofroni published his autobiography in 1806, incidentally the first book to be printed in Bulgarian. It was originally entitled *Nedelnik* (Sunday) and contained, in addition to the main autobiographical section, a preface of various sermons and homilies. Between 1806 and 1809, still clearly influenced by the new educational concepts of the European Enlightenment, Sofroni translated a number of works into Bulgarian including *Aesop's Fables*, *The Mythology of Cynthippus the Philosopher* and *Theatron Politikon*. *Theatron Politikon* was Sofroni's last known publication in 1809 and included ideas of liberty relating particularly to the reformation of social relationships. Sofroni writes in his introduction to the book:

> I, humble in zealousness for my people, have worked and translated from Greek into Bulgarian, because this book is very useful and necessary to men. And not only to the rulers who are in power, in that it will teach them gently how to rule their states and subjects justly and honourably, but it is also necessary and useful to everyone. [90]

In Bucharest Sofroni busied himself not only with literary activity but continued in his political struggles on Bulgaria's behalf. For example, during the third Russo-Turkish War (1806-1812) he was actively engaged in political manoeuvring. After the fiasco of the first Russo-Turkish War he was well aware that Russia's political and military aid was essential if any hope of Bulgarian liberation was to succeed. He urged upon his fellow Bulgarians the need for cordial Russo-Bulgarian relations. It was therefore with the blessing and authority of Bishop Sofroni that the Bulgarian émigrés made contact with the Ministry of Foreign Affairs in St. Petersburg in the hope of receiving Russian aid in any future plan for liberation. Shortly after the outbreak of war he sent a letter to the Russian authorities, which spoke of the close ties of blood and religion that existed between the Russians and the Bulgarians, and offered Russia the help of the Bulgarians in the war. The letter also included, perhaps for the first time, a Bulgarian plea to be liberated by the Russian army, and the desire to become part of a greater Russian Empire. This indeed was a premonition of Bulgaria's future fascination with *Dyado Ivan* (Grampa Ivan - Russia) – but in this instance it is important to note that Bulgaria saw the immediate result of their liberation as union with Russia. Thus, in his *Appeal to the Bulgarian People* he urges his fellow-countrymen to welcome the Russian troops as brothers.[91]

Bishop Sofroni of Vratsa, or humble Stoiko Vladislavov, must be regarded as an extremely influential figure in the history of Bulgaria's cultural and spiritual awakening. Perhaps of even greater importance than Father Paisii of Hilendar, for his exploits put into practice what Paisii had only preached. He not only propagated the ideas of the European Enlightenment but also modelled his ministry on them. He aspired, through his ecclesiastical role, to reform social relations, to fight against the ignorance of his contemporaries, to introduce a new educational model, to break the yoke of slavery that entrapped his fellow Bulgarians and engender new international political relationships, which would help achieve the liberation of his people. He must also be considered an equally influential figure in the sphere of Bulgarian literature. Apart from being the author of the first modern book printed in Bulgarian, he is important for his insistence that future books be written in the vernacular, rather than Old Church Slavonic or Greek. He was not only the first person to copy Paisii's *History*, but also the first to re-copy the original into a vernacular Bulgarian edition, enabling it to be read widely. He was greatly influenced, as was Paisii, by the humanist ideas of the European Enlightenment, perceiving knowledge and education as being of paramount importance in the resurrection of the Bulgarian people. He thus assumed the role of educator with a vision for a new model of education, making him the forerunner of future Bulgarian school reforms, beginning in the 1830's. Thus, in the fields of politics, education, spiritual and cultural awakenings Bulgarians have many reasons to acclaim Bishop Sofroni.

CONCLUSION

This chapter has endeavoured to explain the religious and social context of Bulgarians in the Ottoman empire during the period prior to the National Revival. Attention has been drawn to the 'double-yoke' of Bulgaria's oppression under Ottoman political, social and economic control combined with Greek religious, cultural and economic subjugation. It was in these circumstances that the Bulgarian peasantry began to revolt, not out of nationalistic desire, or anti-Islamic sentiment but due to economic and social hardship. It is beyond doubt that the Ottoman conquest and extended process of Islamisation impeded the development of Bulgarian culture and stifled national identity. Allegations of Islamic persecution against the Christian population and Church extending over five centuries, however, is simply not borne out by the archival evidence. Although faced with moments of persecution the Church was not imperilled by Islam, the greater danger came from its oppression by the Greeks and the Constantinople Patriarchate. This fact is corroborated by Paisii of Hilendar. It is important to note that Paisii never incited his fellow countrymen to revolt against the Ottoman authorities. It was enough for him that Bulgars regain a knowledge of whom they once had been, and a vision of whom they could be again, within the Ottoman empire. What was of specific importance to Paisii was that Bulgaria would stand against the ecclesiastical hegemony of the Greeks. Bishop Sofroni of Vratsa embodied and developed Paisii's desires. Although he criticised both Ottomans and Greeks, his criticism of the Turks was political in nature as he understood that Bulgaria's freedom would only be achieved through separation from the Ottoman empire. Inherent in Sofroni's own desires was the idea of Bulgaria regaining spiritual, cultural and territorial independence, but only through unification with

Russia. Although the harsh and occasionally violent Ottoman regime was mentioned by Paisii and Sofroni, they neither overstressed nor embellished its nature. An investigation of Ottoman and Bulgarian archives from this pre-National Revival era concurs with their understanding and confirms the conclusion that although the Ottoman authorities were viewed as conquerors, unwanted by Bulgarians, their five centuries' rule of Bulgaria was marked more by tolerance than oppression of the Christian population. The Bulgarian catastrophe theory must therefore be considered anachronistic, the fabrication of a later nationalist sentiment that invokes Paisii and Sofroni, while neglecting their historical realism.

3
THE JOURNEY TOWARDS CULTURAL AUTONOMY

This chapter will examine events surrounding the cultural regeneration of Bulgaria which grew in intensity during the nineteenth century. It will achieve this by investigating the underlying circumstances that made renaissance possible. It will look at the political perspectives of the Ottoman Tanzimat reform programme and its effect on the economic and social conditions of Bulgaria. The chapter will concentrate specifically on the development of education in Bulgaria from the medieval religious model to the advent of the secular 'New Bulgarian' model and the emergence of a culturally aware Bulgarian intelligentsia. The chapter will also look at foreign influences upon the cultural development of Bulgaria and will analyse the Ottoman Vilayet Law of 1864, specifically designed to discourage developing national and international cultural tendencies. This will provide a framework from which the chapter will consider the role of the Bulgarian Orthodox Church during this period of cultural awakening, in which it claims to have kept alive Bulgarian cultural, educational and linguistic traditions. From this foundation the Bulgarian Orthodox Church professes to be the most important indigenous agent of National Revival – a claim that will be critically assessed as the chapter moves to its conclusion.

TOWARD CULTURAL REVIVAL

For the Balkans, enveloped within a weakening Ottoman Empire, the eighteenth century was a time of awakening and enlightenment. Bulgaria, during the first half of the century, remained largely untouched by the changes that were transforming Europe or by the growing cultural and national awareness amongst the Greeks and Serbs. By the end of the eighteenth century the repercussions of Napoleon's victories over Austria were affecting all Balkan peoples. In 1809 Napoleon created the Illyrian Provinces from territory ceded by the Austrians, comprising part of the far western Balkans, resulting in the emergence of modern nationalism in Croatia, Slovenia and Serbia. In northern Bulgaria Osman

Pazvantoglu took advantage of the chaotic conditions and in 1795 declared his region independent of Ottoman central government, spreading the message of the French revolution, *liberté, égalité et fraternité.*[1] These external events hastened the process of cultural and national awakening in Bulgaria, but her national revival could never have occurred without the simultaneous decline and reform of Ottoman imperial structures.

Economic, Social And Political Change In The Ottoman Empire

By the early nineteenth century the Ottoman empire was a major world power whose territories included vast areas of Europe, Asia and Africa. Behind its impressive façade, however, Ottoman administration was in a state of serious decline. Dubbed the 'weak man' of Europe, the empire's once successful administrative system was in a state of terminal meltdown; the original provincial administrators, complete with their excellent bureaucratic training and strict merit system of advancement, had given way to the officeholder who bought his position and treated it as a personal investment that should yield the highest financial profits. This resulted in the exploitation of the peasantry with minimum benefit to Ottoman central government. The most serious problem was the failure of central government to exercise authority over the *ayân* class – the local administrators and notables – who turned their areas of responsibility into personal fiefdoms: "Ottoman government was government in little more than name".[2] Escalating anarchy created the urgent necessity for a reorganisation of imperial structure with the primary purpose of re-establishing the authority of central government.

The era of Ottoman reform began in the last year of the reign of Sultan Mahmud II (1808-1839) who promulgated the Gülhane Rescript (1839) that regulated administrative and military expenditure and prepared the way for more extensive legislation in the Edict of Reforms of 1856. The reforms aimed not only at re-establishing central governmental control with a diminution of the Sultan's power, but also reconstituted the very nature of the state by introducing equal rights and responsibilities of non-Muslim and Muslim subjects. In 1829 a new clothing law sought to eliminate visual differences amongst males by requiring the adoption of identical headgear; by appearing the same all men would presumably become equal. This law anticipated the later Tanzimat decrees of 1839 and 1856, namely, the 1839 edict, the Hatt-i

Sherif, which elaborated further the need to eliminate inequality and create justice for all Ottoman subjects, Muslim and non-Muslim; and the 1856 imperial edict, the Hatt-i Humayun, announced by Sultan Abdulmecid I (1839-1861). This reiterated the state's duty to guarantee equality between the people of the empire and also created a concept of common Ottoman citizenship (*Osmanlili*), introducing for the first time the idea of Ottoman patriotism in an attempt to stem rising nationalist/ separatist movements.[3]

The Constantinople Patriarchate, fearing a loss of primacy amongst the empire's Christians, opposed these reforms particularly where they affected the internal administration of the Christian *millet*-s. The Hatt-i Humayun required each Christian community to elect a local assembly of laypersons as well as clergy to implement reform of its own administration and submit their results for the Porte's approval. The ecclesiastical hierarchies interpreted this as a direct attack on their traditional authority. The Greek Metropolitan of Izmir, for example, is reported to have commented when the firman was replaced in its ceremonial pouch after its official promulgation: "God grant that it not be taken out of that bag again".[4] Despite patriarchal resistance the reforms went ahead, and between 1860 and 1862 the internal structure of the *millet*-s were reorganised as the principle of secular participation in ecclesiastical leadership was implemented. In Bulgaria the Hatt-i Humayun was reinforced by the findings of the Grand Vizier, Kibrisli Mehmet Pasha, who reported widespread Patriarchal corruption.[5] However, as only Greeks were eligible for election to these lay positions, the Bulgarians continued to have virtually no representation. Indeed, by 1865 only two of sixty-five Assembly members were Bulgarian. Thus, while the 'reformed' millet embraced the secular principle, it continued to be charged by a spirit of Hellenic superiority.

The implementation of these reforms was complicated by external pressures on the Porte imposed by the European powers, each of whom saw patronage of different Christian communities within the Ottoman Empire as a means of political influence. Russia thus presented itself as the patron of the Orthodox community, while France and Austria competed for the protection of the Catholics, and Britain for the small Evangelical or Protestant communities that were coming into existence at this time.[6] The *millet* reform therefore involved several paradoxes: While the reorganisation was intended to eradicate abuse, corruption continued; although the stipulation of fixed salaries for higher clergy was intended to reduce corruption, it encouraged financial dependence on *ex gratia* payments by European consuls. As for the Porte's desire to extend the principle of popular government and increase the loyalty of minorities to the Ottoman state, the fact that the reorganisation retained the *millet* as a socio-political unit served to reinforce the lack of homogeneity among Ottoman peoples. Although the power of the clergy was reduced and a degree of secularisation introduced, lines of religious distinction did not disappear and indeed began to take on the additional dimension of nationalism that was disseminated through secular education. Thus, *millet* reform actually militated against the Ottoman vision of *Osmanlilik*. It can been concluded, therefore, that "the old clerical obscurantism, which kept the mass of non-Muslims in ignorance" would have been a better ally toward continued Ottoman dominion.[7]

Bulgarian Cultural Renaissance

By the mid-nineteenth century European influence and Ottoman reform combined to stimulate cultural awakening in Bulgaria. This was due in large part to the work of pioneer Bulgarian educators whose work was only made possible through subsidy received from the rising class of wealthy Bulgarian merchants and artisans, who equally would not have appeared had it not been for the Ottoman reform programme. One of the first reform measures introduced by Sultan Mahmud II was the liquidation of the janissary corps in favour of a regular army based on the European model, with European military training, weaponry and uniforms.[8] It was primarily to the Bulgarian farmers and producers of cloth that the Porte turned for its source of supply to feed and clothe this new army. As a result the farmers grew wealthier, as did the manufacturers of *aba*, a coarse woollen cloth, and *gaitan*, a decorative lace used to adorn uniforms. Large scale purchase of *aba* and *gaitan* began in the 1820's, and by 1848 the Porte had concluded a number of commercial agreements with the trade guilds of Bulgaria to build factories in Sliven and Plovdiv.

A consequence of military reform was the increased pressure to amend the system of land ownership in Bulgaria. This had been tied, in theory, to the Ottoman practice of levying soldiers, as well as taxes, for the sultan's military forces. The hated *sipâhi* system of military recruitment and taxation was rendered obsolete by the introduction of a professional army, and during the 1830's it gradually diminished. New land tenancy agreements were drawn up that enabled wealthy Bulgarians to purchase property. Thus, whilst the peasantry continued to encounter difficulty, Bulgarian merchants and manufacturers grew increasingly affluent. The economic revival had cultural and political repercussions as these new merchants began to exert their influence upon Bulgarian society. As their contact with the outside world increased they were influenced by new ideas, in conjunction with increased political and social freedom and with the necessary finances, businessmen and trade guilds began to invest in Bulgaria's cultural renaissance.

Cultural Renaissance: Education

Although the Bulgarian Orthodox Church claims to have kept alive the country's cultural and educational traditions throughout the Ottoman period, a major expression of Bulgaria's national revival was its investment in secular education during the nineteenth century: "Without the educational movement the Bulgarian national revival would have been impossible."[9]

Bulgaria's medieval educational system, centred within its many monastery complexes, had been eliminated as a result of the Ottoman conquest in the late fourteenth century. Monasteries were destroyed, scholars were killed, and others were deported to Asia Minor, while some took part in the mass migrations to Serbia, Romania and the Ukraine. However, during the second half of the fifteenth century, the consolidation of Ottoman power over the whole Balkan region witnessed a gradual revival of Bulgarian education in the form of ecclesiastical 'cell schools'.[10]

For three centuries (15th-18th) these cell schools offered the only education available to Bulgarian Christians. Typically they operated within monasteries or convents, although some later appeared in private homes and businesses. The teachers were predominantly monks or priests. Thus the Church claims: "the monasteries and the cell schools were the last flickering light of Bulgarian civilisation."[11] Documentary evidence tells us that during the fifteenth century seventeen cell schools opened in Bulgaria, twenty-nine were added in the sixteenth century, another thirty-one in the seventeenth century, and seventy-five in the eighteenth century, by the end of which there were no less than one hundred and fifty-two cell schools in Bulgaria.[12]

The number of students in a monastery school would normally have been quite small, between ten and twenty, with tuition consisting of mastering the basic elements of reading, writing and arithmetic, as well as instruction in Church Slavonic and Greek. The curriculum was specifically religious in character, with students learning the Psalter, the Gospels and the Book of Hours, along with other Church books. Secular knowledge appears to have been largely ignored, and most of the students became priests or monks. The cell schools therefore represented a system of clerical education, following the medieval, religio-scholastic model.

Scholars of the Bulgarian National Revival period, such as M. Arnaudov, I. Shishmanov, B. Penev and H. Gandev, have nonetheless argued that religious cell school education maintained a minimum of knowledge without which the awakening of Bulgarian economical, political and spiritual progress would have been impossible. They claim that despite the low standard of education the cell schools ensured the formation of a socially active group who emerged as the spiritual restorers of Bulgarian society during the eighteenth century. To this degree they contend that a denial of the value of the 'cells' is unjustified.[13] It must be recognised, however, that the sum total of learning to be gained from these schools was reading and writing in a language that meant very little outside of the Church. The church's elementary educational programme was incapable of meeting the needs of the emerging commercial class of Bulgarian merchants.

Bulgarian aspirations towards secular education undoubtedly stemmed from Greek cultural influence that introduced the ideas of the European Enlightenment. By the second half of the eighteenth century the first signs of Greek spiritual and cultural restoration could be perceived. In many towns of the Ottoman empire Greek educators opened secular schools in which they taught mathematics, philosophy, history, languages, natural history and science. It was to such schools in Istanbul and Bucharest that the Bulgarian economic elite sent their children, and it was not long before Greek schools opened in a number of Bulgarian towns. It was within these schools, as distinct from the old 'cell schools', that Bulgarian students began to receive an education that prepared many for future participation in Bulgaria's National Revival, students such as Vasil Aprilov, Ilarion Makariopolski, Georgi Rakovski, Petur Beron, among others.

The success of secular Greek education prompted the reform of the traditional cell schools, a need which had been advocated in the previous century by Paisii Hilendarski and Sofroni Vrachanski. For example, Sofroni wrote:

> Ah! Reckless Bulgarian stupidity! The sombreness and gloominess of drunkenness, they cannot manage to find a wise schoolmaster or teacher to teach the children wisely... so they walk as the blind in the darkness. Oh, foolish and unwise people! It appears that the other Christian nations teach wise philosophy. Now then look and ask what you can do. Why do you not spend money for schools and for academies and for teachers of grammatics and philosophy?[14]

Sofroni's appeal illustrates an orientation towards renaissance thinking in his desire to construct a modern secular educational system in Bulgaria. One may argue that the cell school system had achieved a level of success with progressive graduates such as Paisii and Sofroni. However, although Paisii and Sofroni were products of medieval religio-scholasticism it was not the system that influenced the reformist activities of both men, which were borne more precisely from their individual experiences of European Enlightenment teaching on Mount Athos.

Sofroni Vrachanski's desire for modern secular schools imbued with Bulgarian national character highlights one of the major problems of Greek education in Bulgaria. Greek schools mediated a spirit of Hellenic superiority and nationalism. The teachers preached the concept of *megali* – the creation of a 'Greater Greece' and nurtured an admiration of Greek culture within their students. Many Bulgarians succumbed to Greek influence but others refused to submit to the Hellenising ideals of their tutors. For example we know that pupils from the Andros Greek School formed a secret 'Slavo-Bulgarian Philosophical Society'. The students were undeniably influenced by Greek teaching as it heightened their awareness of nationalist ideals, but rather than accept the *megali* paradigm they directed their nationalist fervour toward Bulgaria and the plight of their own people.[15]

This led to the creation of the first Hellenic-Bulgarian school in Svishtov in 1815.[16] This school and others that followed taught the same range of subjects as Greek schools but with the addition of Bulgarian language. Many of the graduates went on to infuse new life into the reformation of Bulgarian education and by the late 1820's they were at the centre of the spiritual and cultural revival of Bulgaria that had begun in earnest. They urged the patriotic *chorbadzhi* – town leaders and wealthy businessmen – to support the reformation of traditional education in their towns and aided by the activities of trades guilds they advocated the construction of new school buildings. The Hellenic-Bulgarian school may therefore be considered as a transitional educational form between the medieval religious model and what is known as 'New Bulgarian education'.[17]

Thus through the early nineteenth century there arose a strong united Bulgarian movement for national secular education that embraced the whole country. However, the educational movement acquired real strength and growth through the 1830's-40's with the introduction of the monitorial method of teaching commonly known as the Bell-Lancaster system, the essence of which was that one teacher would instruct a large number of pupils by enlisting the aid of the more advanced students to help the younger children.[18] An exceptional role in Bulgarian education was played by Dr. Peter Beron (1800-1871), one of the first Bulgarians to understand the need to construct a wholly Bulgarian educational system. He was born in Kotel where he attended his local cell school. He later studied at the Greek school in Bucharest before graduating with a medical degree from Munich University in 1831. He is remembered in Bulgaria for his innovative educational booklet *A Primer with Sundry Precepts* published in Brasov, Romania in 1824, in which he expounded his educational ideas categorically rejecting the religious cell school model and advocating a completely Bulgarian secular and nationalistic model in its place. He understood that Bulgarian education would only be successful if mediated through the spoken language of the people and thus wrote his *Primer* in the common vernacular.

Through the initiative of Vasil Aprilov, a wealthy Bulgarian émigré from Odessa, the first Bulgarian secular school using the monitorial model and teaching in the vernacular was established in Gabrovo in 1835 to serve, "all of Bulgaria".[19] Aprilov belonged to that part of Bulgarian society that Paisii Hilendarski had berated as becoming Greek. However, under the influence of the Russian scholar Yuri Venelin (see next section) he adopted Pan-Slavism and sought to redeem his earlier Greek bias by helping rebuild Bulgarian national consciousness. He perfectly exemplified the process of change that took place from Paisii's era to the middle of the nineteenth century. In 1833, at Aprilov's suggestion, the influential leaders of Gabrovo requested before the Metropolitan of Turnovo, that the Church support the opening of Bulgarian secular schools in his region. The Metropolitan initially refused, only to succumb to the pressure of local community support for educational reform. He recommended that a Bulgarian priest, Neofit Rilski, be appointed to the post of schoolmaster and on 2 January 1835 the school opened marking a significant development in Bulgarian education and a major leap in her cultural revival.

The success of the New Bulgarian educational movement played a decisive role in the forming of Bulgaria's national consciousness during the National Revival period. Nevertheless, although the argument for a secular approach to educational revival had been won, its cultural direction was still an issue of contention. Four contending positions struggled to dominate each advocating its own idea for the future direction of Bulgaria's educational and cultural development: Firstly, the leaders of the National Action group believed that Bulgaria's cultural renaissance would be achieved only on the basis of her national traditions without any foreign cultural or political influence; secondly, the Graecophiles believed that Greek language, literature, culture and education were the only means of securing a better Bulgarian future; the third grouping consisted of Russian émigrés, including Aprilov, who were influenced by Pan-Slavism insisted that Bulgaria's future development should be closely associated with Russian culture, language and literature; the final group believed that the Ottoman empire would eventually reform in the spirit of western liberalism and culture, thus ensuring the proper conditions for the cultural and educational advance of Bulgarian society within the framework of a remodelled empire.

Comprehending fully the development of the secular educational movement, this researcher's assessment of the role of the Church in shaping Bulgaria's educational revival in the nineteenth century is more qualified than the conventional claims of Bulgarian nationalist historiography. The Church's educational role in medieval and early Ottoman times is not in question, and the cell school system did preserve an indigenous educational tradition through the centuries in which there was no alternative. The expansion of the cell system in the eighteenth century demonstrates the effort of the Church to respond to the growing demand for education, while at the same time failing to produce the kind of education that the commercial elite required. Although it can be argued that the cell schools provided a transition to modern education they remained pre-modern themselves and eventually gave way to Greek and later to Bulgarian initiatives in secular education that focused on the nation without the mediation of the Church. The clergy acquiesced in this change reluctantly for it clearly signalled a diminution of one of their traditional conduits of power over the general populace. This was in line with the Ottoman Tanzimat reforms which, among other things, were designed to develop a balance between secular and clerical authority in the administration of their empire's Christian communities. Thus it is impracticable to build a simple bridge between the cell school system and Bulgaria's National Revival. It is impossible, therefore, to sustain the claim of traditional Bulgarian scholarship, that the Church fulfilled a major role in keeping Bulgaria's cultural and educational traditions alive when in reality it was losing its influence to shape the direction of Bulgaria's National Revival intelligentsia.

RUSSIAN AND TURKISH INFLUENCE ON BULGARIAN CULTURAL ASPIRATION

The development of education in Bulgaria introduced a number of contending foreign influences that sought to promote their own politically and/or religiously motivated ideas for the future direction of Bulgaria's cultural revival. Russian influence, particularly in the form of Pan-Slavism, proved to be a principal foreign agency guiding Bulgaria's cultural renaissance. Originating in seventeenth century Russia, Pan-Slavism developed as an intellectual and cultural movement during the nineteenth century and was intended to promote the political and cultural unity of all Slavs. The philosophy was steeped in Eastern Orthodox tradition and dreamed of restoring Constantinople, or later of establishing Moscow, as the capital of an Orthodox Christian empire, which implied the liberation of all Balkan Slavs from Ottoman authority, under Russian direction. Throughout the Russian empire supporters of their 'little Slav brothers' established benevolent societies, raising funds for Bulgarian refugees, finding employment for émigrés, and scholarships for Bulgarian students to study in Russian educational establishments. Thus the propagation of Pan-Slavism in Bulgaria was a decisive factor influencing the direction of her cultural development specifically oriented towards Russia. However, it was the work of one man in particular who ignited Russian intellectual and cultural interest in Bulgaria.

Yuri Ivanovich Venelin (1802-1839)

If Paisii Hilendarski re-introduced Bulgarians to their history, it was the Russian, Yuri Venelin, who fired the historical and national imagination of the leaders of the Bulgarian national revival with an influence that overshadowed Paisii until the latter's reputation was restored by historian Marin Drinov in 1871.

Venelin was born in Carpathian Hungary in the village of Velika Tibava in 1802. His father was a Uniate priest whose premature death destined the young Yuri to fulfil his family's wish that he study theology. However, his dislike of the subject led to him changing that destiny when he enrolled in Lvov University to study history. After graduating he was given a teaching post in Kishniev Seminary, and it was during this period that Venelin first encountered Bulgarian refugees who had fled their country as a result of the Russo-Turkish Wars.[20] This first contact with Bulgaria proved decisive in guiding the rest of his life. In 1825 he travelled to Moscow and become acquainted with a number of influential Slavophiles, among them Mihail Pogodin, the editor of *The Moscow Gazette*, who encouraged him in his historical research and influenced his pro-slavophile views. In an article for the *Gazette* Venelin voiced for the first time his future Bulgarophile predilection:

> In their language we conduct our services today, and in that language we wrote almost up to the time of Lomonosov – the cradle of the Bulgars is indivisibly linked with the cradle of the Russian people.... While we [the Russians] moan over the fate of the Greeks, while we discuss whether or not the eagle of Byzantium should rise again – we do not remember the Bulgars; not even one Slav has wept over the body of the dead lion. [21]

This article would be the foundation for his first major publication in 1829, a 230-page historical work entitled, *The Ancient and Present-Day Bulgarians in their Political, Ethnographic, Historical and Religious Relationship to the Russians. Historical-Critical Researches.*[22] His research caused a commotion within the academic world of Slavic studies questioning all existing theories relating to the origins of Bulgaria. The problem of Bulgarian origins, or Bulgaristics, had become a central issue in nineteenth century Slavic studies as arguments revolved around the interrelationship between Slavic peoples and their languages.[23] Safarik, for example, claimed that Bulgarian was merely a dialect, a "sub-species", of the Serbo-Macedonian language.[24] However, the common understanding was that the Bulgarian language was non-Slavic, having its origins in Turko-Tatar. The controversial nature of Venelin's work, however, was that it claimed to have uncovered the Slavic origins of the Bulgarian people, and assigned them to a pre-eminent place in the history of all Slav peoples.

As a result of his research Venelin was awarded a scholarship from the Russian Academy of Sciences that enabled him to conduct a two-year field trip to Bulgaria and Macedonia where he collected historical, philosophical and archaeological materials. He arrived in Bulgaria in 1830, finding the country in turmoil after the Russo-Turkish War of 1828-29.[25] For his own safety he restricted his travels to Varna, the Dobrudzha and Silistra. This was sufficient for him to complete a 300-page manuscript entitled, *Grammar of the Present-Day Bulgarian Dialect* that he presented to the Russian Academy when he returned to Moscow in 1831.

In 1849 he published a second book on Bulgarian history, with financial aid from a Bulgarian merchant, entitled, *Critical Researches on the History of the Bulgarians, by Y. I. Venelin. From the Arrival of the Bulgarians on the Thracian Peninsula to 968, to the Subjection of Bulgaria by the Russian Grand Prince Svyatoslav.*[26] The crux of this book was his assertion that the medieval missionary brothers, Cyril and Methodius, were Bulgarian and not Greek, and that Macedonia belonged to Bulgaria: "Macedonia is the name of a country, but its inhabitants are Bulgarians, who can also be called Macedonians because they live in Macedonia. Therefore, Macedonian means Bulgarian."[27]

Venelin's research had opened an important door for the evolution of the Bulgarian National Revival. By negating the Turkish origins of Bulgarian language and culture, he lifted the burden of historical guilt from the Bulgars, for now, as Slavs, they had reason to struggle against the cultural burdens placed upon them by centuries of Ottoman domination. His publications created a sensation among the Bulgarian intelligentsia and began a trend which would draw the centre of Bulgarian intellectual, spiritual, cultural and political gravity towards Russia.

Venelin's most ardent supporter was the Bulgarian émigré, Vasil Aprilov, who was converted to the cause of Bulgarian nationalism after reading his work. As Aprilov developed his Bulgarian school network, it became the medium through which Venelin's pro-Bulgarian propaganda was disseminated among the new class of students, secular and nationalist in orientation. Aprilov provided financial backing for Venelin's third book, *On the Birth of New Bulgarian Literature*, published in 1838, and it was under Venelin's influence that Aprilov published his own work, *The Dawn of New Bulgarian Education*, in 1841, both books proving highly influential in Bulgaria's cultural revival.

Yuri Venelin must be credited as being the founder of nationalist romanticism within the Bulgarian National Revival movement, and as "oracle and arbiter" of all things Bulgarian.[28] His academic reputation within Russia raised awareness of Bulgaria transforming it from being a neglected and insignificant country, elevating it to a position of pre-eminence in Slavic national, cultural and linguistic consciousness.[29] For this reason he holds a place of honour within Bulgarian society, being recognised today as a saint of Bulgaria's National Revival period. Bulgarian nationalists erected a marble tombstone on his Moscow grave, on which is etched the epitaph: "He reminded the world of the oppressed but once famous and powerful Bulgarian people and passionately desired to see their rebirth. Almighty God fulfil the prayer of They servant."

The Moscow Slavonic Charitable Committee and its Mission to Bulgaria (1858-1876)

Having accepted Venelin's hypothesis of Bulgaria's pre-eminence amongst the Slav nations, Russian Pan-Slavic societies began actively to promote their mission in Bulgaria during the second half of the nineteenth century. Particularly significant in Bulgaria's ongoing national and spiritual restoration was the work of the Moscow Slavonic Charitable Committee (MSCC). With its introduction in Bulgaria we observe an intermingling of Russian charitable acts and Russian political machinations.

The MSCC applied to the Russian government for approval toward the end of 1857, and was recognised officially on 26 January 1858. Its letter of application expressed the motivation behind the organisation. The letter criticised the growing influence of western Christian mission in Bulgaria, especially through the activities and propaganda of the Jesuits who were perceived as "destroying the influence of Russia" and "eroding Orthodoxy with cosmopolitan and universal education".[30] In addition to the Jesuits, the letter named the following groups as enemies of Bulgarian Orthodoxy: the Polish émigrés, the School of St. Lazur in Rumelia (Eastern Bulgaria), the Roman legation in Constantinople under the leadership of the Bulgarian, Bishop Kazanov, the influence of the

Maltese College in Turkey and the presence of Roman Catholic and Protestant missionaries in Bulgaria.[31]

Christian missionary interest in Bulgaria introduces a subject somewhat different from the central theme of this chapter. However, as it was raised as a major reason behind the creation of the MSCC, brief comment is necessary. Missions were predominantly a feature of the nineteenth century, although this was truer of the Protestants than of the Catholics. Roman Catholic aspirations on Bulgaria were much older, originating during the struggle for Christian dominance between East and West in the ninth century. Subsequently, repeated and temporarily successful efforts were made by Rome to acquire jurisdiction over the Bulgarians. During the seventeenth century the Counter Reformation movement sought to gain territory in the Balkans through the use of the Uniate formula. Although this movement gained a number of Bulgarian converts, its essentially non-Bulgarian nature deprived the Catholics of gaining lasting significance. Hence when Roman Catholic missionary activity revived in the nineteenth century, a small national catholic element was already at hand. On the other hand, Protestant missionary involvement in Bulgaria was purely a nineteenth century phenomenon. As with the Catholics, political considerations were not entirely separate from Protestant missionary work, and owed a great deal to the benevolence of foreign diplomats in the Ottoman empire. However, the central feature of the Protestant missionary movement was the Bible, its translation into the vernacular, its distribution, and its use to promote literacy. Nonetheless, as with the Roman Catholics, the Protestant missionary movement's non-Bulgarian nature relegated it to playing only a small and somewhat insignificant role in Bulgaria's national revival.

The MSCC also criticised the influence of the Turks and Greeks on Bulgaria, stating that the Bulgarians, as the largest 'Slavic tribe' in the Ottoman empire, merited the help of other Slavic Orthodox peoples. To support the struggling Bulgarian Church they proposed the following measures: To provide finances for Bulgaria to support the Church, schools, and other beneficial establishments (they quote as examples, the Community for Bulgarian literature, and Bulgarian national, cultural/community centres)[32]; to provide educational literature and ecclesiastical materials for the use of Orthodox societies and to provide scholarships for promising young Bulgars to study in Russia.[33]

After receiving official recognition the Moscow Committee energetically engaged in the propagation of its Pan-Slavic objectives throughout Bulgaria. Naiden Gerov, one of the leaders of Bulgaria's Odessa emigrant population, persuaded Russian patrons to support the Bulgarian cultural and ecclesiastical cause and especially the Bulgarian Orthodox Church in its growing dispute with the Ecumenical Patriarchate. Gerov and the MSCC spoke on every aspect of the Bulgarian Church, particularly "on the non-Slavic Greek oppression of Slavic Bulgarians".[34] The apparent altruism of their argument must be qualified by the fact that Russian Orthodoxy claimed Moscow to be the 'third Rome'.[35] Thus the charitable goals of the MSCC were pursued, not merely for themselves, but in the political interest of creating an independent Slavic Orthodox state within the ecclesiastical orbit of the Moscow Patriarchate. However, Pan-Slavic ideology was not always consistent with regard to Bulgaria. When the nineteenth century Greek-Bulgarian Church dispute initially broke out, the Pan-Slavist movement was for a time unable to decide where its loyalties lay: "the Russian Orthodox Church was spiritually subordinate to the Greek Patriarch in Constantinople. But the romantic vision of Russia restoring Byzantium could hardly be realised with Greek participation".[36] Thus, Pan-Slav, Russian Orthodox and Russian government policies began to coalesce in a pro-Bulgar, anti-Greek direction.

The appearance of the Moscow Committee in 1857-58 was connected directly to Russia's dire external political situation. After the Crimean War (1853-56) Russia had fallen into international isolation. The Paris Peace Treaty rescinded the territorial gains that she had made through military victory. However, the Tsarist government in St. Petersburg was unwilling to abdicate their interests and influence among the Orthodox populations of the Ottoman empire. Since he could no longer play a leading role in European politics, the Tsar sought alternative ways to maintain Russian influence. The Pan-Slav movement proved to be a powerful instrument in this direction, the MSCC providing a medium through which the Russian government could pursue its political aims.

Neither was the MSCC's emphasis on the Slavic character of Orthodoxy innocent of political intent. The Bulgarians had traditionally identified themselves as being 'Orthodox' rather than 'Slav'. It was Venelin's influence, as we have seen, that encouraged educated Bulgars to welcome the nomenclature 'Slav', but the predominantly peasant population remained 'Orthodox and Bulgarian'. This remained the case during the nineteenth century, as is evident from a multitude of archival documents – letters from village communities, school and church boards which almost always identify people simply as Orthodox, without reference to their Slavic roots.[37] In an attempt to unite their 'Slav-Orthodox' brothers, the MSCC actively fought against "western Christian propaganda" whose activities they declared were "dangerous for Russia, Bulgaria, the Slavs and the Orthodox".[38] Russian diplomats in Constantinople were particularly cautious of the activities of the influential Bulgarian, Dragan Tsankov, in his connection with the Roman Catholic Church, as he attempted to increase the influence of the Uniate Church in Bulgaria. Russian unease had been further provoked by a letter from Archimandrite Peter, of the Constantinople Russian Church, who cautioned the Russian government: "... not to trust and not to assist this Bulgarian [Tsankov] who was being influenced by questionable emissaries."[39]

The MSCC sent a representative, A. Rachinski, to investigate these matters further. He arranged a meeting between the Russian ambassador, Prince Lobanov-Rostovski and Dragan Tsankov to discuss the Uniate question and some of the articles published in the magazine *Bulgarian Literature*, in which Tsankov had advocated the idea of Bulgaria's former royal family contacting the Pope as evidence of the "indisputable leadership of the Roman Pope" in matters pertaining to Bulgarian church and society.[40] Following this meeting the ambassador reported directly to the Director of the Asian Department, in a letter dated 18 April 1859, stating that Tsankov and his articles were "harmful" and that he should be removed from the editorial staff of the magazine forthwith.[41]

MSCC representative A. Rachinski travelled on to Bulgaria to continue his investigations into the progress of "western religious propaganda". In two letters addressed to the Chairman of the Moscow Educational Board and to prominent Slavophile, A. N. Behmetiev, Rachinski comments on the absence of any reliable Orthodox religious education in Bulgaria advising: "...we must act quickly before the strong influence of insidious Jesuit politics prevails."[42] He describes the worrying content of Catholic teaching, especially their emphasis on Bulgarian history and the country's close connection with Rome, highlighting their 13th century union which had secured Bulgaria's independent Patriarchate; as union with Rome had secured Bulgaria's ecclesiastical independence in the past, so, he feared, it could again. He criticised the dispassionate and neutral position of the Russian Church, warning that this would only help the West succeed in discrediting the Patriarchate and secure Bulgarian union with Rome: "The West entices the Bulgarians with the idea of union and with this idea undertaken to achieve national independence."[43] In a second letter he suggested a number of ways in which the activities of the Uniate movement in Bulgaria could be curtailed including: the establishment of a pro-active Bulgarian Orthodox fraternity and the need to convince the Ecumenical Patriarch to accept Bulgarians onto the Holy Synod. He also made known his intention to visit a number of the new Bulgarian secular schools to find out to what extent "it was possible to expect interest for his suggestion to create children strong in the Orthodox faith."[44]

Rachinski's letters express the serious misgivings within the Pan-Slav movement regarding the influence of western religious propaganda in Bulgaria. The connection of Bulgaria with western missions was seen as being disastrous for Orthodoxy, the Slavs, and especially for Russian interests in the Balkan Peninsula. The letters are evidence of the initial construction of a programme to oppose these trends, which included making contacts with diplomatic representatives in Bulgaria, Constantinople and high-ranking state representatives in Russia.

The Moscow Slavonic Charitable Society played a significant role in directing the development of Bulgarian cultural and ecclesiastical independence. It was also instrumental in expanding Russian influence in Bulgaria and the Balkans during the unfavourable period after the Crimean War. In achieving these two diverse goals we observe a degree of synchronisation in the activities of the Pan-Slav movement and official Russian state politics. The MSCC thus succeeded in realising its priorities of strengthening Russian influence among the Bulgarian population, and using the Bulgarian Orthodox Church as a means of disseminating Slavophile identity among the Bulgarian population.

Midhat Pasha (1822-1883) and the Danube Vilayet

As part of the continuing Tanzimat reform programme and in response to what the Porte considered to be insidious Russian influence and Bulgarian national resurgence, the Ottoman authorities sought to develop a new policy in its Bulgarian province. A completely different system of provincial administration was required, which, while securing the authority of central government, would provide an element of latitude for local officialdom, making administration efficient and expeditious. The Vilayet Law (1864) was the result, the aim of which was to eliminate local discontent and therefore indigenous support for foreign intervention within the region.

The chief architect of the new law was the Grand Vizier, Fuad Pasha, who had previously dealt with Greek separatist movements after the Crimean War. In a letter to Sultan Abdulaziz (1861-1876) in 1863, he warned of other nationalist separatist movements emerging on the Balkan Peninsula encouraged by European intrigue.[45] In the Vilayet Law he aimed to re-balance central and provincial authority, and to advance equality between Muslims and non-Muslims, on the assumption that with the guarantee of individual rights, an increased sense of *Osmanlili* citizenship would both counter the threat of nationalist and religious unrest.

In order to test this new system the Danube or 'Tuna' Vilayet was created as a 'pilot area' in effect a 'super-province' combining the three eyalets of Silistra, Vidin and Nish. It extended from the Danube River to the Balkan Mountains, approximately the northern half of modern Bulgaria. The administration of this experimental province was given to one of the empires most efficient and forward-looking provincial governors, Ahmed Sefik Midhat Pasha. Born in Constantinople, the son of Pomak parents, Midhat had entered the Grand Vizier's Secretariat on completion of his education and was rapidly promoted to the *Medjliss-Vala* (Grand Council of State) as Sanie.[46] By 1851 he was First Secretary to the Grand Council, in which capacity he was dispatched to the provinces of Damascus and Aleppo to settle local disputes. Success brought him to the attention of the Grand Vizier, Reshid Pasha, who appointed him to a post within the Superior Council of State.[47]

In this new role he was deputed to settle disturbances in the province of Adrianople in 1854. It was here that he developed his particular leadership style of bringing together local notables, Muslim and Christian. Having been given the chance of airing their views on what troubled their region, he would then have them agree on a plan of action, from which he tolerated no subsequent dissent.[48] In 1861 he was appointed Vali of the Nish eyalet to accomplish what he had previously achieved in the Adrianople province. It was during this spell that he envisaged a new and innovative plan for territorial reorganisation and provincial government, which would not only suppress trouble but would seek to prevent its return. This plan would evolve to become the Vilayet Law.

As governor of the Danube Vilayet, Midhat Pasha used his organisational skills initially to pacify the province without the use of armed force. Depending on local consultations, he established that grievances turned on two main problem areas: the absence of any road network, which made it exceedingly difficult for tradesmen to access any commercial markets and rampant brigandage throughout the region that rendered life and property insecure.

He then struck a bargain with the regional leaders: to recall all Ottoman troops in the vilayet to their barracks and to undertake civil improvement throughout the region, on the condition that local leaders would use their influence to placate their fellow countrymen and discourage emigration and separatist activities. His bargaining skills were successful, as the vilayet became a hive of industry: 3000 kilometres of paved roads,[49] around 1400 bridges, street lights, public buildings and schools were constructed. Model farms were created, complete with European machinery; a ferry service began on the Danube; brigandage was effectively stamped out with the establishment of local gendarmerie, and agricultural banks were created, with a view of relieving the difficulties of the mainly peasant population.[50]

As a result of his governorship, agriculture and industry began to flourish bringing peace and prosperity to the province. This provided the framework in which Midhat addressed the deeper underlying cultural/religious issue. He understood that the New Bulgarian educational movement played a decisive role in forming Bulgarian national awareness in the minds of Bulgaria's emerging intelligentsia. He was also sensitive that the appeal to Orthodoxy was an integral part of incipient Bulgarian nationalism. Therefore, he determined to establish a secular school structure that embraced all people, with the purpose of cultivating the concept of Ottoman citizenship among Bulgarian Christians and Muslims who, by studying together and enjoying the advantages of secular education together, would see their future within a reformed Ottoman polity rather than looking abroad, especially to Russia.

Entirely new schools would be created in the vilayet, based neither on Christian cell schools or Islamic *medresses*, but on secular European models. The success of Midhat's educational directive is evident from reports in the vilayet's own newspaper, *Tuna*. For example, its very first issue from March 1865 announced the creation of a provincial printing office solely for the publishing of educational literature.[51] Later the newspaper reported that the first publication from this printing house would be an alphabet book for free distribution to every pupil.[52] Midhat's appreciation of the necessity for a unified educational system which would diminish Bulgarian national sentiment and Russian interference can be demonstrated by his governmental decree: "If children above the ages of five or six are not sent to school, and if older children are not sent either to school or for vocational training, the parents will be held responsible."[53] Later that same year Midhat instructed the deputy mufti of Pleven that, "schools were above everything else in importance" and that the mufti should make the necessary finances available for multi-faith schools, and if they were not available, he should create them.[54] He announced that a junior school would be opened in every town and a senior school within the administrative centre of every *sanjak*.[55] However, the success of Midhat's school building crusade can be clearly demonstrated by comparing the number of Bulgarian schools with Turkish mixed schools. By 1877 the Bulgarians had established 1,504 schools throughout the Balkan region.[56] Against this number Midhat opened a total of 2,890 schools, not in the Balkans as a whole, but solely within the Danube Vilayet, 150 *medresses*, 2,700 junior schools and 40 senior schools.[57] Midhat Pasha's reforms within the Danube Vilayet created conditions of peace and prosperity, where the regions children were educated together in harmony.

In only four years Midhat Pasha succeeded in dealing a powerful blow against Bulgarian separatists and Russian instigators. Bulgarians within the vilayet where more content than any time previously with their existence under Ottoman control and saw no immediate reason to change their situation. Why then is the vilayet experiment deemed unsuccessful in Bulgarian eyes? An explanation may be sought from the massive influx of refugees into this region in 1864. From the 1830's onwards the Ottoman empire had experienced an extensive demographic population shift when over one million people, almost entirely Caucasian Muslims, migrated to the empire. This was accelerated by Russia's defeat in the Crimean War (1853-1856), and a last great migration of Tartars and Circassians into the empire in 1864.[58]

Around 500,000 starving refugees marched towards Bulgaria and Macedonia, with the vast majority settling in the Danube Vilayet. Their arrival was not unwelcome as central Ottoman government considered that the refugees would help serve as a cushion of defence along the Serbian and Danubian borders. It is recorded that the population of Varna increased by fifty percent overnight due to the influx of refugees.[59] This created tensions with the resident population, and resulted in the eviction of Bulgarians from their homes and villages.[60]

Without provisions the refugees began to terrorise the Bulgarian countryside: "…taking vengeance on their non-Muslim neighbours in a manner hitherto unknown in the Ottoman empire."[61] Consequently many Christians fled once more across the Danube into Romania, where they joined the Bulgarian nationalist cause. Whereas previous lawlessness in the region of the Danube Vilayet had been indiscriminate – as, for example, under the rule of Pasvanoglu some fifty years previously – the new conflict assumed definite confessional contours. Muslim refugees targeted Bulgarian Christians. The lines of confessional conflict were more sharply drawn than at any time since the Ottoman conquest. Thus an event beyond Midhat's control fatally damaged his efforts to neutralise the Bulgarian separatist movement.

Midhat Pasha's administration of the Danube Vilayet demonstrates both the potential of Ottoman reform and its inherent weakness. He showed that it was possible to modernise the administration and infrastructure of an Ottoman province by regulating and cultivating a sense of common Ottoman citizenship among its inhabitants, both Christian and Muslim. The Grand Vizier, Fuad Pasha, announced on May 15, 1867, that the empire had found "… a form of administration corresponding altogether to the needs of the country, to the customs of the population, and to the demands of the concept of civilisation which presses upon the empire from all directions."[62] Yet, inter-confessional concord, founded on administrative reform and economic advancement, was vulnerable to a reversal of social and economic circumstances. This proved to be the case in a matter which was not of Midhat's making, and quickly exceeded his control, with the movement of war refugees into the Danube Vilayet. In retrospect this was one of the Porte's biggest blunders, marking the beginning of the end of its western empire. Had Midhat's model been allowed to continue without such interference, Bulgaria's cultural and national journey might have been very different. Despite his success as governor, Midhat was removed from office, and with his demise the last best hope for *Osmanlilik* citizenship was squandered.

CONCLUSION

This chapter has considered the claim of the Bulgarian Orthodox Church that it was the most important indigenous cultural agent of Bulgaria's National Revival. In highlighting the factors which actually prompted cultural revival, it becomes evident that these did not initially include a consciousness of the past gained through reading Paisii, or the religious educational traditions of Bulgarian cell schools, but rather foreign influences, particularly via Greece and Russia. These were contacts gained through commerce and education, and through the seepage of international secular ideas into the Balkans. However, Bulgaria's cultural awakening could not have taken place without the upheaval of reform experienced in the Ottoman empire during the late eighteenth and early nineteenth centuries – upheaval which brought about the profound economic, social and political changes without which Bulgarian nationalist sentiment could not have been translated into action.

What clearly emerges from this chapter is that the medieval religious traditions of Bulgarian Orthodoxy were rejected by the emerging intelligentsia, who considered the Church to be archaic and therefore inadequate to meet the requirements of Bulgaria's national progress. Consequently, the Church experienced a weakening of its traditional authoritative position within Bulgarian society. With the implementation of the *Tanzimat* reform programme the laity was given increased responsibility within *millet* administration resulting in a further diminishment of ecclesiastical authority, and with the development of secular education, the Church lost its influential role within Bulgarian society. Although the Bulgarian Church strove to maintain its cultural identity, its 'distinctiveness', through the tradition of medieval church education, using Old Church Slavonic as a defence against the Islamisation and Hellenization policies of the Ottoman and Greek authorities, it is evident that these traditions were unwanted and disregarded by Bulgaria's intelligentsia. Cultural identity based on religion rather than on the idea of nation was the aim of the Bulgarian Church at this moment.

This research supports the conclusion that cultural awakening and nationalist romanticism did not originate within the Church, but through secular enlightenment thinking, particularly through the agency of Greek education and Pan Slavism. Therefore, the claim of the Bulgarian Orthodox Church that during this period of history they were the saviour of Bulgarian tradition, culture, language and education is somewhat questionable and should be considered the product of latter nationalist embellishment which sought to enhance the mythical importance of the Church.

4

THE STRUGGLE FOR BULGARIAN
ECCLESIASTICAL INDEPENDENCE

The re-establishment of an independent Bulgarian Church, after its dismemberment in the fourteenth century following the Ottoman conquest, was not the aspiration of every Bulgarian Christian. Rather, spiritual and cultural resignation characterised Bulgarian society during the fifteenth to eighteenth centuries. As this chapter will reveal Bulgarian ecclesiastical independence was not realised until 1872. Through an examination of nineteenth century Bulgarian archival sources the chapter shall endeavour to answer why autonomy took so long to achieve. The overwhelming influence of the Greek Patriarchate which had so distressed Paisii Hilendarski slowly began to infuriate Bulgarian communities. The chapter will investigate the vicissitudes of this Bulgar-Greek dispute and map the journey towards Bulgarian ecclesiastical independence. External forces shall also be assessed to discern if foreign influence affected the direction of the Bulgarian Church movement. Finally the chapter will critically analyse the Bulgarian Orthodox Church's claim that it was central to the National Revival movement supporting liberation from Ottoman domination, inspiring the people with bravery and courage to strive for national freedom.

THE EMERGENCE OF THE BULGARIAN CHURCH MOVEMENT

The Bulgarian-Greek ecclesiastical dispute originated in 1393, following the Ottoman conquest, when the Bulgarian Patriarchate was abolished and the remains of the Church made subject to the Ecumenical Patriarchate in Constantinople. The Bulgarian ecclesiastical hierarchy were removed from power and replaced by Greek clergy. Initially Bulgaria's new religious leaders maintained the taxation arrangements of their predecessors, but soon their demands increased and continued to escalate thereafter. As a result of ongoing financial crises the Sublime Porte discovered a lucrative source of revenue deriving from the selling of religious office offering the Patriarchal throne and other church appointments to the highest bidder. During the centuries of Ottoman domination only the wealthiest Greek families could afford the cost of ecclesiastical office, thus Greeks came to dominate every Church office in the empire. As these clergyman expected to recoup their expenses church taxes escalated, ultimately placing a heavy economic burden on the poor.

It was the increased tax burden imposed by the Greeks that first provoked Bulgarian discontent as the oppressed expressed their dissatisfaction at the economic pillage of the Ecumenical Patriarchate.[1] However, this early discontent merely manifested itself in attempts to secure protection from the Ottoman government against the ruthless exploitation of the Greek clergy. The first sign of any organised movement against the Greek Church authorities can be witnessed in the nineteenth century conflict between the Bulgarian population and the Greek clergy. This conflict contained a new element, that being a desire to replace Greek bishops with Bulgarians, which although isolated and at first unsuccessful developed into a national movement calling for an independent Bulgarian Church.

Archival sources indicate that the first recorded conflict to contain this new element arose between the Bulgarian town leaders and the Greek bishop of Vratsa during the 1820's. At the end of the eighteenth century the town of Vratsa, in north-western Bulgaria, became the centre of a newly created eparchy. Until that time the town had been subordinate to the Metropolitan of Turnovo. However, due to Vrasta's remoteness and the level feudal unrest caused by the *kurdzhalistvo* period it had been nigh impossible to collect taxes. As a consequence the Patriarch created the Vratsa eparchy in 1781 and ordained a permanent bishop to the region.[2]

The inhabitants of Vratsa expressed their discontent at receiving a Greek bishop by ignoring demands to pay their ecclesiastical taxes. Indeed, the failure to collect these taxes was reported to have been the reason for Bishop Antim's removal in 1813.[3] Learning from their failure the Patriarchate, alongside the appointment of another Greek bishop to Vratsa, announced that a Bulgarian, Dimitraki Hadjitoshev, would work as his deputy having the responsibility to gather taxes.[4] Nevertheless, giving the position of tax collector to a Bulgarian did not alleviate the situation as we read in a letter from Bishop Methodius to the Metropolitan of Turnovo in 1821 that the inhabitants of the eparchy refused to be brought into line and pay "that which is due."[5]

Hadjitoshev wrote to the Metropolitan directly asking him to reduce the crippling level of taxation but received the reply that this would be impossible as the Metropolitan also had to meet his demands to the Patriarchate. For this reason relations between the bishop and the town leaders deteriorated and Hadjitoshev joined his fellow Bulgars in seeking the removal of Bishop Methodius. At the beginning of 1824 he composed a statement arguing against the further appointment of Greek bishops to the eparchy and sent it to neighbouring town leaders asking them to countersign it. However, they refused to do so afraid of repercussions and advised the leaders of Vratsa not to forward the statement to the authorities.[6] These actions did not remain unnoticed and in a personal letter to Hadjitoshev the Metropolitan warned him "to be as one voice with [Bishop] Methodius for the sake of not causing a disturbance amongst other Christians," or he would be forced to report the unrest to the Ottoman authorities without pity for the people of Vratsa.[7] Consequently Bishop Methodius reported Hadjitoshev to the Patriarchate, presenting him as a troublemaker and a rebel, insisting that he be sent to Constantinople to answer directly for his actions. At the request of the Patriarchate the Porte issued an order on 21 November 1824 for the arrest and interrogation of Dimitraki Hadjitoshev. The inhabitants of Vratsa actively campaigned for his release before Patriarch Chrysanthos I (1824-26) who eventually granted their request in 1826. Imprisonment had not eroded Hadjitoshev's anti-Greek convictions as upon his release he immediately attempted to replace Bishop Methodius with the Bulgarian archimandrite Gavril Bistrichanin.[8]

The conflict had begun with the general dissatisfaction of the Vratsa inhabitants directed against the economic exploitation of the Ecumenical Patriarchate. The dispute progressed, however, beyond the limits of the initial conflict with their request for a Bulgarian bishop, no doubt hoping that a Bulgarian would be tolerant toward their financial predicament. The leading figure in this movement was Dimitraki Hadjitoshev, the only person in a position to stand with confidence before the Metropolitan and defend the interests of the Bulgarian people. The fact that after his death the movement waned reveals that the Bulgarians of the Vratsa eparchy were not yet sufficiently prepared to continue the struggle.

At the end of the 1820's, in a completely separate incident, the Bulgarians of the Samokov eparchy also took a stand against Greek Patriarchal authority. During the period of Ottoman control until 1766 the eparchy had been part of the Ipekska Patriarchate, later falling under the authority of the Ecumenical Patriarchate. With this decision the former

Bulgarian Metropolitan was forced to relinquish his post.[9] It appears that the eparchy was left for a number of years without a Metropolitan, as the first ecclesiastical representative from Constantinople arrived in 1772. From the town chronicles it is evident that the first Greek Bishop earned the respect of his flock during his forty-seven year reign in office[10]. The Greek hierarchy who succeeded him, however, were not held in the same high regard. Indeed we read from a contemporary letter that "the Samokov Christians watched the abuse of power which the Greek bishops forced upon them, they wept before the Constantinople Patriarch... begging for a worthy bishop who they could elect."[11] In their lament to the Patriarch the people suggested a Bulgarian, Neofit Rilski, the abbot of Rila Monastery for the position of bishop. This first attempt to select a Bulgarian proved to be unsuccessful as yet another Greek, Ignatius II (1830-1837), arrived as Metropolitan.

However, the clash between Bulgarian and Greek clergy within the eparchy of Turnovo had the farthest-reaching consequences for the development of the emerging Bulgarian Church movement. Turnovo was one of the most important regions of Bulgaria its eparchy embracing the largest part of the country. Turnovo had been the capital city of Bulgaria at the time of the Ottoman conquest and remained an important administrative, ecclesiastical and commercial centre through the centuries of domination. From the nineteenth century the town played an increasingly important role as a centre for the rising Bulgarian artisan community. Alongside an accompanying increase in Bulgarian confidence Greek influence in the region decreased. These social/cultural changes were reflected in the religious situation with an increasing dissatisfaction amongst the population of the eparchy toward the Greek clergy. This disharmony reached its peak with the arrival of Greek Metropolitan, Panaret on 6 June 1838. He was described as being "a mad repulsive Greek...who swears in Church and for no reason arrests Bulgarian clergy, forcing them to dig iron ore from the regions mountains...."[12]

Outraged by his behaviour the town leaders of Turnovo demanded that Panaret be removed and put forward the name of a Bulgarian as his replacement. The choice of Neofit Bozveli (1785-1848) would prove to be inspired as he would emerge as one of the most important characters of the Bulgarian Church movement. Bozveli was not an arbitrary selection, he had been intricately involved in regional social activities for some time and was one of the main protagonists behind the demands for Panaret's removal. Bozveli was another product of Hilendar Monastery on Mount Athos, who after leaving the monastery busied himself in patriotic preaching, teaching and literary activities. He spent two years travelling through the Turnovo eparchy engaging in the social problems of his fellow countrymen and actively campaigned against Greek clergy gradually directing his protests towards Metropolitan Panaret.[13]

Once the decision to stand for the post of Metropolitan had been taken Bozveli left for Constantinople to receive Patriarchal endorsement of his nomination arriving in the spring 1839. The leading Bulgarians of Turnovo signed a request on behalf of the eparchy supporting Bozveli's nomination and took the unprecedented action of presenting it directly to the Porte.[14] News of Bozveli's attempt to gain governmental support soon reached the Patriarchate. They could not allow the appointment of a Bulgarian, particularly such a bitter opponent as Bozveli, to the largest ecclesiastical region of Bulgaria. The Patriarchate therefore made every effort to frustrate the mission of the Turnovo delegation and in response immediately proposed a Greek candidate, Neofit Byzantos, at the same time offering a financial incentive to the Turnovo leaders. With this Patriarchal bribe the majority of the town leaders switched their support to the Greek cause and Byzantos was elected in August 1840. To alleviate Bulgarian dissatisfaction the Patriarchate appointed Bozveli as the Metropolitan's deputy promising that he would, in time, be promoted as Bishop of Lovech.

The attitude of the new Metropolitan towards his Bulgarian subjects was antagonistic from the start and relationship with his deputy very quickly became strained, so much so that Bozveli refused to remain in his post and fled Turnovo for the sanctuary of Lyaskovski Monastery. This action was used to the Metropolitan's advantage when he accused Bozveli of disobedience demanding that he be punished for dereliction of his duties. Subsequently, in March 1841, Bozveli was arrested and exiled on Mount Athos.[15] Deprived of guidance and leadership the Bulgarians in Turnovo stayed their activities against the Greeks until the summer of 1844 when Bozveli was released.

The Bulgarian Church Movement in Constantinople

After his release Neofit Bozveli returned to Constantinople where he had previously made contact with a number of influential people from the large Bulgarian colony during his visit in 1839. At this time it is estimated that between 30-50,000 Bulgarians lived and worked in the

Galata district of the Ottoman capital, including successful merchants, master craftsmen and thousands of migrant workers employed in the state's manufacturing workshops.[16] The most important contact Bozveli acquired was that of Ivan Stoyanovich Mihailovski, better known by his ordained name of Ilarion Makariopolski. Makariopolski was yet another product of Hilendar Monastery who had been educated in an atmosphere of ardent Greek nationalism and Bulgarian animosity. The Bulgarian educator Vasil Aprilov had secured him a scholarship to study in Russia but the Greek ecclesiastical authorities forbade this privilege. Thus, when Bozveli met Makariopolski he was resident in Constantinople festering with anti-Greek emotions. The two became friends and quickly reached the conclusion that Constantinople would be the ideal centre to fight against the Patriarchate.

In Constantinople they found fertile ground for their activities as many of the colony's educated Bulgarians were already aware of their 'Bulgarianess'. They quickly gained the ear of leading Bulgarians and succeeded in winning them to the anti-Greek ecclesiastical cause. Nevertheless, a large part of their success was achieved purely by engaging in their priestly roles; Bozveli and Makariopolski ministered to the Bulgarian community, creating a small unofficial church within the 'Hambar' and conducting the Slavonic liturgy for leading Bulgarians within the privacy of their homes.[17] In doing so the Bulgarian community came to discern their 'distinctiveness' within predominantly Greek Christian society and their need for an independent place of Bulgarian Slavonic worship.

In September 1844 Bozveli and Makariopolski met Mihail Chaikovski, a Polish agent working in conjunction with the French Embassy, who advised the two Bulgarians to present a petition before the Porte elucidating the needs of their fellow-countrymen.[18] As a result of this meeting and complete with a mandate to represent the Bulgarian people before the Porte, Bozveli and Makariopolski formulated a petition composed of six basic requests:

- That Bulgarian Christians have the right to elect Bulgarian bishops to their eparchies.
- That they be allowed to extend Bulgaria's school network.
- For permission to publish newspapers in the Bulgarian language.
- To erect a Bulgarian Church in Constantinople.

- To establish mixed law courts in Bulgaria; in which Bulgarians would be protected from Greek hegemony.
- For permission to form a Bulgarian delegation, independent of the Patriarchate, that would express national demands directly before the Sublime Porte.

Initially the Ottoman authorities showed interest in the Bulgarian requests and during 1845 Bozveli and Makariopolski were frequently received before the Ministry of the Exterior and the Grand Vizier to further expand on the Bulgarian Church question. However, the anti-Greek activities of Bozveli and Makariopolski alarmed the Patriarchate and in an attempt to neutralise their threat Patriarch Meletios III attempted to divide the two leaders by offering Bozveli a lucrative position within the Patriarchate and later the Metropolitanship of Trapezund (in north-eastern Turkey). When Bozveli refused to accept either position he and Makariopolski were exiled, on the authority of the Patriarch, to Mount Athos where Bozveli died on 12 June 1848.

The Church movement had developed somewhat from its earlier uncoordinated escapades as despite the death of one of its principal leaders the Constantinople Bulgarians vowed to continue their fight against the Patriarchate. They immediately concentrated their struggle on the building of a Bulgarian Church in Constantinople and Alexander Exarch (1810-1891) was set the task of obtaining permission to build this church. With the assistance of Stefan Bogoridi, a nephew of Sofroni Vrachanski and confidante of the sultan, a firman was granted (1849) permitting the building of the Church. This firman proved to be immensely important as it was the first Ottoman document to refer to the *bulgarmiletani*, thus officially recognising a distinction between the Bulgarian people and the Greeks.[19] Bogoridi gifted the Church movement a prime location within the Phanar district of Constantinople for the building of the church.[20] The site was consecrated on 9 October 1849 and a large church subsequently built. The success of the Bulgarian community in Constantinople prompted the spread of discord against Greek clergy throughout Bulgaria, which only now coalesced into an organised national Church movement.

Foreign Involvement in the Bulgarian Church Dispute

The evolving struggle between Bulgarians and the Constantinople Patriarchate was dependent, at one time or another, on external factors which either impeded or facilitated the Church question. Primarily this dispute affected the Ottoman government as the Bulgarian request for ecclesiastical independence disrupted the administrative status quo established by the Porte after the conquest of the Balkan Peninsula. Thus the Porte insisted it play the role of supreme arbiter during the dispute cleverly balancing its support between each side. In so doing the Porte established a pattern of contradictory politics: Ottoman government could not ignore the position of the Ecumenical Patriarchate who through the centuries had assisted in strengthening Ottoman dominance over the Christian rayah; neither, on the other hand, could the Ottoman authorities ignore the desires of a flourishing national movement that had its raison d'être in the proclamation of the Porte's reform programmes. Consequently Ottoman government had to constantly reconsider its position in regard to this delicate situation, a position further complicated by the attitude of the European powers to the Eastern Question.

French and Polish Participation

France had been one the first European powers to establish diplomatic contact with the Ottoman empire in 1535 in an agreement between Suleman I (1520-1566) and Francis I (1494-1547). By means of this agreement France acquired all trading privileges with the empire, quickly brushing aside competition from Dubrovnik, Genoa and Venice, so much so that by the eighteenth century three-quarters of the empire's average annual trade was executed through France.

Alongside political concessions the French also acquired a number of religious privileges. Within the sixteenth century agreement it was stated that French subjects would not be troubled because of their religion; thus the immunity of Catholics, their clergy and institutions were guaranteed under this agreement. Gradually the Ottoman authorities recognised the rights of the French to protect, not only their own subjects, but also the subjects of other European states who travelled under the French flag.

Under this protection and with the co-operation of French diplomats many Catholic missionaries successfully operated within the Ottoman empire. This missionary movement became particularly active after the creation of the Jesuit order in 1540 and after Pope Gregory XV's congress on the dissemination of the faith the Catholic mission established itself in Bulgaria.[21] Catholic propagation proved successful amongst Bulgarian Orthodox believers due to their complicated national, political and social position under the 'double yoke'. Many converted to Catholicism to benefit from the privileges and protection of the Catholic Church. Throughout the nineteenth century French diplomacy was particularly active in the politics of the Porte competing against the strengthening position of Russia.[22] Thus, in 1841 the French ambassador fought to secure a new firman protecting the ancient rights and religious privileges of the French. At the same time the French protested against a corresponding acknowledgement for the rights of the Eastern Orthodox granted at the insistence of the Russians. In response to increasing Russian influence the French raised the question of consolidating their political and religious influence in the Ottoman empire particularly among the resurgent Balkan nations. The resultant plan had a number of concrete aims: Together with the Vatican the French government would send Catholic clergy into the Balkans who would attempt to unite the numerous separate Catholic communities; they would propagate the faith and establish new educational institutions organised by the Lazarists; and seek to open new consulates throughout the Ottoman empire.[23] This organisational plan for French cultural-religious expansion was gradually applied in Bulgaria.

Large part in introducing the French to the Bulgarian situation was played by the Polish emigrant community in Paris led by Prince Adam Czartoryski (1770-1861). For thirty years he directed Polish agents, scattered throughout Europe and Asia, engaged in activities directed against Russia in hope of re-establishing a Polish state. The antagonism between this enemy of Poland and the Ottoman empire determined the pro-Ottoman orientation of the Polish emigrants. This created a contradiction in Polish diplomacy, in that while they were united with every Slav nation in their struggle for independence they were also eager to assist the Porte in its reform programme. Czartoryski commented: "Whilst we [the Poles] are not ready, until then we will support the Ottoman state with all our strength; as every premature move of the Slavs will be thrown as booty into the hands of the Russians, therefore we should lead them towards Poland."[24]

The desire, so clearly outlined in the words of Czartoryski, coincided with the aims of France and the Porte and led to tripartite collaboration. Therefore in 1840 we observe the Polish community in Paris considering how to expand contact with the Bulgarians. The most successful suggestion was a programme entitled, 'The Project for Slavic Fellowship (1840)', the purpose of which was to "propagate civilisation by means of establishing the influence of the French" and would be "in total agreement with the Lazarists."[25] This included two points, establishing contact with Bulgarians in Paris and establishing contact with Alexander Exarch (the influential Bulgarian who had organised the building of the Bulgarian Church in Constantinople and who also held strong French sympathies).[26] At the same time Czartoryski organised a network of Polish agents in Bulgaria led by Mihail Chaikovski. Travelling throughout Bulgaria these agents made contacts with the Bulgarian population and acquainted themselves with the problems of the nation. In so doing they did not fail to notice the contradictions between the Bulgarian people and the Greek Patriarchate. It was in this conflict that Chaikovski perceived opportunity to strike a blow against the traditional prestige of Russia amongst the Orthodox Balkan nations. The Poles quickly opted to support Bulgarian demands and actively assisted the Bulgarian Church movement, influencing many of the leaders of the movement including Neofit Bozveli and Ilarion Makariopolski.

The efforts of the Polish agents to draw the Bulgarian people away from Russia failed. The primary desire of the Bulgarians to have their own bishops was shared by Chaikovski, who reckoned that a first step towards striking a blow against the Constantinople Patriarchate would be the ordination of "at least three Bulgarian bishops in Bulgaria." The second stage of the Polish plan foresaw complete separation from the Patriarchate and the creation of an independent national Bulgarian Church, which would deeply insult Russian pride. It was then hoped that subsequent difficulties created by Russian dissatisfaction would eventually lead to the incorporation of the Bulgarian Church with Rome. In this task the role of the Lazarist mission would have been important, as they were to educate and convert the spirit of the Bulgarian Church movement toward Catholicism. Hence the Poles played a vitally important role in the Bulgarian Church movement acting as an instigator and an intermediary between the Bulgarians and the Porte. However, Polish actions provoked such a hostile reaction from the Russians that when they ultimately relied on the Ottoman authorities to settle the Bulgarian-Greek dispute, at the decisive moment the Porte gave way to fierce Russian pressure.

Undeterred the French charged with the idea of separating the Bulgarians from Russian influence continued to work toward this end. In a memo dated 16 January 1849 the French Minister for Foreign Affairs suggested a number of proposals for Ottoman reforms which included the appointment of Bulgarian bishops and even a Bulgarian Patriarch.[27] These proposals were handed to Grand Vizier Ali Pasha by the French ambassador. Ali Pasha's response toward the idea of Bulgarian separation from the Greek Patriarchate revealed great insight. He expressed misgivings that an eventual Bulgarian Patriarchate would be a strong instrument in the hands of Russia, falling under Russian influence, rather than that of the Greeks. At the same time he promised the French ambassador that the Porte would seek to restrict the powers of the Greek clergy in Bulgaria. The Grand Vizier's words made a strong impression on the French ambassador: "I need to confess that the thoughts of the minister on the probable consequences on the creation of a Bulgarian Patriarchate deservedly have good reason."[28]

That moment came to define the future attitude of the French toward the Bulgarian Church question, namely that they did not need to be directly involved in the dispute. Rather, they needed only support the aims, reforms and authority of the Ottoman empire who the French considered to be a barrier against "the ambitions of barbaric Russia."[29] Nevertheless, they still endeavoured to weaken Russia's influence in the region by promoting the idea of union between the Eastern Orthodox and Catholic Churches – announced in a Papal encyclical dated 6 January 1848. To this end the Catholic Slavic Institute was established in Paris (1850), for the preparation of Latin missionaries amongst the Eastern Orthodox Slavs. A comment by the head of the institute reveals a leading motive behind its purpose: "... there is nothing that would strike a strong blow against Russia than the unification of the schismatic churches of the East with the Catholic Church."[30]

Russian Interest

Whilst the French had received religious privilege from the Ottoman government on the basis of a sixteenth century alliance, Russia needed war and strength of arms to gain any acknowledgement of legal rights and privileges within the empire. As a result of the 1st Russo-Turkish War (1768-1774) and the Treaty of Kucuk Kaynarca Russia obtained permission to build an Orthodox Church in Constantinople and protect those who worshipped there. A clause in the treaty guaranteed the freedom of worship for Orthodox Christians in the Ottoman empire and sections 16 and 17 guaranteed the specific safety of Orthodox

Christians in Bessarabia, Moldavia, Romania and the Russian Archipelago. Subsequently, this concession became the pretext under which Russia claimed the right to intercede on behalf of all Orthodox subjects of the sultan.[31]

With her victory in the 4th Russo-Turkish War (1828-1829) Russia stabilised and expanded her economic, territorial and political foothold in the Ottoman empire. During this period Russian policy towards Turkey changed. A covert committee was charged with drawing up the future direction of Russian Near Eastern politics that would benefit Russia through the preservation of the Ottoman empire, rather than seeking its collapse. In essence the government of Nikolas I understood that in the near future Russia would not be in a position to break the territorial status quo in the Near East as the western European powers would not permit this.[32] Russia's new pro-Ottoman policy was applied during the Turkish-Egyptian conflict of 1832-33 and for their assistance in overcoming the Egyptians the Ottoman government of Sultan Mahmud II (1808-1839) entered into the Hunkiar-Iskelesi Alliance Defence Treaty (1833). This resulted in Russia and Turkey promising to consult on everything that would bring about mutual peace and security.[33]

By means of these treaties Russia was recognised officially as the protector of Orthodox Christianity in the Ottoman empire. The role of 'protector' emerged during the eighteenth century when the Eastern problem was at the forefront of Russian politics. During this period the emphasis on the 'kinship tie' between Russia and Byzantium brought about the myth that the Russian Tsar's were the inheritors of the Byzantine emperor, called upon to rescue the Orthodox faithful from the Islamic yoke: "The idea of religious messianism served as a reason and a cover for the expansionist goals of the ruling circles in the East."[34] As a result of this belief Russian support was given solely to the Ecumenical Patriarchate, the personification of Orthodoxy within the Ottoman empire.

The idea of universal Orthodoxy, rather than that of independent Slavonic religious communities, became the cornerstone of Russian Near Eastern politics. Thus any attempt to introduce a split within Orthodoxy was received as a hostile act. This principle of ecumenical harmony predetermined the attitude of Russia towards the Bulgarian Church question. Nevertheless, it appears that Russia was ignorant of the complexities behind the Bulgarian dispute. They were so completely absorbed in the struggle against Catholicism that the Bulgarian-Greek dispute found Russian diplomats unprepared and uninformed concerning the contradictions between the Bulgarian people and the Patriarchal authorities. Indeed in 1844 the Russian vice-consul, who was supposed to be the chief informant on Bulgarian events, stated that there were no existing contradictions between the Greek clergy and the Bulgarians. Thus when Neofit Bozveli and Ilarion Makariopolski went before the Porte requesting Bulgarian ecclesiastical independence the Russian government was dumbfounded.

Russian diplomatic correspondence from this period reveals that the Polish agent Mihail Chaikovski was considered to be behind these "seditious ideas".[35] This supposition was further proven when a Bulgarian resident in Constantinople, Hadji Alexander, reported that it was Polish agents "who raised the idea of a separate administration for the Bulgarian national clergy."[36] This unanimity between the Bulgarians and the Polish agents further determined the position of Russian diplomacy towards the Bulgarian Church movement. Russian ambassador V. Titov protested against Bozveli and Makariopolski calling them "destroyers of the Greek Church and supporters of the Polish and French clergy." Titov went on to insist that Chaikovski be expelled from Constantinople as his activities were in "complete contradiction with the agreements between Russia and the Porte."[37]

The reaction of Russia towards the Bulgarian situation was indisputably a result of her traditional political/religious outlook, seeking to preserve the ecclesiastical status quo of the Balkans. Nevertheless, Bulgarian collaboration with an enemy of Russia forced the Tsar's government to stand against them, convinced that the anti-Greek movement had been inspired by their Polish rivals with the aim of undermining Russian influence amongst the Slavic peoples of the Balkans. This conviction was entirely due to a lack of information concerning the nature of the Bulgarian-Greek dispute and it was only later that Russian diplomats comprehended the underlying difficulties and the main trends in the development of the Bulgarian people in this struggle.[38] However, with the onset of the Crimean War Russia's Bulgarian conundrum would take an unexpected turn.

The Crimean War (1853-1856)

The motives behind the Crimean War were many, complex and beyond the scope of this research. The immediate cause of the war was, however, directly linked to Franco-Russian religious rivalry in the Ottoman empire. Although the war did not affect Bulgaria directly, its consequences would have dramatic effect upon the Bulgarian Church question. The war ended in Russian defeat at the hands of a coalition of British and French forces and the resultant Treaty of Paris (1856) proved both humiliating and unpalatable for Russia. The Treaty rescinded Russia's role as sole 'protector' of Orthodox Christianity in the empire, replacing it with a five-power collective protectorate of Britain, France, Prussia, Austria and Russia. As a result Russian influence within the Porte, which had steadily increased since the Treaty of Kucuk Kaynarca (1774), rapidly declined.

Under the terms of the Paris Treaty the European powers demanded that Sultan Abdulmecid grant further concessions to his Christian subjects. In line with this they accepted the sultan's second great document of the Tanzimat, the *Hatt-i Humayun*. Particularly meaningful for the Bulgarians was the paragraph within this document guaranteeing the right of every ethnic and religious community to have independent representation in Constantinople. This declaration rekindled the flame of the Bulgarian-Greek dispute encouraging the Bulgars to believe that finally the law was on their side. Thus the *Hatt-i Humayun* provoked another step in the development of the Bulgarian Church dispute that had advanced, from merely seeking protection against Greek economic pillage, to requesting Bulgarian bishops and now demanded a complete break from the Ecumenical Patriarchate and the creation of an independent Bulgarian Church (particularly as they were now recognised as *bulgarmiletani* – a separate ethnic Bulgarian and Orthodox Christian community).

In response to the terms of the *Hatt-i Humayun* the leaders of the Church movement wrote to every town in Bulgaria asking them to send a delegate to represent their region before the Porte. By the end of 1856 forty representatives had arrived in Constantinople and the following year they presented around sixty petitions to the Porte demanding an independent Bulgarian Church.[39] The activities of the delegation in Constantinople exerted influence on the pace of the Church dispute, so much so, that by the end of the 1850's every Bulgarian eparchy was disputing the rights of Greek clergy in their region.[40]

In the autumn of 1857 the Porte ordered Patriarch Cyril VII to convene a Church Council to discuss the developments of the Bulgarian situation and institute appropriate reforms. The Council sat for almost two years but could not reach a settlement as the Greeks continually frustrated discussions regarding an independent Bulgarian Church. As a direct result of Council negotiations Ilarion Makariopolski was appointed as Bishop to the Bulgarian Church in Constantinople in September 1858. Nevertheless, the generally unproductive outcome of the Church Council convinced the leaders of the Bulgarian Church movement that the time had come to take decisive action and break with the Patriarchate. On Easter Sunday, 3 April 1860, within the Bulgarian Church in Constantinople, Ilarion Makariopolski publicly declared Bulgarian ecclesiastical independence. By omitting the name of the patriarch from the liturgical prayers and replacing it with the name of the sultan, he symbolised Bulgaria's rejection of Patriarchal authority and loyalty to the sultan. In response to this action another Church Council was summoned in 1861 attended by the Patriarch's of Constantinople, Jerusalem, Alexandria and Antioch. This Council condemned Bulgarian actions anathematising all those associated with the incident, especially Bishop Makariopolski. Undismayed the Bulgarians instructed the Patriarchate that the independent Bulgarian Church would be known as the 'Bulgarian People's Christian Church'.

The Uniate Movement

A number of Bulgaria's ecclesiastical leaders had supported the Easter action of Makariopolski in the hope that it would force the hand of Russia to support their cause freeing the Bulgarian Church from its ties with Constantinople. Unfortunately for them St. Petersburg persisted in its support of the Patriarchate and universal Orthodoxy. This inevitably strengthened the confidence of those who believed that Bulgaria would be better off seeking alternative foreign advocacy.

Through the proficient work of French diplomacy and Roman Catholic missionaries, trained in the Catholic Slavic Institute in Paris an appealing 'middle-course' was offered to the Bulgarian people. This middle-way did not totally reject Orthodoxy. It offered communities the genuine possibility of religious self-government, retaining their beloved Slavonic Orthodox liturgy, while recognising the Pope rather than Patriarch as its spiritual head. A leading proponent of the Bulgarian Uniate movement was Dragan Tsankov, who with French financial assistance published the newspaper *Bulgaria* which advocated Uniatism as the only possible solution to Bulgaria's present situation. This formula achieved considerable success with many Bulgarian parishes accepting union with Rome. It must not be assumed, however, that the reason behind these conversions was anti-Orthodox sentiment, rather they were borne of pro-Bulgarian nationalistic frustration as is indicated by the inscription on the Uniate Church in Kukes: 'On March 1, 1858 we recovered our national tongue.'[41]

In December 1860 a group of leading Bulgarians in Constantinople signed an act of union with Rome nominating as their spiritual head Josef Sokolski, abbot of Gabrovo Monastery. On April 2 1861, Pope Pious IX consecrated Sokolski as Archbishop and appointed him as his representative in Bulgaria. The Porte, glad that a solution had been found to the Bulgarian problem, which did not increase Russian influence, welcomed the success of this movement. Thus on his arrival in Constantinople Sokolski and the Bulgarian Uniate Church were presented with a *berat* officially recognising the new Church.

The Russians zealously followed the activities of this new Church and its ardent Catholic missionary supporters. Alarmed by the dramatic increase of French influence, gained at Russian expense, the Russian government organised the removal of the Uniate archbishop from Bulgaria to Odessa. We can only speculate whether this action was a kidnapping or a personal request from Sokolski for assistance? What is clear is that a few months later it was reported that Sokolski had reverted to Orthodoxy. In a letter to his fellow Bulgarians he rejected Catholicism and encouraged all the leading figures of the Uniate movement to do likewise. The Uniate Church remained without a spiritual head until 1863 when Raphael Popov was appointed to the vacant post of archbishop.[42] However, by then the Uniate movement was in disarray.

Although short lived the Uniate movement had one major consequence. The Russians who had until then opposed the creation of an independent Bulgarian Church realised that they were in danger of losing their influence in the Balkans completely if they did not alter their traditional policy on the ecumenical harmony of Orthodoxy. In the midst of these difficulties direct Russian involvement in Ottoman Near Eastern politics became a necessity. Due to the importance of this task one of Russia's foremost diplomats was appointed to the foreign ministry post in Constantinople. Nikolai Pavlovich Ignatiev (1832-1907) was appointed as Foreign Minister in June 1864 and promoted as Russian Ambassador to the Porte in 1867. In a strategy aimed at eliminating Russian obstacles created by defeat in the Crimean War and the Treaty of Paris, thus restoring Russia to a prominent place in Ottoman affairs, Ignatiev immediately established four objectives that would indirectly affect the Bulgarian question. Firstly, that Russia must take steps to restore its influence over the Balkan Christian population; secondly, that Russia had to intimidate the Ottoman government to show that it was still a force to be reckoned with; thirdly, the Russian Foreign Ministry would direct its efforts at breaking up the accord of the European powers, which in Ignatiev's opinion was "fictitious and based on exceptional circumstances"; and finally, Russian diplomacy must combat the dominant position of France at the Porte.[43]

BULGARIAN ECCLESIASTICAL INDEPENDENCE

The diplomatic and personal archives of Russian ambassador, Nikolai Ignatiev, provide us with a glimpse behind the complexities of the Bulgarian question during the period 1864-1870. Although written from a Russian perspective they nevertheless give us opportunity to appreciate the fundamental issues in the ongoing struggle for Bulgarian ecclesiastical independence. In Ignatiev's attempt to achieve his four-stage objective he encountered a number of obstacles, the most serious of which was the dispute between the Bulgarians and the Greeks. He understood that his ability in dealing with this dispute would affect future Russian diplomacy in the Balkans. However, from the onset we witness a clear modification in Russia's Bulgarian policy, when he comments: "My principal preoccupation in this question is to procure for the Bulgarians, without breaking from the Greeks, a national form, while defending them from the efforts of catholic propaganda and thus conserving them to Orthodoxy and to our [Russian] influence."[44] While continuing to seek the unity of Orthodoxy and thus maintain the supremacy of the Constantinople Patriarchate, Russia was now willing to support Bulgaria in an attempt to have independent national representation.

With this overall objective in mind he worked closely with the leaders of the Bulgarian Church movement attempting to assist the Bulgarians achieve some of their original aims. In April 1865, through Ignatiev's direct intervention, Patriarch Sophronios III (1863-1866) promised the leaders of the Church movement that the Patriarchate would seek to replace Greek bishops with Bulgarians in the eparchies that desired this.[45] Having established this concession the Bulgarians urged the Russian ambassador to help them obtain permanent representation on the Patriarchal Synod. For the Greeks this was a step to far and refused the request.[46]

The enmity between the Greek and Bulgarian clergy was so intense that Ignatiev attempted to arrive at a mutually agreeable settlement via another more progressive direction. He achieved this by gathering together a number of leading businessmen from both communities in an ad hoc committee to discuss the Church question. Unhindered by ecclesiastical differences or by canon law this lay committee presented an alarming project before the Church authorities. As well as supporting a level of Bulgarian representation on the Patriarchal Synod its most startling proposal allowed the Bulgarian Church a level of administrative autonomy within the Danube Vilayet.[47] Not surprisingly the Patriarchal Assembly, which met in April 1866, denounced these proposals as "heretical" and an infringement of "the natural rights of the Greeks." They also claimed that allowing the Bulgarians representation in Constantinople would ultimately be a threat to the Patriarchate and rejected the findings of the ad hoc committee.[48] The Bulgarian-Greek dispute had reached impasse yet again.

Ignatiev quickly realised that the Porte was implicitly involved in encouraging this deadlock and advised St. Petersburg that Ottoman policy toward the Bulgarian-Greek dispute was one of divide and conquer.[49] This policy can be clearly discerned throughout the years of the Church dispute in the Porte's practice of making mutually exclusive promises to either side. For example, telling the Patriarchal authorities that they would never support Bulgarian aspirations, while simultaneously pledging to help the Bulgarians. The words of the Porte were simply meant to appease both parties while keeping them at loggerheads with one other. The complexity of the situation is easy to see. The Russian ambassador understood that the Greeks and the Bulgarians had to reach an agreement with each other without interference from the Porte. Unfortunately, the Bulgarians were unable to foresee a time when the Greeks would ever concede to their requests and thus placed all their hopes on Ottoman intervention – therefore the circle of impasse persisted.

The Cretan Uprising (1866-1868)

We observed that as an indirect consequence of the Crimean War the Bulgarian Church question advanced considerably. So now with the Cretan Uprising, an unrelated event would positively affect Bulgaria finally breaking the perpetual cycle of impasse. The details behind the Cretan revolt again are beyond the subject matter of this research, suffice to say that failure to promulgate promised reforms on the island caused the Christian inhabitants to rise in protest against the Porte. This quickly evolved into open revolt supported by large numbers of Greek troops and in the summer of 1866 the Ottoman military contingent surrendered. After the insurgents had dispersed the Ottoman forces reformed and wreaked revenge on the islanders.[50] The Greek government, with aspirations of territorial advancement, declared its support for Crete creating an immediate breakdown in Greek-Ottoman relations.

This local insurgency soon took on international proportions and in the midst of the crisis Bulgaria became an important pawn. In order to win the support of the Bulgarians, to unite against the Porte, the Greek government advised the Constantinople Patriarchate to be more sympathetic in its attitude towards the Bulgarian Church question. We cannot tell if Patriarchal sympathy played a part but the Bulgarians during the crisis did support the Greeks in their struggle, so much so that Naiden Gerov reported that the Bulgarians were following the crisis with such sympathy "that it would seem as if there were no quarrel between them and the Greeks."[51] The Porte concerned that insurrection might also break out in Bulgaria promised the leaders of the Church movement that the independent Church question would be settled to the satisfaction of the Bulgarians. Russia followed these events closely and considered that "now the decisive moment has come to sustain the efforts of the Christian populations in Turkey in their efforts to free themselves."[52] Russian ambassador Ignatiev believed that the time had arrived for St. Petersburg to denounce the Treaty of Paris and in the view of the Cretan Uprising, to favour national insurgency among the Balkan peoples, predicting that if Russia acted the Ottoman empire would quickly fall.[53]

In light of Greek conciliatory machinations toward the Bulgarian question Patriarch Sophronios III, the ardent anti-Bulgarian, resigned from office. In his place and with Russian approval former Patriarch Gregory VI (1835-1840) was re-elected to the Patriarchal throne (1867-1871).[54] The new Patriarch, responsive to the political climate, was immediately set the task of formulating a settlement agreeable to all sides (I say all sides because Russian ambassador Ignatiev intricately involved himself in the whole process). So involved were the Russians that Gregory VI presented his proposal firstly to Ignatiev for Russian approval. The proposal accepted for the first time the creation of an independent Bulgarian Exarchate within the borders of the Danube Vilayet. The magnitude of this proposal and the involvement of the Russians suggest that it had not been widely circulated within the Patriarchate, if at all. If authentic it signalled a remarkable change in the attitude of the Patriarchate as until this moment the Constantinople Patriarchate had argued from Canon law that any separation would have been contrary to the laws of Orthodoxy. From the personal records of Ignatiev we discern that the proposal was formulated without Synodal approval. The Patriarch and the Russian ambassador hoped through time to convince the Holy Synod of its benefits and when the time was favourable they would officially present the proposal before the Patriarchate and the Porte for approval.[55]

Nevertheless, there were still a number of problems within the proposal. Firstly, it had to be approved by the Greek authorities; secondly, even though it presented a major concession on behalf of the Greeks it still might not be acceptable to the Bulgarians. For although granting a level independence within the borders of the Danube Vilayet the plan completely ignored the needs and desires of Bulgarians in Thrace and Macedonia and failed to recognise the independent status of the Bulgarian Church in Constantinople. Even so ambassador Ignatiev believed that "if they [the Bulgarians] have retained any grain of political sense and the slightest true devotion to the cause of Orthodoxy, they must accept this unexpected chance, which appears finally to prepare the way for a solution to a question long considered unsolvable."[56]

As soon as details of Gregory's proposal leaked out Greek nationalists responded negatively calling the Patriarch "a traitor to the Great Idea," believing that the plan would compromise future Greek glory.[57] A number of Bulgarian Church leaders also refused to accept Gregory's proposal demanding that Ohrid (in Macedonia) be established as the centre of any new Bulgarian Church. Ignoring the Patriarchate completely they petitioned the Porte directly for an autonomous Church province combining the Danube Vilayet, Macedonia, Thrace and the Bulgarian Constantinople Church.[58] By ignoring the concessions of the Patriarchate the Bulgarians again placed all their hopes upon the Porte. Thus through 1867-1868 we witness the leader of the Bulgarian 'extremists' Stoyan Chomakov making a number of declarations of loyalty before the Sultan, which the Russian ambassador regarded as an act of treason before Russia, Bulgaria and Orthodoxy.[59]

Toward Independence (1868-1870)

When the promises of the Porte failed to reach fruition an inner conflict broke out in the Church movement between the 'extremist' and 'moderate' factions.[60] The focus of the dispute centred on the Porte's 'double-dealing' tactics that had resulted in Bulgarian disillusionment and distrust of the Ottoman government. Ambassador Ignatiev took advantage of this predicament to support the moderate faction and their figurehead Bishop Paisii who sought reconciliation with the Patriarchate.[61] In this spirit Paisii and Patriarch Gregory VI held a series of consultations between May-June 1868 during which they tried to reach a mutually acceptable compromise.[62]

In an effort to scupper the reconciliation process the Porte announced a six-point programme that met Bulgarian demands in full, allowing them to have their own churches, bishops, an independent Bulgarian Synod and a primate based in Constantinople.[63] The consequences of this action soon became evident. By accepting the Porte's plan the Bulgarians saw an immediate end to their struggle. The Patriarchate, however, saw this action as an infringement and threat upon their position as the defender of Orthodox Church rights. The Russian ambassador said of the announcement: "It is essentially Machiavellian and if it was adopted, dissension, instead of being lessened, could only increase. The presence of the Bulgarian Synod at Constantinople, where the Ecumenical Synod already sits, would obviously perpetuate the rivalry and the discord between the two groups."[64]

The leaders of the Bulgarian Church movement, anxious to bring their dreams to fruition, proceeded to prepare for an independent Church in line with the Porte's promises and an executive committee was elected to set up the new Church. They sought to maintain relations with the Ecumenical Patriarchate but stated that if Gregory VI refused to resume negotiations they would seek the support of the Russian Synod. In November 1868 Gregory VI did refuse categorically rejecting Ottoman and Bulgarian actions, declaring them to be in violation of Canon law. In response the Bulgarian executive committee declared publicly that they were no longer interested in a bilateral agreement with the Ecumenical Patriarchate.[65] Responding to the Patriarchal repudiation Grand Vizier Ali Pasha called on all Bulgarian bishops to convene in Constantinople to prepare the statutes of the new Church. Upon their arrival, without the permission of the Patriarchate, Gregory VI accused them of committing "an unprecedented act of subordination."[66] Nikolai Ignatiev blamed Patriarch Gregory VI directly for the direction the Bulgarians had taken as his refusal to negotiate with the executive committee, in Ignatiev's mind, had left Bulgaria with no choice but to break with the Patriarchate.[67]

As the Bulgarians waited impatiently in Constantinople for the final settlement on the Church question political events yet again altered the course of the movement's progress. With the unstable situation on Crete flaring up once again (1868-69) the focus of the Porte diverted from Bulgaria. Graeco-Russian political relations deteriorated as Greek nationalists blamed Russia for their lack of support in this latest uprising. By early 1870 it became clear that the Porte was in no hurry to settle the Bulgarian question. Several Bulgarian bishops then asked the Russian ambassador for advice on how to secure a firman quickly. He advised them to emphasise that growing unrest in Bulgaria, motivated by similar agitations in Crete and Montenegro, could break out at any time if a firman was not granted for the Bulgarian Church.[68]

Ignatiev's advice and willingness to be involved after the Cretan Uprising introduces yet another change of direction in Russian-Bulgarian policy which now supported the immediate establishment of a totally independent Bulgarian Church. This policy change, spurred on by anti-Greek overtones, can be witnessed in Ignatiev's appeal to the Grand Vizier to officially acknowledge an independent Bulgarian Church before another Patriarchal Assembly could be convened, thus presenting the Patriarchate with a *fait accompli*. This policy change is further supported by an encoded message directed to Russian Foreign Minister Gorchakov in which Ignatiev informs his superior that Ali Pasha accepted "full well the expediency of my advice."[69]

The Bulgarian Exarchate

On 12 March 1870 the Ottoman government issued a firman authorising the establishment of a separate Bulgarian Church.[70] However, the new Church would not be completely autocephalous, rather it would be recognised as an Exarchate, spiritually subordinate to the Ecumenical Patriarch but in regard to matters of internal administration fully independent. The Church movement had achieved its ultimate aim the recognition of Bulgaria as a distinct *ethnos* and the establishment of religious and cultural self-determination for her people. Having won the war of attrition Bulgaria's Church leaders were now satisfied with their position within the Ottoman empire. History constitutes this moment merely as a stepping stone towards further national development ultimately leading to the political liberation of Bulgaria from Ottoman rule. After the firman's proclamation the Church movement's activities advanced towards the practical construction of the Exarchate. Foremost it was necessary to draw up the statutes that would govern the new Church as required by section 3 of the firman. To this end the bishops, who were already present in Constantinople, elected a temporary administrative body that would prepare draft statutes, guide the Bulgarian Church through the separation and final establishment of the Exarchate and organise a Church Synod and Council.[71] On 13 March 1870 the bishops and thirty-nine of the most eminent Bulgarians from Constantinople gathered for this purpose and by means of a secret ballot elected ten lay people and five bishops to the Temporary Council.

The deliberations of the Temporary Council raised new issues for the Bulgarian people. No longer hindered by the predominance of Greek clergy debate arose around the hierarchical organisation of the new church. The roots of this dispute can be traced to a letter, dated 24 February 1870, in which Dr. Chomakov the leader of the extremist faction comments that the new church should have a Synod and Council composed with a broad participation of laymen rather than traditional "aristocratic despotism."[72] His opinion précised one of two opposing streams of thought. Petko Slaveikov and Todor Ikonomov championed Chomakov's progressive attitude on the Council arguing that there could be no division between ecclesiastical and lay authority in the Church because there was no actual barrier between secular and spiritual work: "The Church is not only the spiritual; the Church is every gathering of the faithful, all people."[73] They continued by arguing that the new Church would be beneficial to the nation only if it was democratic, established in the spirit of the new times, rather than maintaining the stratified dogmatic and complicated Church hierarchal structure of the past. In line with this thought process they also promoted the necessity of regularly changing those in the Exarchate's leading positions, as neglecting to do so would lead to the ideal condition for despotism.[74]

Opposing the progressive element was Peter Odjakov who argued not on the basis of modernity but from tradition and Church Canon. He commented that the leading Church position of Exarch should not even be elected but determined solely by terms of seniority.[75] He emphasised that the Metropolitan of the oldest Bulgarian eparchy, Turnovo, rightly should be placed on the Exarchal throne. His views gave total priority to the clergy, ignoring the secular element, as he viewed the role of the Church as being purely representative of Bulgaria's spiritual life.[76] As he continued, in his attempt to prove that the Church had neither civic nor political aspects, it became clear that his predilection was the product of ambition to prove that Turnovo should be the seat of the Bulgarian Exarchate, rather than Constantinople. Hidden deeper behind Odjakov's contentions, however, lay the interests of the ultra-conservative element of the Council who were intent on securing the nomination of Ilarion Makariopolski as Exarch. Makariopolski had been a leading figurehead of the Bulgarian Church movement since its inception, he had argued on behalf of his people, been exiled and imprisoned for their benefit and he was one of the men who had made independence possible. Now he offered his services to the Bulgarian nation.

It appears, however, that personal ambition rather than ideology had taken precedence in Makariopolski's actions. Archival materials collated during this period reveal that he promised the leaders of the Turnovo eparchy a four thousand-groshta 'reward' if they elected him as Exarch.[77] To further ensure his selection his supporters chose a representative, N. Minchoglu, from the Turnovo eparchy to "control and guide" the people towards this decision.[78] Therefore as the Temporary Council worked on the draft statutes in Constantinople Minchoglu visited every community in the Turnovo eparchy reporting in November 1870 that every town and village of the eparchy would nominate Makariopolski.[79] Although Odjakov's anti-progressive contentions were undoubtedly argued from Church Canon, his assertions were somewhat blackened by subordinating them to meet the specific interests of one man, Ilarion Makariopolski. Despite the political manoeuvring of Makariopolski the selection process did not go smoothly and when he saw that even within the Temporary Council his election was not guaranteed he left the conference.[80]

The Council finalised drafting the statutes for the Exarchate in September 1870 after which they called on every Bulgarian community to elect a representative to sit on the National Church Council. The National Council opened for business on 23 February 1871 under the chairmanship of Bishop Ilarion of Lovech composed of fifty people (eleven clergy and thirty-nine laity).[81] On 27 February 1872 the first Exarch of the Bulgarian Church was elected by the National Council.

Exarch Antim I, the former Metropolitan of Vidin, then travelled to Constantinople to receive official recognition from Sultan Abdulaziz on 15 April 1872. Thereafter the Bulgarian delegation presented itself before the Patriarchate to receive the conformation of Antim I. However, rather than pronounce his conformation Patriarch Anthimus implored Antim I to denounce his position and return to Vidin. Ignoring this request Antim read a proclamation declaring the independence of the Bulgarian Church. This led to the Ecumenical Patriarch pronouncing the Exarchate to be schismatic on 16 September 1872, citing the basis for the schism as philetism.[82]

The Bulgarians viewed this pronouncement positively convinced of the justice of their cause and the legitimacy of their actions. Indeed, the schism brought the Bulgarian people together in even greater national unity. Russian ambassador Ignatiev commented that the schism had "excited among them dreams of political independence."[83] Rather than dampening enthusiasm the schism actively encouraged Bulgarian revolutionary elements to take up arms and fight for political independence.

The Exarchate and the Revolutionary Liberation Movement

The Exarchate was the ultimate prize for the National Church movement, giving self-determination to and recognition of the Bulgarian nation. It was now a legal institution recognised as the official representative of the Bulgarian people before the Ottoman government. This position defined both its role and activities; it had legal resources to protect the Christian population, it could be involved in the cultural and educational advancement of Bulgaria and it had the possibility to extend the Exarchate's borders by seeking the unification of Bulgarians in disputed eparchies.

The ability of the Exarchate to implement this power, however, was hampered by the Porte. Born within the world of Ottoman politics and validated only by means of a governmental act the Exarchate was completely dependent on and subordinate to her political master, her existence dependent on the will of government officials. Thus the Bulgarian Church existed by establishing its loyalty to the Porte. The Exarchate was "shackled like a horse and bound by its leg," hindering its true political voice.[84]

The lack of actual power and the perpetuation of political bondage led many to believe that, whilst the Church movement had been advantageous to the nation, it no longer had any positive role to play. So as the Exarchate struggled to secure its position other groups sought complete national autonomy from the Ottoman empire through revolutionary means. Although these activities reached their height during the second half of the nineteenth century random incidents had occurred previously. During the Russo-Turkish Wars thousands of Bulgarian volunteers had joined the Russian army hoping that tsarist victory would bring them a better life. Many more fought with the Serbs (1804-1814) and again with the Greeks in their War of Independence in the 1820's. Emboldened by experience many volunteers sought to instil the concept of attaining independence through armed uprising in Bulgaria.

One of the most significant revolutionary events occurred in 1841 when Bulgarian émigrés in Greece and Romania formed a loosely connected revolutionary union that planned to organise and equip armed detachments (*cheta*) that would enter Bulgaria and incite revolt. The first of these *cheta* detachments was organised in Braila, Romania, led by Vasil Hadjivulkov and a Serbian, Vladislav Tatic.[85] In 1841 they crossed the Danube and landed on Bulgarian soil hoping to precipitate general rebellion. The attempt failed miserably. Nevertheless the characteristics of the *cheta* movement became the model for all future Bulgarian revolutionary activity.

Georgi Rakovski (1821-1867) was hugely influential in Bulgaria's revolutionary development. He evolved these activities from spontaneous risings to become an organised ideological revolutionary movement. He was convinced that liberation could only be achieved through *cheta* tactics. Thus he began to organise and train volunteers to join his 'Bulgarian Legion' to organise revolutionary activities in Bulgaria. In 1861 he founded the newspaper the *Danube Swan* through which he promoted his ideology:

> Let no one imagine that freedom can be won without blood and costly sacrifice! Let no one wait for some one else to free him. Our freedom depends on us! Let each one inscribe deep in his heart as a holy thing the thrilling words 'freedom and death', and with a flaming sword let him march to the field of battle, under the banner of the invincible Bulgarian lion.[86]

His greatest achievement, however, lay in the creation of the Bulgarian Secret Central Committee founded in 1866. This committee brought together many who would become Bulgarian national heroes,

Karavelov, Levski and Botev. His combination of military action, inspirational writing and political intrigue disturbed the Ottoman Porte and played a large part in bringing a conclusion to the Church question. The Porte had hoped that the creation of the Exarchate would extinguish the fiery rhetoric of the insurgents.

Rakovski's protégé Vasil Levski (1837-1873) best fits the romantic revolutionary tradition in that he wished to achieve Bulgarian independence through mass peasant revolt. Born in Karlovo on 6 July 1837 his family wanted him to enter the priesthood. Thus in 1858 he entered the monastery of St. Spas in Sopot and the following year was ordained as a deacon in the Church. His interest was never fully on the divine but rather focussed on the mortal hardships of his fellow countrymen. So much so that by 1861 he had reached a personal dilemma, whether to serve the Church or the Bulgarian people. He revealed his decision in a letter: "...in 1861 I dedicated myself to my country, to serve her till death and to do the will of the people."[87] In 1862 he abandoned his ecclesiastical duties and joined Rakovski's 'Bulgarian Legion' in Serbia. From 1868 on, after establishing himself as one of the leaders of the revolutionary movement, he travelled around Bulgaria promoting the revolutionary message which for him was not only national but also socially inspired. The initial years of the Exarchate's existence therefore coincided with the time of Levski's revolutionary awakening and his travels around Bulgaria when he sought to construct a network of revolutionary committees.

These activities did not go unnoticed; indeed many insurgent actions dismally failed due to the vigorous underground surveillance network of the Ottoman authorities. However, it would be a mistake to consider that all Bulgarians were united in this anti-Ottoman struggle as the majority of the population opposed these actions. The creation of the Danube Vilayet had made many Bulgarians content with their lot. They were experiencing for the first time an element of prosperity and tranquillity and saw no need to stir up trouble with the Ottoman authorities. The desire not to rock the boat can be witnessed in the abject failure of the April Uprising of 1876. This uprising has taken on mythical proportions in Bulgarian history, emphasising the brutality of the Muslim barbarian and the stalwart, honest and heroic character of the Bulgarian Christian.[88] It was meant to be the crowning achievement of the revolutionary movement, with uprisings occurring simultaneously throughout the country removing the Ottoman tyrant from Bulgarian territory after five centuries of domination. Hastily conceived, poorly planned and ultimately because of lack of popular support from within the country it met the same fate as its predecessors. For example, the revolutionary committee had expected three hundred armed volunteers to gather in the town of Chirpan, only twenty-four appeared. Similarly throughout the country only handfuls of men turned out in support of revolution.

The Bulgarian Exarchate had been vehemently opposed to the activities of the revolutionary committee. Church archival records prove beyond doubt that the Exarchate gathered information on anti-Ottoman activities which they passed directly to the Porte, information that helped capture influential revolutionary leaders and ultimately led to the failure of their activities. This is somewhat disturbing as the Bulgarian Orthodox Church and Bulgarian national history claim that the Exarchate was at the centre of the movement supporting Bulgarian liberation:

> The Bulgarian exarchate emerged as the one church and political entity which sublimated the quintessence of the religious and patriotic in the embattled Bulgarian people, inspiring it with the bravery and courage to strive for national freedom. The role of the exarchate is in this respect widely recognized and duly appreciated.[89]

Despite this pro-Exarchate nationalistic rhetoric the church's anti-revolutionary policy had been openly reported in the Bulgarian press during 1872 as the official stance of the Exarchate.[90] This was not a new policy as we know that the Church had been acting on it some years previously. The Eparchial Church Board of Plovdiv removed Vasil Levski from the priesthood because of his activities against the state in 1864.[91] The Church hierarchy continued to follow Levski's activities particularly closely as they were concerned that his revolutionary activities could sacrifice their own newly won freedom. In connection with their ongoing investigations the National Church Council ordered the detention and flogging of the Metropolitan of Samokov in November 1872 to find out more about Levski's plots against the state.[92] Their investigation led to Levski's arrest for conspiracy against the Ottoman government and his death by hanging in Sofia in February 1873.

Insurrections in Bulgaria and the surrounding Balkan states reflected the instability of the Exarchate as they increased the suspicion of the Porte towards the Church. On 4 August 1875 at the height of growing unrest Exarch Antim sent a confidential letter to all his Metropolitans urging them to "continue in your work whatever the circumstance" and to encourage their flocks to stay calm and show their loyalty to the Sultan.[93] This letter was one of many censuring rebellious activities and urging demonstrations of loyalty toward the Porte. These censures originated after Grand Vizier, Mahmud Nedim Pasha, ordered Antim I to meet with him to discuss the loyalty of the Bulgarian people.[94] In response the Exarch stated that the Bulgarian Church was not involved in any rebellious activity against the Ottoman state and that every eparchy in Bulgaria would defend against "troublemakers". The Grand Vizier expressed the satisfaction of the sultan and thanked the Exarch for his assurance of loyalty from the Bulgarian people.[95]

In line with this policy Metropolitan Gregory of Ruse worked closely with the regional Ottoman authorities. He despised those who sought to violate "order and tranquillity," and insisted that "these madmen" be delivered into the hands of the authorities.[96] In this respect he commented:

> Dedicated to the interests of Orthodoxy, of the Church and the people, we need to display dignity, perseverance and energy to reveal fully the falseness of these scoundrels, who do much harm in the people.[97]

The French Consul in Ruse wrote of Metropolitan Gregory that he was a most intelligent and capable man "whose conduct from a Turkish perspective was correct," but in the eyes of the Bulgarian revolutionaries "he was completely compromised."[98]

In December 1875 the National Church Council sent a circular letter to the Metropolitans, reminding them once again that they were obliged to help the Porte in the gathering of information regarding "any mischief or violence." Furthermore they were to send weekly reports to Constantinople of all activities in their region.[99] In doing so the Exarchate aimed to show the Porte that the condition of the Christian community was improving, but also sought to protect themselves from any future rebellious acts. In February 1876 church reports began to filter through notifying the government of growing unrest amongst "Bulgarian agents" who were planning an uprising in the spring. Therefore it was the Bulgarian clergy who spearheaded the drive to gain the Christian community's loyalty to the Ottoman government at the moment of Bulgaria's greatest bid for national freedom. Indeed immediately after the April Uprising of 1876 the Exarchate appealed for people to "seize the troublemakers" and turn them over to the authorities.[100]

After the April Uprising (1876)

With the assistance of the Exarchate the April Uprising was thwarted. As a rebellious action it had been nothing less than a disastrous shambles, but it would have an irreversible affect on Bulgarian history. The Ottoman authorities were able to crush the rebellion, however, this was accompanied by months of violent retribution as regular Turkish troops and bands of *bashibazouks* scoured the countryside fearful that fresh insurgency would break out. The British government, through their envoy in Constantinople, Sir Henry Elliot, encouraged this Ottoman action: "About five thousand troops have been dispatched from here [Constantinople] and I believe no exertion should be spared for assuring the immediate suppression of a movement which, if allowed to spread, will become extremely serious."[101] As reports of the retribution began to circulate it became apparent that the uprising had not only been thwarted it had been eradicated and a massacre had ensued.

The *Daily News's* Constantinople correspondent, James MacGahan, was one of the first international reporters to write on the awful consequences of the April Uprising:

> I have just seen the town of Batak with Mr. Schuyler, the American Consul. Here is what I saw. On approaching the town on a hill there were some dogs. They ran away and we found on this spot a heap of skeletons with clothing. I counted from the saddle a hundred skulls, picked and licked clean, all women and children. We entered the town. On every side were skulls and skeletons charred among the ruins. There were skeletons of girls and women with long hair. We approached the church. Here the remains were more frequent, until the ground was literally covered with skeletons and putrefying bodies in clothing. Between the church and the school there were heaps. The stench was fearful. We entered the churchyard. The sight was more dreadful. The whole churchyard was deep with festering bodies partly covered – hands, legs, arms, and heads projected in ghastly confusion.... The church was still worse. The floor was covered with rotting bodies. I never imagined anything so fearful. There were three thousand bodies in the churchyard and church... In the school two hundred women and children had been burnt alive. All over the town there were the same scenes.... The town had nine thousand inhabitants. There now remain one thousand two hundred.[102]

The American Consul in Constantinople, Eugene Schuyler, after investigating these events also wrote: "Old men had there eyes torn out and their limbs cut off, and were then left to die, unless some more charitably disposed gave them the final thrust. Pregnant women were ripped open and the unborn babies carried triumphantly on the point of bayonet and sabre, while little children were made to bear the dripping heads of their victims."[103] A tide of opposition arose around the world in response to what became known as the 'Bulgarian horrors'. British Prime Minister Benjamin Disraeli dismissed reports of the atrocities as "inventions" which prompted William Gladstone to denounce Turkey and Disraeli:

> An old servant of the Crown and State, I entreat my countrymen, upon whom far more than perhaps any other people it depends to require and to insist that our Government, which has been working in one direction, shall work in the other, and shall apply all its vigour to concur with the other States of Europe in obtaining extinction of the Turkish executive powers in Bulgaria. Let the Turks now carry away their abuses in the only possible manner, namely by carrying off themselves... This thorough riddance, this most blessed deliverance, is the only reparation we can make to the memory of those heaps on heaps of dead; to the violated purity alike of matron, of maiden and of child; to the civilisation which has been affronted and shamed, to the laws of God, or, if you like, of Allah; to the moral sense of mankind at large... No Government ever has so sinned, none has so proved itself incorrigible in sin, or which is the same, so impotent for reformation. If it be allowable that the executive power in Turkey should renew at this great crisis, by permission of authority of Europe, the charter of existence in Bulgaria, then there is not on record, since the beginnings of political society, a protest that man has lodged against intolerable misgovernment, or a stroke he has dealt at loathsome tyranny, that ought not henceforward to be branded as a crime.[104]

The atrocities also caused major disagreement between the Exarchate and the Bulgarian people. The brutal retribution had made it abundantly clear that the nation could no longer live under the present conditions within the Ottoman empire. Thus under pressure to survive Antim I and the Holy Synod had no choice but to change their sympathies, from supporting the Ottoman government to advocating the Bulgarian national cause. The National Church Council proposed that a Bishop's Commission be formed to lead an investigation in the regions where the atrocities had occurred. Their plea was ignored.[105] Thereafter an unofficial Bulgarian enquiry was undertaken led by a student from the

Bulgarian Royal Medical School, Atanas Shopov. Through the summer of 1876 Shopov visited the regions affected by these events. His final report included information on the scale of the destruction and the number of lives lost in Bulgaria, which according to differing accounts fluctuated between thirty-to-fifty thousand. Complete with Shopov's report the Exarchate established a 'National Commission', which gathered and systematised all the information, translated it into English and French and then disseminated it through diplomatic representatives in Constantinople.[106] After collating the information the urgent need of the victims was recognised and it was decided that the Exarchate should develop humanitarian activities "for the material and moral relief of those affected."[107]

The activities of the Exarchate between the April Uprising (1876) and the War of Liberation (1878) reveal a major change of direction. The general unrest, which resulted from Ottoman retribution in conjunction with the anger of the Bulgarian people, forced the Exarchate to rethink their strategy. It was only after some hesitation that Antim decided to support the ground swell of anti-Ottoman opinion, knowing what the consequences could have been for the Exarchate. However, he came to the conclusion that to rely on the Porte to improve the situation in Bulgaria would have been a waste of time: "We will wait for nothing, I have waited for an answer to our requests before the Turkish government long enough."[108] Seeking protection from further retribution, the Exarch wrote to the Russian Synod, begging the Tsar for his protection and deliverance, emphasising that the uprising had been the result of the intolerable situation arising from fanatical Muslims' implementing a plan to exterminate all Bulgarian Christians.[109]

In December 1876 the ambassadors of the European powers in Constantinople met to press the institution of reforms by the Porte. The Exarchate dispatched a Bulgarian legation to appear before this gathering, further influencing Europe in favour of the Bulgarian national cause. The Russian and American ambassadors, Ignatiev and Schuyler, prepared a series of draft proposals for establishing an autonomous Bulgarian state: a major problem being whether to create a large entity embracing all the lands of the Bulgarian Exarchate, or to divide them into two separate units, which would overcome a number of objections. The Porte rejected both proposals. The Ecumenical Patriarchate took advantage of the circumstances and the Exarchates new anti-Ottoman policy, calling the Bulgarians and Exarch Antim disturbers of the peace.

Under the circumstances the Porte forced Antim I to resign. The deposed Exarch responded: "Once a Greek Patriarch was hanged and the result was the liberation of Greece. I will gladly give my life if my people may by this act become free."[110]

Simultaneous with events in Bulgaria there had been a Conference in Berlin, in May 1876, which had discussed the issue of Serbian independence from the Ottoman empire. The European powers dismissed the suggestion. Weary of the fruitless deliberations Serbia and Montenegro formed an alliance and began to prepare for war with Turkey. On 19 June 1876 war broke out but by October the Serbian army was defeated. Another catastrophe was prevented when Russia intervened demanding an immediate cessation to military activity. For a short time it looked as though stability had been achieved, but Russia, enthused by Ottoman disarray and angered at the failure of the Porte to accept their Bulgarian proposals, declared war on the Ottoman empire on 24 April 1877.

The political machinations of the Bulgarian Exarchate have been dealt with during the period 1875-76. However, after Antim's removal from office the Holy Synod again reiterated their support for the Ottoman government when, on 1 May 1877, new Exarch, Josef I, sent a circular letter calling for the loyalty of the Christian population towards the sultan. The Moscow Slavonic Charitable Committee appealed to the Bulgarian people to support the liberating Russian army, but in response the new Exarch ordered the people "to take immediate action against the ill-intended aims of the malevolent scoundrels."[111] On 15 June 1877 the Russian army crossed the Danube and set foot on Bulgarian soil near Svishtov. The liberation of Bulgaria had begun. With this action the Ottoman Minister of Foreign Affairs, Savfet Pasha, informed the Exarchate that a 'Commission for Military Assistance' would be set up in Constantinople to which the Synod elected Parteni Velichki as their representative.[112] At the climax of Bulgaria's national struggle we witness the Exarchate again fully supporting the aims of the Ottoman government over the desires of their own people.

San Stefano and Berlin

After eight months of fighting the Russian army marched through the small town of San Stefano, less than seven miles from Constantinople. At the imminent collapse of Turkey in Europe the Porte sued for peace before Constantinople fell into Russian hands and on 19 February

1878 the San Stefano peace treaty was signed. The Ottoman government was compelled to sign a treaty which fulfilled Russia's territorial dreams. Primarily through the establishment of a vast new Bulgarian state the treaty gave Russia strategic domination over the Balkan region. 'Greater Bulgaria', as it became known, comprised of around 176,000 sq.km., stretching from the Danube to the Rhodopes in the south and from the Black Sea in the east to Macedonia; as far west a Ohrid and as far south as Kostur. It even had access to the Aegean Sea. The treaty's territorial terms were greater than any Bulgarian could have hoped for. Its signing was regarded by Bulgarians as the official end of five centuries of Ottoman rule and is still celebrated annually as Liberation Day.

Bulgarian nationalists had achieved their goal. With an independent Church and State the nation was free. A letter of gratitude was sent to Tsar Alexander II complete with 230,000 Bulgarian signatures, including Exarch Josef's.[113] However, Bulgaria's hour of triumph was brief. A major weakness within the San Stefano Treaty lay in the fact that it was exclusively a Russian creation. The European Powers feared the potential influence Russia could exert through Greater Bulgaria and insisted that its boundaries be redrawn. All interested parties gathered at the Congress of Berlin (13 June - 13 July 1878) to redress the balance of power in the region.[114] Russia had already accepted that San Stefano Bulgaria would be dismembered. This had been accounted for in their plans – Russian ambassador Ignatiev had prepared draft proposals for establishing an autonomous Bulgarian state, one large, the other small in 1876. Therefore, the reduction of Bulgarian territory from 176,000 sq.km. to 96,000 sq.km. was acceptable to Russia, being part of a calculated long-term strategy. For Bulgaria, however, the Berlin settlement was a traumatic experience, in the space of four months the national mood had moved from jubilant triumph to humiliating defeat. They realised that external forces had dismembered their country to satisfy their own interests. Stefan Stambulov, the future Prime minister of Bulgaria, remarked that as Russia had not been willing to defend the integrity of the Bulgarian nation she should never have undertaken to liberate it.[115] Greater Bulgaria was divided into five separate regions. Ultimately the Bulgarian nation, as with the Exarchate, although the goal of Bulgarian nationalism, was the creation of external events.

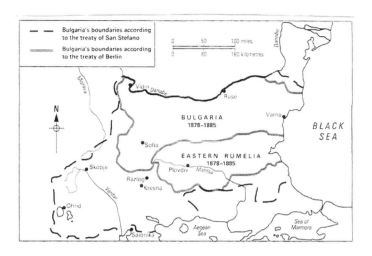

Fig. 3 Bulgaria according to the Treaties of San Stefano and Berlin

CONCLUSION

Through this chapter we have advanced from a time when Bulgarian national awareness and religious self-confidence was only developing, to the conclusive stage of realising their dream of an autonomous Church and independent nation. After almost five centuries under the double-yoke of Ottoman and Greek subjugation Bulgarians had taken action to promote and safeguard their history, culture, language, and ecclesiastical heritage.

The chapter has demonstrated that the dream of an autonomous Bulgarian church did not emerge until 1844, a desire instigated by French/Polish intrigue. The ecclesiastical dispute originated with the economic burden caused by Patriarchal over-taxation. Local town leaders came to the conclusion that by replacing Greek Church hierarchy with Bulgarians their hardships would end. Thus the first phase of the Church movement was to decrease the economic burden and the second the appointment of Bulgarian bishops. These local disputes coalesced into a national movement only when the struggle moved to Constantinople. In the Ottoman capital Bulgaria's most influential businessmen gave the movement new impetus and raised its awareness within the

Porte. However, it was only after the involvement of foreign political agents, working to achieve the national aims and objectives of their own governments that the possibility of recreating an independent national church germinated in the Bulgar psyche.

This fact does not negate the work of the Bulgarian Church movement. However, it does ultimately question the desire of Bulgarian ecclesiastical hierarchy to escape the confines of the Ottoman empire. Even after the establishment of the Exarchate in 1872 and in the midst of growing nationalistic fervour that emanated from Bulgarian émigrés in Greece, Serbia and Romania, Church leaders continued to encourage loyalty toward the sultan. The Exarchate clearly never accepted the principle of armed struggle and therefore stood against the activities of revolutionary elements. This position resulted not only from their obligations towards the Ottoman authorities but also from the spiritual irreconcilability of violence against 'God's authority'. As a whole the Exarchate championed the idea of evolutionism. According to this stream of political thought church efforts needed to be directed towards the spiritual, economic and social prosperity of Bulgaria from within the Ottoman empire, seeking its reformation and restoration with the aim of expanding the spiritual, cultural and political rights of the Sultan's Bulgarian Christian subjects. They believed that the question of Bulgaria's political independence would be realised eventually, but only after the wider Eastern Question had been resolved. Thus the Exarchate dismissed revolutionary thinking. However, the brutal retribution of the Ottoman authorities upon the Bulgarian population after the April Uprising completely amended their mindset. Nevertheless, at perhaps the greatest moment in Bulgarian history when she reclaimed national independence, in 1878, the Exarchate yet again struggled to maintain the loyalty of the people towards the sultan.

The combination of these factors: the absence of a Bulgarian Church movement until the nineteenth century, the concept of an independent national Church appearing only after foreign instigation, the Exarchate's constant desire to remain within the Ottoman empire; its struggle against revolutionary elements and even at the moment of liberation the Exarchate's proclamation of loyalty towards the sultan, must bring into question the claim of the Bulgarian Orthodox Church that it was central to the success of Bulgaria's National Revival. By the evidence of this research it would appear that the role of the Bulgarian Orthodox Church during this vitally important national period has been embellished, so much so that every Bulgarian connects the Church to the liberation of the nation. National Revival romanticism has given birth to the affirmation that the Bulgarian nation survived through the centuries of Ottoman domination owing to the Bulgarian Orthodox Church – the evidence of this and preceding chapters suggests this is not historical fact. On the basis of the evidence presented in this chapter it would be more correct to assert that the ecclesiastical struggle of the Bulgarian Church movement played a defining role in the revival of Bulgarian national self-consciousness and helped accelerate the process of national consolidation.

5

DEVELOPING RELATIONSHIPS:
THE CHURCH, STATE CONSOLIDATION,
NATIONAL UNIFICATION AND WAR (1878-1945)

After five centuries of Ottoman domination an autonomous Bulgarian state was established in 1878. Following the euphoria of 'San Stefano' and the dejection of the 'Berlin' treaties, the nation was placed under Russian provisional administration. The Congress of Berlin stipulated that the Russian administration, under the leadership of Prince Alexander Dondukov-Korsakov, would require handing over power to the Principality after nine months. As a result two main objectives demanded the attention of the Russians and Bulgarians: a Bulgarian national constitution had to be drafted and a suitable prince elected. To achieve these ends a constitutional assembly was convened in Turnovo in February 1879 composed of 231 Bulgarian representatives that included members of the clergy.

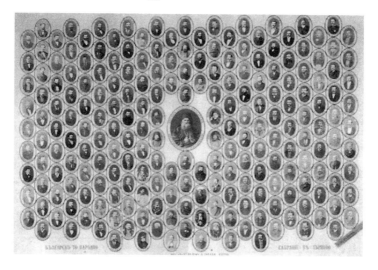

Fig. 4: The First Bulgarian Constituent Assembly (1879)

The San Stefano Treaty, signed on 3 March 1878, should have created the basis for a new relationship between two national institutions, the Bulgarian State and the Exarchate. From its inception, however, this association proved awkward. The dramatic events of 1878 had brought chaos to the work of the Exarchate. Having attempted to rally the people to remain within the Ottoman empire, whereby the Exarchate would have been the sole political, legal and spiritual representative of the Bulgarian people, the ecclesiastical hierarchy now found itself subservient to the secular national authority which it had once opposed. The burden of responsibility fell on the shoulders of Exarch Josef I (1840-1915) to reconstruct the work of the Exarchate, to renew the peoples trust in the work of the Church and to re-establish the Exarchate to a place of pre-eminence within Bulgarian society. This task was exacerbated by the decision of the Congress of Berlin to revise the territorial allotment of 'San Stefano', dividing the eparchies of 'Greater Bulgaria' over five regions: the political independence secured by 'San Stefano' was preserved only in the Principality of Bulgaria, Eastern Rumelia received a level of internal autonomy but remained under the authority of the Sultan's government, Macedonia and Eastern Thrace were returned to the Ottoman empire, a number of Bulgarian eparchies such as Nis and Pirotska were annexed by Serbia and Southern Dobrudja was placed under the authority of the Romanian Church.[1] In the diversity of this geopolitical quagmire the Exarchate was recognised as the only national institution which could connect the dispersed Bulgarian population to the Bulgarian nation.

This chapter will examine the relationship that developed between Church and State from the establishment of the Bulgarian State (1878) to the end of the Second World War (1945). Through an investigation of contemporary scholarship, Bulgarian Central State, Military and Church archives it will seek to comprehend the role of the Church through this seminal period of Bulgarian national evolution. Within a framework of political, ecclesiastical, national and international events the chapter will attempt to express the boundless changeability in interrelationships between Church, State and society during the period investigated.

STATE ESTABLISHMENT AND CHURCH RELATIONSHIP

From the onset of the parliamentary process a strained relationship developed between State and Church. While the State desired to establish itself as the main authority in Bulgaria, it realised that the Exarchate would be a necessary medium in achieving any future aspiration toward national unification. A major section within the first Bulgarian Constitution (Turnovo, 1879) therefore dealt solely with the issue of Church and State. A problem immediately arose, however, around the generally accepted formula within Eastern Orthodoxy, 'One Church – One State'. If this were applied to Bulgaria's present predicament their Exarch would have required leaving Constantinople and relocating within the Principality. If this had occurred the Exarchate would have lost ecclesiastical jurisdiction over the Bulgarian Christian population remaining in the confiscated territories. This would have been an immense blow to Bulgaria especially after the tragedy of the Berlin settlement, as by 1879 the number of Bulgarians outside of the Principality outnumbered those within. After heated debates the National Assembly voted to accept Article 39 into the Constitution, which stated:

> The Principality of Bulgaria constitutes an inseparable part of the jurisdiction of the Bulgarian Church, subject to the Holy Synod – the supreme spiritual authority of the Bulgarian Church, wherever it may exist.[2]

Directed by patriotic enthusiasm and political aspiration to re-unify the nation on the basis of the San Stefano Treaty the National Assembly made what many considered to be an ill-founded decision, guaranteeing not only its solidarity with the Bulgarian Orthodox Church, but its subordination to the Holy Synod.[3] In doing so the Assembly ignored the warnings of the Liberal Party who claimed that by accepting article 39 they would create an obstacle for the future development of Bulgarian independent government.[4] After consideration Exarch Josef assessed that in the interests of the Bulgarian people and for the integrity of the nation the seat of the Exarch required to remain in Constantinople. Only from there would he be in a position to support the "enslaved populations and protect them from the high-handed manner of the Turkish authorities and from any foreign attempt [Greek, Romanian and Serbian] to spread religious propaganda."[5] Thus, on 9 January 1880, Exarch Josef departed for Constantinople to rebuild the dishevelled Exarchate. Despite receiving support from the National Assembly the Sublime Porte was unhappy with this political/religious arrangement. The Ottoman authorities warned Exarch Josef that they did not acknowledge and would not take into consideration any constitutional laws of the Bulgarian Principality, particularly relating to the Bulgarian Church. In a letter to the Metropolitan of Plovdiv, Exarch Josef commented:

> The Porte claims that Bulgarians from the Principality do not have the right to participate in the government of the Exarchate in Constantinople or to control the Church as if it is totally independent.... The Porte will not permit the application of Church laws decided by the Principality, or the Principality's Metropolitans to participate or affect the election of any future Exarch or the statutes of the Holy Synod.[6]

In response the National Assembly voted that the Holy Synod should be based in the new Bulgarian capital of Sofia[7] while the Exarch would remain in Constantinople.[8] In practise this meant that the Exarchate and the Holy Synod would operate as two separate entities. As the Exarchate remained an integral part of the Ottoman establishment, subordinate to the sultan and his government, Exarch Josef comprehended that the Holy Synod would not have the jurisdiction to exercise power over the Church beyond the Principality.[9] He therefore considered that it would be impossible to apply Article 39 of the Constitution. In his diary he recorded:

> The Porte has decided not to give me authority in the Macedonia and Odrin Thrace vilayets as their administration would not be run solely by the Exarchate in Constantinople, but also by the Synodal members from the Principality. Article 39 of the Turnovo Constitution is therefore impracticable for the Bulgarian Church in the Principality.[10]

Hence one of the fundamental problems for the Orthodox Church within the Principality was the impossibility to govern itself whilst remaining part of the Exarchate. Likewise the Exarchate would never be allowed to operate freely whilst it remained connected to the independent government of Bulgaria.

Necessity required that the Bulgarian Church in the Principality become a self-governing body separate from the Bulgarian Exarchate. This Church would be administered by a Holy Synod, consisting of Metropolitans whose eparchies lay within the independent state's borders and who would be appointed by the Bulgarian National Assembly. Their activities would come to be regulated on the basis of the Adapted Exarchal Statute (1883). The remaining Church territories would be governed by the Exarch and a separate Synod of Metropolitans from Rumelia, Macedonia and Thrace, appointed by the Porte. Its activity would be based on the old Exarchal Statute (1872) in accordance with Ottoman law. Consequently the leadership of the Bulgarian Orthodox Church was divided working with two sets of laws in two very different politically controlled regions with divergent national interests. The ecclesiastical hierarchy did attempt to synchronise the work of the Sofia Synod and Exarchate. This entailed representatives from Sofia working closely with the Exarchate and special Exarchal delegates being resident in Sofia to work as an intermediary with the Principality's Synod.[11] By means of these representatives the ecclesiastical hierarchy attempted to bring unity to the two halves of the Bulgarian Church. However, this enabled the Exarch to intervene on administrative questions within the Principality, at times without the agreement of the Principality's Synod, which began to raise problems between the Holy Synod, the National Assembly and the Exarchate.

These difficulties did not endear the Church to the increasingly powerful political elite who were resentful of the prevailing influence of the Church in the running of the Principality.[12] This reflected negatively upon their relationship and found expression in an intensified anti-ecclesiastical attitude, which aimed to restrict the authority of the Church in the running of the Bulgarian state, minimising their social significance and public role. By amending the Bulgarian Constitution the government began to regulate on the rights of the Bulgarian Church, making it increasingly dependent on the state and restricting the rights of its employees to participate in the political life of the Principality.[13]

In the initial years after the establishment of the Bulgarian State all Bulgarian Orthodox clergy had been eligible for election to parliament and thus actively participate at every level of national political decision making. In 1880, however, Peter Karavelov's Liberal government included within the National Assembly's electoral statutes an amendment to Article 27 which stated that the powerful and influential 'black' clergy would not be eligible for election to the national forum.[14] A subsequent alteration to the electoral law permitted the election of bishops to the National Assembly, but denied the rights of the parish clergy.[15] Finally in 1883 the government of Dragan Tsankov introduced an addition to the article on election according to which, "persons, who receive a salary, pensions or assistance from the state treasury with the exception of MP's and elected civil representatives of the regions, town councils and judicial delegates…may not be elected as national representatives."[16] This addendum denied the rights of bishops to be elected to Bulgaria's national forum as according to Article 99 of the Exarchal Statute, also adopted in 1883, every bishop now received a salary directly from the state. The anti-clerical faction within Bulgarian politics had succeeded in removing all vestiges of ecclesiastical power from the National Assembly. These decisions were made absolute by the government of Stefan Stambulov who voted that in the interest of national liberty and for the restoration of the Bulgarian state all clergy would be denied access to any national political forum.[17]

A further development in this strained Church and State relationship can be traced to the National Assembly debate on budget considerations for the Bulgarian Church and the introduction of salaries for the clergy. Although the Exarchate in Constantinople functioned as an official Ottoman institution it was financed by the Principality of Bulgaria. This created a practical contradiction – it was the Porte who allowed the Principality to finance the Exarchate but not to participate in its daily functioning. The Second Bulgarian National Assembly (1881) chose to limit the finances of the clergy within the Principality. Emboldened by the anti-clerical attitude of the liberal government they announced that Metropolitans from all the major eparchies would receive an annual salary of 8,000 francs, somewhat less than the 14,400 proposed by the Holy Synod. In response the Metropolitan of Turnovo commented: "The clergy are not herdsmen, neither are they hired labourers of the community, you cannot change their material condition at the convenience of the national representatives..."[18] In contrast the very same National Assembly increased the salaries of the Metropolitans working outside the Principality to 14,400 francs. In reply to a question regarding the unbalanced increase in salaries for the Exarchate's staff Exarch Josef replied that if the Bulgarian government had not provided sufficient funds the clergy would have returned to the Principality.[19] It would appear that the National Assembly were willing to pay the Exarchate's clergy an increased salary to remain in those territories deemed politically important to the nation's future plans.

This reveals another factor which disrupted the unity of the Bulgarian Church, not merely the difference in salary, but the distinctive working conditions and activities of the clergy engaged in Bulgaria and in European Turkey. The Bulgarian clergy in the two sections of the Church were faced with divergent problems. In the Principality priestly functions were limited to clearly defined religious and charitable activities, but in Rumelia, Macedonia and Thrace the accent of the clergy's work was on the preservation of Bulgarian national self-consciousness, particularly through the strengthening and consolidation of Bulgarian school networks, in which they encouraged emotional, spiritual and political connection with the Principality with a view to their eventual integration.[20]

That the Church's budget considerations were politically motivated can be supported by the government's lack of interest in the education of its Orthodox clergy. The question of poorly educated Bulgarian clergy had been a concern both during and after the National Revival. Having desired to replace the Greeks with their own national clergy the Exarchate faced the dilemma of not having sufficient qualified Bulgarian priests to fill those posts. Russian Prince Alexander Dondukov-Korsakov, leader of the provisional administration, had been so concerned by this deficiency that he personally provided funds toward the establishment of a Divinity School in Samokov.[21] This seminary was the only specialist school preparing clergy for the needs of the Bulgarian Orthodox Church through the first half of the 1880's. Despite this the school was closed in September 1886 by decision of the National Assembly, without asking for the advice or consent of the Holy Synod. Church-State attitude in the Principality was being defined by factors of foreign policy. Having Bulgarian clergy present in strategic territorial positions was clearly of importance for future advancement toward national unification, while seminary education was not. At this preliminary stage of autonomous national development this research would consider that the Exarchate was being used as a strategic pawn in Bulgarian geopolitics.

Church and Monarch

Following the drafting of the Bulgarian Constitution the second major concern of the State was the selection of a prince. The successful candidate, suggested by the Russian tsar, was the German Protestant, Prince of Hesse, Alexander von Battenberg. He was a nephew of the tsar and related through marriage to the British royal family. From an international perspective he was an excellent choice appeasing both the European and Russian governments. The Bulgarians also approved of Alexander as he had served with the Russian army during Bulgaria's War of Liberation (1878), as a liaison officer under General Gurko. In

July 1879 the National Assembly conferred the title Prince of Bulgaria on Alexander I.

Despite receiving a rapturous welcome in Bulgaria Alexander faced immediate difficulties with the Principality's liberal political establishment particularly over the issue of his lack of power. He fully comprehended the importance of future unification with the disputed territories, but in doing so he equally understood the need to establish a disciplined and well-equipped army. He therefore desired to transform Bulgaria into a strong militaristic state. However, his powers were severely restricted leading him to comment that the Turnovo Constitution was "ridiculously liberal," which led to heated debates with the government who stated, "the National Assembly makes the laws, the Prince proclaims them."[22] Thus the Prince found it practically impossible to work with the Liberal government or the Turnovo Constitution and sought to abolish both those obstacles which stood between him and absolute power.[23]

When the National Assembly re-convened on 5 July 1879 it did so under the new leadership of Conservative Todor Burmov. The Prince had appointed a new Prime Minister by royal decree, overriding constitutional law. By so doing Burmov's government proved compliant and voted unanimously to accept all of the Prince's constitutional demands.[24] Only a few months later, however, the Liberals once again were voted into government. Alexander I refused to acknowledge this electoral result and by another decree appointed a second Conservative government, this time presided over by the Metropolitan of Turnovo, Vasil Drumev. In the midst of political and constitutional chaos the Holy Synod convened a special council following Alexander's 'constitutional coup' to discuss the question, how and by what right should the Church in the Principality be governed? This resulted in the production of a draft-bill entitled 'The Exarchate's Statutes – Changes in the Principality.' On 4 February 1883 Prince Alexander approved this Church bill, generally known as the Adapted Exarchal Statute, in which he was given an element of power in Church government.[25]

Prince Alexander now believed he could govern the Principality effectively and without hindrance. He was immediately confronted, however, by Tsar Alexander III who demanded that Bulgaria defer to Russian political ambitions. Subsequent relations between the two countries deteriorated, especially when the Russian officers within the Bulgarian army declared publicly that they took their orders from the tsar and not from the Bulgarian Prince.[26] Russian relations declined so much that even the Liberals who had opposed the Prince now considered that Bulgaria had merely exchanged Ottoman for Russian tyranny. A unified political national front developed to oppose Russia's autocratic demands culminating in the formation of a new coalition Liberal-Conservative government. Thus, for the first time there was a semblance of political unity in the Principality, the common basis of which was the "prodigious hatred that developed of the Russian yoke which had become increasingly intolerable."[27] However, this anti-Russian sentiment was not unanimous. The Church challenged the government's attitude towards Russia once again fuelling its conflict with the State. Church hierarchy and especially the 'black clergy' pleaded for political and spiritual adherence to Orthodox Russia, who they considered to be the natural protector of Eastern Orthodoxy and the Bulgarian Church.[28]

Russophile Ideology

Considering the history of the National Revival and the work of the Russian government in helping establish the Exarchate the presence of strong Russophile tendencies within the Bulgarian Church is unsurprising. While Russia had succeeded in enhancing the Slavic element of Bulgarian identity it equally had not neglected to emphasise its Orthodox component. Thus the rhetoric of 'common faith' with 'Mother Russia' had important place in Bulgarian ecclesiastical circles and was commonly encapsulated in pro-Russian, pro-Slavic, anti-Western and anti-Turkish language; so much so that the conviction began to circulate that during the five centuries of the Ottoman yoke the Bulgarian people would have been eradicated if it had not been for the Church and "every real Bulgarian owed that preservation...only to Russia".[29] Those who opposed Russia were therefore considered to be against the Church and represented as "enemies of our Orthodox faith and our Slavic nation."[30] Hence when government reporter D. Petkova commented that "Orthodoxy and Slavism" were "idiotic naiveties" she was lambasted for ignoring her "faith and origin," for Orthodoxy and Slavism, it was suggested, had been for Bulgaria, "two anchors to which it owed the redemption of its life and its resurrection as a nation".[31]

Russophobe Ideology

Despite the Church's pro-Russian predilection the Principality's government and her national press depicted the Church and Russian Orthodoxy as backward, associating them with "colonialism", "ignorance" and "parasitism."[32] The state newspaper *Nezavisimost* presented the Church and Russia as reactionary, often using the religious metaphor of 'the bell' as a substitute for the 'yataghan', the curved sword which had been used as a symbol of Ottoman subjugation.[33] Even terms such as 'Orthodoxy' and 'Orthodox Russia' acquired disparaging connotations, so much so that Russia was considered to have taken the place of the Phanar in her attitude towards Bulgaria.[34] At its worst the press said of Russia that it offered a "raped and debauched Orthodoxy."[35] These designations were first and foremost an attack on Russia's autocratic policies towards Bulgaria. However, they became inseparable from criticisms of the Bulgarian Church in their sympathy and support of Russia. At every level of society 'Orthodoxy' was being challenged as to whether it was a crucial component in Bulgarian identity. Attempting to differentiate between the terms 'faith' and 'nation' Z. Stoyanov wrote:

> All these nations Russia liberated not as Greeks, Serbs and Bulgarians but as Orthodox. But as soon as they announced that their nationality was dearer and higher to them, we see what has happened in our country today. It is a pity that the Russian diplomats cannot understand the simple truth, that our national desires were planted long before Orthodoxy.[36]

On 24 March 1884 six parliamentary representatives introduced a proposal before the National Assembly that encapsulated the religious/national issue. They asked for a new article to be added to the section on religion which clearly stated: Proselytism is prohibited.[37] The proposal was based on an 1879 report composed by a fifteen member parliamentary commission for inclusion in the first Bulgarian Constitution. The original proposal referred not to foreign missionary activity but specifically to the proselytising activities of the Greek, Serbian and Romanian Orthodox Churches. However, it had been rejected after the Liberal Party's ecclesiastical purge. Nevertheless the proposal was reintroduced and justified in the following manner:

> The Commission, while recognising the tolerance and liberty of the Assembly, cannot allow these two principles to be exploited and directed against the interests of the State and of social order.... Everyone is free in his or her religious conviction, but with the zeal of those who promote the systematic and public changing of these convictions, the Commission considers this as impudence, in which it is necessary to restrict the liberty of conscience....[38]

The proposal was consistent with the spiritual and nationalistic characteristics of Orthodoxy which required to defend itself against the activities of foreign religious propaganda. Proceeding from this understanding the proposal stressed that the State needed to be conscientious of the fact that the Bulgarian Orthodox Church was the central pillar of Bulgarian national identity and unity.[39] After debating the issue, however, the need to prohibit Proselytism was deemed unnecessary by the National Assembly. The opposing argument of P. R. Slaveikov was accepted by the Assembly, to reject the proposal "not because Proselytism is dreaded by the faithful, but simply because it is an anachronism, indecent to the faith; for her it is degrading and according to our original Constitution this prohibition... has nothing to defend against."[40]

The significance of this rejection can be witnessed some years later when in 1892-93, Article 38 of the Constitution was amended to allow the government of Stefan Stambulov to provide jurisdictional basis for the establishment of a Roman Catholic monarchy in Bulgaria. Due to the primacy given to the Orthodox Church within the first Constitution it was accepted that the monarch should confess the Orthodox faith. It was agreed, however, that the first prince, Alexander I, would be exempt from this ruling, but any future monarch and their family would require to profess Orthodox Christianity.[41] The principal ideal behind this demand was that the Prince and his subjects be united in one faith – Orthodoxy. Therefore any future monarch would have three important obligations: to be/or become an Orthodox believer, to have an Orthodox marriage and to produce an Orthodox heir. Stambulov's government wanted to ignore these requirements as they created an obstacle to Bulgaria's new Catholic Prince Ferdinand.

The Holy Synod had ascertained from government sources that the second Bulgarian Prince would not be expected to respect the doctrines and statutes of the Orthodox Church. In response the Synod announced that if Prince Ferdinand and his wife Klementina remained loyal to Catholicism they would not be recognised or blessed by the Bulgarian Orthodox Church.[42] Following this declaration Stambulov's government sought to amend Article 38. The Church opposed these alterations, Metropolitan Kliment and the Sofia Synod denouncing the actions of the government as traitorous. Exarch Josef equally opposed the government by publishing a number of acrimonious articles in the Church's press.[43] A maddened Stambulov, in return, publicly criticised and slandered the Exarch, accusing him of living a licentious and debauched life. The

Principality's government went even further, threatening to discontinue subsidies to the clergy in Macedonia and Thrace and even to separate from the Church in the Principality if they did not agree with the Constitutional amendments. The government warned that if the Church did not stop its campaign against government and Prince they would ban the Church's newspaper, *Novini*. In his diary Exarch Josef recorded:

> They [the government] have threatened me, that they will take action against *Novini*, if it writes again on this subject and I answered that even if they imprison me in a monastery, I will continue to write. I have one question, if the faith of the nation is in serious danger, am I not allowed to express an opinion? Who then in Bulgaria can express an opinion or vote against the government?[44]

Threatened with financial ruin, separation from the state and the removal of their public voice the Bulgarian ecclesiastical hierarchy had no alternative but to restrain their monarchical objections.

Fundamentally the selection of Prince Ferdinand had been unconstitutional as it clearly violated Section 38 of the Turnovo constitution. It would be accurate to state that Ferdinand himself had no intention or desire of becoming Orthodox. The Austrian diplomat Stefan von Buran wrote in 1893: "The Prince often comments that he is considering joining the Orthodox Church, but only as an outward gesture, not in veneration or sympathy of their historical outlook."[45] This subterfuge is further testified by Ferdinand's personal secretary:

> He [the Duke of Parma] helped us to contact the Holy Father, who showed an interest in Bulgaria and her Church, through a union of the Bulgarian Prince with a Catholic Princess, this union may even lead to lifting the schism of Photius setting the country under the supremacy of the True Church... But for this aim to be achieved we need to alter Article 38 of the Constitution of Bulgaria... with a view and in the interest of the good, that this may be accomplished through some future project whereby the royal heir is secretly baptised into the Catholic faith, but publicly follows Orthodoxy, thus ripening the question of a union between Rome and the Bulgarian Church?[46]

The premarital agreement of the Bulgarian Prince confirmed his desire to establish a Catholic dynasty at the expense of the Bulgarian Constitution and the Orthodox Church. It contained a special clause stipulating that the children from the marriage of Ferdinand and Maria-Louisa of Parma would be raised in the Catholic faith, a pledge made before Pope Leo XIII (1878-1903). The promise is attested by the baptism of the Prince's first two children into the Roman Catholic Church. Only three years after the making of this solemn pledge, on 2 February 1896, Ferdinand's first son Boris was re-baptised into the Bulgarian Orthodox Church. The reason for this compromise was obvious: firstly, the Orthodox baptism of his son was the only way for Ferdinand's monarchy to be acknowledged by Russia and the other European states and secondly, Ferdinand was aware that if he were ever to abdicate Boris may not automatically be given the throne as he was a Roman Catholic.

After this public demonstration of loyalty to Bulgaria and Orthodoxy Ferdinand's personal secretary recorded a meeting between the Prince and Prime Minister Stoilov: "We allowed our son to be baptised only after Russian demands. Nevertheless according to my agreement [with the Pope] we are obliged never to mix his religious upbringing. I therefore give you fair warning that his upbringing shall continue to be fully Catholic."[47] The Prince's allegiance to Catholicism is proven beyond doubt in a personal letter from Ferdinand to Pope Pius X (1903-1914) where he confesses:

> The Bulgarian people are separated from Rome only temporarily. They will soon by political, rather than by religious means, see how their sovereign and his royal heir's faith differs from their religion. Russia, the liberator and protector of the Bulgarians, will share in this knowledge and will decline to pardon or support this nation. I continue to promise to raise my son in the bosom of the Roman Church... But this needs to remain completely secret, in view of the fact that this declaration and my pledge could compromise forever the future of my dynasty.[48]

Apart from snippets of information it is difficult to follow closely the correspondence between the Saxe-Coburg dynasty and the Vatican. Nevertheless from the information presented it is clear that private agreements were made without consultation with the Orthodox Church and contrary to the Bulgarian national constitution. It is also certain that to the present day not one member of this dynasty has entered into marriage with a Bulgarian or with an Orthodox believer. Regarding this predicament it is interesting to read the reflections of Dr. K. Stoilov, an influential member of Stambulov's government and future Prime Minister who voiced his concerns in his diary:

Orthodoxy is our dominant faith. At this moment it is acknowledged that the State by necessity has to have an Orthodox dynasty. Orthodoxy is a national institution, not only religious; our existence is connected with the Orthodox faith. Our National Revival is connected to her. Freedom of religion does not adapt to the voice of the State, the voice of the State therefore needs to be Orthodox. "Freedom of religion" here is a superficial argument. In this essential question the Prince is not even with the people.... The Prince or his heirs from another faith will never be united with the people, they will always remain foreign.

The Exarchate supports the unity of the Bulgarian nation. But unity with her is impossible if ruled by a Prince from a different religion. It is not correct that the Prince marry without changing religion. The parents of the royal heirs need also to have an interest and insight into the future of their children. A prince or princess who comes under these circumstances shall be from the beginning against our nation; they will despise our history and our tradition... The dynasty will remain foreign, like an exotic plant. My ideal for the Bulgarian State is that it is an Orthodox State... because I want an Orthodox dynasty.... We should be against foreign religious propaganda in our courts.[49]

After the fall of Stefan Stambulov from power the Church did not call for retribution, but rather asked for loyalty towards the Prince, considering "should another dynastic crisis occur, we are all lost."[50] Responding to Kliment's act of loyalty the Metropolitan was invited by Dr. Stoilov's new government to lead a Bulgarian Parliamentary delegation to Russia in July 1895. In dialogue with Tsar Nicholas II he succeeded in persuading him of the necessity to acknowledge the Bulgarian Prince and renew diplomatic relations between Russia and Bulgaria. Russia set as a precondition for reconciliation that the Bulgarian heir to the throne, Prince Boris, be baptised into the Orthodox faith, which occurred on February 1896. After this condition was met Russia acknowledged Ferdinand I as the legitimate Prince of Bulgaria.[51] Russia and the Bulgarian Orthodox Church had attained their desire the monarchy's public show of loyalty. The weight of historical evidence, however, proves beyond doubt that no member of the Bulgarian monarchy has ever actively adhered to Eastern Orthodoxy.

The National Question and Union with Eastern Rumelia

By June 1884 the political situation within the Principality had changed significantly. The constitutional crisis generated by Prince Alexander had been settled and the Turnovo Constitution restored ending the era of rule by monarchical decree. Petko Karavelov's Liberal party was re-elected to government and once again the political focus centred on the issue of national unity.[52] On this occasion Church and State were in full agreement that the confiscated territories had to be returned to Bulgaria. To this end both national institutions actively promoted the unification of Eastern Rumelia with the Principality.

When San Stefano Bulgaria was dismembered and the two autonomous states of the Principality and Eastern Rumelia formed it created a hindrance to the economic development of the region. Custom controls were established between the two States creating the irritant that Bulgarians had to pay taxes on locally produced goods transferred between north and south. This created major economic complications for the Sofia government, which cannot be ignored, as during this period industry was better developed in the south, particularly in the area of tobacco and wine production, while the Principality was predominantly a cereal producer. Add to this the annual tribute of 80 million gold groschen which Rumelia had to pay to the Porte and Bulgaria's heavy financial burden becomes clear.[53] Many business projects which could have aided economic prosperity in both States were frustrated by the Ottoman government.[54] Demonstrations were common in the Principality and Rumelia, staged by politicians, tradesmen and academic's calling for a union of the two states, as this was the only way for the country to advance economically.[55] Unification was therefore considered by both Bulgarian states as a remedy to their dire economic predicament. It may be argued therefore that the unification of Eastern Rumelia with the Principality was a decision based on economic necessity, rather than on the romantic idea of national and religious unity.

Economic and political factors served to strengthen the conviction of the population that unity was absolutely essential. Prince Alexander I also realised the tremendous significance to his monarchy if unification succeeded. He therefore encouraged the Rumelian activists in their struggle for unification and supported the military in their plans to instigate a coup. Social, economic and political conditions thus favoured unification. The only foreign power to support the unification movement was Russia. This can be attested by their insistence that a special clause be inserted within the *Dreikaiserbund* treaty (1881) which secured the non-intervention of Russia, Germany and Austria-Hungary if and when unification occurred.[56] It is evident that the Russian government was not only in favour of unification but also desired to take a lead in achieving this end. Thus from the onset of Prince Alexander's reign the Russian government had supported him believing that Bulgaria's unification should take place under his patronage. By 1884, however, Russia not only refrained from supporting the candidature of Prince Alexander as the future ruler of a united Bulgaria but was of the opinion that he should no longer occupy the throne of the Principality. Thus the situation arose that Russia, the only foreign power who had declared the necessity of unification, now urged its postponement.

Despite this prevarication preparation towards unification intensified. The Bulgarian Central Revolutionary Committee reformed with the objective of uniting every Bulgarian under foreign rule in one state.[57] Rallies and demonstrations were organised nationally. Although Prince Alexander had been informed of the possibility of a revolutionary coup in Rumelia he was unsure if and when this would actually occur. Therefore when the activists announced, on 18 September 1885, that the unification of Eastern Rumelia with the Principality had been accomplished he was undecided whether to accept or denounce the act. If he were to accept the leadership of a united Bulgaria he would violate the Berlin Treaty and possibly anger the European powers. However, if he rejected the act of union he would lose the support of his own people. He was persuaded to accept and later announced "behold in me the ruler of a united north and south Bulgaria."[58] Accompanied by his Prime Minister, Prince Alexander departed for Plovdiv to legitimise the union. On 21 September 1885 the Prince entered Rumelia to rapturous welcome from the population. The Rumelian Governor-General resigned gracefully declaring "I am a Bulgarian and shall not call in the Turks. I wish happiness to the Bulgarian people."[59] The Sofia government took over the administration of Eastern Rumelia while Church administration within the united state fell under the remit of the Sofia Synod leaving the Exarchate to tend Macedonia and Thrace.

The Russians were infuriated by Alexander's action as they had wanted to lead the way taking, once again, the role of Bulgaria's national saviour. They did not oppose the union per se, but rather the Prince's duplicity in stealing their glory. In response Tsar Alexander III ordered all Russian military personnel to leave Bulgaria making it vulnerable to attack. Accordingly the Bulgarian army were given orders to enter Southern Bulgaria and take up positions along the Turkish border to repel any Turkish backlash.

Serbian-Bulgarian War (1885)

Bulgaria's vulnerability to attack became evident, but not from the expectant route, when the Serbian government presented Bulgaria with an ultimatum – Grant us territorial concessions, or war! The Serbian army deployed along the frontier with Bulgaria and King Milan announced that he would not withdraw his army until his claims for territorial compensation were satisfied. The Serbs realised that the unification now gave Bulgaria an important strategic advantage in the territorial struggle for Macedonia. Thus by conquering western Bulgaria the Serbs intended to sever the government from her Macedonian aspirations. This was no fantasy as Prince Alexander's personal secretary had previously commented: "We must succeed with the unification of north and south Bulgaria... We must bring down the Rumelian government and unite in the interest of Macedonia."[60] With this in mind Serbia declared war on Bulgaria on 13 November 1885 and thereafter her troops entered the Principality. With a larger and better equipped army the Serbian High Command expected to win the war quickly and easily, declaring that in a few days they would take Sofia and the war would be over.

The Bulgarian population were alarmed because their western border lay unprotected, the majority of their army being deployed along the Turkish border. Bulgarian military command decided to leave one-third of their troops at the Turkish border and dispatched all others to defend against the Serb aggressor. The order was given to amass the Bulgarian troops near the town of Slivnitsa – on the road from Belgrade to Sofia. On 17 November the Serbs appeared in front of the Slivnitsa defences and the decisive battle commenced. The battle was concluded on 19 November 1885 with the Serb army being utterly routed. Following the intervention of Austro-Hungary and Russia the Treaty of Bucharest was signed on 3 March 1886 restoring the pre-war *status quo*. Russian historian S. Tatishchev comments: "the question of Bulgarian unification, so long and futilely discussed by diplomats, was now resolved irrevocably and in spite of them."[61]

On 15 January 1886 Prince Alexander sent a telegram to Sultan Abdulhamit II (1876-1909) requesting that he be officially recognised and appointed ruler of Eastern Rumelia. At the conclusion of the armistice with Serbia the Great Powers accepted that to restore the *status quo ante* in Rumelia would have been impossible and therefore deemed that the unification should be recognised. Thus Alexander was appointed ruler of Eastern Rumelia, not as Prince over a united Bulgaria but as Governor-General of Rumelia, thereby bypassing any violations to and resolving the need to amend the Berlin Treaty.[62] Thereafter a Bulgarian delegation travelled to Russia to request Russian recognition of the unification. This delegation was led again by Metropolitan Kliment of Turnovo, the ardent pro-Russian, who was assured that Russia had not objected to the unification, but rather to the manner in which it had been proclaimed, without the consent of Russia. German chancellor Bismark had warned the Bulgarian Prince before the act of union that if he acted independently of Russia he would eventually be forced to abdicate: "…but if you wish to remain in Bulgaria, then give yourself up to Russia unconditionally…. I advise you to restore good relations with Russia."[63] Despite this warning Alexander acted independently of Russia who indeed never forgave the Prince and in August 1886 St. Petersburg successfully conspired with its agents and military supporters to forcibly depose the Prince replacing him with Prince Ferdinand of Saxe-Coburg.

The Bulgarian Exarchate in Macedonia and Odrin Thrace

The union of north and south Bulgaria consolidated Bulgaria as a nation. It failed, however, to resolve completely Bulgarian national aspirations that would only be appeased by re-creating 'Greater Bulgaria' through the integration of Macedonia and Odrin Thrace. According to statistical data from the end of the nineteenth century approximately 2.26 million people occupied Macedonia of which 52.31% were Bulgarians and in Odrin Thrace the population numbered almost one million of which 42.37% were Bulgarian.[64] Those Bulgarians remaining in Ottoman territory were inclined towards union with their motherland, their aspirations fed by the fact that the Porte had not yet implemented Section 23 of the Berlin Treaty, which promised to introduce sweeping reforms within the region.

Rather than provoke another war in the region the Bulgarian government preferred to support the work of the Exarchate in their efforts to unite these regions. Thus, Exarch Josef I expressed to the Chairman of the Holy Synod in Sofia that it was time to gain control and gather under their administration every Bulgarian in the remaining vilayets of European Turkey. The Exarchate's objective was to engender within the estranged population awareness and love for the fatherland and to cultivate in them the idea that every Bulgarian had one national spirit and faith united under the wings of the Bulgarian Orthodox Church. To achieve this end they concocted, with the government, a plan to affect a 'cultural evolution' through the Exarchate's educational work. The conviction was that they first needed to prepare the spirit of the people before taking political steps to gain their liberation. Exarch Josef defined this mission as a debt to the entire Bulgarian race.[65]

One major problem obstructed their way. After the Liberation all Bulgarian schools in Macedonia and Thrace had been transferred to the supervision of a Turkish educational commission, in an attempt to bring Christian education more closely under the control of the Ottoman state. However, in the summer of 1890, with the assistance of Prime Minister Stambulov, the Exarchate obtained from Sultan Abdulhamit II, under the rubric of the 1870 firman, permission to appointment Bulgarian metropolitans in Ohrid and Skopje. Four years later Veles and Nevrokop also received metropolitans and in 1897 the same privilege was granted to the eparchies of Bitolya, Strumnitsa and Debur. By the end of 1912 the Exarchate had established another eight eparchies in Macedonia: Kosturska, Lerinska, Vodenska, Solunska, Poleninska, Serska, Melnik, Dramska and another in Thrace. In this region alone the Bulgarian Church operated 1600 churches, 73 monasteries and 1310 clergy. The lifting of religious restrictions benefited the Exarchate's educational plans as, in 1891, the Grand Vizier announced that Bulgarian religious schools could be re-opened under the direction and responsibility of their own clergy. Later, in 1893, the Porte declared that Bulgarian schools would now be completely independent of the Turkish Commission. Following this announcement the educational work of the Exarchate increased in strength and by 1912 administered some 1373 schools and 2261 teachers within the eparchies of Macedonia and Thrace.[66]

The religious, educational and nationalistic activities of the Exarchate created a barrier opposing the equally active propaganda of the Serbs and Greeks. Despite being paid significantly more than their fellow clergymen within the Principality the working conditions of the Exarchate's clergy were not comfortable. The regions remaining under

Ottoman control were becoming increasingly insecure as Bulgars, Greeks, Serbs and Turks sought to establish territorial claims on the land. So distraught were the Bulgarian clergy in the midst of this turmoil that many fled to the safety of the Principality abandoning their parishes. In response Exarch Josef issued a circular letter prohibiting metropolitans from allowing their clergy to abandon their parishes, "the offenders should be pursued and punished according to the regulations of the Holy Church."[67]

Ilinden Uprising: Macedonia (1903)

Ecclesiastical unhappiness highlighted the increase of nationalistic tension in the region. As the situation deteriorated insurgent detachments were dispatched by the Internal Macedonian Revolutionary Organisation (IMRO) in order to prepare the ground for an expected full-scale military intervention by the Bulgarian army in Macedonia and Thrace. As before these revolutionary actions were at variance with the evolutionary policies of the Exarchate. Worried by the increasing intensity of revolutionary rhetoric Exarch Josef warned Prince Ferdinand not to push Bulgaria into war with Turkey because "war would be a catastrophe for the entire Bulgarian race. This moment will be fateful and because of this we need to be resolute and efficacious." However, events came to a head on 2 August 1903, during the Celebration of St. Elijah (Ilinden), when the insurgents roused the people to stand against Ottoman domination in Macedonia. Even the local priests blessed banners emblazoned with slogans 'Freedom or Death' which were carried by the Bulgarian inhabitants as they set fire to hundreds of homes in an effort to drive Muslim families from Macedonia. Bridges were destroyed, roads blocked and major social disruption ensued.[68]

Exarch Josef had to use his influence to intercede before the Porte to save as many towns and villages as possible from retribution. Nevertheless this did not stop a total of 119 villages being burned, 8,400 homes destroyed and thousands of Bulgarians fleeing to safety. Consequently Bulgarian influence in many regions of Macedonia decreased enabling the Greek and Serbian Patriarchates to take ecclesiastical control of the Exarchate's vacated eparchies. In the end Exarch Josef could only grieve as the work of the Exarchate, which had been established over ten difficult years, was decimated. In the midst of the ensuing chaos he reiterated: "Revolution will not rescue Macedonia, only evolution and education."[69] Five years later, in a letter to the Minister of Foreign Affairs, General S. Paprikov, Exarch Josef confirmed his conviction that "the policies of the revolutionary committee put our objectives in chains."[70]

Exarch Josef I was so adamant in his arguments against the activities of IMRO that many of its activists called for the government to sentence him to death for treachery against the Bulgarian state. It is recorded that the Exarch had asked the Macedonian Bulgarians to remain calm and loyal subjects of the sultan and in so doing had followed exactly the same course of action as his predecessor during the War of Liberation (1878). In this situation the impossible predicament of the Bulgarian Exarch becomes evident. He was in a religio-political office created by the Ottoman government, he was a subject and employee of the sultan and had he not remained loyal to the sultan the Exarchate would not have survived and a far worse retribution would have fallen upon the local Bulgarian population. However, in remaining loyal to the sultan and preserving the work of the Exarchate Josef was ridiculed as being disloyal to the Bulgarian nation, state and society.

The Young Turk Revolution (1908)

From the political debacle which followed the Ilinden Uprising and the devastation of the Exarchate's work the opinion emerged that Bulgaria's Macedonian aspirations would be best served through developing diplomatic relationships with her neighbours. The government therefore sought accommodation with Turkey agreeing to withdraw support of any future insurgent movement.

The Ottoman government itself was undergoing a lengthy period of dramatic change. Continued weakening of its empire had led to increased opposition against the incumbent Hamidian regime. Opposition coalesced around the 'Young Turk' movement, a group who had been forced underground after the suspension of the Ottoman constitution in 1877.[71] They formed the Committee for Union and Progress (CUP) with the objective of removing Sultan Abdulhamit and restoring the Constitution. A major commitment of the CUP was to lessen foreign interference in the running of the empire. This aim was justified again when, after the Porte's harsh repression of the Ilinden rising, Austrian and Russian governments met in Murzsteg to discuss intervention to avert another crisis in European Turkey. The Ottoman army had been unable to eradicate the guerrilla threat completely or protect the civilian population due to a very practical problem – the army had not been paid. To prevent further bloodshed foreign interference had once again forced the Porte to accept an international commitment which it could not fulfil. This proved both humiliating and frustrating to Mahmut Sevket Pasha, commander of the Ottoman Third Army, who threatened that should the situation continue the Hamidian regime would fall.[72] The CUP seized the opportunity and supported the military in their predicament calling at the same time for the reinstitution of the Constitution.

Displaying political acumen Sultan Abdulhamit temporarily preserved his position by restoring the Constitution and announced democratic elections. The CUP were voted into power and after a brief political struggle succeeded in deposing Abdulhamit replacing him with his brother Mehmet V (1844-1918). The government of the CUP immediately convened a parliament to represent all the Ottoman provinces, including Eastern Rumelia. Included in the parliamentary agenda was Midhat Pasha's now famous and impassioned call to create an increased sense of *Osmanlili* citizenship to counter the threat of nationalist and religious unrest. By reminding Bulgarians of Rumelia's vassal status the Turkish government stirred up nationalist disquiet. Rather than provoking hope within Bulgaria the 'Young Turk' revolution and the call to engender Ottoman citizenship, re-galvanised Bulgaria's national ambitions – from a Bulgarian perspective the revolution had emphasised Ottoman weakness. Exploiting the ensuing political chaos Bulgarian Prime Minister Alexander Malinov (1867-1938) declared Bulgaria's complete independence from the Ottoman empire in October 1908. Prince Ferdinand simultaneously accepted the title 'Tsar of Bulgaria'. Presented with *faits accomplis* the new Ottoman regime grudgingly accepted the situation. Bulgaria and what remained of Ottoman Europe had taken their first steps along the road which would end in the Balkan Wars of 1912 and 1913.

THE WAR YEARS (1912-1945)
Balkan Wars (1912-1913)

In the twenty-seven years that separated the Serbo-Bulgarian War of 1885 and the outbreak of the First Balkan War in 1912 Bulgaria underwent a staggering transformation becoming one of the most militarised states in Europe.[73] After experiencing extreme vulnerability after the unification and the Ilinden fiasco the Bulgarian National Assembly decided to create a modern army with strong offensive capabilities, spending almost a third of its budget annually on arms accruement.[74] Conscription was also introduced for men up to forty-six years of age and so on the eve of the Balkan Wars Bulgaria could field some 350,000 men.

On 13 March 1912 Bulgaria and Serbia signed a diplomatic treaty agreeing that any future division of Macedonia would be three-fold: Bulgarian, Serbian, and a third disputed zone whose control would be mediated by Russia.[75] A few months later a Greek and Montenegrin alliance followed.[76] The formation of this Balkan League united the former antagonists against Turkey. The goal of uniting all Bulgarians in one territory had been an indispensable part of the Church's ideal for the nation. Therefore as the Balkan League pushed for the expulsion of the Ottoman government from Balkan territory and war mongering intensified so did the voice of the Church, offering its support stating they would welcome a war as it would be a 'just retribution' for all that had went before.[77]

On 8 October 1912 when Montenegro, invoking a long-standing border dispute, declared war on the Ottoman empire they were supported not only by their Balkan neighbours but also by the Bulgarian Orthodox Church. Amongst the multitude of documents preserved in the Central Military Archive and in the Library of the Institute of War History lie some which reflect the presence of the clergy in the war. These documents portray mass ecclesiastical support for the military campaign, not only from the hierarchy but also from among the parish clergy, many of whom embarked with the first wave of soldiers to war. The significance and dimension of their activity has largely been ignored in modern Bulgarian literature. Wherever present the clergy were at the centre of the military action. It is recorded that priests carried ammunition to the battlefront, drove transport, assisted in medical duties on the frontline, worked in the typhoid hospitals and followed on the heels of the army persuading Islamic survivors of the conflict to convert.[78] One British diplomat recorded an incident in a village at the battlefront when after the fighting had moved on "the priests, with threats and blows endeavoured to force the people to renounce their religion."[79]

Fig. 5: Preparing to baptise Muslims during the First Balkan War

**Fig. 6: The Muslim who is bent over bares his head to receive baptism
performed by a Bulgarian Orthodox priest**

Sultan Abdulhamit had not been particularly concerned at the declaration of war assuming that his empire could not be defeated. German field marshal, Colmar von der Goltz, regarded the Ottoman European defences as "one of the best in the world..., there is no need to strengthen it as it is as unassailable as Gibraltar."[80] However, the nationalistic fervour and desire for vengeance indwelling the Bulgarians were not taken into consideration. This war had been the first real opportunity for the Bulgarian people to avenge the five centuries of Ottoman domination and prove to the world that, although they had received their liberation through foreign intervention, it was their destiny by right. Within two weeks Turkey's unassailable defences had crumbled and the capture of Constantinople by Bulgarian troops appeared imminent. The Bulgarian National Assembly were not in favour of entering Constanti-

nople but Ferdinand and his military commanders were intent on celebrating their victory in the imperial city.[81] The lure of Constantinople
momentarily deflected their attention from a troublesome situation
which was developing in Macedonia.

When the Bulgarian troops arrived in Macedonia, after their
success on the eastern front, the Serbs and Greeks were already there and
refused to concede the previously agreed territories to Bulgaria. Thus
when the Ottoman government sued for peace and according to the
Treaty of London (30 May 1913) ceded all its territories in Europe
(except Albania), the Balkan allies found themselves with a multitude of
problems arising from the division of territorial gains. When the
National Assembly learned that Serbia and Greece had concluded an alliance against Bulgaria the military high command immediately planned
to attack their former allies. However, when Romania and Turkey also
became involved, taking the opportunity to regain lost territory, the Bulgarian army was simply too stretched to fight on four fronts and had no
alternative but to sue for peace. History had repeated itself, as within the
span of only a few months Bulgaria's supreme triumph had descended to
embarrassing defeat. The ensuing agreement in the Treaty of Bucharest
(10 August 1913) carved up Macedonia in three pieces the smallest of
which was given to Bulgaria. Romania was given Southern Dobrudja
and Eastern Thrace was returned to Turkey.

This course of events was heralded as a national catastrophe and
from a diplomatic and ecclesiastical perspective it certainly was. Nevertheless the Bucharest settlement presented a mixture of losses and gains.
There remains a general feeling that Bulgaria had been robbed of Macedonia, yet the Pirin region of Macedonia was incorporated into the
country. The western part of Thrace remained Bulgarian territory, the
only major loss was the Dobrudja to Romania. All in all Bulgaria came
out of Bucharest intact and indeed enlarged. But even sober retrospective
calculation of these events cannot assuage the solemn mood of the
nation. That mood was embodied in a letter sent to all Bulgarian clergy
by Metropolitan Josef of Turnovo:

> Rivers of blood, tens of thousands of homes desolated, left by young
> widows, thousands of miserable orphans wandered the country...
> onerous sacrifices, massive efforts were made by our people to secure
> our freedom, but beautiful Bulgaria was once again nailed to the cross
> – bloodstained like a wingless bird or an eyeless corpse. Macedonia,
> Dobrudja, Seres and Kavala – those wings and eyes of young Bulgaria

– robbed from our body... that is why Bulgaria must begin a holy war, sent from God, because she is led by the name of truth, against injustice.[82]

The Balkan Wars and the Treaty of Bucharest destroyed what was left of the already decimated work of the Exarchate in Macedonia and Thrace. Metropolitans and priests fled their eparchies as the Serbian and Greek Patriarchates forcibly gained control and Exarch Josef was ordered to move the seat of the Exarchate to Sofia.[83] On 28 November 1913 Exarch Josef, failing in health, arrived in Sofia where he was met by Tsar Ferdinand and representatives from the government. Stepping from the train Bulgaria's ecclesiastical leader openly lambasted his monarch blaming him for this national catastrophe:

Your Majesty, end the search for the perpetrator of the Bulgarian catastrophe outside of Bulgaria, because they are here inside Bulgaria. They are in the person of Your Majesty, in your former and present advisers.... They are in the regime of Your Majesty... From this difficult position today I have a way out: Your Majesty, for you to abdicate and to leave your Orthodox successor to the throne to unite around him the parties and people and with God's help, and with the assistance of our Holy Church to return the gloriousness and majesticness to Bulgaria.... To remain on the Bulgarian throne would be fatal for Your Majesty and for Bulgaria, for the simple reason, that you Your Majesty shall never have the faith, consequently we cannot support your politics. Even I, a simple, humble, national church worker, do not have faith in you because my faith in your diplomatic ability and skills bring me inexpressible grief and disappointment. I am prepared to be candid today... I am a witness to the ruin and destruction of Macedonia, to the breaking off of the Dobrudja, of a bloodstained Thrace, and witness to the rape of Bulgaria. A witness to the tragic death of the most idyllic Bulgarian product – the Exarchate.... I cannot, Your Majesty, remain composed and exemplary with the fact, that after your political disasters you still claim the Bulgarian throne.[84]

The Balkan Wars had not ended favourably for Bulgaria, indeed they had initiated a period of conflict in Europe which would last until 1945. This era encapsulates, however, the nationalistic and territorial aspirations of the Church that had evolved to be the foundational principle of its relationship with the Bulgarian nation.

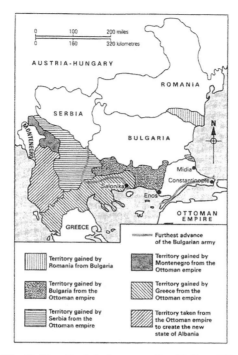

Fig. 7: Territorial changes after Balkan Wars

Bulgaria and the Great War

When World War I commenced one year later one country more than any hungered for revenge. So much so that on the eve of war Tsar Ferdinand stated "the purpose of my life is the destruction of Serbia."[85] As a result of their former allies duplicity Bulgaria was prepared to take whichever side enabled them to avenge her embarrassment. German diplomats sought to persuade Bulgaria to side with the Central Powers of Austria and Germany promising the government control not only of Serbian Macedonia, but also Southern Dobrudja, Eastern Thrace and Adrianople. Having agreed on the spoils of war over 800 000 Bulgarian men took their positions on the Eastern Front.

Bulgarian interests in the consequences of the 'greater war' were non-existent. The country's entry into the war must be understood solely in conjunction with its own specific objectives – the restoration of 'Greater Bulgaria' – it may be judicious then to recognise this Eastern conflict as a Third Balkan War. The First World War in the Balkans served only to underline the animosity which had developed following the Congress of Berlin. Therefore once Bulgarian troops occupied Macedonia and Thrace the national commitment to the greater war effort faded.[86]

In the midst of this militaristic situation the Bulgarian Orthodox Church sought to re-establish their presence in Serbian controlled Macedonia. To achieve this end an ecclesiastical commission was dispatched, under the leadership of Metropolitan Josef of Turnovo, with a mission to "instil spiritual desire for the Bulgarian Church."[87] According to data from the reports of the Bulgarian High Command there were around 147 clergy working in the region. The Holy Synod collaborated with military High Command to develop regulations for the ecclesiastical commission whose work was divided into three areas: an educational and cultural character with the aim of supporting Bulgarian troops; to help direct charitable donations to the frontline; and finally to advance the faith in the recently liberated territories by 'leading' the populations to the Bulgarian Orthodox Church.[88] For his role in assisting the military and national effort Metropolitan Josef was elected to the Holy Synod and for his services to the German Fatherland was presented by the German High Command with the Iron Cross II Class.[89]

However, as German hopes of victory faded the Bulgarians placed their expectations on America. The USA had not declared war on Bulgaria and in President Wilson's 1918 announcement regarding national self-determination that:

> All well defined national aspirations shall be accorded the utmost satisfaction that can be accorded them without introducing new or perpetuating old elements of discord and antagonism that would be likely in time to break the peace of Europe.

The Bulgarian nation saw opportunity to retain their territorial gains.[90] Wilson's Commission of Inquiry although sympathetic towards Bulgarian aspirations, concluded that the needs of the three Balkan states that had supported the Allied cause, Romania, Serbia and Montenegro, should take precedence over Bulgaria.

Therefore at the conclusion of the Great War Bulgaria experienced yet another national catastrophe. According to the terms of the Treaty of

Neuilly, which Bulgaria signed on 27 November 1919, the newly gained territories were once again taken from them. This was a heavy blow for the political, spiritual and economic life of Bulgaria. The Bulgarian Church once again lost their eparchies in Macedonia and Thrace, what is more the Treaty of Neuilly no longer protected the minority rights of the Bulgarian population under foreign rule. After another humiliating defeat the country's infrastructure began to disintegrate. As hundreds of thousands of angry and disillusioned troops returned from the war demonstrations opposing monarchy and government became prevalent, taking on a more volatile character as rioting and looting proliferated. Calls for the removal of Tsar Ferdinand deteriorated into rebellion and on 27 September 1918, BANU leader Alexander Stamboliski was proclaimed President of the breakaway Radomir Republic:

> Today the Bulgarian people break the chains of slavery, throw down the despotic regime of Ferdinand and his henchmen, proclaim them enemies of the people, proclaim themselves a free people with a republic form of government, and hold out the hand of peace and understanding to the peoples of Europe. From this day Tsar Ferdinand and his dynasty and the former government are fallen.[91]

Although the rebellion was crushed two days later it achieved two ends. Tsar Ferdinand, realising his future was untenable, abdicated in favour of his son Tsar Boris III (1918-1943) on 3 October 1918 and secondly, it marked a profound shift in the country's political direction with the communist and socialist parties becoming increasingly powerful. The weakening of Church authority coincided with a further diminution in Church-State relationships during the inter-war period.

The Bulgarian Orthodox Church and the Second World War
The work of the Bulgarian Exarchate, for the first time since its establishment, was limited within the borders of the Principality. Consequent defeats in the Balkan and Great Wars resulted in drastic territorial concessions restricting the Church's ecclesiastical jurisdiction, leading to a temporary cessation of its aspiration toward the restoration of Greater Bulgaria. In surrendering its wider parameters the Church was able, during the inter-war period, to concentrate its efforts on strengthening the Bulgarian Church within the Principality.

In November 1940 Metropolitan Paisii of Vratsa was invited to meet with the director of the Board for Civil Mobilisation, General Sava

Bakurdjiev, at the Ministry of War. General Bakurdjiev praised the productive role of the Orthodox Church in Bulgaria's history and expressed the positive role he felt the Church could play in influencing the nation's future. He particularly enthused Paisii regarding the Church's role in changing the prevalent national negativity connected with the possible disruption of yet another war, to inspire the confidence of the people towards the government, to remove the spirit of defeatism after the catastrophes of the Balkan and Great Wars, to encourage the economy and to prepare the nation for war. Metropolitan Paisii replied that the Church was willing to assist the Board in their request, adding that the most important need was for the spiritual mobilisation of the nation.[92]

The General was surprised at the enthusiasm and readiness displayed by Metropolitan Paisii. However, the Holy Synod had already debated these issues, convening the previous year to discuss the Church's future. In November 1939 the Holy Synod had assembled to discuss the ailing condition of the Church, its relationship with the State and the role it played in the spiritual life of the nation. During heated discussions Metropolitan Stefan of Sofia raised the question "can we claim that our Church is in good order and that our liturgical life is manifest with joy and piety? The truth is that the hierarchy of our Church is far removed from the people, which is not beneficial. Let us confess that in many cases we are only a shadow of what we should be."[93] The statement succinctly underlined the fact that the BOC had reached a nadir in its relationship with Bulgarian nation, state and society.

This can be construed as a conclusive moment in what had been a continuous slow, self destruction and social marginalisation of the Church that had occurred since the establishment of the Bulgarian State. Perceiving this to be true members of the Synod listened carefully to Metropolitan Stefan. Following his statement three turbulent meetings took place on 23, 24 and 27 November 1939, where the Holy Synod of the Bulgarian Orthodox Church took full inventory of their situation, of relationships between the high clergy, parish priest and the laity and in problems of communication with the civil authorities. These contained such awful revelations that a nameless Metropolitan commented: "We cannot enter into the records everything which is inadequate in our Church life, if we do there is not other choice but to cover our heads with ashes and abandon our position."[94]

This act of self-deprecation did not materialise as their discussions resulted in the general conviction that the Church could not desert its divine mission. To fulfil this mission the Synod agreed that they needed to develop in two general directions: to restore the Bulgarian Church's canonical status as a Patriarchate and to return to 'our glorious past' to that moment of glory at the establishment of the Exarchate and to the harmony of Social-Church relationships at that time. One may forgive the Synod of wearing rose-tinted spectacles as this research has shown that relationship to be illusory from its inception. Metropolitan Stefan emphasised that the Church needed to assert its ties with and its love for the nation and in doing so the divine mission of the Church would be fulfilled. This comment surreptitiously divulged the perception that the Church was the nation, not the State and her strength resulted from the support of the nation rather than from the benevolence of the State and for this reason the Church needed to be present at every level and aspect of society and could not watch indifferently as the State moved purposefully forward in power. With political insight Metropolitan Boris of Nevrokop continued:

> Today we have a State which has absolute authority, which tells us that everything is subordinate to the State. This spirit will penetrate into our nation and will continue to create obstacles for the Church. But if the Church is aware of the spirit of the new times it can still be of beneficial influence... We need to be ready, even though it may not be our desire that the state will want to separate from the Church.[95]

For the first time, since the crisis of the monarchy in 1879, the Church voiced its most fearful thought – separation of Church and State – but now the Holy Synod considered that this was not some vain threat but rather future inevitability. With this in mind the Holy Synod commissioned a special programme to secure the church's future and strengthen her social relationships with the nation. The Synod appointed two commissions to investigate and develop these matters further. The first was entrusted to report on the church's social, educational and relational character and the second to comment on its economic situation.[96]

The findings of the first commission on education and disciplinary matters are more pertinent to this research as they comment on the relational character of the Church with the Bulgarian nation. One of the first points the commission proposed, as necessary toward the Church's survival, was the introduction of religious instruction in the secular school network, suggesting that a minimum of four hours per week be set aside for participation in a religious educational programme. It also proposed the creation of a Theological Faculty within the University of Sofia to further opportunities for religious education at a higher level. In line with these educational proposals it was decided to create a 'Child and Student Orthodox Christian Society' aimed purposefully at stimulating an interest in the Church within Bulgaria's youth. Every Metropolitan was encouraged to organise children's clubs and choirs which would follow a centrally produced programme of events. Child friendly literature was published that included liturgy, poems and songs. Special attention was given to families, who the commission reported had been neglected and even alienated from the life of the Church. The Synod sent out an "imperative obligation" to all parishes to embrace families in the mission of the Church. New Christian societies were formed to organise crèches, after-school groups, children's summer camps and day homes for the elderly, to assist working families. Soup kitchens and night shelters were to be established for poorer members of society.[97]

The reports of both commissions established the foundation for the practical application of a substantial, long-term programme of activities aimed at affecting every level of Bulgarian society restoring the Church to a place of prominence within the nation. General Bakurdjiev's request to the Church, to assist in alleviating the mood of the nation and to prepare them for a war which was advancing inevitably towards Bulgaria, arrived at the conclusion of the commission's findings. This meeting of interests provoked the discussion between the General and Metropolitan Paisii in November 1940. The commission reports were accepted by the Supreme Council on 29 November 1940. Alongside the results of the 1939 consultation arose the general consensus that the Church needed to support the nation particularly during periods of war: "In the days of world conflict the Church's duty in this is immense, thus as the protector of freedom and independence in Bulgaria we seek a new spiritual and moral revival in Bulgaria."[98]

The ecclesiastical hierarchy's willingness to prepare the nation for war began to filter through to parish level. Local priests were given guidance enabling them to combine teaching on Christian doctrine with the militarism of the political situation, promoting the idea of a 'just war'.[99] In doing so the Exarchate sought a compromise from the government, for as well as supporting the nation they were striving to strengthen the Church. Therefore the government agreed to assist the BOC in seven concrete directions. Firstly, every statesman, municipal worker and soldier would be obliged to attend regular public worship;

the Exarchate would be able to take a prominent role in state youth organisations such as, 'The Young Defenders'; Eastern Orthodoxy would be given preferential place within State legislation, whilst all other 'sects' and 'religious propagandists' would require legal approval; the Exarchate would receive financial assistance from the State to build a church in every town and village; they gained permission to establish chaplaincies in every hospital, prison and military barracks; full-time military chaplains would be appointed who could prepare the troops spiritually and morally for war and finally they received permission to produce a range of religious educational textbooks to instil, "a complete spiritual-moral ideology in the heart of the reader."[100]

As this agreement was being finalised the Bulgarian government made a military pact with Germany, allowing Hitler's army full access to Bulgarian territory. The German invasion of the Balkans in the summer of 1941 offered, in the light of past events, a somewhat risky resolution to Bulgaria's unfinished programme of national unification. Nevertheless with German approval the Bulgarian army re-entered Macedonia and Western Thrace declaring that "all former Serbian and Greek subjects shall become Bulgarian, unless they expressly request otherwise".[101] The Holy Synod reacted quickly to the changing situation. Having predicted this outcome they had prepared a secret project in April 1941 to incorporate its Balkan neighbours within the Exarchate: "to embrace the Bulgarian Orthodox population in every territory of the Balkan Peninsula...."[102] The Church proclaimed that the project to liberate Bulgarian soil was historically justifiable and expressed God's supreme will.[103] In the ensuing euphoria following their territorial gains the Synod sent a message to the German and Italian governments thanking them for their help in completing Bulgaria's national union.[104] The Exarchates newspaper even glorified Adolf Hitler as the "liberator of a long-suffering Macedonia and restorer of the borders of San Stefano Bulgaria."[105]

The Exarchates praise of Germany has led Macedonian authors to comment that the Bulgarian Church was working "in the service of the fascist invaders," destroying Macedonia's national structure.[106] Greek historians also claim that the Bulgarian Church was implicit in national discrimination and terrorism of the Greek-Macedonian population.[107] This criticism equates with Bulgarian records from the time which comment that one of the most difficult problems in governing the new Bulgarian eparchies was to do with the presence of Serbian and Greek clergy. The Bulgarian Interior Minister, Ivan Popov, explicitly recommended that the Exarchate should not become involved in any work which would harm its prestige.[108] In debating this issue with the Interior Minister the Church hierarchy judged that "it was a question of prestige for our [Bulgarian] Church to abandon the Greek clergy and to reduce them to beggars."[109] Later the Exarchate introduced a programme of enforced deportation of 'alien populations' from Macedonia and Thrace. In contradicting the wishes of the Bulgarian government we perceive a very different Bulgarian Church hierarchy from the one which was eager to cooperate with the government during the Balkan and Great Wars. The hierarchy now followed its own objectives and in so doing claimed it was, "protecting the unity of the Bulgarian nation."[110]

The growing confidence of the Church can be witnessed again in its stand against the government in opposition to the deportation of Bulgarian Jews to Katowice, Auschwitz and Treblinka. The number of Bulgarian Jews was small compared with other European states, numbering 48 400 according to the 1934 census. Bulgaria's anti-Jewish policies can be traced directly to its alliance with Germany during the Second World War, beginning with the introduction into her legislature of the Law for the Defence of the Nation in October 1940. This was aimed generally at preventing any action against the State but specifically targeted the Jewish population. The deportation issue entered a critical phase with the arrival in Sofia of SS Hauptsturmfuhrer Theodor Dannecker in January 1943. The deportation of Jews from Thrace and Macedonia began in March 1943 and by the end of the month 11,343 people had been murdered. However, when the deportation of Jews within Bulgaria was proposed opposition arose. The Metropolitan of Plovdiv contacted the Bulgarian government to intercede on behalf of the Jewish inhabitants of Plovdiv vowing to lie across the rails in the path of any train which attempted to deport Jews from his eparchy.[111] Metropolitan Stefan of Sofia warned his king: "Know Boris, that God watches your actions from heaven."[112] The Church even organised a mass demonstration against the government's anti-Jewish policies on the traditional Christian holiday of Sts. Kiril and Methodius (24 May 1943). Statements from the Holy Synod, such as the one directed at the Bulgarian government on 15 November 1940, spoke against the new Law for the Defence of the Nation. It can be proven therefore that the intervention of the Church certainly assisted the Jewish cause in Bulgaria saving many thousands from certain death. There is ambiguity, however, in this stance. The

BOC continues to take the moral high ground for their role in protecting its Jews, a role which was praised once again at the 60th anniversary of the liberation of Auschwitz, but what of the Jews and Gypsies who perished in Macedonia and Thrace, after all these lands at this moment in time were under the ecclesiastical jurisdiction of the Bulgarian Church. Despite this there has never been any mention of remorse from the Bulgarian Church hierarchy for the deaths of over 20,000 Jews and Gypsies from those territories which were deemed by the BOC to be theirs by holy right.[113]

The Exarchates programme for the spiritual mobilisation of the Bulgarian nation had proven successful. So much so that by 26 June 1944 the Holy Synod could state that the Church acted as a mediator between nation and state and as an interpreter of the national will before the executive powers and in this role voiced its opposition against the politics of the Bulgarian government.[114] This testified not only to an evolution in political understanding within the ecclesiastical hierarchy at the end of the Second World War but also to the success of the Church in raising its prominence within Bulgarian society.

CONCLUSION

This chapter has uncovered an important but generally untouched aspect in the development of Bulgarian State-Church relations. Although the Bulgarian Orthodox Church continues to proclaim its central and crucial role in Bulgarian history and an equitable relationship with Bulgarian State the years from 1878-1945 unveil a somewhat different story. The Church, far from being raised on a pedestal for its role during the National Revival period, was increasingly distanced and then restricted completely from having a voice in national politics. The National Constitution regulated on the rights of the Bulgarian Church making it dependent on the state. Therefore, the period from the establishment of the Bulgarian state (1878) to the end of the Second World War (1944) was extremely difficult for the Church. The ecclesiastical hierarchy were forced to construct a new model of interrelationship between Church and State to ensure its survival. Although the State did not desire close ties with the Church, the Church was clearly indispensable to the State particularly for fulfilling its aspirations toward national unification and the recreation of 'Greater Bulgaria'. Being the only national institution which represented the Bulgarian people outside the

Principality, the Orthodox Church became an important mechanism of Bulgarian geopolitics. Thus, after the separation of the Exarchate and the Sofia Synod we witness the Exarchate's clergy receiving preferential treatment from the Bulgarian government to remain in those territories deemed important by the State. The Bulgarian Church willingly accepted its role as spiritual and national enlightener, in so doing attempting to strengthen its troubled bond with the Bulgarian government. The Church fully supported the government in its unification attempts and even accompanied the military to the battlefront in order to protect and expand the nation. The desire of the Church to be a central part of the nation cannot be doubted.

Bulgaria's Church hierarchy, however, found it increasingly difficult to operate in the modern world of secular politics. The Exarchate's former position as sole Bulgarian arbiter on all things spiritual, political and judicial had been taken away and now the Church found itself powerless in society. When the Church did speak out against injustice, as in the monarchical crisis of the 1890's, the government simply threatened complete separation of Church and State. The ecclesiastical hierarchy therefore had no choice but to be compliant to the desires of the government in order to survive. However, as a result of subsequent defeats in the Balkan and Great Wars territorial concessions ensued restricting the Church's ecclesiastical jurisdiction, enabling the hierarchy to concentrate their efforts on strengthening the Bulgarian Church within the Principality. In so doing they realised that to survive as a national institution they had to re-assert their influence upon Bulgarian society. During the inter-war period, before Second World War, the Church introduced a new successful strategy permitting them to fully support the aspirations of the nation, while not entirely conforming to the appeals of State, therefore increasing their own general popularity within society. Despite the animosity which existed throughout the period the Bulgarian State remained protective towards the work of the Bulgarian Church as it continued to be a useful instrument in Bulgarian foreign affairs. Therefore, at the end of the period investigated through this chapter the Bulgarian Orthodox Church found itself in an improved situation from that in 1879. Although remaining voiceless in the national political forum the Church could now claim to be a true mediator between society and State. This proves beyond doubt the success of the ecclesiastical commission's special programme to secure the church's future and re-assert her social significance in and relationship with the nation. Recognising the improved position of the Church within society the government acquiesced to the desires of the Church, as seen in their seven-point concession of 1940. Unfortunately this newly placed confidence in the Church dissipated when the Soviet Army entered Bulgaria in September 1945. When the Fatherland Front assumed power later that year fate determined that the relationship between Church and State would develop very differently.

6

THE CHURCH AND THE COMMUNIST REGIME
(1944-1989)

This chapter will examine the development of Orthodox Church-State relations under communist administration, from the coup of 9 September 1944 to the regime's fall in 1989. It will focus on the years 1944-1953, a period in which the government developed policies towards the BOC that would dictate Church-State relations until 1989. This will be achieved by consulting Bulgarian Central State and Central Party Archives as well as the records of the BOC. The aim of this research is not to analyse all government policy relating to religion but rather to investigate those policies which led to the deteriorating situation in which the Church was placed in the employ of the State. The Communists controlled Bulgaria from 1944-1989, a forty-five year period in which the Bulgarian Orthodox Church became increasingly overwhelmed by the materialistic and atheistic policies of the Soviet inspired government. Even so there remained a discernable Church-State relationship throughout the period, a relationship which ranged from toleration to cooperation. This chapter will consider whether the BOC's chosen *modus vivendi*, was inescapable or if there was an alternative to the symbiosis of the cross and the hammer and the sickle.

The Red Army crossed the Danube and entered Bulgaria on 8 September 1944 seizing control of the country the following day. Having supported the Axis Powers the incumbent Bulgarian government was removed and replaced by the Fatherland Front (FF), a coalition of four anti-fascist political parties: the Zveno Party, the Communists, the Agrarians and the Social Democrats. The FF government has generally been associated with the communist regime. However, it must be recognised that from the point of view of contemporary society many Bulgarians considered there to have been a real opportunity for the country to have developed democratically along a western pattern. An integral part of the new political structure was the creation of local FF committees, which by the end of 1944 numbered over seven thousand. Amongst wide ranging powers committees were given the authority to appoint provincial governors, mayors, police officials and teachers. During the first year of FF control a nationwide anti-fascist purge was organised and coordinated through these local committees. One of the major targets of this purge was the BOC, accused of collaborating with the Nazi regime. The coup of 9 September fundamentally altered the foundational position of the BOC in the new Bulgarian State. Although the relationship of the Holy Synod with the previous government had been strained it had not opposed the introduction of Bulgarian military in Macedonia and Thrace as this had increased BOC authority. Thus the Church and its clergy were accused of being fascist sympathisers and enemies of the new State. Consequently many Orthodox clergy were liquidated during the blood-letting which accompanied the anti-fascist purge.[1] This purge is commonly portrayed as being instigated by the communists, however, the Soviet military authorities had not welcomed violence and insisted on the establishment of People's Courts to try those accused of collaboration with the previous authorities. In the first six months following the establishment of courts official statistics record that a large number of clergy were tried and imprisoned for anti-State activities, while others were sent to labour camps without sentence.[2]

The example of the anti-fascist purge highlights one of the initial problems tracing the political line regarding Church-State relations in Bulgaria under communism immediately after the war. The terror unleashed against the clergy was not solely the prerogative of the communists but was condoned by all four coalition parties, three of which had no particular love of communism. Thus although the communists dominated the FF government under the leadership of Georgi Dimitrov, a one-party communist system was not imposed until the end of 1947 after the signing of the Paris Peace Treaty. In retrospect Church-State relations during the period researched in this chapter fall into three distinct phases, rather than one prolonged period of unchanging communist rule: the period of coalition rule (1944-1947); the Stalinist inspired regime (1948-1952); and finally the post-Stalinist phase (1953-1989).

COALITION RULE (1944-1947)

During this initial phase the communists faced the primary task of converting the FF coalition into a one-party communist system, whilst simultaneously securing international recognition of that regime. Imitating Soviet policy Bulgarian communist leaders, having witnessed

Moscow's attitude towards the Russian Patriarchate, discerned the usefulness and role of the national Church in its regime legitimising campaign. This inhibited the communists from taking any drastic action against the BOC during this coalition period. Nevertheless their aims can still be defined as steering towards separation of church and state. This initial pro-church position presented opportunity for the Holy Synod and the FF coalition to deal with a number of major unsolved problems within the BOC – above all the election of an Exarch and the lifting of the schism.[3]

The Election of Exarch Stefan (21 January 1945)

Stoyan Georgiev Shokov was born in 1878 in the Rhodope village of Shiroka Luka. From 1893 he studied in the Samokov Seminary later attending the Kiev Theological Academy. In 1904 he took the monastic pledge and accepted the name Stefan. Later that year he was appointed as Exarchal Protosingel in Constantinople and from that moment accompanied Exarch Josef everywhere until his death in 1915. Following Exarch Josef's death Stefan left to further his theological education in Switzerland. Whilst studying there Stefan was brought to the attention of Bulgarian diplomatic staff in Berne to assist them in making contacts with western churches. The following year Stefan was asked to join the Bulgarian political delegation which signed the Neuilly Peace Treaty.[4] In 1921 he was promoted to the position of Metropolitan of Martsianopol and the following year was elected as Metropolitan of Sofia.

He had rapidly emerged as one of the most prominent figures in the BOC. Undoubtedly contacts with western diplomats contributed to the speed of his advancement after 9 September 1944 and as one of the founders of the Bulgarian ecumenical movement he was in regular contact with international Church leaders. He also had a level of political acumen and was not afraid to express his opinions. For example, when Tsar Boris was married according to Roman Catholic rite Stefan insisted that his monarch also receive an Orthodox service of blessing which he personally performed in Sofia's Nevski Cathedral. Stefan had also been openly opposed to the militaristic union of Bulgaria with Nazi Germany and had played a central role in protecting Bulgaria's Jewry. He was close political friends with the leadership of the FF government, including Prime Minister Kimon Georgiev Stoyanov and Minister of Defence Damyan Velchev. Apart from politics Stefan had been a long standing member of the Bulgarian Holy Synod both as Exarch Protosingel and Metropolitan. All of these factors contributed to the prominence of Stefan and as one of the most appropriate figures to lead the BOC.

His first recorded public statement was heard on Radio Sofia in 1944. In an address entitled, 'The Spirit is not Extinguished' he expressed his desire for the development and progress, not only of the new Bulgarian State, but of the BOC. He shared the belief that from that moment the two institutions should work together for the happiness and future prosperity of the Bulgarian nation. He considered that the FF government should serve, not wield power, and was categorical that the BOC "cannot and should not be outside the purview of the loyalty, needs and love which the FF government have shown as the ideal for tomorrow's Bulgaria." The main part of his address was given over to the changing international situation of Bulgaria and stated that the nation, "should receive from the Soviet Union and her allies a real possibility to work in peace to progress in their work and demonstrate their recognition, loyalty and love toward their greatest benefactor... who first offered them an olive branch." For this reason he declared that Bulgaria should be strongly united with Mother Russia.[5]

Simultaneously the church newspaper *Tsurkoven vestnik* published a series of articles entitled, 'The Message of Stefan Metropolitan of Sofia to the Russian People.'[6] He emphasised that the years during which Bulgaria was an ally of Nazi Germany were "years of heavy and ruinous slavery in our land, that have devastated and corrupted our morals!" He concluded by proclaiming that Nazism had been the enemy of the entire Slavonic race and should be crushed by Russia, America and Great Britain. However two statements should draw special attention to this message. Firstly where he writes:

> Bulgaria saw a lucky omen in this, that in Moscow, at the heart of our liberators and not elsewhere, should be achieved justice for our nation...,

and secondly where Stefan comments:

> Our nation hopes that the illustrious and great Russian nation from today will rule over the family of Slavonic nations as a genuine elder brother, and under its wise and mighty influence the smaller Slavonic nations will not lose their identity or their national ideals, but should unite together in family unity to strengthen their awareness of their Slavonic unity.

He was categorical that the fate of the Bulgarian people should be decided in Moscow. The question is frequently asked of these statements, how much did Stefan accommodate to the wishes of the coalition government, or where these comments completely his own inspiration? Although rising quickly through the ranks of Orthodox hierarchy Stefan was subordinate to the presiding chairman of the Holy Synod, Metropolitan Neofit of Vidin (during the period when the position of Exarch was vacant Chairman of the Holy Synod was the highest position in the BOC). Thus it would have been expected that Neofit's would have been the prominent voice within the Church. His activities never received the publicity of Stefan's. Take for example a letter of Neofit's dated 20 September 1944 in which he welcomed the new authorities and expressed the full support of the BOC for the government. This letter was disregarded and has remained neglected within Church archives.[7] Why were Stefan's words, basically the remarks of a deputy, promoted as the voice of the BOC over and above those of its leader? Later events may explain this enigma.

On 3 October 1944, Neofit Metropolitan of Vidin resigned as Chairman of the Holy Synod and also as a member of the Synod. On 14 October the Synod communicated this situation to Prime Minister Stoyanov and on 16 October they elected Stefan as the new Chairman of the Bulgarian Holy Synod.[8] On 20 October 1944 the new Chairman visited the Soviet legation in Sofia where he received a letter from the Russian Patriarch (dated 5 October 1944), which was addressed personally to 'Metropolitan Stefan, Chairman of the Holy Synod'. However, on 5 October 1944 Stefan still remained an ordinary Synodal member. The Patriarchal message suggests that the appointment of Stefan had been agreed in advance by Moscow.

On 18 December 1944 the FF permitted the Holy Synod to conduct elections for a new Exarch and a Church-Electoral Council. The government, however, took the unprecedented action of amending the laws connected with the election of an Exarch, allowing not only ecclesiastical delegates but also governmental delegates on to the electoral council (the Foreign Minister, the Chairman of the Treasury, a representative from the Bulgarian Academy of Sciences, the Director of Religious Affairs and three other representatives from the FF). According to official procedure, seven days before the election the Holy Synod in a private vote would choose three Metropolitans as candidates to the Exarchal throne. These names would be passed on to the Foreign Minister for governmental approval, after which the Synod would convene a National Church Council. 75% of the National Council would have to be in attendance for any vote to take place and a 66% majority would be required to be elected as Exarch. After the vote was completed the Synod would notify the Foreign Minister again who would sanction the induction of the new Exarch. The electoral procedure would be finalised when the Exarch declared an oath of allegiance to the Bulgarian State.

The significance of the new regulations are realised only after considering a document from the archives of the Bulgarian Communist Party. This is in the form of a telegram sent by T. Kostov (Chairman of the Party in Bulgaria) to G. Dimitrov (leader of the Bulgarian Communists resident in Moscow) on 25 December 1944: "The decision has been taken to elect Metropolitan Stefan as Exarch and for him to attend the Church Council in Moscow as head of the Bulgarian Church."[9] This decision of State preceded the Church election by almost a month. Therefore the announcement of those standing for election, the convocation of a National Church Council and the election itself were merely scenery for the clandestine activities of the communists. Thus when the National Church Council met for the election on 21 January 1945 it comes as no surprise to find that Stefan was approved by an 84/90 majority.

In his acceptance speech Exarch Stefan pointed to the cause which had made his election possible, the political changes of 9 September 1944. For him the FF was not only political doctrine but "a kiss of life for the Bulgarian nation," which had created the conditions for the restoration of harmonious relationships between Church and State. He then turned his attention to the government declaring "We are with you, our faith will not be an obstacle to your work."[10] It would appear that the endorsement and election of Exarch Stefan had been engineered not only by the Bulgarian government but also from Moscow.

The Lifting of the Schism (22 February 1945)

Alongside the BOC the FF government inherited an ecclesiastical schism which had remained unresolved for over 70 years. Less than a year after coming to power, however, the proclamation of schism upon the BOC had been revoked. On 28 February 1870 an Ottoman *firman* had restored the BOC under the form of an Exarchate. The resulting document had raised questions regarding which eparchies came under the jurisdiction of the new Church creating contradictions between the Exarchate and the Ecumenical Patriarchate, as both claimed jurisdiction over the eparchies of Macedonia and Thrace. The ensuing disagreement led to the proclamation that the BOC was schismatic on the grounds of philetism.

Initially schism had not troubled the Bulgarian Church, as it had allowed its leaders opportunity to organise the Church without outside interference. However, after the Liberation of Bulgaria (1878) and particularly following the Unification of the Principality with Eastern Rumelia (1885) the schism began to weigh heavily on Bulgarian church life. All attempts to remove it were unsuccessful, the fundamental reason being the problem of transferring the headquarters of the Exarchate from Istanbul to Sofia. The Bulgarians had been adamant that the Seat of the Exarchate must remain in Istanbul because only from there had the Exarchate been successful in defending the interests of the Bulgarian population which remained outside of Bulgaria's independent borders. In this way Orthodox Bulgarians from the Principality, Eastern Rumelia, Macedonia and Thrace remained under the jurisdiction of the Bulgarian Exarchate, despite the fact that its citizens resided in different national States. That is why the BOC became the figurehead for the movement to restore Greater Bulgaria.

At the end of WWII the re-allotment of the Balkans into zones of influence between the USSR and her allies changed that situation. For the new Bulgarian authorities the solving of this ecclesiastical problem became politically important, necessitating the merger of church eparchies within Bulgaria's national borders. This would cease opportunity for interference from external factors, such as the Ecumenical Patriarchate and at the same time would make the BOC increasingly dependent upon the State. Therefore at the end of WWII the loss of Macedonia and Thrace was deemed an acceptable sacrifice and a final resolution to the question of the schism a real possibility.

The minutes of the Holy Synod and its correspondence with the Ecumenical Patriarchate reveal the mechanisms used to achieve resolution of this problem. On 21 November 1944 the Synod took the first step by sending a letter to the Russian Patriarchate requesting it to mediate between the Bulgarian Exarchate and the Ecumenical Patriarchate in their attempt to lift the schism.[11] It was no accident that on the very day of the election of the Bulgarian Exarch the Synod announced the momentous decision to transfer the seat of the Exarchate from Istanbul to Sofia, removing the fundamental obstacle for the removal of the schism.[12] Thus when the Ecumenical Patriarch was informed of the election of Exarch Stefan he was also presented with an official request for a restoration of 'fraternal and canonical relations' between the Holy Ecumenical Patriarchate and the BOC. To accept this request the Constantinople Patriarchate would have to recognise and accept the Bulgarian Church as being fully autocephalous and would therefore require revoking the schism. Therefore after receiving the request a BOC delegation was invited to Istanbul to undertake negotiations for the removal of the schism.

The Patriarchate was represented by four delegates and the negotiations were chaired by Maxim Metropolitan of Halkidiki. After an initial synopsis of the history of the schism Sofroni Metropolitan of Turnovo spoke:

> I want to emphasise that the Bulgarian Holy Synod, clergy and nation on 21 January in Sofia elected a new head of the BOC, His Beatitude Exarch Stefan with his residence in the capital of the Bulgarian kingdom – Sofia, not in Istanbul, as was the case with previous Bulgarian Exarch's. This fact I believe is significant as it gives assurance to the Ecumenical Patriarchate of the good spirit and new direction of the BOC, to open the way to facilitate the restoration of canonical relations between the two churches.[13]

With the main obstacle removed a special sitting of the Patriarchal Holy Synod was convened on 22 February 1945 which resolved to reverse the condemnation of schism pronounced on the BOC in 1872, to restore canonical relations between the two churches and finally to declare the autocephaly of the BOC.[14]

Consolidation and Cooperation

Following the election of Stefan as Bulgarian Exarch and the revoking of the schism relations between Church and State developed in two directions: consolidating connections between Church and State and drawing closer to the Russian Orthodox Church. In the first few months of the FF government there are no records of any particular contradictions or conflicts between the BOC and the new authorities, apart from the fascist element which the government maintained remained within the BOC. This is illustrated in a letter from Georgi Dimitrov (Moscow) to Traicho Kostov (Sofia) dated 21 October 1944:

For now it is unnecessary to raise the question of separating Church and State. Now we need to prepare by means of the FF Committee's to tactfully eliminate the churches pro-German and Nazi orientated Church workers.[15]

Following this correspondence the FF implemented a judicial policy directed against clergy with fascist connections. The People's Court accordingly sentenced over 90 clergy finding them guilty of criminal connections which had led to conflict between Church and State.

During this initial period the BOC openly supported the initiatives of the coalition government. Nevertheless, they remained under close surveillance to observe whether they deviated from the government's political plan. This is testified in another communiqué between Dimitrov and Kostov from 13 November 1944:

> Comrade Traicho, our neighbours have information from Sofia that the head of the Bulgarian militia Glavinchev is a Macedonian nationalist, and a former terrorist. Begin the work for his arrest, but use discretion in this task, and ignore the instructions of the Central Committee of our Party. At this present time Glavinchev is preparing to arrest every member of the Holy Synod, with the exception of Metropolitan Stefan, for this reason, the Synod in 1944, in their appeal to the government on questions of domestic and foreign politics, expressed their opposition to the partisan movement... The arrest of members of the Synod will no doubt produce a negative impression from amongst the members of the coalition parties against our own Party... Therefore be aware of the treacherous provocateurs who desire to discredit our Communist Party.[16]

Dimitrov's mention of 'neighbours' refers to the intelligence activities of the KGB in Bulgaria who were of the same opinion as the BCP that the BOC were central to achieving their political goals in Bulgaria. This communication reveals the power struggle which was occurring during this initial period between the Communists and the other FF Parties. It is interesting that the communists did not allow the arrest of the Holy Synod, as it would be seen to harm their image, while the other party's sought to undertake the judicial anti-fascist purge of the clergy. Dimitrov continued sending orders from Moscow regarding the Church and on 18 December 1944 dispatched the following instruction:

> We do not have any interest in forcing the question of separating Church and State. Our efforts at this moment need only to be directed

towards putting the BOC in the service of the FF authorities. And this is perfectly attainable....[17]

In an effort to achieve this goal a special Communist Party committee was established. By the end of May 1945, however, a problem between Church and State emerged. Traicho Kostov reported that the Church Committee had decided to take a more direct approach in the running of the Church as they wanted to democratise the Church and limit the rights of the Exarch who was beginning to exhibit the tendencies of an anti-communist and anglophile political agitator.[18]

This allegation reveals some important truths about Exarch Stefan, particularly as the implication behind his election victory had been that he was a communist plant. It appears that although his election was engineered, it was not because of his communist sympathies but because Stefan was generally a most useful and acceptable figure to head the BOC. Indeed, Georgi Dimitrov himself commented on Stefan "I consider him a sly person, but at this moment to be a useful person."[19] No admirer of communism perhaps, Stefan was still eager to create strong connections between Bulgarian and Russian Churches. Stefan saw in the Russian Church a model for the BOC's relations with the Bulgarian government and believed it to be a potential protector. Hence on his visit to Moscow in June 1945 to attend the installation of the new Patriarch, Exarch Stefan raised the theme of Orthodox unity, expressing his hope that the Russian Orthodox Church would rescue the East, calling the new Moscow Patriarch "leader of all Slavonic Orthodox Churches."[20] On his return from Russia Stefan addressed a personal letter to the leader of the Bulgarian communists reporting not only on his visit but also on the decision of a recent Bulgarian Church conference to "support the Fatherland Front in Bulgaria." He continued: "We completed this work unanimously and enthusiastically for the glory of Russia and with fervent loyalty to the new state of the FF...."[21]

From this document we see the Exarch having direct contract with Dimitrov promising the support of the BOC. He comprehended that Dimitrov was the key figure behind the FF government who determined domestic and international political questions concerning the destiny of Bulgaria. Although no admirer of communism he accepted that his role and future of the Church meant involvement with the communists. These documents prove invaluable as they reveal the aims of the Communist Party leadership and the hopes of the BOC. They show the delicate condition of relations between Church and State in the first months of the FF government, attempting to survive the anti-fascist purge whilst being fully supportive of government initiatives. Under Soviet military control, however, could the direction of Bulgarian politics ever have been in doubt? As the communists garnered power the policies of the coalition fell into line with Soviet politics. In this situation the FF government took its first steps to curtail the role of the Church in Bulgaria by infiltrating the parish clergy, instigating a power struggle between the lower and higher clergy and by removing religious education from schools.

The Priests' Union

In their efforts to curtail the Church the communist's realised that by altering the balance of power, by increasing the authority of the lower clergy and laity and correspondingly decreasing the influence of the Holy Synod, the ensuing power struggle could fulfil their concept of creating a truly democratic 'people's church'. To achieve this they had to infiltrate and instigate change within the parish clergy. The organ of the Church chosen for this purpose was the Priests' Union (PU). The PU had been established in the summer of 1903 as a professional and charitable organisation of the Bulgarian clergy. However, after the coup of 9 September 1944 the raison d'être of the Union changed.

At the time of the coup the Secretary of the PU had been Father Dimitar Andreev. Due to the allied bombing campaign of Sofia the Board of the PU had been unable to meet for nine months. Therefore by the time they convened on 7 October 1944 the political coup had already occurred. The meeting turned out to be lengthy and turbulent lasting two days. In his initial address Andreev emphasised that the coup d'état should be considered as a revolutionary act and explained to his compatriots that the FF government was already talking about reforms within the Church.[22] The main topic discussed over the two days was, what should be the attitude of the PU be to the new political situation. After examining the government's proposals for Church reform the Board issued a statement declaring that although the PU was an apolitical organisation it would support the new authorities.[23]

Despite offering their support a second meeting of clergy convened in Sofia (12 October) which concluded:

> We need to immediately seize from their hands, the administration, accounts, and work of the Union and pass them into the hands of others, more contemporary and imbued with the spirit of the new time.[24]

Accordingly a Temporary Committee was elected to govern and lead the PU's activities in this new political era. On 17 October 1944 the FF government approved the reports and actions of this reactionary gathering and officially appointed the Temporary Committee to govern the PU led by Dimitar Kotsaliev.[25] On 24 October it was announced that the former Secretary Dimitar Andreev would be transferred to another post.[26]

In the months following the takeover the new PU Board produced a programme of activities for the Union encompassing two basic goals: to support the principle of 'people's rule' in Bulgaria and to implement reforms within the BOC. The XXVII Congress (4-6 June 1945) was the first national convocation of the newly established PU. Although representatives from the Holy Synod had attended previous Congresses they declined from attending this one. Exarch Stefan commented that the emergence of serious differences and contradictions between the hierarchy of the BOC and the leadership of the PU made their attendance impossible. The introductory speech of D. Kotsaliev set the tone for the Congress:

> On 9 September our nation was removed from the chains of long years of oppression – political, economical and spiritual. From this date we begin to build a new freedom, an independent and democratic Bulgaria.

He then appealed for:

> Commitment to the historical and epoch-making changes... we are ready to understand correctly the spirit of the new time... we are capable of active participation in the construction of FF Bulgaria. Only then will we receive a place in the societal life of the new State.[27]

At its conclusion the Congress delegates sent a telegram to the National Committee of the FF assuring them that the Bulgarian clergy would support every effort of the government in the building of a new liberated and prosperous people's Bulgaria.[28]

The central question during the Congress, however, had not been whether or not to support the State, but rather to debate the future direction and actions of the PU. The question was raised by Georgi Bog-danov, Chairman of the Committee for Recommendations on Control and Reform of the BOC. He proposed that Board members of the PU be granted the same constitutional rights as bishops and that the lower clergy be granted a greater voice in the administration of the BOC, thus realising the demands of the FF that the BOC truly become "the people's church". It was explained that if accepted the changes meant that the BOC would be ordered and governed only by the lower clergy. The Holy Synod refused to enter into negotiations with the PU on this matter.[29] In agreement with these proposals the Congress elected a nine member governing council under new chairman, Georgi Bogdanov, who inci-dentally had been a member of the Communist Party since 1923.

Through early 1946 Bogdanov and the Board of the PU clarified their project to establish the BOC as a "democratic and progressive institute". To achieve this goal they proposed the creation of a Supreme Church Council, composed of parish clergy and laity, who would take away a large part of the functions of the Holy Synod.[30] The XXVIII Congress of the PU (26-27 July 1946) sanctioned these proposals by re-electing Bogdanov and his Board. By the end of 1946 the relationship between the PU and the Holy Synod had reached a critical point. In a report to the Central Committee of the Communist Party the PU charged the Holy Synod of holding "reactionary opinions" and of having nega-tive attitudes towards the more progressive clergy who they considered to be members of the Communist Party. The most prominent report, however, concerned Exarch Stefan, who was assessed by Bogdanov as a "pronounced reactionary, antagonistic to every reform in the Church and hostile to every good, democratic and progressive church employee."[31] The following year the PU tried unsuccessfully to reach an agreement with the Holy Synod on the democratisation of the BOC. During its XXIX Congress the PU delegates once again supported the demand for "complete democratisation of the BOC," in which the parish clergy and laity would be given "equal share in the government, organisation and life of the Church."[32]

However, after the Paris Peace Conference in 1947 Bulgaria's international and domestic political situation altered significantly, per-mitting the BCP freedom to construct a new Constitution which would permit the construction of a socialist society separating Church and State. In this evolving situation the Holy Synod agreed to work in coop-eration with the State authorities.[33] Therefore, although the PU continued to demonstrate complete loyalty to the policies of the government its raison d'être became defunct and thus became an organisation superfluous to requirement.

By decision of the Politburo the XXXII Congress of the PU in 1950 did not take place. The reason provided for its non-event was continued conflict between the PU and the Holy Synod.[34] In light of the new political situation the continuation of conflict succeeded in bringing about the removal of Georgi Bogdanov as the Chairman of the Union in 1951. His replacement, Ivan Yuliev, was elected with full agreement of the Holy Synod.[35] It is obvious that during his period in office Georgi Bogdanov had performed his assigned tasks to the letter but in the new political climate his leadership became unnecessary. From 1944 the PU had actively fought for the Communist Party within the structures of the BOC, to subject the Church to the new regime. When this problem was resolved in 1947 the need for the PU dissolved. The Priests' Union continued but deprived of its political raison d'être had to reinvent itself as a socialist cultural-educational organisation within the Church publishing reports, lectures and essays under the direction of the State authorities.

The Removal of Religious Education from Schools

One of the major steps the FF government took to precipitate the separation of Church and State was the removal of religious instruction from Bulgaria's school network. Ecclesiastical involvement in education, which had once been considered vital in establishing national awareness, particularly after the Liberation (1878) was now considered an anachronism opposed to the cultural development of a socialist Bulgaria and was therefore maligned by the communists. Immediately after the coup of 9 September 1944 the Ministry for People's Education (MPE) released a memo stating that religious instruction would be withdrawn from the school programme, as would the reading of prayers before and after school, arguing that "religious instruction is strongly divisive due to its reactionary aims and in the view of the FF authorities it appears to be an obstacle to the implementation of education."[36]

Although disapproving of these actions the Holy Synod did not react hastily to political manoeuvring. One of the reasons for their restraint was the guarantee given them within the Bulgarian Constitution, particularly article 80, which insured the Holy Synod special rights in the area of religious education in Bulgaria. Constitutionally the government could not prohibit religious instruction. Thus in response the MPE issued another memo in May 1945 entitled, 'Concerning the Optional Teaching of Religious Instruction in Primary Schools and Junior High Schools.' On paper this appeared to answer the concerns of the Church, as guaranteed in the Constitution. In practice, however, the new provisions continued to hinder the BOC. The Church was still deprived of teaching in secondary schools, the hours they could teach elsewhere were reduced, but the important word in the memo was 'optional' as this created a loophole for local school authorities, appointed by the FF. The word 'optional' enabled them to frustrate the implementation of religious education under the pretext of having other obligations to the students, therefore by-passing constitutional requirements.[37]

Despite this setback the Holy Synod received an unexpected bonus at the beginning of the following school year (1945/46) when they were informed that the BOC could use vacant school rooms for the purposes of religious education.[38] This resulted from the tolerant position towards the Church held by the newly appointed Minister of Education, Stoyan Kosturkov (29 September 1945 – 31 March 1945). He was a leading member of the Social Democratic Party and although a member of the FF coalition opposed the growing influence of the communists. The power struggle within the coalition government enabled the BOC to persevere with religious education during that school year. Unfortunately Stoyan Kosturkov was soon replaced as Minister of Education, under the pretence of failing health, by Dr. R. Angelov, a member of the Communist Party. With his induction communist policy was reinstated and religious instruction brought to an end with the proclamation of Edict No. 151 from 15 January 1946:

> Every Bulgarian citizen is free to confess any religion. To secure this freedom and to remove unavoidable conflict and disturbances in connection with religion and religious education I ORDER that schools are to remain completely neutral towards religion. Religious instruction, under whatever form shall not be permitted....[39]

Exarch Stefan voiced his opposition in a letter to Prime Minister Georgiev, demanding that Edict No. 151 be repealed. He also expressed hope that the government would respond to "the wishes of the Bulgarian people... to educate their children in religion."[40] Petko Stainov, Minister of Foreign Affairs and member of the Zveno Party (9 September 1944 – 31 March 1946) supported the BOC in this matter. In a letter to the

Prime Minister he shared this opinion: "I consider the undertakings of the MPE to be wrong and harmful and must be revoked or modified."[41]

In an attempt to silence the growing voice of opposition the State security services characterised Church education and clergy before the National Committee of the FF in this manner:

> They actively work for the conversion of school age children.... The pulpit is used as a platform to address their criticisms against the FF and their policies, reinforcing this with God's words and stating that the authorities are acting against God. They speak against our Young Pioneer Organisation. They are turning Christian society into a reactionary force....[42]

Thus when the National Committee of the FF convened to consider matters surrounding Edict No. 151 they came to the conclusion that religion was totally incompatible with education and agreed that it had no place in Bulgarian schools.[43] The opposition of the BOC, the Education Minister and the Foreign Minister were either ignored, or the person in question removed from the equation. Thus when Exarch Stefan met with Prime Minister Georgiev in July 1946 he reported back to the Synod that the Church had no option but to accept the decision of the government on the removal of religious education from the Bulgarian school network.[44]

In their increased efforts to separate religion from societal life the FF government also introduced a new law on marriage. This made civil marriage ceremonies the only legally recognised method of union, at the expense of the Church service (March 1946). It appears that as the Communist Party consolidated power within the coalition the process to separate Church and State increased. Thereafter the government took control of church buildings which were used for charitable purposes and then removed every aspect of charitable work from the jurisdiction of the church. In this manner the FF authorities, dominated by the Communist Party, applied pressure on the BOC to subordinate it to the greater aims of the Party. It is important to emphasise that the aim was not to destroy but to transform the BOC.

Georgi Dimitrov and the Bulgarian Orthodox Church

The importance of the BOC for the Communist Party was explained in a speech given by BCP leader Georgi Dimitrov from 1946 in which he laid the foundations for the socialist State's acceptance and even support of the Church as a national institution. On 26 May 1946 the millennial commemoration of the death of St. Ivan Rilski was celebrated in Rila Monastery. The Bulgarian Communist Party leader and Chairman of the Central Committee of the FF, Georgi Dimitrov, participated in this event by giving a speech entitled, 'The Bulgarian Church's Role and Tasks.'[45] After the initial political machinations of the coalition authorities Dimitrov's speech set the agenda for future relations between the State and the BOC. In view of the length of his speech, which bore the mark of his time in the Soviet Union where he served as General Secretary of the Comintern (1935-1943), this section will concentrate on the significance of the speech for the BOC's relationship with socialism. It is here for the first time that we comprehend the State's distinction between the Church as a historical and a national institution.

A major section of Dimitrov's speech concentrated on the significance of the BOC within Bulgarian history. He honoured the Church for its historical efforts in preserving national self-awareness in the Bulgarian people during the era of Ottomanization and Hellenization, stressing that there would be no democratic Bulgaria if the BOC had not protected the nation from oblivion. For this reason he expressed the gratitude of both the FF and the Communists to the national Church of Bulgaria.[46] After praising the BOC's historical mission he turned to the contemporary situation and its demands on the Church and discussed the long-term expectations regarding the relationship between Church and State. He demanded total obedience from the Church in following the new political direction stating that by doing so the Church would live up to its patriotic past. He challenged the Church to support the government's plan to abolish the monarchy and establish a republican constitution. For this reason he ordered the ecclesiastical hierarchy to desist from praying for the monarchy during the liturgy.[47] Moving on from this point Dimitrov delivered his expectation that the BOC would become the true church of the people, accepting the republican and progressive policies of the State. He stated that he did not want only declarations of loyalty from the BOC but action.[48]

The Communist Party leader's congenial tone then faltered as he criticised the members of the Holy Synod for being people with 'ossified minds and deeply conservative views,' who needed to move forward with the times. To make himself unambiguously clear he alluded to the fate of the Russian Church at the time of the October Revolution, suggesting that if the leaders of the Church had supported the people rather than the counterrevolution the Russian Church would not have had to endure its unfortunate fate. To emphasise the point further Dimitrov concluded his speech by addressing himself directly to the hierarchy of the Bulgarian Church, encouraging them to learn from the Russian experience for only by doing so would there be unity between Church and State.[49]

Dimitrov's praise and acknowledgement of the BOC's national significance determined a pattern of acceptance and even support for the BOC in comparison with other religious institutions. He also clearly stated, however, the limitations which the Church hierarchy would have to operate under or face disastrous consequences. The speech revealed that as a religious institution the BOC was presently not in harmony with the aims of the new government and particularly the communist's who held power within the coalition. Within this seminal discourse the BOC would find its *modus vivendi* based on Dimitrov's acknowledgement of the church's national and historical mission.

The 'Dimitrov' Constitution (4 December 1947)

Throughout the period of coalition rule the government had worked in accordance with the National Constitution (Turnovo, 1879). In preserving the Constitution they required to adhere to Article 39, according to which the State in its relationship to the Church was subordinate to the Holy Synod. Consequently the BCP avoided raising the question of separation of Church and State favouring to conduct its policies toward "putting the BOC in the employ of the FF authorities."[50] Nevertheless, following the referendum on the abolishment of the monarchy and the establishment of republican government (September 1946) the FF government was able to candidly place on their agenda the constitutional separation of Church and State.[51]

The Holy Synod attempted to impede separation by seeking guarantees which would regulate relations between Church and State in any constitutional review. The Synod saw no objective reason to separate Church and State, however, as this was a probability they wanted the new Constitution to preserve the rights and freedoms of the Church.[52] In connection with this the Holy Synod convened an extraordinary Church Assembly in Rila Monastery (1 November 1946) to discuss the draft bill of the new Constitution. The delegates accepted a report to be sent on behalf of the BOC to the Bulgarian National Assembly. It emphasised the historical service of the BOC to the Bulgarian nation and State and pointed to the words of Prime Minister Georgiev who had defined the BOC as "the true national Church," and to the comments of Georgi Dimitrov when he expressed the gratitude of both the FF and the Communist Party to the patriotic clergy of the BOC.[53] The report proposed making textual alterations to the draft bill: To amend Article 63, the article of separation, by adding to it that the BOC was still acknowledged by the State to be a legal entity in public law[54]; secondly, the Synod proposed that "the BOC should benefit from the liberty of internal self-government, in cult, in doctrine and in finance," and then contradicted this by suggesting that the State should assist in subsidising the Church.[55]

The report was signed by every Bulgarian bishop and delivered to Georgi Dimitrov. Afterwards Foreign Minister Georgi Kulishov promised that the Church report would be examined by the Parliamentary Commission editing the Constitution. On 11 March 1947 the chairman of the Parliamentary Commission stated that any attempt to preserve the old Constitution, according to which the dominant faith in Bulgaria was Eastern Orthodoxy, would contradict the new Constitution concerning its guarantees of freedom of conscience and religious liberty. Therefore every proposal put forward by the BOC was rejected and on 4 December 1947 the new 'Dimitrov Constitution' was unanimously accepted officially separating Church and State.

By the end of this first phase of communist control the government had secured the internal autonomy of the BOC, not for the benefit of the Church but rather to allow the State free hand to intervene in Church matters without external interference. Manipulating people loyal to the government into positions of ecclesiastical authority the communists were able to pass laws on education and marriage facilitating the move towards full separation. The most important development for Church-State relations was the introduction of the 'Dimitrov' Constitution whereby the Bulgarian Communist Party gained complete control of the FF and freedom to implement Stalinist inspired policy in Bulgaria.

THE STALINIST REGIME (1947-1953)

The new Constitution launched the second era of the communist regime. After receiving international recognition of its one-party State a series of tough measures against the BOC were designed not only to press home its separation but to make it completely subordinate to the State. The fresh wave of repression which surged against the clergy, ending with the removal of Stefan from the Exarchal throne, encapsulates the concerted campaign of the authorities to turn the BOC into a compliant cadaver. Two documents from the Party archives illustrate the State's intentions towards the BOC during this period and explain the decision of the Holy Synod to support the communist regime. The first is a Report from General Yonko Panov, Deputy Minister of the Interior in charge of State Security from 1949; the second is the Report of Anton Yugov, Minister of the Interior, to the Central Committee of the BCP. The Reports discussed the political state of affairs in the BOC, specifically the attitudes of the Holy Synod towards the communist government and proposed how to deal with the situation.

Repression of the Clergy

From 1944 to 1953 three separate waves of repression rose against the clergy. The first had been the anti-fascist purge which occurred over the first twelve months of coalition rule. Apart from the many priests who were murdered during the chaos of that period, a further one hundred and fifty-two were sentenced by the People's Court, thirteen sentenced to death and another thirteen to life imprisonment. During the same period forty-five members of the Holy Synod were arrested, twenty-five disappearing without trace.[56]

A second and very different wave of repression hit the clergy from 1948 onwards. This took the form of infiltrating people loyal to the government into senior positions of Church administration. For example, an edict from the Directorate of Religious Affairs (DRA) withdrew authority from Bishops to appoint their own deputies, making it compulsory for those deputies to be appointed by the government.[57] The Synod's attempts to reach a compromise over these appointments, "to combine with the DRA" failed because the State wanted prerogative on who be appointed to these influential Church administrative positions. D. Iliev, Director of the DRA, commented that these structures had in the past concealed hardened enemies of the People's Republic of Bulgaria and for this reason the Ministry of the Interior viewed the question of deputies as one of the issues which would determine either a good or bad relationship between the BOC and the National Council. Iliev cited, as an example of a good working relationship between Church and State, the words of Russian Patriarch Sergi from 16 July 1927:

> Church workers who do not approve of the relationship between Church and State, should abandon ecclesiastical life, and not be an obstacle to the life of the Russian Orthodox Church.[58]

The DRA informed the Synod that the appointment of deputy's would be executed through State administrative channels as the Church had previously refused to accept their decision. This obstructive stance resulted in over 200 members of the clergy being accused of opposition activities against the People's Republic of Bulgaria. One of those accused, Father Ilia Lupanov responded:

> I have forty-two years of service as a teacher, parish priest and Bishop's Deputy. Throughout that time I have been an active leader with the responsibility to instruct other Church leaders. From then until now I have not belonged to any political organisation. I have always been loyal to the ruling authorities. Until 9 September 1944 I served, as did every citizen, as an employee of the fascist powers, I never spoke against it, but neither did I insult the partisan movement.

Father Lupanov concluded by saying that from September 1944 on he had been totally loyal to the People's Republic.[59] Many of those accused during this wave of repression, such as Father Lupanov, were later released without charge. The stigma of accusation, however, was never forgotten as those clergy were branded anti-communist and pro-fascist. In consequence they were denied the opportunity to work and were thus fated to a life of poverty and isolation.

A third wave of political repression commenced in 1950 affecting every level of clergy but targeted the ecclesiastical hierarchy. This was applied by placing the administrative services of the Church under governmental control, including the allocation of pensions. As a consequence not every member of the clergy who reached the age of retirement automatically received their pension. Individual cases were brought before a Pension Commission (1950-1953), part of the Regional People's Council of Workers. The archives show that during this period thirty-three Archpriests, eleven eparchy Treasurers, ten Archimandrites, eight Abbots and five Protosingels were denied their pensions.[60]

Investigation of the archives also revealed documents testifying to judicial forms of repression against individual Metropolitans. Take the predicament of Philaret, Metropolitan of Lovech who was arrested in April 1948 after a financial audit of his eparchy discovered a number of discrepancies. The archival evidence reveals, however, that his arrest and imprisonment were no more than a subterfuge to secure his vote in an attempt to remove Exarch Stefan.[61] This research also uncovered twenty-four instances of fabricated criminal charges of black market-eering against members of the clergy, for purchasing the likes of flour, wax and other items connected with the preparation of the Eucharist or the making of candles. The records do not explain that the State allow-ance granted to the parish clergy was simply not sufficient to purchase materials necessary to exercise the church's most fundamental acts – the Liturgy and the Eucharist. In this predicament priests were forced to solve the problem by purchasing the necessary goods on the black mar-ket. An example of this was the arrest of Father Ivan Hadjiev from Stara Zagora who was sentenced to ten years imprisonment and fined 100,000 leva for purchasing materials to manufacture Church candles.

These acts of repression were intended to undermine the confidence of the church and its clergy. It became abundantly clear that if clergy did not toe the communist line they would become like pariah in society. The subjugation of the Church to the desires of the State clearly took place on many different social and political levels – Church and State separation, the degradation of Christian ceremonies, such as marriage and the humiliation of its clergy.

The Expulsion of Exarch Stefan (6 September 1948)

The coup to remove Exarch Stefan represents one of the most important acts of repression in the history of the BOC. The Bulgarian public were first notified of Stefan's 'retirement' in an announcement published in *Tsurkoven vestnik* on 21 September 1948 which stated:

> The Holy Synod of the BOC announces that on the 6th of this month, His Beatitude Exarch Stefan by word of mouth and in writing handed in his retirement to the Holy Synod... after considering the condition of his health he has retired from his heavy load and after giving important consideration to his spotless character, we unanimously decided to accept his retirement and release him from his duties as Exarch of Bulgaria and Metropolitan of Sofia.[62]

Until the opening of the BCP archives this event had engendered differing explanations, but today the archival documents provide us the opportunity to investigate the event thoroughly. Although Stefan's appointment as Exarch appears to have been engineered by the FF authorities, criticism of him arose soon after his election. Georgi Bogdanov, Chairman of the Priests' Union, regularly reported on the Exarch's activities to the Central Committee of the Communist Party. For example, only three months after Stefan's inauguration Bogdanov reported:

> Towards the end of the month a delegation of the BOC will depart for the Soviet Union. The delegation will be led by His Beatitude Exarch Stefan, who will be accompanied by a number of ecclesiastical personnel. The personnel who the Exarch has chosen to accompany him are well known in the Church community, as being people with anti-communist and pro-fascist sympathies who hold negative attitudes towards the Soviet Union... I reckon that those selected are not only unsuitable, but their departure for the Soviet Union is a provocation to the government of the Fatherland Front, and thus towards the Soviet Union.[63]

In a later report from 12 December 1946 G. Bogdanov commented:

> Recently I reported that Church leaders were not giving the more progressive clergy any opportunity to advance, thus giving evidence of and demonstrating their reactionary opinions and hostile attitude towards those they know are members of our Party. In this situation the head of the BOC Exarch Stefan has been revealed as a pronounced reactionary opponent of every reform in the Church and is hostile in every respect to democratic and progressive Church employees... His conduct was particularly aggressive during a session of the Holy Synod, when before every bishop he declared that we should purge, not the good bishops and clergy, but the progressive and left-wing clergy who have lessened discipline in the Church and for this need to be judged. Here he is meddling with the message of our beloved leader and teacher, Chairman of the Party, Dr. Georgi Dimitrov.[64]

As a result of these reports Exarch Stefan was put under close surveillance by the security services who quickly assessed that the Exarch was an enemy of the Party.[65] Despite the incriminatory accusations of the reports they were never acted upon during the period 1944-1947, probably due to the unsettled domestic and international position of Bulgaria. However, following the signing of the Paris Peace Treaty and the introduction of the new Constitution surveillance on Stefan was intensified. Another report from the Chairman of the Priests' Union exemplifies the intrusiveness of the surveillance: "According to reliable information the Exarch is suffering from an incurable disease. It has advanced so quickly that it is creating a lot of confusion within his staff."[66] It is reported that Exarch Stefan departed for Karlovy Vary in Czechoslovakia in July 1947 where he remained for over two months. There is no information to suggest that this trip was in any way connected to illness. On the contrary it is recorded that during his journey he met with Church leaders from Yugoslavia, Hungary and Czechoslovakia to discuss a forthcoming Pan-Orthodox Consultation in Moscow.

Intensified government pressure upon members of the Holy Synod created a division among the Metropolitans of the Church. The most influential of the Metropolitans were members of the 'God and Bulgaria' group, known for their devotion towards Bulgaria and their uncompromising attitude towards the faith; they included Exarch Stefan, Mihail of Russe, Boris of Nevrokop, Sofroni of Turnovo, Kliment of Star Zagora and Neofit of Vidin. The progressive Metropolitans influenced by the Communist Party were Paisii of Vratsa, Kiril of Plovdiv, Josef of Varna, Philaret of Lovech and Nikodim of Sliven.[67] Archival sources suggest that there was also a division of attitude towards Stefan at governmental level. Documentation reveals that Prime Minister G. Dimitrov was inclined to support the head of the BOC whereas Foreign Minister V. Kolarov was insistent that Stefan be removed immediately.[68]

As the politicians deliberated Stefan's fate the Orthodox Churches prepared for a Pan-Orthodox Conference to be held in Moscow (8-18 July 1948). Among the important topics to be discussed at the conference was the attitude of the Orthodox Church towards the Orthodox Ecumenical movement. Exarch Stefan was one of its founding members and actively promoted the view that the Slavonic Orthodox Churches needed to be more involved in the movement worldwide, particularly in the work of the WCC in Geneva. As preparations commenced Stefan was criticised by Russian Patriarch Aleksi for the BOC's position on ecumenism.[69] The Bulgarian political authorities extracted a promise from Stefan that he would support the position of the Moscow Patriarchate (Moscow against – Constantinople for WCC involvement). However, upon his arrival in Moscow, in conversation with Metropolitan Krutitski, Stefan shared that he had prepared a report in defence of the ecumenical cause.[70]

Stefan's change of heart provoked a panicked response at Church and government levels. Stefan was immediately subjected to pressure by the Russians to oppose ecumenism.[71] Unable to alter his position Bulgarian Foreign Minister V. Kolarov sent Stefan a telegram stating that the Bulgarian government would restore the BOC to the status of Patriarchate if he refrained from supporting the ecumenical cause. Prime Minister Dimitrov, who was undergoing medical treatment in Moscow, also met with Stefan and by enticing him with the title of Patriarch succeeded in changing Stefan's position.[72] Nevertheless, it would appear that this was the final act which cost Stefan his position as Exarch.

While Stefan was being offered the Patriarchate in Moscow, D. Iliev director of the DRA met with Synodal members Paisii of Vratsa, Boris of Nevrokop, Sofroni of Turnovo and Mihail of Russe, all of whom objected to this proposal. D. Iliev commented on this meeting: "It was interesting to observe the leaders of the Holy Synod as one stand against the declaration of Exarch Stefan for Patriarch. Their statements reveal quite clearly the discord at Stefan being offered this position, in view of the trouble which he has caused in Moscow."[73] Iliev skilfully manoeuvred the heated discussions on Stefan onto reasons why he should be removed from office. Therefore when Exarch Stefan returned to Bulgaria he was faced with a *fait accompli*.

A few days after his return from Moscow the Holy Synod emerged with a decision on the 'retirement' of Stefan on the grounds of his poor health. Following this on 10 September 1948 the Politburo accepted decision No. 52 which stated: "We accept the retirement of the Exarch, his deputy the Metropolitan of Ruse will remain in charge for the time being."[74] In this manner the Communist Party found a means of removing Stefan without the evident engagement of the State. Investigation of the archival sources reveals, however, that pressed by the government and betrayed by his colleagues, Stefan was forced to step down.

In another historical and political era Stefan may have been recognised as one of the great Bulgarian Church leaders. He had been a true patriot, desirous to see Bulgaria play a political role in Europe, as a leading ecumenist he wanted the Bulgarian Church to be internationally involved, as a faithful Orthodox believer he had supported both the Russian and Constantinople Patriarchates while at the same time fighting to secure the autonomy of his own Church. He had been the main obstacle hindering the infiltration of people loyal to the communist government into positions of influence in the BOC and he had been the figurehead defending the Church's right to self-government. Now that obstacle had been removed the Communist Party seized the opportunity to assert its influence fully upon the Holy Synod therefore enabling the government to control the BOC from within.

Yonko Panov and Anton Yugov's Report (August 1949)

The following section presents two documents which remained confidential until the fall of Todor Zhivkov's government on 10 November 1989. They are crucial in comprehending fully this second period of communist rule as they discuss in detail the political state of affairs with the BOC and propose how to deal with the Church. They were authored by Yonko Panov, Deputy Minister of the Interior in charge of State Security and his superior Anton Yugov, Minister of the Interior. Both documents were later combined to form one report which was presented to the Secretariat of the Central Committee of the Politburo (BCP).

After the successes of previous purges on the Church and with the removal of its "strong man" [Exarch Stefan], the report suggested that there should be a further purge directed against the Holy Synod, removing the strongest opponents of the regime from Church leadership, particularly Mikhail of Russe, Sofroni of Turnovo and Neofit of Vidin. This was intended to frighten the remainder of the Synod into submitting wholly to the demands of the State. After this initial purge of Church hierarchy it was proposed that the eparchy's of the BOC be reduced from eleven to three in number. This was by far the most radical part of the proposed plan intended to make the remaining Metropolitans totally compliant to the wishes of the State. It is unclear from the sources investigated whether these proposals were leaked to the Holy Synod or not, it is clear that they were never fully acted upon. Perhaps they were only intended to instil fear because soon after important changes did occur within the Synod. Mikhail of Russe, who had been *pro tem* President of the Synod 'resigned' and was replaced by Paisii of Vratsa. However, he also proved to be uncooperative and was ousted in December 1950. Kiril, Metropolitan of Plovdiv then took control of the BOC and was rewarded for his obedience by becoming the first Patriarch of the Bulgarian Church since the Ottoman conquest in 1393.

Secondly, it was proposed that stricter judicial measures be taken against the Church in order to transform the BOC into a truly socialist Church. In conjunction with this the Law of Confessions was introduced on 24 September 1949. The introduction of this law was yet another stage of separation and subjugation, isolating the Church not only from

Bulgarian society but from every international religious institution as well. The law re-emphasised the State monopoly on education and forbade the BOC from organising any activities which involved children (art. 20). The publishing activities of the Church were put under the strictest controls of the State with every sermon, speech or parish letter having to be approved (art. 15). Every appointment and dismissal to and from the Church was dependent upon the decision of the Directorate of Religious Affairs (DRA) (art. 12). The Church was prohibited from sending any of its students abroad to further their education and every domestic theological student had to be vetted by the DRA (art. 14). Any contact between the BOC and foreign religious institutions also required to pass through the DRA (art. 22) and finally no donations would be accepted from abroad without the permission of the DRA (art. 24).

The Law of Confessions enabled the DRA to carry out State directives, to place clergymen loyal to the regime into key positions in the Church; for example, the General Secretary of the Holy Synod, Director of Culture and Education, Director of Finance, Director of Publications, Editor of *Tsurkoven vestnik*, the Rectors of the Seminaries and Theological Institute and the Abbots of Rila, Bachkovo and Troyan Monasteries.[75] As well as infiltrating people loyal to the State into the Church the report also recommended that the Party "strongly persuade" some of the Metropolitans at the top level to work for them. The author uses the Bulgarian words *obraboti* (обработи) and *podraboti* (подработи), suggesting the cultivation of chosen individuals to become agents of the State. These agents would then be able to manipulate those loyal and progressive Church workers into positions of authority.

In the light of these proposals did the Holy Synod have any option but to "join in the hymnology of the Communist Party?"[76] Whether they condoned, tolerated or compromised is of no real consequence, the truth of matter is that the Synod were faced with their ultimate dilemma, either accept being an instrument of the communist government or watch the Church be destroyed. The proposed purges would have taken place and the eparchy's would have been reduced and placed under the control of communist sycophants. The ultimatum which faced Kiril as he guided the BOC was to accept the brutal conditions but keep an Orthodox believer at its head, or resign the Church into the hands of the atheistic State. The Panov-Yugov report discloses the harsh reality of life for the BOC during this second period of Communist Party rule in Bulgaria – a period where the Church hierarchy accepted that they had no choice.

The Restoration of the Patriarchate (10 May 1953)

The restoration of patriarchal dignity to the BOC was a peculiar end to the evolution of Church-State relationships following the sternness of this second phase of communist rule. However, there had been raised expectations within the BOC, especially after the election of a new Exarch and the lifting of the schism that the restoration of the Church's Patriarchal title would ensue. As early as 1946 the government had explored the advantages and disadvantages which would have followed the restoration of the Patriarchate. The DRA were divided in opinion. Some considered it necessary, in accordance with Canon Law, to seek the approval of the Ecumenical Patriarchate and others such as Alexander Chuchulain said there was neither historical nor canonical obstacle which would require the involvement of foreign interference in accomplishing this act. He reckoned that the Church should not make any independent decision on this question because it was a purely political question which needed only the consent of the government.[77]

Before any decision was taken on the question of restoration G. Bogdanov, Chairman of the Priests' Union, suggested that it would be prudent to introduce new Exarchal Statutes, produced in conjunction with and acceptable to the new political regime.[78] Towards the end of 1946 the Holy Synod sought the approval of the government to convene a National Church Council as this would be the only means of altering the Exarchal Statutes to accord with the spirit of the new times. The request was refused, however, on the grounds that the introduction of the new Bulgarian Constitution was imminent and would affect the Statutes of the Church. For this reason they suggested that it would be better to await its legislation.[79]

The Holy Synod published a statement in *Tsurkoven vestnik* (15 February 1947) that immediately after the new Constitution had been accepted they would convene a National-Church Council to approve any alterations to their Statutes. This statement raised alarm bells in the communist ranks. Thus, on 25 February a special session of the National Council of the FF was convened where I. Harizanov responded to the statement of the BOC. His comments concentrated on the forthcoming Church Council and any eventual changes they would make to the Exarchal Statutes. According to Harizanov, the decisions of the Church Council would be provoked by the conviction of the Metropolitans that "the present time was opportune for the reorganisation of the Church and Statutes, but obviously in their own way and for their own advantage."

He therefore suggested that it was necessary to prepare for this eventuality.[80] In Harizanov's opinion an accumulation of power in the hands of the Synod was dangerous due to the fact that at the beginning of 1947 there was less then a fifth of Orthodox clergy under the influence of the FF and another fifth were considered to be 'active reactionaries' against the FF, the great danger being that the FF had no direct control over the majority of the clergy. For this reason he suggested that the National Church Council be set for a later date and organised by the FF not by the Holy Synod.

Thus for reasons of State security the decision to restore the Patriarchate was postponed until the BOC was completely under the control of the State. Edict No. 29 of the Council of Ministers passed on 17 September 1948 charged the Ministry of Foreign Affairs with completing any necessary alterations to the Exarchal Statutes with a view to democratising the BOC.[81] It was the retirement of Exarch Stefan, however, that signified the beginning of a new stage in the development of relations between the State and the BOC. After securing control of the Church and its hierarchy the Politburo agreed to re-commence talks on Patriarchal restoration.[82] However, now Moscow and the Russian Orthodox Church also supported this action, in an effort to raise the authority of the BOC thereby enabling it to fight alongside other Orthodox Churches against the Vatican and the World Council of Churches in Geneva.[83]

When Foreign Minister, Mincho Neichev, reported considerable progress in the democratisation of the BOC, at the beginning of 1951, the government considered that the time was auspicious for restoring the Patriarchal title to the BOC. It is significant that the date of the restoration's approval by the Bulgarian Politburo on 3 January 1951 preceded the decision of the Third People's Church Congress by two years (10 May 1953). The decision fulfilled the heartfelt aspirations of the Holy Synod restoring the church's Patriarchal title after 560. However, the restoration had serious consequences for the Church. The reinstatement of its Patriarchal title had been a purely political decision and although the decision was supported by the Orthodox Churches of other socialist countries it was rejected by the Ecumenical Patriarchate, a situation which lasted until 22 July 1961 when the Bulgarian Patriarchate was universally accepted. For this reason the BOC actually became a subsidiary organ of the State, recruited into the communist structure, despite its constitutional separation. Thus, by the end of the second period of communist rule, with its separation and subordination secured, if the

BOC had a role to play in Bulgarian society it would be dictated by the Communist Party.

THE POST-STALINIST PHASE (1953-1989)

The induction of Kiril to the patriarchal throne on 10 May 1953 coincided with the death of Stalin and marked the third and final phase in Church-State relations during communism. Although there was a moderation of Stalin's model of socialism during this period, this had no bearing upon relations with the Church. The persecution of church personnel and the judicial and constitutional acts separating Church from State during the first two periods of communist rule had achieved their purpose and now under its complete authority Church and State developed an equilibrium, the State administering and the BOC obeying the rules. Patriarch Kiril commented on this relationship: "We render to Caesar the things that are Caesar's and to God the things that are God's, that is rendering to God faith and to the State complete loyalty."[84]

In this spirit of cooperation the BOC, for the remainder of the era, became an instrument of communist propaganda. One of the major questions to arise during this period was how the BOC should carry out its propagandist functions for the State. The Directorate of Religious Affairs defined these functions as: being fully supportive of the State; for all clergy to be members of the FF or the Communist Party; to support the nationalisation of private industries and encourage collectivisation[85]; to acknowledge from the pulpit that the State is above the Church; to oppose anti-communist and anti-Russian propaganda from the pulpit and finally to place portraits of government officials in the Church as well as icons and promote loyalty and affection towards Bulgarian State leaders. These responsibilities became the *modus vivendi* for the BOC under Kiril. In particular the Patriarch promoted "the way of tolerance" and highlighted "patriotic service" as a common ground where Church and State could join forces to cultivate patriotism and pride in Bulgaria's history, heroes and achievements.[86] However, Kiril's *modus vivendi* signified an elementary variation in the BOC's reason for being and also revealed a major difference in the principles of Kiril and Exarch Stefan. For Stefan the Church first and foremost was in service to God within the confines of the State; for Kiril the Church's patriotic service to the State was faith in God.

Following the death of Kiril on 7 March 1971, Maxim Metropolitan of Lovech was appointed to the patriarchal throne. His position had been approved by the Communist Party leadership before the death of Patriarch Kiril and following a period of political machination the Holy Synod was coerced into accepting the government choice.[87] It appears that the BCP preferred the compromising attitude of Maxim and the fact that he was younger than any other candidate could promote longer term stability within the Church. Maxim therefore brought nothing new to the Church, indeed his ingratiating leadership followed the course plotted by Kiril, echoing the political proclamations of the socialists.

Reinterpreting National History

Throughout the communist era the BOC was held in a position which distinguished it from other religious confessions within Bulgarian society. The differentiating factor was the overlap of identity between church and nation through Bulgarian history. This determined the Church's discriminatory treatment under communism but was also reflected in the politically and ideologically controlled academic research of the period. An example of this can be observed in the re-interpretation of the BOC's historical role, particularly during the period of Ottoman domination, which was used as a justifying principle in government policy relating to its contemporary Turkish-Muslim population. The conception of the BOC as the preserver of Bulgarian religious-national identity, which prevented total assimilation into Ottoman society became a key theme of politically biased academic research. Emerging from this interpretation the *continuity theory* developed which considered that the BOC under Ottoman rule was the creator of Bulgarian national and cultural continuity. Fundamental to this concept was the communist researcher's acceptance and accentuation of the nineteenth century *catastrophe theory*, which depicted the centuries under Ottoman control as years of Islamic despotism when they allegedly committed genocide, persecuted Christians and coerced their conversion to Islam. Common to both the *continuity* and *catastrophe theories* was the understanding that the Ottoman Conquest resulted in a dramatic reduction in Bulgarian national identity.[88]

Political control of the religious and historical sciences in Bulgaria made history an ideological discipline under the Communist Party, designed to defend and promote socialist principles.[89] An example of how this operated can be found in the fourteen-volume work *History of Bulgaria* which first appeared in 1979. This project was initiated by the Tenth Bulgarian Party Congress (May 1968) and authored by only the most trusted scholars who had the confidence of the Party and who agreed to follow its ideological guidelines: to characterise Bulgaria's history as a heroic sequence of events from ancient times to today, marked by the struggle against slavery and oppression and by social progress.[90] For the purposes of this research we shall concentrate on Volume Four of *History of Bulgaria* (1983) entitled *Ottoman Rule 15-18 centuries* edited by Hristo Gandev, Svetana Georgieva and Bistra Svetkova.

The influence of the *continuity* and *catastrophe theories* were clearly portrayed in this volume as even from the introduction the patriotic and heroic character of the Bulgarian people are contrasted with the violence and brutality of Ottoman rule. Indeed from the outset the editors rejected any view which described the Ottomans as benign to their Christian subjects as being due to a poor reading of original sources.[91] Negativity towards Islam proceeded through the volume, characterising it as a fanatical, aggressive and repressive regime with a systematic ongoing policy of forced conversion.[92] Bulgaria's demographic disaster is described in detail and attempts to prove the assimilation process.[93] From the ashes of destruction the researchers emphasise the bravery of the Bulgarian Church in maintaining and developing Bulgarian language, culture and history. However, the political research which controlled *History of Bulgaria* was blighted by two fundamental shortcomings. The interpretation of five continuous centuries of violently enforced Islamic conversion did not explain why the Ottomans abjectly failed in their assimilation policy; secondly, the distorted depiction of Ottoman rule in Bulgaria which painted a black and white picture of hostility between Christianity and Islam was simply erroneous. The evidence gathered during the compiling of this research would suggest that the archival evidence presented in Chapter Two of this thesis proposes a more accurate interpretation of history, that being, although periods of violence did occur the five hundred years of Ottoman rule in Bulgaria were distinguished not by violence but rather by toleration towards the Christian community which allowed Bulgarian society to develop and prosper through the Ottoman period into the era of National Revival.

It would be a mistake to consider all Bulgarian historiography from this period to be being politically misinterpreted. Take for example the

work of Svetana Georgieva from 1979 where she presents three varia-
tions on the character of Ottoman rule in Bulgaria: the first view derived
from Turkish research views the Ottomans as liberators of the Balkan
peoples, freeing them from feudal oppression enabling them to live in
order and social harmony; secondly she delivered the interpretation
exhorted by the *continuity* and *catastrophe theories*; and thirdly she proposed a compromise that views the moment of conquest as violent,
drastically altering Bulgaria's historical and cultural direction, but also
in time bringing stability and prosperity to Bulgarian society.[94] Another
example of critical analysis from this period can be found in the work of
Antonina Zhelyazkova. She concluded that Islamisation during the
Ottoman period was the result of a progressively slow religious change
rather than a continuously violent assimilation process.[95] However, as
her conclusion went against the view of the Party as promulgated in
History of Bulgaria Zhelyazkova's work remained unpublished until
after the fall of the communist regime. Therefore those who were critical
of the Party's historical-political paradigm were simply ignored and
remained unpublished until after the communist era.

Historical analysis based on the principles of Marxist-Leninism
therefore faced no criticism or opposition in creating a generally false
interpretation of Bulgarian Church history. This re-interpretation was the
perception which the communist government wanted to instil within
Bulgarian 'Christian' society.[96] The key to understanding that perception
lay in the State's national ideological interpretation of religion and
nation, connecting Bulgarian national history and the BOC, to form and
justify its confrontational religious policy to separate Muslim religious
and national identity. Although the BOC does not seem to have been
intricately involved in drawing up these historical conclusions, they did
not oppose them. Quite the opposite, the Church in its role of 'patriotic
service' embraced them and in its efforts to survive the communist era
adopted them within its *modus vivendi*. Its role as faith provider, educator and enabler had been denied them within society and now the Orthodox Church readily took on and evangelised its role as Bulgarian
national and cultural saviour in an attempt to preserve a prominent role
within society.

The Process of National Rebirth[97]

Responding to socialist inspired misinterpretations of history the late 1970's and early 1980's witnessed Bulgaria's Muslim population become the object of a massive assimilation campaign that focussed on changing their names from Arabic-Turkish to Slavic-Bulgarian. In this manner the authorities attempted to obliterate any remaining vestige of Ottoman rule in Bulgaria. During this period almost one million people, an eighth of the Bulgarian population were forced to change their names.[98]

By the end of the Ottoman era there had remained within the independent Bulgarian State a sizeable Muslim minority amounting to between a fifth and a quarter of the population.[99] Bulgarian governments conducted a policy of hegemonic control in an attempt to maintain the supremacy of the ethnic Bulgarian Christian population, thus keeping the 'Turkish' Muslim minority in an inferior position. This control did not attempt to integrate or assimilate the minority into the majority. In the long term it appears that the future of the Muslim population was envisaged mainly in terms of emigration to Turkey.[100] When the communists came to power in 1944 similar policies ensued. They attempted to divest themselves of as much of the Muslim population as possible forcing 150,000 across the Turkish border between 1949-1950 and the remainder of the population were given a level of cultural autonomy, foreseeing this as a step towards integrating the Muslim minority into a transnational communist society.[101] This was expected to come about through gradual cultural and economic fusion over an indeterminate period. By the late 1970's these policies had failed to fulfil the expectations of the communist leadership. These factors lead Todor Zhivkov, Chairman of the Communist Party, to adopt an enforced renaming policy. This campaign included more than simply changing names: Turkish language media, press, radio and television were banned; speaking Turkish in public places was forbidden; mosques were closed down and celebration of Ramadan was outlawed.[102] This resulted in a massive wave of emigration during 1989 when a further 300,000 Bulgarian Muslims fled to Turkey.

One of the most important forces behind this process derived from the findings of the research for *History of Bulgaria*. G. Filipov, President of the Council of Ministers referred to this fact in a speech where he cited *History of Bulgaria* to describe Bulgaria's tragic fate under Ottoman slavery, which he stated was a period when the people were violently and systematically Turkified and Islamicised. This fact was intended to signify the governmental belief that the majority of the Bulgarian State's contemporary Muslim population were actually ancestors of those forcibly converted Christians. He continued to argue that the Islamic community would only find their true destiny by returning to their Bulgarian roots, accepting the name changing policy and liberating themselves from their religion.[103] This argument was accentuated when the *catastrophe theory* was advanced by Petur Petrov, one of the Bulgarian historians directly implicated in the re-naming campaign of the 1980's. He re-popularised the *Chronicle of Metodi Draginov* (see Chapter 2), using it to categorically demonstrate the enforced conversion of the predecessors of Bulgaria's Islamicised population thus proving they belonged to the Bulgarian and not the Turkish race.[104] However, the justification behind Filipov's impassioned speech and Petrov's misinterpretation was eliminated on 10 January 1990 when the Bulgarian News Bureau published a declaration undersigned by sixty historians who were/or had been associated with the Bulgarian Academy of Sciences. The declaration stated that these historians had been forced by the Communist Party to participate in the name changing campaign, particularly in providing proof of forced religious and cultural assimilation and in doing so had overemphasised the role of the BOC in Bulgaria's Ottoman history.[105]

Despite the statement from the historians associated with the Bulgarian Academy of Sciences the BOC remained silent. Throughout the period of the rebirth process the BOC was mute. Almost sixteen years since the collapse of the communist regime and the Orthodox Church continues to zealously promote its role as Bulgarian national and cultural saviour, as promulgated in *History of Bulgaria*. Nevertheless, the role of the BOC within Bulgarian society has been irrevocably damaged by these events, no more so than in the area of Christian-Muslim dialogue. This research has uncovered evidence that discussions did occur between the BOC and the Directorate of Religious Affairs on events surrounding the rebirth process. During an interview with a former archivist from the Church History Institute she graphically recalled two meetings which occurred in the mid-1980's in the former Ecclesiastical Academy. Representatives from the DRA and the State Security services discussed with leading clergy the BOC's attitude towards the renaming campaign. The Church leaders candidly stated that it would be better to link the National Rebirth process firstly with the Christianization of the Muslim population and then secondly to discuss their true nationality.[106] The religious dimension in this atheistic political campaign cannot be ignored because for the Muslim minority name changing meant more than simply a name: their name was a primary indicator of their ethno-religious identity.[107] This is exactly what the Orthodox representatives understood and why they considered conversion to be a primary factor in this political process and by all indications the Muslim population associated renaming as Christian conversion.[108] As a result of these findings we have to recognise the implicit involvement and support of the BOC in this campaign particularly as this has been refuted until now, not only in the silence of the BOC but also in avenues of academic research.[109]

CONCLUSION

During the period 1944-1953 the institutional problems which had plagued the BOC for many years were solved: an Exarch was appointed, the schism removed, its full autocephaly recognised and finally its Patriarchal rank was restored. However, analysing the fate of the Church during the first few years of communism reveals that its old problems were simply replaced by new ones – this time the very nature of the BOC was endangered as it struggled to stand against the determined and ruthless policy of the State to control the Church. It was unable to carry out its evangelical, educational or charitable duties – the very duties which had secured its relationship with Bulgarian society during the War Years. Without that security and after the official declaration separating Church and State the BOC became subordinate to the will of the Communist Party.

The three phases of communist controlled government were designed to gradually achieve this goal of containment, subordination and cooperation. The first two stages from 1944-1953 were years of preparation, developing the BOC for its role in service to the State. From 1953 onwards the Church as an organ of the State, was at times coerced and at others, willingly cooperated with the communist regime. Thus the Church once again became a political tool this time used in the interests of the Bulgarian Communist Party.

This chapter began by claiming that throughout the period of communist rule there remained a discernable Church-State relationship that ranged from toleration to collaboration. This relationship clearly deteriorated as the phases of communist control upon the Church intensified. This was graphically illustrated in the differing leadership styles of Exarch Stefan and Patriarch Kiril. Although Stefan is commonly portrayed as a communist sympathiser the findings of this research would oppose that characterisation: He was an ardent Bulgarian patriot who wanted to secure the authoritative place of the Church within the nation, but in so doing realised that the BOC would have to cooperate with the new regime. As communist measures against the Church increased, however, Stefan's tolerance toward government policy decreased, a dilemma witnessed during the Moscow Pan-Orthodox Conference. In the end his efforts to protect the Church, to maintain its independence and promote ecumenism against the desires of the Sofia and Moscow governments made him a dangerous and undependable figurehead to lead the BOC.

The leadership of Patriarch Kiril was very different deciding that collaboration was the best policy. Kiril and the BOC have been lambasted for their policy of accommodation during his reign, but unlike Stefan he had no choice but to accept the government line. The Church by now had been fully recruited into the apparatus of the regime and the role of the BOC was presented to Kiril as a *fait accompli*. In his efforts to protect the integrity of the Church he had to willingly subordinate himself to the desires of the State. Nevertheless, in the midst of one of the most brutal assimilation campaigns of the 1970's and 1980's his decision to slavishly follow the Party line and support the suggestion that the Church play a leading role in the government name-changing campaign suggest his motivations were somewhat different than Stefan's. He willingly accepted the new political role given to the BOC by the State, that of Bulgarian national saviour and protector. However, in promoting this role it may be suggested that the integrity of the BOC was critically damaged

The fact remains that the Church hierarchy had little choice but to work within the constraints of the regime. As with most totalitarian regimes the border between collaboration, toleration and resistance ceased to exist. The accepted *modus vivendi* of the Bulgarian Holy Synod prevented the implementation of the Panov-Yugov plan allowing the BOC to survive the communist years emerging wounded but alive. Perhaps the better question to ask then is 'would the BOC survive in a democratic society after the fall of communism?' The truth is the price of survival has been very high. Maxim, the former Metropolitan of Lovech succeeded Patriarch Kiril after his death in 1971. He extolled the leadership of Kiril and stressed that the BOC would be guided by his great example. Thus, for the remainder of the communist period and some may argue to the present day the Church has followed the Party line espousing the cause of Bulgarian nationalism. No doubt in an effort to ensure its continued existence the BOC accepted the role the communist regime had gifted to it: a role engineered by politically reinterpreting history to reveal the brutality of the Ottoman period and proclaiming the BOC as the saviour of Bulgarian culture, language, religion and national awareness.

7
POST-GLASNOST, CONTEMPORARY BULGARIA AND THE ORTHODOX CHURCH (1989-2005)

The communist regime collapsed on 10 November 1989 after reigning supreme in Bulgaria for forty-five years. During one of its final public acts Peter Mladenov, Head of State of the Republic of Bulgaria and Chairman of the BCP, appeared on the occasion of the traditional celebrations at the monument of national hero Vasil Levski accompanied by two official representatives – Dobri Jurov, Minister of Defence and Maxim, Patriarch of the BOC.[1] This public gesture was intended to emphasise the restoration of the Church to its former position as an official representative of the Bulgarian State. Political gesturing did not succeed in gaining the BOC a position of respect in democratic Bulgarian society.

This chapter will examine why the BOC has failed to reassert itself as a dominant force in Bulgarian society by tracing the convoluted progression of church leadership as they entered into the new democratic era up to the present day. The hierarchy of the Church has generally been considered to be a corrupt instrument of the former communist State. Therefore, as Bulgaria sought to break from its communist past the BOC suffered as a consequence of its previous association. This dichotomy between past and future has threatened to divide the BOC. Insecurity within the Orthodox Church, created by public criticism and bitter internal dispute, has hindered my research into contemporary issues in Bulgaria. Access to contemporary documentation from Church archival sources was denied. Thus the information collated toward completion of this chapter comes from a variety of sources including: personal interviews, survey questionnaires, group discussions, contemporary Bulgarian press and inter-church debate.

A NEW ERA
Complications Post-Glasnost
Since 1989 Bulgarian society has been in a condition of radical transformation and the State is presently in a process of rapid moderni-

sation, as it seeks entry into the European Community on 1 January 2007.[2] In the midst of fifteen years of upheaval the Bulgarian public have sought a stable factor in societal life. As the self-proclaimed creator of 'national and cultural continuity' the BOC would have been expected to have been that stabilising force for the nation. However, rooted in the past and contaminated by allegations of communist infidelity, the Church has struggled to be that anchor. Indeed, in the days following the former regimes collapse on 10 November 1989, the involvement of Church leadership with the socialists had been so complete that, the BOC could not even join in the jubilant nationwide celebrations. As one religious commentator voiced:

> One would have expected that the Church would have been on the front line leading the nation with crosses and holy banners, with tears and exaltations of joy. Instead, it was nowhere to be seen. The Church hid, and it is still in hiding from the faithful.[3]

A significant problem has been the BOC's inability to adapt towards the new conditions. Its ability to apply adequate strategies in the face of radical change seems to have been seriously impaired. This dilemma stands contrary to what in the past had been the Bulgarian Church's forte – that ability to modify externally whilst maintaining its unchangeable doctrinal nucleus. This contemporary problem can be traced directly to the BOC's interrelationship with the former communist regime. Under that regime the Church had a place in society by which it was able to maintain its ritualistic independence, but in everything else was subject to and dependent upon the State. Consequently the Church had no autonomy or voice within society remaining a passive observer. As a result the BOC is presently set up in such a way that, at least for the time being, it appears incapable of undertaking adequate steps to respond to the current needs of society and continues, by habit or inertia, to be passive.

Caught up in such rapid and thoroughgoing change many Bulgarians have sought to rationalise their existence. The BOC has failed to ease their predicament. The message of the Holy Synod to contemporary Bulgarian society has been negligible and therefore connections between the Church and local communities are disintegrating. While other Christian Churches and various faith groups seek to attract Bulgarian society through various measures, particularly by means of charitable activity, the BOC looks to answer its problems by means of the State – through its apparatus and power. Nevertheless, Bulgarian society is very different now, it is less accepting and is unwilling to remain mute whilst the church does nothing to assist the people. Thus a Bulgarian sociologist has commented that as society continues to be modernised, the State can no longer safeguard the Church, whether it is historically important or not. Therefore if the BOC want to remain an active force within contemporary democratic Bulgaria the Church "must adapt or die."[4] Despite this dramatic ultimatum it must be clarified that the author referred not to Orthodox dogma, but rather to the Church's way of existence in the community and its attitude towards society. This is the key element essential to the preservation and future of Orthodoxy in Bulgaria. As this chapter will reveal, however, the BOC no longer possesses the means to be forceful in contemporary society. Its marriage to the State, that ancient formula which proved successful in the past, today has been damaged and proves ineffective. Despite this and regardless of the inactivity and weakness of the Holy Synod this has not deprived the BOC, at the level of public opinion and societal consciousness, of having an influence and a certain role in society.

This 'religious' role is not one connected to the doctrinal institutions of the Church, but is united rather to its historical and cultural experience which has determined the religious self-definition of Bulgarians. Thus in the face of mounting problems the BOC champions its historic/cultural role before society. Attempting to maintain a prominent place in the nation Church leaders proclaim the Church as the 'saviour of the Bulgarian nation'. It is no surprise then that the majority of Bulgarians consider themselves to be Eastern Orthodox.[5] During the gathering of research data when individuals were asked about their Christian affiliation, 86% defined themselves as Eastern Orthodox. Only 9% of those questioned considered themselves deeply religious. Added to this when asked, "When you face a difficult personal problem, where do you look for help?" Only 0.7% responded that they would go to their local priest or Orthodox Church. The comparison between these figures reveals the distance between peoples declared religious affiliation and the real presence of religion and the Church in people's everyday circumstances.[6]

Table 1
Christian Affiliation

Eastern Orthodox	86%
Roman Catholic	0.5%
Protestant/Evangelical	0.1%
Unsure	13.4%

Table 2
Depth of Religious Feeling

Deeply religious	9%
Slightly religious	48%
Not really religious	30%
Completely unreligious	11%
Unsure	2%

Table 3
Where do you look in a crisis?

Spouse	55.8%
Family	33%
Friends	35.2%
Myself	24.9%
God	3.2%
Priest/Church	0.7%
Clairvoyant	0.9%
Never have problems	3.7%

After analysing the collated information regarding the BOC, this research would conclude that: the contradiction between 'religiousness' and affiliation to Christianity is due to Orthodoxy being comprehended, not as religion, but as a national and cultural identification. Therefore declarations of affiliation are not based on doctrinal belief, formal bonds of membership or attendance of the Orthodox Church but rather refer to individual and corporate socio-cultural comprehensions of Bulgarian history.

During a number of group discussions undertaken as part of this research the question was asked, "What practical steps can the BOC take to resolve this negative situation and become a dynamic force in Bulgaria once again?" From the ensuing deliberations four suggestions emerged: It was expressed forcefully that the BOC was not meeting the needs of individuals, or society. For the Church to satisfy these needs it was agreed that the Holy Synod required to shed light upon what had happened in the past, in its dealings with the communist State and secondly give an opinion regarding what was occurring in Bulgaria now, to prove that it cared for every level of life in the nation. It was considered that the Church should prepare a 'social charter' and present a systematic plan of action that would enable it to meet the needs of contemporary Bulgarian society. Thirdly, it was argued that the BOC must work with the disenfranchised, the elderly, the poor, the hungry and the suffering – an area which presently it is almost completely absent from. Lastly, it became obvious that many difficulties in the Church had arisen due to the character of communications between Church hierarchy and society, therefore the style of language and form of communication must change to free itself of archaic formalism.[7] The major emotion which emerged from every group discussion was this, "if the Church will not lead and comfort us, then who will?" Bulgarian society is ardently seeking a strong shepherd and loving pastor to provide a unifying and calming voice amid the tumult of change. The majority opinion is that the BOC is not providing that succour.

INTERNAL SCHISM AND THE BULGARIAN ORTHODOX CHURCH

The crisis in the Church, what is generally regarded as a deeply compromised, corrupt and procrastinating Church leadership, unwilling or powerless to react to the changes occurring in Bulgarian society and incapable of responding to its critics, has been exasperated by internal schism which has brought the BOC to its knees. Throughout its history the BOC has suffered many vicissitudes but never until 1992 had it faced internal schism. This division was not based on doctrinal conflict but rather had its origins, at face value, in concerns to break free from its links with the communist past.

The Communist Regime Falls (1989-1991)

Although the communist regime collapsed in 1989 Bulgaria continued to be haunted by its spectre until 1991. The first democratic elections, in June 1990, were won by the Bulgarian Socialist Party (BSP), the renamed Communist Party. This in part may explain why the leadership of the BOC remained silent during the celebrations of communism's downfall, as it awaited the nation's future direction after the political fallout. If the Synod had spoken out against the former regime its image would no doubt have risen admirably in public opinion, but that would definitely have had a detrimental affect on its relationship with the socialist State, on which the BOC would rely for its economic existence.

Fig. 8: Patriarch Maxim

In an effort to allay public criticism Patriarch Maxim announced that he would convene a National Church Council sometime later in 1990, which would respond to the nations questions and fears regarding the Church.[8] A young renegade priest, Christopher Subev, was elected on to the Council's preparatory commission, a man who would come to play a major role in fomenting future schism. Born in 1946 Subev had graduated in atomic physics from Sofia University. As a student he led a group called the Che Guevara sympathisers. His strong communist leanings opened the way for him to further his career in Moscow. However, after two failed marriages he returned to Sofia and took his monastic vows in 1980. In 1988 he formed the 'Independent Committee for the Defence of Religious Rights, Freedom of Conscience and Spiritual Values,' a dissident movement which called not only for Church renewal and reform but also for the removal of Maxim from the Patriarchal throne.[9] The Synod must surely have been aware of Subev's background before appointing him? Perhaps fearing an embarrassing backlash the Church decided to postpone the National Council until further notice. A wise move considering that soon after Subev became one of the leading political characters in the opposition party, the Union of Democratic Forces (UDF). In his political role but clad in priestly vestments Subev publicly called for the hierarchy of the BOC to repent of its sinfulness during the communist era to "exorcise the demons which still prevailed in the Church."[10]

Simultaneously plans to remove Patriarch Maxim were afoot within the Church. Radko Poptodorov, a professor in canon law from Sofia Theological Academy, attacked the Holy Synod, condemning them for their subservience to the former regime. He pointed out that the Synod had not been appointed in accordance with Canon law, but rather by the authority of an atheistic regime. He contended that the Synod's incompetence had fostered religious apathy and moral decay in Bulgaria and for these reasons the Holy Synod should be replaced. These denouncements came to form the argumentation on which the forthcoming schism would base itself.[11] In May 1990 Poptodorov resuscitated the defunct Priest's Union in effort to stimulate reform. Responding to pressure from the PU the Holy Synod agreed once again to form a preparatory committee to organise a National Church Council, the only body which could canonically replace Patriarch and Synod. The committee disintegrated in chaos during its first meeting. Pressure upon the Synod did not abate as another movement for renewal in the Bulgarian Orthodox Church demanded that a National Council be convoked immediately to answer to the families of those priests who had been martyred during communism, particularly as the facts implicated the Holy Synod in their deaths.[12]

Breaking with the Past (1991-1993)

In October 1991 Bulgaria's second free elections were won by the UDF with a 67% share of the vote. In the minds of the people this truly was the end of communism. The new democratic government agreed and without hesitation introduced plans to break with Bulgaria's communist past. Father Christofer Subev was appointed chairman to a Commission for Religious Affairs and immediately set to work opposing the incumbent Orthodox establishment who had been closely connected to that communist past. On 9 March 1992 the government released a statement declaring that the election of Patriarch Maxim in 1971 had been conducted in violation of the statutes of the BOC and the Law of Confessions and therefore he required to be removed from his position.[13] When Maxim refused to respond the Holy Synod was ordered to apply for formal registration, reducing the Orthodox Church in Bulgarian law to the same rank as any other religious denomination, Christian or non-Christian. At this point four Metropolitans – Pimen of Nevrokop, Pankrati of Stara Zagora, Kalinik of Vratsa and Stefan of Veliko Turnovo issued their own statement: "We testify that the violation of the statutes in Maxim's election for the Patriarchate in 1971 renders his service illegitimate and must be terminated." They concluded by calling for the election of a new Patriarch.[14]

A few days later three of the Metropolitans met with Prime Minister Dimitrov, who assured them that the government would support them in their stance against Maxim. With this guarantee on 19 May 1992 Pimen, Pankrati and Kalanik announced themselves to be the new and legitimate Holy Synod of the BOC, along with Metropolitan Sofroni of Ruse and another five bishops – Antoni, Hilarion, Nestor, Nahum, Galaktion and one Christofer Subev. On 25 May, recognised as the date when the schism commenced, the UDF government declared that Maxim and his Synod no longer represented the Orthodox Church in Bulgaria, in their place the Bulgarian State officially recognised the new Synod with Metropolitan Pimen as its chairman *pro tem* (from this point on the schismatic Synod shall be referred to as the 'Provisional Synod').

Reproach and animosity between supporters of the rival synods deteriorated into violence when on the evening of 31 May the newly promoted Bishop Subev, along with an escort of armed minders, occupied the headquarters of the Holy Synod in Sofia. The State Prosecutor and the police refused to intervene in the affair, which led to the accusation from the BSP that the UDF government were implicated in this criminal action.[15] A few days later, the leaders of the schism, Pimen, Subev and Poptodorov attempted to take control of Alexander Nevski Cathedral, the spiritual heart of the BOC. Pimen intended to conduct the Ascension Day Liturgy, however, priests loyal to the Holy Synod refused the intruders access to the altar. Pimen was forced to begin the service from the floor of the Church but had to stop when Maxim's call to worship was heard from behind the iconostasis.[16] Following this embarrassment the Provisional Synod turned their attention toward an alternative Church property, Sofia Theological Seminary, appointing Radko Poptodorov as its new Rector. While the seminary was vacant during its summer break armed supporters of the Provisional Synod seized the property. Responding to this action Bishop Gregori, the displaced rector, students and concerned families, gathered at the gates of the Seminary in an attempt to voice their disapproval. During the demonstration a number of the students managed to enter the building, overpower and expel its occupiers regaining it on behalf of the Holy Synod.[17]

While supporters of both Synods traded blows, striving to gain control of Church property, the UDF government pursued its own relentless policy to remove the Holy Synod from power. On 3 June 1992 it ordered that funds within the bank accounts of the Synod be transferred into a new account in the name of Pimen and his Provisional Synod.[18] State interference appalled many, whatever their reservations regarding Maxim, some even suggested that these intrusive actions amounted to caeseropapism. What strained the credibility of all level-headed Bulgarians was how the Provisional Synod could be promoted as any less compromised than the other. The three leading Metropolitans of the Provisional Synod had generally been regarded as the most compromised during the communist era. The choice for the Bulgarian public therefore was between two groups of compromised Metropolitans who had been elected during the communist regime, the arguments used to discredit the one could equally be used against the other. Krasimir Kunev of the Bulgarian Helsinki Committee succinctly commented "unfortunately the people who organised the split were not the right people in terms of moral qualities."[19] Therefore, as the dispute progressed the public began to treat the situation with indifference.

President Zhelyu Zhelev asked the Constitutional Court to address the matter of the schism and in particular the role of the government's Board of Religious Affairs (BRA). On 11 June 1992 the Court ruled that provisions under which the BRA had acted against the Holy Synod were themselves unconstitutional, however, it was left to the Supreme Court to make a decision on which was the legitimate Synod.[20] On 2 July the Supreme Court rejected the constitutional ruling and continued to support the Provisional Synod.

On 22 July the Holy Synod retaliated by accusing the Provisional Synod of setting up a schismatic Synod in violation of Holy Canon. They proceeded to convene a Council of Prelates, to function as a Church Court whose sentence declared that the members of the schismatic Synod should be defrocked, and Bishop Subev excommunicated.[21] The Provisional Synod rejected these rulings on the grounds that Maxim and his Synod were not legitimate and convened a Court of their own. On 18 August the rival court proclaimed that Maxim was deposed and the remainder of his Synod were ordered to retire to monastic life.[22]

On 6 November 1992 the Constitutional Court ruled that both Synods were invalid. The expectation was that the schism would now collapse and the Provisional Synod would return to the bosom of the Holy Synod. Instead the dispute continued to drag on as mutual recrimination and denunciation steadily eroded Bulgarian church life.

**Fig. 9: Cartoon by Georgi Chaushov from 1992 showing
the loss of Public respect for the Bulgarian Orthodox Church**

Under Socialist Protection (1993-1997)

The UDF's policy and strategy toward the religious dispute antagonised many. Nevertheless, its desire to break with Bulgaria's communist past was widely welcomed. The government's intervention in Church affairs must be considered a serious error of judgement, however, for in doing so its arguments against communist State involvement in the

Church were rendered invalid. Dismayed by these events the government's coalition partner switched their support to the BSP, subsequently the government of the UDF collapsed. We can conclude therefore that despite the low membership of Bulgarian public in the Orthodox Church, Orthodox sentiment and tradition continue to play a powerful role in society and State. From the information presented it would appear that a government's supportive or hostile attitude towards the BOC was sufficient to keep it in power or not.

Table 4
Membership of Orthodox Church

Active membership	0.5%
Non-active membership	2.5%
Consider themselves Orthodox but not members	97%

Hence, after the Socialist Party were returned to government it determined to support the canonical Holy Synod, assuming a role as defender of the faith – a faith which its communist predecessor had attempted to ruin. The BSP immediately reversed the decision of the previous government restoring the status of the Maxim, his Synod and the Church to the consternation of the Provisional Synod. This section will chronicle the actions of both branches of the BOC during this second period of socialist control until February 1997 when the BSP was forced to resign from government.

For Maxim and the Holy Synod the return of the BSP offered a welcome period of consolidation and restoration as they sought to convince the Orthodox world of their validity. The political change favoured them and in realisation of this fact the schismatics sought reconciliation with Maxim. In the ensuing negotiations the dissident Metropolitans even offered to take responsibility for the schism if they were restored to their previous positions.[23] In an act of good will the Provisional Synod returned the Synodal headquarters in Sofia into Maxim's hands. Despite this conciliatory move a number of complications continued to hinder negotiations which resulted in the Bulgarian government asking Ecumenical Patriarch Bartholomeus to mediate between the two parties.

The Ecumenical Patriarch arrived in September 1993 to find the dispute as heated as ever. Each Synod refused to concede to the other, but the main issue of contention was Maxim's refusal to reinstate the schismatic Metropolitans to their former eparchies. Bartholomeus disapproved of Maxim's intransigent approach but could do nothing to alter it. Thus, on 15 December the Holy Synod, against Bartholomeus' better judgement, announced that it would elect new Metropolitans to replace the wayward bishops, who had now been officially demoted, but not excommunicated.[24] Unwilling to accept this decision the schismatics walked away from the negotiations. This development concerned many, as it appeared that the State was interfering in Church affairs yet again. Indeed some have suggested that the socialists were responsible for the failure of the negotiations, pressing Maxim to take sterner measures against the Provisional Synod, thus continuing and even widening the schism.[25]

The question of who was the power behind the Holy Synod was clear in the minds of the Bulgarian people, the BSP. The same question asked of the schismatics, however, created confusion. This was exacerbated in July 1994 when Pimen stipulated that no order of his could be implemented without prior approval of a special board.[26] This led to the conclusion that the schism itself was being prompted by businessmen, hiding behind the ecclesiastics, manipulating them in order to prevent the Church from reclaiming any of the property which had been appropriated during the communist era.[27]

By 1995 pressure upon the schismatics intensified. On 17 April the Holy Synod convened a second Prelates Council to approve of the excommunication of Metropolitans Pimen, Pankrati and Kalanik and accept the repentance and welcome Metropolitan Stefan back into the Church. Stefan had been one of the original signatories at the withdrawal of the dissenters, however, his signature was found to have been either forged or obtained under false pretences as Stefan had been in the latter stages of Alzheimer's. The original nucleus of the Provisional Synod split on 16 December when Pankrati and Kalanik having sought forgiveness for their actions were also received back into the patriarchal fold.[28]

In an effort to restore lost ground, reignite interest within Bulgarian society and ultimately raise the profile of the Provisional Synod Pimen announced the convocation of a National Church Council to elect a new Patriarch in place of Maxim, to occur in Sofia on 2-3 July 1996. He applied for a three million leva subsidy to pay for the National Council from Deputy Prime Minister Svetoslav Shivarov. His request was refused on the grounds that the BSP recognised only one Orthodox Church in Bulgaria, led by Maxim and his Holy Synod. Shivarov added that any attempt to create a second Orthodox Church would be considered a threat to the stability of society and therefore national security and thus would violate Article 37(2) of the Bulgarian Constitution.[29]

Despite government objections the schismatic National Church Council assembled with 150 delegates in attendance. However, there was no representation from the canonically recognised international Orthodox Churches, only the non-canonical Orthodox Church of Macedonia, the Kiev Patriarchate and the Ukrainian Church were represented. Nevertheless the Council continued to elect Pimen Patriarch of the Bulgarian Church, despite the fact that 55/150 delegates abstained from voting. New statutes were also introduced creating a 37 member Synod, two thirds of which would be clergy and one third laypeople. Participation of the laity at Synodal level was unprecedented in Bulgarian history.[30]

The enthronement of a second Patriarch plummeted the schism and the BOC in general, to new depths of despair within society. While the government refused to recognise any of the decisions of the Provisional Council the Bulgarian press dubbed the schismatics as the "Church of the UDF."[31] The Holy Synod reacted strongly condemning the actions as sterile acts of darkness, they continued:

> Those who have seceded from the unity of the Church convened an uncanonical, anti-church and anti-national Council. This irresponsible gathering dared to adopt statutes contrary to the canons and traditions of Holy Orthodoxy. They instituted some kind of Synod for themselves and elected a pseudo-patriarch – the excommunicated former Metropolitan Pimen.... The act committed by the schismatics is an event of absurdity and shame in the centuries-long history of our Church and our State. Regrettably, prominent public figures, with their attendance and irresponsible statements at this pseudo-council, proved its anti-Church character.[32]

Later Maxim's Holy Synod pronounced an anathema on Pimen, the direst ecclesiastical punishment possible.[33] These antics reduced the BOC to a ludicrous level in public life even being lampooned in the national press.

By the close of 1996, however, another more serious problem confronted the nation. Bulgaria plunged into economic crisis, inflation topped 300 per cent, banks collapsed, the public faced starvation and civil war became an imminent possibility. The crisis was explained by an economist in this fashion:

> The BSP had adroitly harnessed the old unaccountable methods of administrative control [from the communist era] to new links with western partners and produced a society where money haemorrhaged out of the system into the shadowy black economy which existed beside and fed off it.[34]

As the BSP government faced its toughest political crisis since the fall of communism Patriarch Maxim blessed their presidential candidate Georgi Pirinski, endorsing the Holy Synod's support of the socialists.[35] On the other hand the growing street demonstrations against the government were blessed by Patriarch Pimen. The two branches of the schismatic church clearly displayed their political colours before the nation. On 3 November 1996 UDF candidate Petur Stoyanov was elected President. As the economic crisis worsened the Holy Synod retreated in silence as Pimen's Synod seized the initiative. By January 1997 those involved in daily demonstrations had risen from tens of thousands to over one hundred thousand. Pimen called on the Bulgarian people not to submit to the "godless ruling politicians" and he and his Synod expressed solidarity with the "long suffering people in their just protest."[36] On 4 February 1997, in the face of national opposition, the BSP government was dissolved to make way for new elections. The UDF swept to power, the political transfer from the BSP to the UDF signifying yet another transfer of power within the religious realm of the nation, from Maxim to Pimen, as the Provisional Synod gained yet another lease of life.

A New Religious Policy (1997-2001)

At his presidential inauguration Petur Stoyanov voiced his desire to unite the BOC, thus both Patriarchs were invited to his swearing-in ceremony on 22 January 1997. In an effort not to cause embarrassment protocol insisted that the Patriarchs attended dressed in priestly attire, rather than their patriarchal vestments. Maxim observed protocol and was cordially greeted by Stoyanov. Pimen, in what we can only surmise was a choreographed act, arrived in full patriarchal garb. Maxim and his party swiftly departed, leaving Pimen to administer the presidential oath.[37] The following year Stoyanov admitted in an interview that he had wanted to receive the presidential blessing from both patriarchs, a rather ludicrous and unrealistic suggestion.[38] Whether this act was choreographed with Presidential approval or purely an act of opportunism by Pimen it undoubtedly delivered the message that the UDF supported the Provisional Synod.

The Bulgarian people were by now truly disillusioned with the continuing fracas between Maxim and Pimen. Having lost sympathy for either side Dimitrina Merdjanova succinctly expressed public opinion when she explained that Bulgarians wanted a new patriarch from another generation, someone who was not tainted, someone who cared for people and who would attract people back into the community life of the Church.[39] UDF policy towards the schism may well have been intended to fulfil these desires, nevertheless, by reinstituting their 1991-1993 policy, to purge key institutions [including the BOC] of corruption from their communist past, they could only succeed in digging up old ground. Therefore instead of searching for new avenues of reconciliation the new government reiterated that Pimen was the only legitimate Patriarch and Maxim and his Holy Synod were again denied official recognition.[40]

Indignant Maxim protested before the European Court of Human Rights in Strasbourg after which the government noticeably became less confrontational.[41] Indeed, Maxim was even chosen to bless the Bulgarian Army on Armed Forces Day (6 May). However, when Prime Minister Ivan Kostov assumed office on 21 May the traditional blessing of the waters was celebrated by Metropolitan Innokenti from the Provisional Synod.[42] Efforts to appease both sides of the schism increased when the government suggested that a National Church Council be convened to end the dispute by ecclesiastical means, the deputy Prime Minister even promised that the government would not intervene in the process.[43] The conciliatory tone of the government lasted all of two weeks when Veselin Metodiev, Director of the BRA, attempted to scupper the National Council by rejecting the BOC's request for 15 million leva to finance the event and vowed to do everything in his power to prevent it being held.[44]

In spite of government attempts to hinder it, only the fourth National Church Council in the history of the BOC assembled from 2-4 July 1997. The expectations of the nation rested on this Council hoping that the schism would finally be resolved, that Maxim would retire and a new younger Patriarch would take the reins of the canonical Church. The Council achieved one major objective before it commenced, with representatives from every canonical Orthodox Church present, the legitimacy and canonicity of Maxim, the Holy Synod and the BOC were affirmed.

In a report dealing with the state of the BOC the Holy Synod strongly denounced the schism and those who had brought it about, the Provisional Synod and UDF:

> Absolutely without justification the Holy Synod was declared to be a 'Communist tool,' the prelates – 'red bishops' and 'servants of the former totalitarian communist administration.' A campaign with evil designs for 'renewal' and 'decommunisation' of the Church was organised, which led to an intolerable schism.... There began manoeuvres based on the so-called absence of registration of the Holy Synod, placing the Church in humiliating conditions caused by administrative interference with its constitutional and legally recognised rights.[45]

This was by no means a public apology for past associations with communists, but it did offer comment which the Bulgarian people had been waiting for. It talked about the consequences of wounds inflicted by materialistic atheism and infiltration and control by State organs. It suggested that laws implemented by the communists to control the Church had been exploited by the UDF to instigate and support the schism. A second document contained another important sentence: "We [the Holy Synod] beg the Bulgarian people for indulgence and forgiveness for all that which clergy and laity failed to do in their defence." A public apology, which by implication suggested possible ecclesiastical involvement with the communist State, but still refused to openly admit any direct relationship with the authorities.

The Council to an extent appeased the Bulgarian people but in other areas infuriated them. When proposals from the floor suggested alterations to Church statutes regarding the retirement age of patriarchs and metropolitans Patriarch Maxim refused to allow any debate on the suggestion, perhaps because he was beyond the age put forward for retirement. Also when it was suggested that the personal files of all senior clergy be opened to the public to put an end to bitter allegations against the Holy Synod, Maxim again refused to put the issue to a vote.[46] Finally, when no definitive action was declared surrounding the schism it was realised that the Council had achieved very little, no end to the schism, no resignation from Maxim or Pimen and no announcement on the election of a new Patriarch.

Pressure again fell on the government to find a solution to the dispute. Diplomatic and ecclesiastic methods having failed the government employed intimidation, threats and verbal abuse in an attempt to force the two sides into arbitration. Pimen, realising that opportunities for his Synod were dissipating, consented to arbitration, whereas the Holy Synod, in an act which can only be described as political blackmail, declared that it would be a pity if the pressure which had compelled it to defend its rights before the European Court of Human Rights proved to be a hindrance toward political efforts to join the nation with the European Community.[47] Realising that supporting Pimen and opposing Maxim had achieved nothing the UDF government decided to implement a policy of non-involvement. The exasperation of the government was graphically displayed during the 150th anniversary celebrations of national hero Hristo Botev, when President Stoyanov publicly appealed to both Maxim and Pimen to provide proof of their responsibility and humility and have the courage to bow out to allow a generation of clergy uncorrupted by the old regime to take their place: "Under the Ottoman yoke our clergy were prepared to face chains and death. Today we ask these bishops to make a much easier sacrifice – simply to retire."[48]

Weary of the infighting amongst the ecclesiastical hierarchy lower clergy from both sides attempted to forge some unity. Moved by their efforts Pimen even offered to retire if the BOC convened an extraordinary Council to settle the dispute. However, secretary to the Holy Synod, Metropolitan Gelasi replied:

> Who are we supposed to be negotiating with? This is not a dispute between two sides on an equal basis. With Pimen? Pimen is a renegade, an apostate. We have nothing whatsoever to say to him. A Council? Yes, but only after they crawl back to us on bended knees, and not to discuss disputes about church hierarchy but to talk about millennium related issues.[49]

The intransigent attitude of the Holy Synod frustrated everyone within the BOC. The government's policy of non-involvement with church hierarchy was, however, producing a dividend. Without contact between leaders of Church and State, without a move toward unification, there could be no formal agreement between Church and State on much needed cash subsidies to pay priests wages. This resulted in priests from both sides remaining unpaid for up to six months, many of whom went on strike demanding reunification. Priests from the Vratsa eparchy threatened that if an agreement on unification was not reached they would transfer from the BOC to Russian jurisdiction.[50]

Discontent and frustration amongst the clergy spread to the hierarchy, many of whom called for the resignation of the Holy Synod. Exasperated clergy gathered around Pimen's call to convene an extraordinary Council and representatives from both sides agreed to convene a Council to dismiss both patriarchs and metropolitans and elect new ones agreeable to everyone.[51] The Holy Synod, neglecting the practical issues and mood of the parish clergy, hid behind the safety of canon law and commented that such a council would have no canonical validity.[52]

Unable to heal itself, Patriarch Petros VII of Alexandria arrived in an effort to familiarise himself with the history of the schism. A few days later Metropolitans Meletios and Meliton from the Ecumenical Patriarchate joined Petros to sound out the possibility of a Pan-Orthodox Council to meet in Sofia to finally bring the schism to a canonical end.[53] The Pan-Orthodox Council convened soon after this initial consultation meeting from 30 September–1 October 1998. It was chaired by Ecumenical Patriarch Bartholomeus and was attended by the Patriarchs of Alexandria, Antioch, Russia, Serbia, Romania and Bulgaria, a representative of the Patriarch of Jerusalem, the Archbishops of Cyprus, Albania and Athens and all Greece, the Metropolitan of the Church in Poland, a representative of the Czech and Slovak Church and twenty-two other bishops.

Following accustomed vitriolic attacks from either side negotiations ensued. Encountering the full canonical force of the Orthodox Church upon them the schismatics promptly and publicly repented and expressed their desire to return to the canonical Bulgarian Church under the headship of Maxim. The anathema against Pimen was annulled, but in view of his age [93 years old] he was not reinstated as metropolitan. Thus on 1 October 1998 the end of the schism was proclaimed. Ecumenical Patriarch Bartholomeus very wisely declared before the Bulgarian nation that neither side could claim victory or defeat, emphasising that only the devil had lost.

Stoked by press speculation Bulgarians awaited Maxim's resignation. When this was not forthcoming the UDF leadership shocked everyone by announcing that they did not recognise the ruling of the Pan-Orthodox Council and encouraged dissenters to press for patriarchal elections. Maria Dimitrova, from Kliment Ohridski University in Sofia, comments that talk of reconciliation had been premature because none of the inner church conflicts had been resolved, only the canonicity of the Bulgarian Church had been ascertained.[54] As the events of the Pan-Orthodox Council receded it became clear that it had done little to allay the discontent of those who sought renewal within the BOC.

Faced with continued government criticism Patriarch Maxim complained to visiting members of the European Union's parliamentary assembly monitoring Bulgaria's human rights situation. He claimed that the State was intent on destabilising the Church and refused to conform to the decisions of the Pan-Orthodox Council.[55] The death of Pimen on 10 April 1999 did little to appease the situation, even though it was decided that it would be unwise to elect another 'schismatic' patriarch. Instead Metropolitan Innokenti, widely considered to be the power behind the schismatics, was chosen to be *locum tenens*.

Thus, at the beginning of the new millennium the BOC was considered to be one unified Church without schism. In reality practise spoke very differently. Many of the bishops who had been reinstated during the Pan-Orthodox conference defected creating chaos over diocesan jurisdictions. In practice the hierarchy within the BOC worked as two separate synods each working to outdo the other, the schismatics refusing to do anything which could be deemed tantamount to recognising Maxim's primacy. On 1 January 2001 the Holy Synod ordered the schismatics to fully implement the decisions of the Pan-Orthodox council and acknowledge the authority of Maxim. To bolster this instruction a delegation from the Ecumenical Patriarchate arrived in Sofia to reiterate the council's 1998 condemnation of schism and affirm Maxim as the "only legitimate patriarch."[56]

An End to the Schism (2001- 2005)

By 2001 the two leading political parties, BSP and UDF, had been largely discredited by the Bulgarian public. The appearance onto the Bulgarian political scene of the regal and charismatic figure of Tsar Simeon II, deposed as a child in 1946, ignited Bulgarian hope for the future. Unlikely to revoke its republican ethos and be reinstated as monarch, Simeon established a new Bulgarian political party, the National Movement for Simeon II (NMS) which enticed the Bulgarian electorate with the promise of prosperity in 800 days, through the introduction of reduced taxation, extended social welfare provision and easily obtained low interest loans.[57] On 17 June 2001 his broad based coalition party, won the national election with almost 50% of the vote. Tsar Simeon or more correctly Simeon Saxocoburg duly became prime minister, despite the fact that he had not lived in the country since 1946 and had visited Bulgaria on only a handful of occasions in twelve years. Baptised into the Orthodox Church as a child he had throughout his life worshipped as a Roman Catholic. Would these predominantly western and catholic traits affect State attitudes toward the apparently insoluble schism? Until the present it appears that Simeon's 'unorthodox' background has had bearing on his attitude towards the problems in the BOC, in that he has left it to its own devices, the dispute has in other words been swept under the political carpet.

Despite Simeon's personal lack of interest in the schism his coalition partners have striven to reach a compromise. The dispute continues but has centred once again on ownership of property. Property provides money and money is power. Whilst the two sides literally fight over that property which is presently owned by the Church, the greatest struggle is to gain control of property confiscated by the communists. It has been suspected that the church property scandal has persisted and restitution of property delayed because of financial misappropriation by every Bulgarian government since the fall of the communists.[58] Each government in power has, however, absolved itself on the pretext that if restitution was granted to which side of the church divide should it be given? Criticism of government aside the hierarchy of the BOC also appear to be implicated in claims of financial abuse. Key documents pertaining to ownership of Church property have disappeared from the Church Archive department and recent documents have been neglected, misplaced or destroyed.[59] Others have claimed that Church hierarchy, from both sides, have been involved in sharp practice, even of having links with the Bulgarian mafia.[60]

The most traumatic event in the recent development of the schism happened in the city of Blagoevgrad. In a city church, the legal ownership of which had been disputed since 2000, Stefan Kamberov a parish priest belonging to the schismatic branch of the BOC was brutally murdered. The fact that it was a priest, slain within the church, horrified the Bulgarian people. When information was released that a priest from the canonical Synod had been arrested for his murder the whole nation took notice. When the priest in question, although admitting to the murder, was released without charge, the public were dismayed. What was more worrying was the reason provided for the committing of this terrible act by the Metropolitan of Nevrokop. Firstly, he considered that "nothing wrong" had been committed, as the murder was the "objective conclusion" of the escalation of conflict, the most important aspect of which was that it was provoked by "the other." In this way guilt even for such an extreme act, although unacceptable, should be attributed to "the other." For this reason the Metropolitan refused to accept or place any responsibility on the killer as he had been provoked by the schismatic 'other'.[61]

As result of this awful event the schismatic element retreated from the forefront of church life. As they contemplated the immediate future, in light of judicial and ecclesiastical proclamations, the schismatic clergy feared that they could no longer presume any protection or justice from Bulgarian law. One priest commented that through this atrocity the canonicity of the Church had been transformed from something which was once charged with responsibility and truth into something which vindicates absolutely anything that the Holy Synod opposes and therefore stops providing assurance because of its dogmatic infallibility.[62] The predicament of the schismatics was dealt a further blow when a nationwide police action raided all property belonging to the schismatic clergy. During the night of 20 July 2004 police entered over 90 churches and related properties belonging to Metropolitan Innokenti's alternative synod, ejected all the schismatic clergy and sealed off the churches until new priests were appointed by Maxim. A number of clergy were arrested during the action, but perhaps more threatening were the reports of priests and laypersons being beaten. This brutal attempt to unite the divided BOC was coordinated and approved by the Supreme Prosecutor's Office who protested that they were restoring what belonged to the rightful Church. In doing so, however, it was claimed that a number of human rights were violated, facts distorted, laws interpreted erroneously and outdated laws enforced.[63] This remains the contemporary situation with the schism, the declaration of the Pan-Orthodox Council of 1998, that the schism was healed, remains the official statement of the BOC. In reality the schismatics in fear, for the time being, have gone into hiding. However, resentment over recent events and disrespect for Maxim's leadership continue unabated.

POLITICAL AND JUDICIAL PRIVILEGE
Law on Religions

As a consequence of internal schism the BOC has struggled to maintain a position of respect in Bulgarian public life. This resulted in the Holy Synod lobbying State to politically and legally reconfirm its privileged status within society. This was no easy task as the functioning Law on Religions (1949) had been the product of the communist era and thus favoured anti-religious, secular and materialistic policy and had been created to emphasise the separation of Church and State, removing the privileged status of the BOC. However, after a period of intense campaigning by Orthodox hierarchy, concerned politicians and business people the government agreed to review the Law on Religions. As a result of judicial re-assessment and despite its often precarious legal status during the schism the BOC has been able once again to rely on the support of the State. Indeed, the new Law on Religions which was adopted on 20 December 2002 unequivocally supports the canonical BOC, recognising only one Orthodox Church under Patriarch Maxim and the Holy Synod.[64] The Law was welcomed by the majority of Bulgarians as it not only brought the schism to logical conclusion but also took firm measures to defend Bulgaria and Orthodoxy from foreign 'sectarian invasion'.

Widespread protest against the 'unjustness' of the new Law, however, has shaken the Bulgarian political establishment. Eighteen legally registered religious organisations voiced their concern, the basic premise behind their protests being that all religious bodies in Bulgaria were to be subject to restrictions which did not apply to any other non-government organisation. They were particularly grieved because the BOC had been granted complete immunity from these State restrictions.[65] Whilst accepting the Bulgarian Constitution's affirmation describing the BOC as the nation's traditional religion, the protesters objected to its being granted extra judicial rights which discriminated against other religious organisations.[66] They condemned these as being completely unjust, contravening not only the Bulgarian Constitution but also the Constitution of the European Court of Human Rights which the Bulgarian government had already signed as a prior requisite to its joining the European Community in 2007.

Article 13(3) of the 1991 Bulgarian Constitution, although defining Orthodoxy as the "traditional religion of the Republic of Bulgaria," does not provide the BOC any legal preference vis-à-vis other religious denominations. It does not even define the BOC as an established church, a majority church or any other such term, which could have been interpreted as giving it privileged status. At the height of the schism such statements were problematical, but after the Pan-Orthodox conference of

1998 the canonicity of the Holy Synod and the BOC could no longer be questioned. As it stood, the Constitution did not give clear guidance on how to handle the BOC, being described neither as an established Church or disestablished religious organisation. Therefore when disputed issues came before the judiciary the decision making process was left to the interpretation and discretion of the legislator or judge. It became clear that Bulgarian law needed to be amended to recognise the established nature of the BOC, as well as the developing relationship between Church and State in Bulgaria. As part of this ongoing process amendments were made to the *Persons and Family Act* which dealt with the changing position of the BOC within the nation. Although assisting the predicament of the Orthodox Church it was widely considered to be a major blow to religious freedom in Bulgaria as the amendment stipulated that all religious organisations, apart from those which had been present in Bulgaria for over 100 years, would require re-registering for approval by the Council of Ministers.[67]

It was not only Bulgaria's religious minorities who criticised the new Law on Religions, the Commission on Security and Cooperation in Europe (OSCE) also raised its concerns.[68] In a report published in 2003 the OSCE voiced alarm that Bulgaria's commitments to religious freedom were out of step with the provisions it required to meet to satisfy entry into the European Community. For example, in its haste to pass the Law on Religions the Bulgarian government had neglected to consult with religious communities other than the Orthodox during the drafting process. Also during the review stage of the bill it refused to respond to complaints brought by fifty parliamentary representatives regarding this issue. The OSCE also criticised the Sofia City Court, mandated to deal with all religious re-registration, as it had stalled on issuing registrations since the *Persons and Family Act* was amended in 1994.[69]

The major concern raised by religious minorities and the OSCE regarded the Bulgarian governments recognition of the BOC as the 'traditional church of Bulgaria'. All complainants recognised that the wording of the Law acknowledged the role of the BOC in the nation's history and was also an attempt to settle the saga of schism. Nevertheless, the apprehension was that the positive assessment given by the State to one religion and one creed would explicitly influence the choice of public religious opinion and also automatically give the BOC legal advantage over other religious groups, which had already created conflict over matters of religious registration. The registration system clearly favoured Orthodox organisations and disapproved of non-Orthodox religious bodies. As a result if a religious group was refused official registration it could not legally exist. It was apparent that this system was open to arbitrary and non-transparent decision making by pro-Orthodox civil servants.[70] The OSCE report concluded by stating that the Bulgarian Law on Religions curtailed fundamental freedoms of religious minorities in Bulgaria and should therefore be amended and brought into line with decisions of the Constitution of the European Court of Human Rights.

Other national bodies, such as the European Law Centre in Sofia, appealed to the Bulgarian Courts on the anti-constitutional nature of the new Law on Religions. They argued that reinstating the BOC to a privileged national position, because of what it had achieved during a previous era, meant that Bulgarian history was being re-written purely to equate with the new law. In debating their case they compared this approach to Bulgaria's 1971 Constitution which recognised the historical victory of the Socialist Revolution in 1944 and the wonderful leadership of the Communist Party. Few people would now agree with that assessment and similarly many would disagree with the "indisputable fact" that the BOC merits a privileged place in Bulgarian society today. In arguing this they attempted to explain, that alongside every historical fact rests various differences of opinion, which by necessity excludes imposing historical fact by virtue of law. By adopting the law they claimed that the State had negated the basis for freedom of thought and religion and individual liberty to interpret history. Therefore those who are not Orthodox, or agree to a specific reading of Bulgarian history, may be considered to be political agitators or even a threat to Bulgarian national security.[71]

The desire to re-assert Orthodoxy's privileged status illustrates that the BOC and the Bulgarian State have reverted to 19th century nationalist ideology. Rather than being theocentric the BOC has become religio-ethnocentric, while the State appears to identify its very existence with its intimate relationship with the established religion of the land. This has created a religious agenda full of canonical and theological inconsistency. The desire to be the sole representative of the nation has become so pervasive within the Church that it is somehow forgotten that it does not have any theological foundation. Rather it was born of a legal concept from within Ottoman law, that of the *millet*. The establishment of the *millet* led to ethnic emancipation within the Christian communities of the Balkans and led to the concept of the national Church. The desire of contemporary Church and State appears to be to construct a cultural/ bulgaro-national/orthodox *millet* which has declared war on minority Christian denominations and other non-Christian religions within Bulgarian territory. This *millet* mentality has outworked itself in the form of restrictive and unjust religious/political practice. As a number of international organisations have stated, the BOC must reject this quasi-orthodox theology, which not only deflects from the rich heritage of Eastern Orthodoxy, but may hinder Bulgaria's entry into the expanding European Community.

The Reintroduction of Religious Education

While securing its privileged position under the law the BOC has also endeavoured to re-assert its authority within society by re-introducing religious education into the secular classroom. One of the major programmes implemented by the communist regime, to subjugate the Church and distance it from society, was the removal of religious instruction from the State educational system. Therefore, after the collapse of communism debates immediately arose regarding the re-introduction of religion as a subject into the Bulgarian school curriculum. Constitutionally schools remained secular but politicians were willing to consider amending this policy. Discussion focussed around two options: a complete renewal of the previous religious programme, which would study different world religions and introduce subjects such as law, politics and philosophy; or to reinstate the tradition of religious instruction present in schools before the socialist era, a tradition which included subjects such as: Sacred History, Public Worship, Catechism, History of the Orthodox Church, History of the BOC, Moral Consciousness and Moral Admonition. The second option was clearly not intended to be a general religious education but a specific upbringing within the domain of Eastern Orthodox Christianity.

In 1993 The Ministry of Education issued a statement announcing that their policy would adhere to the existing laws enshrined in the Bulgarian Constitution, which defined schools as secular institutions and therefore should remain independent of any religious beliefs. The issue remained in abeyance until 1997 as the socialist government realised that if it guaranteed access to the Orthodox, it would require guaranteeing equal privileges to other Christian denominations and faith groups. The statement contradicted itself, however, by adding: "The upbringing in

Bulgarian schools is connected with the national united norms of Orthodox Christian ethics and morality...."[72]

By 1997 the UDF's Education Ministry had dropped the language of 'religious upbringing' and talked instead about 'religious education', which intended to introduce the major world religions and equip children to cope morally with the new challenges and dangers of the modern world. The new curriculum aimed to contribute to a mutual understanding and respect between different faith groups in Bulgaria, it would provide a balanced religious world view and the historical role of Orthodoxy would be explained, emphasising its role as national saviour.[73] These newly formulated objectives were intended to conform to the new amendments in the United Nations Human Rights Charter encouraging tolerance toward differing faiths.[74] Thereafter a curriculum was designed to introduce this new agenda and a new M.A. programme in Religion was established to provide staff with additional qualifications to teach it.[75]

Despite these efforts teachers and manuals used for religious instruction continue to favour Orthodox upbringing. The most recent approved school text book, published in 2003, contains sections on Orthodox history, catechism and liturgy. It also proclaims the evils of Islamic rule in Ottoman Bulgaria as encapsulated by the *catastrophe* and *continuity theories*.[76] Therefore the present generation of Bulgarian children are still being instructed in Orthodox superiority over other religious minorities and its biased reading of history has the danger of instilling an inbred fear of 'the other' particularly the Turkish-Muslim. The Bulgarian Helsinki Committee raised the objection that this programme violated the national Constitution, which does not permit any restriction of rights or privileges based on race, nationality, religion or conviction, and accused advocates of Orthodoxy of pushing their faith into a dominant position at the expense of other churches and faiths.[77] A repercussion of this biased approach has been a rise in anti-sectarian hysteria.[78]

Regardless of the efforts of the Church to influence the religious upbringing of Bulgaria's children a survey undertaken during this research revealed that only 2% of those questioned considered that school education had any bearing on their attitude toward religion. It must be recognised, however, that the majority of those interviewed would have been taught under the atheistic socialist system. Nevertheless, it does appear that contemporary schoolchildren's interest in religious education continues to be very low, but this may have more to do with the lack of religious instruction available in schools, due to the continued shortage of suitably qualified teachers. A 2000/01 survey of schools exposed the reality that only 3% of children had any religious classes in their school.[79] From this survey it was discovered that there were only two hundred and sixty-eight qualified persons able to teach religion in Bulgaria's schools, a number clearly incapable of providing an adequate response to the renewed call for Christian education.[80]

Table 5
Who/What has most influenced your attitude toward religion?

Family	60.0%
Friends	25.0%
TV/Press	5.5%
Not influenced	5.0%
School	2.0%
University	1.5%
Church	1.0%

New Hope Emerges From Below

On a cold September lunchtime (2004) seventy people line up in front of a ground floor window in an apartment block next to an Orthodox Church in central Sofia. The queue is made up mostly of elderly women, interspersed with neatly dressed younger men and women accompanied by their children. As they reach the window each person receives a small bag containing oil, rice, butter and half a loaf of bread. Each person also carries a container which is filled with hot soup. This scene provides a microcosm of Bulgarian society and represents the widespread economic hardship of young and old alike. This picture is copied in many places throughout the city, but what makes this one significant is that it is organised by a local Orthodox Parish Church. However, it was not established by decree from above, or financed from the Synod's coffers. It was founded and run by the Pokrov Foundation, a movement of Orthodox laity which is trying to restore genuine parish life and diaconal service to the Orthodox Church in Bulgaria.[81]

The Foundation was established in 1994, originally as a publishing and educational organisation to promote Orthodoxy in Bulgaria. However, after evaluating its mission the Pokrov Foundation came to the realisation that social work was being neglected by the hierarchy of the Church and therefore sought to constitute a programme of work, undertaken by the laity, to meet the pressing social needs of their communities. The presence of the Church in the social life of the local community is considered by them to be one of the best opportunities for Orthodox Christian witness.[82] Despite this fact the hierarchy of the Church remains inactive. Almost sixteen years after the fall of communism the Holy Synod is still unprepared to meet the public demand for a practical and comprehensible outworking of the Christian message in society. Current tendencies reveal that apart from the BOC's 'national' nomenclature Orthodox Christianity is becoming increasingly marginalised as the Church fails to meet the spiritual and practical needs of Bulgarian society.

Today there is a growing conviction that if any change is to occur in the BOC, it can only come from below, from the laity. Alongside this conviction rises an exciting new hope for the Church in Bulgaria. At the heart of this movement the Pokrov Foundation is intricately involved in analysing Bulgarian society, involving people in dialogue and outlining reforms required to renew the BOC. In this way fundamental issues are being tackled which have never before been discussed in the Church: Where are the roots of the Bulgarian Church crisis to be found? Is a radical and more spiritual approach to Bulgarian history and cultural heritage possible? What is the real religious identity of the nation? The Foundation has progressed to become a catalyst for a number of new lay initiatives including the National Orthodox Women's Committee, the Orthodox Education Fund and the Bulgarian National Christian Committee (encompassing leaders from all the major Christian denominations in the country). Most importantly the Foundation has engendered the belief that the BOC must have a vision for ecumenical cooperation, not form above, but promoted by these new lay movements.[83]

It is from these models of contemporary lay ministry which the BOC must take encouragement for the future. Whilst the hierarchy of the church has found it impossible to extricate itself from its communist past, or cope with the demands of pluralistic society and whilst the lower clergy generally remain poorly educated and unmotivated to become involved in parish social life, it is the laity who has taken the lead. Unburdened by canon law or political rivalry the laity has shown the ability to escape from Bulgaria's socialist quagmire. Subsequently the work of the Pokrov Foundation has been perceived by the Holy Synod as being both a strong and positive factor in church life, but also a dangerous and hostile body which reveals the weakness of the BOC and its leadership.

In the face of mounting public criticism, which has called for the dismissal of the entire Holy Synod, it is interesting to find that the Pokrov Foundation oppose this sentiment and support the hierarchy of the Church. In a statement from 1997 the Foundation declared: "The Church crisis is a matter of personal responsibility for everyone baptised Orthodox. Replacing the old bishops through revolutionary or anti-canonical methods cannot be a solution to any problem in the Church, therefore, the role of the lay movements should be actively supported as the only peaceful way to overcome this crisis."[84]

CONCLUSION

The social and political transition from communism to democracy in Bulgaria has proven problematical. The Bulgarian Orthodox Church in its self proclaimed role as national saviour would have been expected to be in a leading position to sustain the needs of society through this turmoil. As events unfolded, however, the BOC was nowhere to be seen, its leadership deigned not to be involved in celebrating communism's downfall. This lack of enthusiasm, the failure of the BOC to lead the Bulgarian nation into a new age and the Holy Synod's political manoeuvrings with the former regime amalgamated to become a major focus of Bulgarian public resentment and hostility toward the Church and its leadership. Bulgarians desired to break completely with their communist past and wanted church leadership to do likewise. Silence and inaction from the Synod, however, were deemed by the public to be a sign of guilt and disinterest.

As the socialists and democrats struggled for political superiority they voiced their approval or disapproval of the Holy Synod's inaction. Those desiring a fresh start in a new era coalesced around the UDF's call for church reform and demanded Patriarch Maxim's removal from office, accusing him of collaboration and uncanonical election. Thus politicians and the State became embroiled in the affairs of the Church. Throughout its history the BOC had suffered many vicissitudes, but never until 1992 had it experienced internal schism. This division was not created by doctrinal conflict, but had its origins in concerns to break free from its links with the former regime. Nevertheless, it would appear that underlying every event surrounding the schism has been a struggle for ownership of Church property, a substantial multi-million source of income in which unscrupulous and malevolent characters have played an important part. At parish level all the public have witnessed is bitter infighting amongst the clergy. A consequence of over ten years of schism in the church has been a reduction in moral and spiritual values, graphically displayed by Orthodox clergy and synod alike, particularly surrounding the events of the murder of schismatic priest Stefan Kamberov.

Ultimately an impotent leadership and a struggling church have encouraged a weak religiousness amongst the population. Qualitative research completed during this investigation revealed that Orthodox Christianity in contemporary Bulgaria is employed as a method of national identification rather than a matter of personal religious belief. Indeed, the BOC as an institution in contemporary Bulgaria does not primarily present itself as a religious body at all but as an integral factor in Bulgarian national history and therefore to be a vital part in national characterisation and identification. Thus the religiousness of the Bulgarian people reveals itself as a nationalist trait.

In an effort to survive, to maintain a dominant role in contemporary society the BOC promotes its salvific historical/cultural role. Unable to extricate itself from past communist associations, or cope with pluralistic democratic society, church leadership has reverted back to a 19th century monolithic model of church-state relationship. The Bulgarian government has reciprocated by raising the BOC to a legally privileged position in the nation, above all other Christian and non-Christian religions. Despite the pride which many Bulgarians have in their national church there are those who wish to be spiritually revitalised and practically supported by their ecclesiastical leaders. However, every act of social work and spiritual renewal which is emerging from the church comes from below. It is the work of lay movements such as the Pokrov Foundation that are renewing the living communal sense of being in the Church, without any supporting initiatives from above. However, the laity want the Church and its hierarchy to be an active and reactive part of society.

To reassert itself as a dominant spiritual force within society the BOC requires obtaining a level of organisational autonomy which does not rely solely on special statutes of State. As Bulgaria prepares to enter the European Community the Church will be compelled to reject its pretensions for singular special treatment – as the unique carrier of Bulgarian spiritual values. By necessity it will have to respect the rights of individuals to choose values different from their own and not enforce Orthodoxy upon Bulgarian society. Through the international requirement to amend the Law on Religion the Bulgarian Orthodox Church will have the opportunity not only to achieve this but also to free itself from its nationalist narrative.

8

NATION, NATIONALISM AND THE BULGARIAN ORTHODOX CHURCH

The Bulgarian Orthodox Church has served Bulgarian nationalism for a thousand years in conditions of infinite diversity.... It is not the gospel that the patriarch and bishops in Sofia hold high for the Bulgarian people.... It is the national cause in its church wrappings that they propagate today.[1]

Spas Raikin's comment on the relationship between the Bulgarian Orthodox Church and nationalism serves to portray the passion which the Bulgarian church holds for the nation. Preceding chapters of this thesis have highlighted that Bulgaria's socio-political environment has been forged by the dominant themes of religion and nation. However, Raikin's comment regarding the BOC serving Bulgarian nationalism for a thousand years will send modern commentators on nationalism into a state of apoplexy. It runs counter to western theories of nationalism as a secular phenomenon that, many claim, only developed with the birth of nation-states in the nineteenth century. This chapter will argue that there is indeed a direct connection between modern nationalism and pre-nineteenth century pro-Bulgar sentiment, bringing together the themes of church and nationalism in Bulgaria that have been discussed previously from a socio-historical perspective. It will also contend, however, that modern Bulgarian nationalism has succeeded in recruiting the BOC as an instrument of its own political purpose, and thus clarify the issues that underlie Raikin's statement. Through an analysis of the development of the relationship between church and nation in Bulgaria this chapter will move towards a clear understanding of this argument in conjunction with contemporary research in the area of religion, nation and nationalism.

DEFINING THE KEY CONCEPTS
Ecclesiastical Nationalism

Peter Kuzmic in a 1992 article argued that nationalism has been one of the major challenges facing the traditional Balkan Churches during the process of replacing communist ideology: "The major problem for the Christian Church and its mission may be the temptation to return to a quasi-Constantinian model of Church-State co-operation. In this process... there is an intense and valid rediscovery of national-religious identity."[2] The weakness of Kuzmic's theory is its situational generality, for in the Bulgarian context, as Raikin has previously implied, the 'quasi-Constantinian model' has never been terminated by the Bulgarian Church. That intimate relationship between church, state and nation is a service which Bulgaria's Orthodox ecclesiastical hierarchy has performed throughout the centuries with enthusiasm and without reservation. For example, after the collapse of communism in 1989 the Holy Synod wrote in support of Bulgaria's new government:

> The Holy Orthodox Church is the traditional confession of the Bulgarian people. The Bulgarian Orthodox Church is linked with the history and the development of our nation. It is a Church of the people, a democratic church.
>
> For more than 1100 years now our church has been educating and cultivating unflinchingly and with zeal the believing fellow countrymen of the mother country and outside it in loyalty to Holy Orthodoxy, which is the history of the nation over the centuries. The Bulgarian Orthodox Church has made an exceptional contribution in keeping alive national self-consciousness, and in creating a rich spiritual culture within our borders...it has helped during the years of slavery to preserve the mother tongue, the morality and the religious and moral traditions of the Bulgarian people. It is with good reason that out Orthodox Church is called a Church of the people.
>
> Our Church has lived and will continue to live with the successes and hardships of the mother country. That is why it welcomes with complete approval the nation-wide striving for a renovating process of the Fatherland's government... With good conscience the church will in every way contribute towards achieving national unity... and will teach the people to labour diligently where their duty requires it.[3]

Such public utterances are evidence that for the BOC religion and nationhood are identical realities, dependent on one another, the nation providing the body and the church the soul to Bulgaria.[4] One of the recurrent themes in the Bulgarian Orthodox press today is the parallel continuity between church and nation, linking that progression historically to the Patriarchates of the First and Second Bulgarian empires. This doctrine is not new. As this thesis has shown, the close identity of church, state and nation has been advanced by every Bulgarian historian from Paisii to the present day and by every leader of the BOC past and present.[5] The church's strength, it appears, is founded more in Bulgaria's particularity and unity with political and national history, than in the ecumenism and mission of universal Orthodoxy. In electing to walk along the path of traditional Bulgarian nationalism the present leaders of the BOC have given the impression that they are seeking to regain a place of dignity and respectability in the hearts of the nation after the problematical years of communism, during which they were accused of compromise and accommodation with the former regime.

Historical Foundations of Nationalism

The foremost difficulty in attempting to define nation and nationalism is to find any agreement within the diverse formulae encompassing the subject. Nevertheless, it is vital to comprehend the historical foundation behind these theories as this will enable us to analyse and interpret them in relation to the subject of this particular research. Within the context of this research the term 'nationalism' is used to convey devotion to a cultural-linguistic collectivity which has manifested itself in its respect toward the history, culture, traditions and religion of a particular nation and seeks to promote a specific culture and way of life identified as that of the nation.[6]

Balkan nationalism was initially affected by the German nationalist movement, particularly the eighteenth century work of philosopher Johann Gottfried von Herder (1744-1803).[7] At the height of the German nationalist period von Herder emphasised the importance of respecting, preserving and advancing national groupings. He argued that nations were not defined by imperial dynastic power structures, but were differentiated by linguistic and historical-cultural factors. This theory coincided with the situation in South-Eastern Europe where religion had been the dominating cultural differentiation in people's lives for a number of centuries. By the nineteenth century Bulgarian nationalism had developed into what has been termed 'Christoslavism', the theory that all Slavs are Christian by nature and therefore are racially Christian.[8] Although few scholars have attempted to argue this from an academic or theological perspective, the belief continues to be implicit in the contemporary religio-cultural debate over the issue 'to be Bulgarian is to be

Orthodox'. Eugene Lemberg rejects the theory that common qualities such as religion, language and culture are what make a nation. He prefers to talk of nationalism as a "system of notions, values and norms…an ideology," which demarcate a group from its environment.[9] In Bulgaria's social predicament during the nineteenth century, however, that defining 'system' was religion. Indeed, sociologists have pointed out that the intimate relationship between nationalist and religious movements in the nineteenth century both had inspirational and revivalist characteristics.[10] Opposing the unifying cultural and ideological theories of nation, and thus contradicting the ecclesiastical Bulgarian definition of nationalism, Eric Hobsbawn suggests that the political and modern nature of nationality were born purely of nineteenth century political machinations.[11]

Both these concepts are based on an original differentiation promoted by Friedrich Meinecke between *Staatnation* (nation-state) and *Kulturalnation* (cultural nation): "We can divide nations into cultural and state-nations: into those which rest basically on a certain commonly experienced cultural possession and those which rest basically on the unifying power of a shared political history and constitution. Shared language, shared literature and shared religion are the most important and effective cultural goods that create and hold a cultural nation together."[12] This differentiation has taken many forms including its most recent articulation between 'modernist' and 'traditionalist' approaches. Every theory, however, follows Meinecke's basic model of separation: modern-political nation or traditional-cultural/religious nation.

Although theorists would prefer to promote one or another of these concepts, this research asks if such a strict demarcation is really possible in the Bulgarian case? Both theories have there place in the context of the Bulgarian nation: the modernist theory explains clearly the progression and development of nineteenth century political machinations, while the traditionalist theory retains significance for what happened prior to and to an extent simultaneously with the modern era. Therefore although contemporary nationalist debate surrounding 'nation-state' versus 'cultural nation' retains significance, in the context of this research it would be profitable to speak of 'cultural nation' and 'nation-state' in parallel, such as the 'cultural nation-state'.

Nationalism has political and cultural preconditions often rooted in the history of a nation. Hence, this research proposes that both the idea and first forms of nationalism in Bulgaria appeared before the nineteenth century and the so-called 'age of nationalism'. Although political nation-states began to manifest themselves simultaneous with the break up of the Ottoman empire, they still continued to be dominated by religious issues. In the Bulgarian situation the demise of Ottoman administration enabled the creation of a Bulgarian *millet*. However, this cannot be deemed to have been as a result of Bulgarian nationalism per se, because a nation did not exist. It is therefore a problem of the language and terminology used. In Bulgaria's nineteenth century struggle for church autonomy it may be better to speak, not of nationalism but of *milletism*. Whichever term is preferred the concept of distinctiveness and separation from the 'other' remains the same. Undoubtedly the modern concept of nation-state has imposed itself as the dominant paradigm but it is not the only one: "The paradox of the nation state epoch lies exactly in the fact that, by ever more intensifying national differentiation, the unity of the same, or similar, historical principles is still preserved."[13]

It is clear that Balkan and particularly Bulgarian nationalism have followed quite a different path from their West European counterparts. The precise geographical territory on which Balkan nations were to exist was unclear, unlike that of the western nations. Therefore those first modern Balkan nationalists had to deal initially with the creation of a national identity within unspecified territorial borders. Religion and the specifics of local ecclesiastical eparchial borders lent themselves to the formation of Bulgarian identity as a nation. Each Balkan group in attempting to produce a history of its own pointed to the ecclesiastical traditions of its national church to emphasise its cultural and territorial difference from its neighbour. Also as the importance of language as a carrier of national consciousness was recognised and consequently the centrality of Bulgaria's role in the birth of the Slavic vernacular strengthened. However, to comprehend the foundational links between church and nation we must look back further still.

Formative Links Between Church and Nation/State

Georges Florovsky noted that Christianity is essentially a social religion whose reference point is society. Christianity by necessity requires to express itself in relation to society and state.[14] That association was reciprocated by the state for the first time in the Edict of Milan, pronounced by Constantine Augustus and Licinius Augustus in 313 A.D. This established Christianity as a *religio licita* thereby giving the Christian religion legal status and making the persecution of its followers illegal.[15] Subsequently, it became the favoured religion of the Roman Empire and later in 380 A.D. the official religion of the Empire, when Theodosius I (379-395) announced Christianity *Cunctos populos* in the Edict of Thessalonica. This created a radically new situation which set the tone for the church's relationship with the state for the next thousand years: the church would serve the empire and the empire would protect the church. As the administrative centre of the Roman empire moved eastwards it inclined toward Greek culture and language and Latin was discarded as the administrative language of Church and State. Consequently religion and state became increasingly linked.[16] As a result of the Great Schism of 1054 and later the sacking and occupation of Constantinople during the Fourth Crusade in the thirteenth century, Byzantine citizens identified the west as their enemy. Consequently bonds between Eastern Orthodoxy and the Byzantine State reinforced so that Orthodoxy and Byzantine nationhood became intricately intertwined.[17] With the Ottoman conquest in the fourteenth century and the establishment of the *millet* system religion metamorphosed to become the sole determiner of cultural identity. The historical equation of religious and political unity equalling national identity was even accepted by 19th century nationalist movements as the framework in which they sought to develop more secular concepts of the nation state.

The tension between the universal and the particular has been ever present within Orthodoxy. This can be identified clearly in the church's practical struggle to express itself as part of the wider catholic Church while simultaneously being part of an independent national or local church. All Orthodox churches belong to the one universal Church, having the same liturgy, creed and canon; at the same time each local church requires to express its own cultural attributes, its historical peculiarities, its independence. Nevertheless, this expression of independence requires to be held in balance with the universality of the Church and in an effort to achieve this equanimity the Ecumenical Patriarchate in Constantinople denounced nationalism within Orthodoxy in 1904.[18]

Despite this denunciation contemporary Orthodox theologians have expressed their dismay that every local Orthodox Church now exhibits nationalistic tendencies. According to John Meyendorff the Church became absorbed in nationalism during the nineteenth century.[19] As a consequence the Balkan Orthodox churches became deeply disunited, affirming their national identities at the expense of Orthodoxy's universal mission. Individual churches treated each other with suspicion and hostility and submitted to what Vladimir Solovyov termed the "provincialism of local traditions."[20] This resulted in the sowing of unwanted division within the churches of the Balkans which affects the region to the present day. Research undertaken during the spring of 1994 revealed that people from every Balkan nation confessed an aversion to their neighbour, Christian or otherwise. For this reason Maros Mpegzos has called nationalism the enemy of the people.[21] The research further suggested that the educational system within the Balkans may be at fault, as it has the propensity to instil a sense of national, cultural and spiritual superiority over its neighbours.[22]

The Bulgarian educational system has been heavily influenced by Paisii Hilendarski's *Slavo-Bulgarian History*. His was the first national revival attempt to single out the Bulgarian national community from other Balkan communities by restoring the memory of a common past. In so doing he sought to implant in his reader's minds the concept that the Bulgarian nation was a fact of history, an existing reality within its own justifiable borders and not something to be created but rather re-established. In order to achieve the emancipation of the Bulgarian nation, through its separation and opposition to others, he set a number of goals before the Bulgarian people: firstly, he emphasised its religious distinction as an Orthodox Christian community; then as a Slavic community he emphasised its distinctive language and culture; and lastly, as a separate ethnic group within the greater Slav community, he advanced the theory of its racial distinction, thereby maintaining the uniqueness of Bulgarians among the Slavic peoples.[23] In this way he established a foundation for future national emancipation by creating a history which emphasised Bulgaria's uniqueness and superiority. Paisii's *History* also created within the Bulgarian educational system a model for proclaiming national superiority: "There are many historical facts and phenomena which may help strengthen our sense of national dignity by bringing to the fore the advantages of our people over other peoples..."[24]

National segregation, although influenced by Paisii, was moulded in the struggle to establish modern secular education in Bulgaria.[25] The struggle centred on the use of Bulgarian language in schools. Indeed, the efforts to restore the Bulgarian vernacular became one in the same as the effort for political emancipation. Thus, during the nineteenth century and in the birth of many of the Balkan nation-states language became a politicised tool. One of the entitlements for becoming a nation-state was justified by the existence of a culture's independent vernacular language.[26] For this reason the struggle for affirmation of the Bulgarian national vernacular became an important step in the struggle for national state sovereignty.

THE DEVELOPMENT OF BULGARIAN NATIONALISM
Pre-Ottoman Bulgaria

The territory comprising of modern Bulgaria was first settled by the Slavs in the sixth and seventh centuries. However, it was not until the seventh century that the area was invaded by the Proto-Bulgars and remained a loosely organised medieval kingdom until the ninth century. Following the ascension of Khan Boris I (852-889) the Bulgarian kingdom progressed from being a somewhat irrelevant and unorganised 'pagan' kingdom to become and independent sovereign Christian empire. Under the rule of Boris an independent Bulgarian national and Christian identity was born, some ten centuries before the birth of the secular Bulgarian nation-state. The evidence provided in the first chapter of this dissertation would suggest that from the ninth century 'nationalism' or 'strong independent cultural identity' has been an integral part of the Bulgarian Church and nation.

In the eleventh century Bulgaria fell under the sway of the Byzantine empire and in the fourteenth century was invaded by the Ottoman empire, remaining under its administration until the late nineteenth century. Therefore, for the greater part of its existence Bulgaria has been under the jurisdiction of a foreign power and during this lengthy period of alien domination Bulgarian national and cultural consciousness almost disappeared. For this reason the year 1762 is cited as a definitive moment in Bulgarian history, for it was then that Paisii Hilendarski completed his *Slavo-Bulgarian History*. Driven by fervent national consciousness and by his fellow Bulgarians abject lack of national awareness Paisii wrote his *History* to prevent the total disappearance of Bulgarian national territory, people, culture and history, which had almost been accomplished by means of the Islamicisation and Hellenisation of the Bulgarian people over five centuries. Through time Paisii's *History* succeeded to spark national consciousness in the Bulgarian people which in turn gave rise to the advent of the Bulgarian National Revival.

Orthodox Christianity and Nation-Building in Ottoman Bulgaria

For Byzantine Christendom the fall of Constantinople was a decisive turning point. In the article entitled "'Imagined Communities' and the Origins of the National Question in the Balkans", by the Greek historian P. M. Kitromilides,[27] the author uses modern theories of nationalism to reassess the traditional comprehension of Balkan scholars regarding the function of the Orthodox Church under Ottoman rule.

Kitromilides argues that Balkan nationalist mythology has obscured a correct understanding of the relation between Orthodoxy and nationalism.[28] Therefore if we are to reassess this relationship, particularly in regard to Bulgaria, we must see through stereotypical nationalist interpretations which promote the view that the BOC played a major role in preserving the ethnic identity of Bulgarians under Ottoman rule and in guiding their national awakening. An explicit claim of this interpretation is the identification of Orthodoxy with nationality and the ensuing recognition of the BOC as a vanguard of Bulgarian nationalism. Kitromilides proffers general criticism of Eastern Orthodoxy as the preserver of collective identity under the Ottomans, however, his criticism is pertinent to Bulgarian historiography's *continuity theory*, which promotes the view that as preserver of Bulgarian collective identity the BOC created the basis for future nation-building and political independence.[29]

First and foremost Kitromilides draws attention to the contradiction between religious and national communities. Basing his criticism on the biblical exhortation of Galatians 3:28 that in Christ "there is neither Jew nor Greek, slave nor free, male nor female, for you are all one in Christ", he argues that Christianity's demand for universalism established the basis for Orthodox ecumenism, which in turn prevented the Patriarchate of Constantinople from being affected by nineteenth century enlightenment ideals which called for national identity and the establishment of separate nation-states. By this interpretation the nationalisation of Balkan church organisation required a radical break from Orthodox canon and tradition that condemned nationalism as phyletism.[30]

Theological reasoning brings to the fore the fundamental and inescapable antimony between Orthodoxy and nationalism, between the incompatibility of the communities of religion and nation. Indeed, when nationalism raised its head the Church met the challenge with open hostility. Remember, for example, the Bulgarian Exarchates response to the nationalist rebels. The Bulgarian ecclesiastical hierarchy refused to support the nationalist cause, which threatened to ruin their relationship with the Ottoman Porte. Instead they handed the rebels, which included some of Bulgaria's greatest national heroes, over to the Ottoman authorities. Kitromilides claims therefore that one of the greatest anachronisms in Balkan historiography consists in its presentation of the Ottoman religious political system as being based on national difference; the difference he argues was based not on national but religious distinction. The only way in which the Orthodox Church could maintain a collective sense of identity among Christians in the Balkans was by emphasising their religious unity. But under the Ottoman *millet* system the mixing of Orthodoxy and nationality implied a radical renunciation of biblical principle and Orthodox ecumenism. For this reason Kitromilides criticises the way that Balkan historiography has uncritically accepted the link between Orthodoxy and national identity, a link which has been traced throughout this research. Bulgarian national historiographical tradition has been premised on the assumption that the BOC played a major role in nation building by preserving collective identity under the Ottomans. The BOC in short is supposed to have created Bulgarian national identity through the years of captivity. According to Kitromilides' assessment, however, we must conclude that if the BOC did indeed contribute to the preservation of Bulgarian collective identity, this distinction was religious not national in content.

Despite Kitromilides' thought-provoking analysis, his article requires additional comment particularly in relation to the specifics of the Bulgarian situation. His presentation of the contradiction between Christian biblical foundations and the birth of national communities, although not incorrect, is utopian. It fails to recognise the complex interrelation between political and ecclesiastical powers prior to the emergence of nation-states. Failure to do so creates a problematic historical vacuum, for since its recognition by the Roman Empire in the fourth century the Christian church has maintained an intensely close relationship to the political powers of the day, a relationship articulated by the classic edict of Emperor Justinian (527-565) in 535: "The greatest blessings of mankind are the gifts of God which have been granted us by the mercy on high: the priesthood and the imperial authority. The priesthood ministers to the things divine; the imperial authority is set over, and shows diligence in, things human; but both proceed from one and the same source, and both adorn the life of man...."[31] There can be no doubt that in Byzantine understanding the emperor and the church were intricately connected in a glorious concept of symphony: a sovereign empire required an autocephalous church. The Bulgars demonstrated that they had successfully adopted the Byzantine model by establishing the Bulgarian kingdom as a fully independent political power with its own self-governing church organisation, albeit in theological and liturgical unity with the Constantinople Patriarchate.

This model entailed a major weakness; if political power collapsed so would the independence of the church. Therefore after the conquest of Bulgaria in 1393 its independent church structure disintegrated and after the fall of Constantinople in 1453 all Orthodox Christian inhabitants of the sultan were incorporated into a single church organisation, under the authority of the Patriarch of Constantinople. The Ottoman *millet* system did not, however, create a radical break from former imperial religious tradition, rather it flowed in logical consequence for the Byzantine imperial church, as it unified in 'symphony' with its new political master. Indeed, the situation was viewed as providential, as the *millet* protected the purity of the Orthodox faith from the danger of Latin Christianity.

From his historical analysis Kitromilides claims that Orthodox churches in the Balkans were neither ethnically nor nationally defined: "The medieval churches were not national churches because their empires were not national; such an assertion in anachronistic."[32] The findings of this research would disagree with that rejection of Orthodoxy as a synonym for national identification in the period prior to the nineteenth century. Kitromilides' anachronism lies again in the technical form of language used. The historical preview of the BOC, in Chapter One revealed that Tsar Boris' goal for his church was to be an instrument unifying Slav and Proto-Bulgar elements in the Bulgarian population resulting in the strengthening of his kingdom. Therefore the Bulgarian medieval church was founded and developed precisely on ethnic and nationalist foundations. History's generalised assumption that this relationship changed only with the advent of modern nationalism is clearly misconceived in the Bulgarian context.

Nevertheless, the fragmentation of the Orthodox *millet* in Ottoman Europe into smaller national units during the nineteenth century did occur as the result of radical western national ideological ideals which transformed the *millet* system and Orthodox tradition into the idea that nation-building must be accompanied by church institutional independence. However, Chapter One of this research suggests that this was not a novel idea, but an ancient one which had been lost in the midst of centuries of foreign domination and re-established by Paisii Hilendarski's *Slavo-Bulgarian History* and the advent of nineteenth century nationalism. As a consequence of the nation-state ideal, the Orthodox *millet* divided into smaller ethnic segments, a situation theologically rejected by the Constantinople Patriarchate. Although Kitromilides strongly argues his position, another question arises concerning Greek-Bulgar ecclesiastical enmity, a religio-cultural struggle which commenced in the fifteenth century. From the evidence presented it is clear that this ethnic dispute was not solely defended on theological grounds, there were also cultural factors present. Therefore what was legally and canonically permitted for the Greeks was seen as sinful when the Bulgarians attempted to protect their religio-cultural legacy.

This critique of Kitromilides' reassessment raises that most contentious question in the ongoing debate on the concept of nation and nationalism: do nations have their origins in the modern political, social and economic conditions of the nineteenth century, or should these roots be sought in more ancient times? Kitromilides asks the same question in another manner: did Orthodoxy become politically instrumentalised in the nineteenth century nation-building movement, or was the Church always an indicator of collective identity, before, during and after the Ottomans? Although the latter view is generally closer to the relationship between church and nation in Bulgaria, as outlined in the *continuity theory*, it would appear to be a matter of degree: to what degree were national characteristics learned or acquired in the modern national construction process, or were they continuations of medieval kingdoms? The modern debate on nationalism may assist us to understand these questions and contribute to our comprehension of the relationship between the Church and national movements in Bulgaria.

Bulgaria During the Period of State Nationalism

The nineteenth century marked a new chapter in church-state relations for Orthodoxy in the Bulgaria. Disparate medieval Balkan societies had been politically unified by the Ottoman conquest and with the establishment of the *millet* system, they were ecclesiastically, culturally and psychologically bound together by the traditions of Eastern Orthodoxy. However, with the import of Western Enlightenment ideals in the late eighteenth and early nineteenth centuries modern concepts of secular statehood threatened to subvert both Ottoman rule and Orthodox unity.

The work of national awakeners, such as Paisii Hilendarski, although emphasising Bulgaria's Orthodox history, actually succeeded in loosening that ancient concept of Orthodox unity, which in turn gave impetus to the gradual articulation of a secular historical interpretation of Bulgarian identity. Those secular inspired patriots aimed to subordinate religion to state power, therefore by accepting the autocephaly of the Bulgarian Church the politicians hoped to control it. Thereafter the church was stripped of its authority and became, in imitation of the western model, an agency of the state.

Through the ensuing Bulgarian national revival period the socio-political process toward independence passed through a number of stages. The first affirmed the cultural and religious character of Bulgarian national identity, then organisations were formed which championed the national cause and lastly elite concepts of nationalism were espoused by the masses in the formation of the secular Bulgarian state in 1878. After the "first great victory of Bulgarian Nationalism", the establishment of the Bulgarian Exarchate (1870), Bulgarians turned their attention to agitating for their separation from the Ottoman empire.[33] Thus towards the end of the nineteenth century the concept of 'nation' became tantamount to Bulgaria. The national revival era spawned a new class of Bulgarians; merchants, intelligentsia and priests, who guided the Bulgarian people, informing them of who they were and perhaps more importantly who they were not. National awareness served to differentiate ethnic Bulgarians from ethnic Turks. National consciousness rose to such levels that many Bulgarians were willing to defend the sovereignty of their land. Thus alongside the struggle for and introduction of an independent national state, including church institutions, army, schools and a state constitution, arose a spontaneous wave of violence against former symbols and reminders of Ottoman-Muslim power. Muslim families were forced to flee, houses were burned and mosques destroyed as the Orthodox Christian population sought to obliterate the characteristics of previous domination.

Once the San Stefano borders of Bulgaria had been reversed by the Berlin Treaty the re-incorporation of lost-territories became the goal of the nationalists. Bulgarian nationalism therefore did not only express a pride in the borders agreed by European politicians, but demanded the recognition of lands that historically belonged to Bulgaria and were now, it was argued, populated by 'ethnic' Bulgarians. Therefore as early as 1878 during debates within the Constituent Assembly it was proclaimed that "... we who are part of this nation shall never be calm... We shall always support the wishes and attempts, of those, who are flesh of our flesh and blood of our blood...."[34]

In this sense the Balkan Wars and to an extent the two World Wars, demonstrated the people's commitment to Bulgarian nationalist cause. For those wars were not fought to fulfil someone else's greater European or global objectives but were undertaken to accomplish the national unification of Bulgaria's dispersed ethnic population within her historically justifiable borders: "Bulgaria has always united in a single entity only the Bulgarian people; the waged wars, in general, are aimed at the unification of the people."[35] However, the liberation of Bulgarians outside Bulgaria's recognised borders was not the only goal of the nationalists; they called for the enlargement of the state to include regions that belonged to Bulgaria in the past: "The place where the substantial portion of our people is left under foreign rule should point to the direction of the country's development in order to assemble all its compatriots under a single culture and statehood."[36] Thus the development of the nation and the longing for the establishment of a Greater Bulgaria were presented as the finest Bulgarian virtues, as the ultimate justice crowning the people's movement towards happiness.[37] Only by achieving this goal would the Bulgarian people be enabled to "grow and improve on the basis of the values which incorporate them into spiritual entities."[38] By this interpretation anything which stood against national unification and the expansionist efforts of the Bulgarian state was deemed unfair and unjust. Hence, the findings of the Berlin Congress were 'unfair' because they lacerated parts of the nation, but war on the other hand, especially the First Balkan War (1912-13), was viewed as being "liberating and legitimate."[39] This value system was structured around two teleological theories: progress is compulsory for humanity and humanity's progress is conditioned upon the progress of nations, which in Bulgaria's situation was feasible only under national unification. Symbolically then 1870 marked the transition from church-nationalism to state-building nationalism and 1878 the passing from state-building to irredentist nationalism, a stage which would last until 1944.

Nationalism, Internationalism and Communist Bulgaria

The communists initially considered Bulgaria's xenophobic concentration on nationalist issues to be a debilitating obstacle in the establishment of their global and domestic policies. Steered by Moscow the authorities of the Fatherland Front sought to remove the hindrance through the creation of a Balkan Federal Republic. This would be built upon the principles of internationalism rather than on the right of the nation. One of the first indicators of this new direction appeared in a school textbook from 1946, which talked about the "emancipation of the people" and the "possibility to realise people's interests". The realisation of people's happiness, it was stated, could be achieved only at an international level and therefore the historical narration of the book attempted to diminish Bulgarian national identity and engender a greater sense of Balkan détente. The textbook implied that continuing on a path of inward national self-absorption and by claiming superiority over fellow communist neighbours would lead to 'catastrophe'; whereas internationalism was linked with the concept of 'salvation': "The new path [communism] which Bulgaria takes on – the path of the people's welfare, Slavic brotherhood and unification – is a path traced by our history, by our historical development. Each deviation from this path has led to national calamity."[40] Through this historical materialistic interpretative lens of Stanev's view of Bulgarian history, the praise of war and struggle for unification, were understood to be "aggressive and catastrophic". Nationalist ideals were to be replaced with an internationalist identity based no longer on universal orthodoxy but communist internationalism.

From the 1970's, however, the communist credo changed substantially. The emphasis became nationally focussed once again with the authorities claiming that all citizens of Bulgaria were Bulgarian. The socio-political reasoning behind this emphasis was to affirm the ethnic identity of Bulgarians, to the exclusion of any religious reference. Bulgarians were treated as one non-religious ethnos.[41] Nevertheless, the xenophobic nationalism of previous Bulgarian generations continued within this appeal to international communism. As shown in Chapter Six of this thesis the Bulgarian Communist Party followed its own nationalist programme which aimed at assimilating every Bulgarian Pomak and Turkic Muslim into one homogeneous Bulgarian population.[42] The BCP used every means at their power, including educational and ecclesiastical resources, to prove that there were no Turks in Bulgaria. Even Bulgarian Orthodox Church history was reinterpreted to justify the government's confrontational policy to separate Muslim religious and national identity.

So why did the BCP undertake the assimilation process? The Bulgarian press suggested that the government had been attempting to defuse virulent Islamic separatist movements.[43] However, a contemporary report on Bulgarian ethnic groupings appears to provide an answer closer to reality. The study reported that Bulgaria's Turkish Muslim population had grown alarmingly, whilst 'Christian' Bulgarian numbers were on the decrease.[44] The Politburo suggested that in this Muslim-growth lay the possibility of an eventual Ottoman-cum-Turkish revanchism, which if unchecked would lead to the Muslims outnumbering the Orthodox Slav population. In this manner the communist authorities showed their national policies to be on par with both post-Ottoman and wartime Bulgarian governments, particularly in their attempts to obliterate any remaining vestige of Ottoman rule in Bulgaria.

Religion, Nationalism and Civil Society in Post-Communist Bulgaria

The preceding chapters have revealed that during the eras of Byzantine, Ottoman, and even to an extent Communist control, the Orthodox Church has been recognised and protected as the traditional religion of the Bulgarian people. However, whenever Bulgaria has entered into periods of independence, democracy, cultural pluralism and/or religious diversity, the discourse on religion, or more precisely the place of the BOC in society, has become increasingly prominent. This agrees with Gunter Rohrmoser's 1989 opinion that "when the question of an alternative to Marxism-Leninism is seriously put…then the symbiosis between religion and nationalism could gain attractive power."[45]

This discourse, prevalent in post-communist Bulgaria, has articulated itself through the introduction of new religious statutes. Immediately after the fall of communism one of the first steps of the new government was to introduce revised laws on religion. As Paul Mojzes remarks: "Throughout the region, constitutions and laws were written that contained guarantees for human rights and religious liberties, bringing Eastern European states in line with the Western democratic civil rights tradition."[46] Initially these new laws guaranteed freedom of conscience and religious liberty, replacing former restrictive laws. In 2002, however, a new bill was introduced favouring the traditional role of the BOC as an "inseparable part of Bulgaria's historical, spiritual and cultural heritage."[47] This decision met with sharp criticism from human activists, politicians, minority religious groups and the European Union. Its adoption has been considered retrogressive, particularly for the development of democratic civil society.[48]

By taking this decision Eastern Orthodoxy, once again, has been advanced as the 'traditional' and 'national' religion in Bulgaria, and all others religions have been deemed alien to the prevailing national ethos. As a result of political and ecclesiastical activity they have been accused of betraying national interests and have become objects of societal intolerance.[49] However, this development is not specific to Bulgaria; it has been a general repercussion which has arisen across post-communist Europe where nations have searched for symbols and myths to provide orientation and identity during a decade of radically changing circumstance. There has been a return to the values of an 'imagined community' that existed in the past. In this sense nationalism has worked as an anti-modern factor in which the nation becomes a transformation of traditional pre-modern realities.[50] Whilst accepting the need to maintain stability in the midst of socio-political chaos, genuine religious freedom can never be achieved through abstract legal and governmental provision for the traditional church:

Experience shows that the framers of the post-communist constitutional provisions for religious liberty generally tended to interpret the notion of religion in Christian terms and even in the terms of the Christian churches traditions for a particular country. This trend nurtured by the common lack of religious culture, not to say ignorance in religious matters...is hardly justifiable at the level of state policy.[51]

Father Innokenti Pavlov, in analysing the preferential treatment of the Orthodox Church, has suggested that these actions are attempts to endorse a new state ideology to replace the spiritual void after the collapse of communism. In addition, however, he identifies an ambition within particular political circles that attempts to promote the Orthodox Church as the new compulsory 'national' ideology in the place of the old.[52] For this reason other religious movements are considered to be an alien threat to the state, and restrictions can therefore be legitimately place on them. Father Pavlov's argument is open to the criticism that it fails to consider the constitutional provisions which explicitly favour a model of separation between church and state. Yet the Bulgarian church-state separation has clearly articulated itself within the terms of the 'accommodationist' approach, or to quote Mark Howe the "liberal principle of tolerance" as opposed to the "radical principle of religious liberty."[53] This explains why Bulgarian governmental preference is still given to the traditional church of the state. In other words, constitutionally defined separation signifies neither neutrality, indifference, or neglect.

Roman Herzog contends that there is nothing improper in this position. In his interpretation the 'accommodationist' approach is proof that the democratic state is developing along acceptable lines, for by acknowledging constitutionally the fundamental principle of human dignity one cannot be indifferent to, or simply reject, the churches or religious communities which have been important to the religious orientation of the nation.[54] According to this view it is only right and proper that the BOC be given a preferential position in Bulgaria.

A contradiction now arises, however, in that post-communist Bulgaria's support of the BOC does not equate with her leanings toward Europe. The Bulgarian Ministry of Education's 1993 textbook set the nation on a new European-geopolitical perspective. This new perspective laid stress not so much on 'national' identification as on 'universal' citizenship in which: "... shared human values and the goal of a united Europe does not in any way contradict national identity."[55] However, it does contradict Orthodoxy's tacit parity with Bulgarian national identity, a contradiction that will require to be voiced within the religious pluralism of multi-cultural European existence.

The 'Fortress Mentality' Within Orthodoxy

This research has exposed the central preoccupation of 'nation' and 'religious tradition' in Bulgaria, both of which have succeeded in creating a powerful unifying effect within society. Ecclesiastical nationalism has been underpinned by the conviction that the church is deeply rooted in the national ethos, so much so that it considers Bulgarian national culture to be unsustainable without the church: "It is not the Church which should fear separation from the state, but the state which should fear separation from the state, as this would separate Bulgaria from her soul."[56] However, as modern civil society has evolved and particularly as Bulgaria manoeuvres to become a full member of the European Union, society has come to oppose this traditional stance. The re-invention of South-East European civil society, mirroring patterns of western democracy and society, is no longer based on principles of ethnic and religious uniformity, but rather is founded on notions such as democracy, pluralism and tolerance. Therefore the Orthodox Church in South-Eastern Europe finds itself in a complex situation. On the one hand it has to recover from the spiritual stagnation it experienced under communism, while on the other it has to come to terms with new social realities, the greatest of which is religious pluralism.

This is a major reason why the BOC has found it difficult to function in contemporary Bulgaria and why it struggles to maintain the patterns of the past and reinterpret its history towards a future in which the Church will once again takes its place at the head of nation and society. This ultimate desire is best expressed in the words of Dostoyevsky's *The Brothers Karamazov*: "The Church is not to be transformed into the State.... On the contrary the State is transformed into the Church, it will ascend and become a church over the whole world – which is the glorious destiny ordained for the Orthodox Church."[57] In this vision the Orthodox Church attempts to supplant the State altogether, reflecting the true *orthos* project of the Church, not to exist with the State as a necessary evil, but to strive to reconstruct the world on Christian Orthodox principles. Dostoyevsky articulates an implicit vision shared by Orthodox hierarchy, which explains the intense struggle to maintain the BOC's traditional role within society.

This 'fortress mentality' is stereotypical of the behaviour of a church seeking to protect itself after enduring the oppression of totalitarianism. It is the reaction of a church which cooperated with the communist regime, initially in order to survive repression and later because it was assured particular privileges. It must be stressed, however, that despite 'survival' the BOC has been systematically and politically used, on many occasions willingly, not only by communism but also by Byzantine and Ottoman powers, so much so that the BOC now perpetuates a model of 'functional religion'. The BOC has never experienced another model and therefore follows this *modus operandi* as its benchmark. For this reason the BOC continues to cooperate with the powers of the day, seeking to survive by promoting a symphonic unity between Church and state in inharmonious times. As a safety feature, this 'fortress mentality' has tended to express itself socially in negative terms, exposing the BOC's unwillingness or inability to interact with contemporary society. Although this situation is largely due to the BOC's refusal to accept cultural plurality and religious diversity, it is also strongly based on Orthodox theology which focuses on the soteriological role of the Church in terms of eschatology. David Martin forewarned that any Church incorporated within a political power structure would eventually be involved in the ruins of that structure.[58] Ina Merdjanova fears that the BOC has become a visible illustration of that omen and has declared that the church must develop relevant theological understandings, practical social explanations and *modus operandi* for a new democratic, pluralistic and diverse European era. The failure to do so, she argues, could have grave consequences for the Orthodox Church.[59]

NATION AND NATIONALISM IN CONTEMPORARY RESEARCH

Research encompassing the concepts of nation and nationalism has attracted attention from a wide range of academic fields. However, in the context of this investigative research Ernest Gellner's social anthropological views and Anthony D. Smith's contribution to ethnicity research have been given special consideration.[60] In this context, Smith's theory will explicate the importance of the national idea, linking together history, religion and politics during the decline of the Ottoman empire, whereas Gellner will put forward the opposing modernist viewpoint.

Gellner is an advocate of the modern hypothesis for the origins of nations and nationalism. He argues that it was from the ashes of agrarian society and the advent of nineteenth century industrial society that modern states were born, unifying populations in common national structures. This national identity connected disparate peoples who, due to the radical change in society, have lost their connection to one another; nationalism was thus the glue which held people together. He accentuates the modernity of nation-states by completely rejecting any attempt to connect his theory to myths surrounding the antiquity of nations: "Nationalism sometimes takes pre-existing cultures and turns them into nations, sometimes invents them, and often obliterates pre-existing cultures... But nationalism is not the awakening and assertion of... mythical, supposedly natural and given units. It is, on the contrary, the crystallisation of new units, suitable for the conditions now prevailing...."[61] Therefore, according to Gellner, nationalism is a modern ideology and the nation-state a modern political entity, both of which emerged entirely due to social conditions in the western world during the late eighteenth and early nineteenth centuries. His specific use of the phrase 'the western world' is an important insertion which lays much of his socio-political theory in relation to the 'non-western' experience of Bulgaria open to question.

However, there are elements in Gellner's 'modernist' theory which remain important in explaining the development of the relationship between religion and nationalism in Bulgaria. It explains, for example, that the construction of a nation and that nation's history coalesce to form the notion that the nation in question has always existed.[62] By this interpretation national ideology retrieves from Bulgarian history the myths and cultural values that characterise contemporary society. It is in this sense that Benedict Anderson uses the term 'imagined communities' to express the phenomenon of modern nations being built on ideas and expectations provided by historians and folklorists.[63]

Critics of the 'modernist' theory reject the supposition that pre-existing cultures are used arbitrarily to support modern national development. Paul James criticises Gellner's approach and proposes a more conciliatory theory which considers a pattern of continuity between medieval and modern nations.[64] He suggests a theory which allows us to say that "while nations do not come into being until they are lived as such (or at least abstractly recognised as such, usually in the first instance by intellectuals or persons lifted out of the face-to face) the social forms which ground national formation are already lived prior to the generalisation of the new sense of historicity."[65]

However, one must consider that the 'modernist' position is generally poorly qualified to analyse nation-building in South-Eastern Europe, as the theory is based on Western European perspectives. The typology of Hans Kohn, whom we could perhaps describe as a contemporary of German nationalist school, is better suited in this context as he differentiates between a West and East European concept of nation.[66] According to Kohn the modern concept of nation emerged as the result of specific western historical and territorial determinants during the eighteenth century. As the concept of nation progressed eastwards those historical and territorial factors differed. The further east the theory ventured, the more mystical and historically fixated its construction became, linking itself to socio-cultural factors such as language, religion and ethnicity.[67]

Kohn's influence upon the more recent work of Anthony Smith is clearly observed in Smith's distinction between a western 'civic' national concept and an eastern 'ethnic' concept.[68] Central to this Eastern European historical interpretation of national development is the vitality of historical myth in construction of national collective identity. Smith maintains that there are clearly identifiable connections between pre-national ethnic groups and modern national communities.[69] The major difference between the continuing existence of Western and South-East European nations is that the existence of the Balkan nations is conditioned by myths based on historical memories. These memories are especially relevant in connection with the Bulgarian national movement's linking of religion and national identity. Smith comments that within these myths the organised religion of a nation often played a prominent role, but with the transformation into the modern era the bureaucratic state took on this role. In the case of Bulgaria the BOC functioned as the head of the *millet* during Ottoman times, as the practical expression of the Bulgarian ethnic community; but as the country developed into a modern bureaucratic state the BOC lost its place and position within society. Therefore, one could propose that the existence of the BOC is equally dependent and conditioned by national myth. Smith postulates further that these 'national myths' normally contain a number of common motifs including: a myth of origin in time; a myth of ancestry; a myth of migration; a myth of liberation; a myth of a golden age (with national heroes and cultural greatness); a myth of decline; and finally a myth of rebirth (or national revival).[70] The majority of these myths are present within Bulgaria's national historical narrative.

The presence of myth in the development and continuation of Balkan nations is not in question here. The debate is rather over its relevance in connection with the linkage of Bulgarian national identity and religion that is advocated by the Bulgarian national movement and the state. From the evidence of this thesis we know that national identity in Bulgaria was shaped during the nineteenth century within the framework of the *millet* system. Bulgarian national myth was therefore created in interaction with an Ottoman social organisation based upon religious criteria, but was undermined by the influence of the western nationalist categories. The development from *millet* to nation-state required the transformation from religious affiliation into national identity. The BOC became instrumentalised in the Bulgarian nation-building process as the historic institution that promoted the national, political and territorial goals of the modern state. The BOC continues to operate as this vanguard of Bulgarian nationalism because the national myth permits the church to be the institution of continuity that connects the Bulgarian religio-ethnic community to the modern nation.

CONCLUSION

Bulgaria's national consciousness, built upon historical, cultural and religious kinship has steered the Bulgarian nation throughout the centuries. In the nineteenth century Bulgarian nationalism achieved three important and positive goals: the creation of an independent church in the form of the Bulgarian Exarchate; the establishment of the Bulgarian

Principality and the union of the Principality with Eastern Rumelia. Once these goals had been accomplished Bulgarian nationalism took on negative xenophobic and irredentist qualities, features which the BOC has promoted and in which they have participated to the present day.

The preceding chapters have revealed how Bulgarian myths regarding the origin of the nation have unfolded within the theoretical framework of contemporary scholarship, corresponding in particular to the work of the German nationalists, particularly von Herder, Meinecke and Kohn and to the contemporary findings of Anthony Smith. Smith's model of ethnic communities transforming into modern nations corresponds to the situation of Balkan people's under the Ottomans as Eastern Orthodoxy acted as the chief mechanism of ethnic persistence among communities: "Religion then may preserve a sense of common ethnicity as if in a chrysalis."[71] His model supports what has been termed in Bulgaria as the *continuity theory*, a supplementary hypothesis to the research paradigm behind the *catastrophe theory*, both of which are integral to the Bulgarian historiographical tradition.

However, Smith's model does not take into account the fact that the *Rum millet* included a number of distinct ethnic identities. Therefore, how could religion, as Smith proposed, provide a sense of ethnic identity when the *millet* was not based on ethnic criteria? For this reason we must modify Smith's interpretation to emphasise that the Orthodox Church under the Ottomans was not an ethnic church, but became so under the political motivation and influence of the modern movement for national self-determination. In the progress toward national independence each ethnic group within the *millet* expressed its own cultural, linguistic and historical peculiarities to distance themselves from the Ecumenical Patriarchate. This tradition was emphasised via the *continuity theory* which invokes a connection between the political and ecclesiastical structures of the Bulgarian medieval kingdoms and the nineteenth century national revival movement.

In the national struggle for an independent and sovereign Bulgarian state, religion and church became political instruments used in order to achieve the national goal. Thus the nineteenth century development of independent nation-states represented not 'continuity' but a radical break with Orthodox tradition and the non-ethnic character of the Ottoman *millet* system. The movement for Bulgarian national independence defined Bulgarian national characteristics by denying *millet* tradition and emphasising the cultural, linguistic and historical differences between both Muslim Turks and Orthodox Greeks. It is interesting that the very same principles were applied by Tsar Boris and his advisors in the ninth century to legitimate early Bulgarian efforts to secede from Byzantium and the Constantinople Patriarchate. Therefore the national idea transformed both Bulgarian medieval religious history and Ottoman political domination. In so doing proof is established that 'nationalism' in Bulgaria is very much an ancient tradition related to Bulgarian ecclesiastical history.

The xenophobic features of Bulgarian nationalism have cloaked ethnic and religious discrimination in patriotic wrappings, placing membership in the Bulgarian Orthodox Church and devotion to the Fatherland above all. This brand of nationalism in Bulgaria is grounded, as was witnessed in previous chapters relating to the National Revival period in a national inferiority complex, which continues to view the Ottoman era as a catastrophic period in Bulgarian history. Xenophobic nationalism also masqueraded behind the Bulgarian communist credo of 'internationalism', as it sought to enforce an ethno-political homogenisation programme in an attempt to submerge the Turkish-Muslim minority into the Bulgarian-Christian majority.[72] The paradox is that the atheistic communist regime used the heritage of the BOC to their advantage, to argue that there were no ethnic Turks in Bulgaria, only Bulgarians whose forebears had converted to Islam under pressure. A representative of the former communist regime candidly expressed:

> Although the Bulgarian national consciousness of some of them may still be blurred, they are the same Bulgarian flesh and blood; they are the children of the Bulgarian nation; they were forcibly torn away and now they are coming back home. There are no Turks in Bulgaria.[73]

Bulgaria's plan to join the European Union in 2007 is ultimately tied up with its struggle for international approval and national dignity. However, the absence of either a democratic image or history suggests that nationalism will continue to maintain Bulgaria's cultural and religious links with history, indicating that Bulgarians are unwilling to put their mythological past behind them. In its quest for relevance and survival the BOC has actively promoted the nationalist cause and in doing so seeks to cement historical links between church and state. In the twenty-first century the church has discovered in nationalism its latest refuge for survival. This is the reason why Raikin, with whom this chapter began claims that nationalism has become a deeper faith for the

BOC than the Gospel. By espousing this philosophy and actively working for the Bulgarian national cause, the BOC believes it can continue to stand with dignity.

CONCLUSIONS

The research reported in this thesis has endeavoured to contribute a new perspective to ecclesiastical history by investigating the evolving relationship of a church and nation in Bulgaria, a country that has claimed insufficient attention among Western scholars. The research was promoted by the observation that the Bulgarian Orthodox Church, celebrated as the cultural liberator and spiritual saviour of the nation, embraces the indefatigable allegiance of 85% of the Bulgarian population, whilst only 0.5% actually attends church on any regular basis. To understand this apparently contradictory situation, the research set out to examine the historical relationship between the Bulgarian church and the Bulgarian nation, with particular attention to the international political turmoil that convulsed Bulgarian history during the Byzantine, Ottoman, World Wars, Communist and Post-Communist eras. By giving priority to Bulgarian language sources it is hoped that an authentically Orthodox and Balkan perspective has been presented, and that this has been analysed in ways that differentiate between nationalistic bias and dispassionate historical reconstruction.

The thesis revealed that the preservation of Bulgarian society throughout its traumatic historical journey has been premised on a direct connection between national and religious identity. The present Holy Synod of the BOC claims that this correlation has preserved the nation through the vicissitudes of Bulgarian history. The thesis has demonstrated, however, that the roles that the BOC has played in this history, and society's national identification with it has been embellished through the creation of a national myth, based upon uncritical advocacy of the *catastrophe* and *continuity theories* established in the nineteenth and twentieth centuries. The predicament facing the contemporary Bulgarian Orthodox Church, therefore, is one precipitated by context and time. As the Holy Synod continues to look to the past to justify the church's future existence, it fails to deal with the present in a constructive way. It thus neglects the spiritual and practical needs of Bulgaria's Orthodox faithful.

The BOC's ability to harmonise with its cultural context has historically been its strongpoint. Chapter One revealed the transformational quality of the Bulgarian church, taking on many different popular national traits, which helped establish the link between church and nation. The radical change that was forced upon Bulgaria when it fell to Ottoman conquest in the fourteenth century confronted the church with a new situation with which it struggled to adapt. However, with the establishment of the Bulgarian Exarchate in 1870, the hierarchy of the church succeeded in re-establishing itself in its historical leadership role, executing its service, both willingly and under coercion before the Ottoman Porte. With the rise of the Bulgarian National Revival, however, the church's evolutionary approach to achieving national independence was opposed by the revolutionary methods of the separatists. By denouncing the latter the Holy Synod found it difficult to reassert the church's authority after the liberation. Although the BOC succeeded in fulfilling an important role, as the only national body which could unite the dispersed Bulgarian population, it never again regained the authority that it held during the last few years of the Ottoman era. From 1878 to the end of the Second World War in 1945 BOC relations with the secular Bulgarian government became sharply polarised, with clergy being denied the right to stand for any governmental position, and from 1945-1989 the church by necessity had to acquiesce to the demands of the atheistic communist authorities. This brief synopsis of the history of church-state relations in Bulgaria underscores one of the main conclusions of the thesis: that the relationship between church and state has varied during the main periods into which Bulgarian history can be divided, and that claims of unfading and indestructible relations with Bulgaria's ruling authorities are therefore exaggerated.

The scientific historian of church-state relations in Bulgaria is therefore confronted with the need to distinguish between imagined and empirical history. James Payton, Professor of History at Redeemer University College, in Ancaster, Ontario, Canada has commented that the role of religion has been neglected as a factor in the history of Eastern Europe.[1] This observation may apply, as was intended, to Western scholarship of the Balkans, but it is not true in respect of indigenous historiography. In the case of Bulgaria religion has been considered a major factor in the history of the nation since the ninth century. As this thesis has argued, however, this religious factor has been steered and interpreted less by the church than by national, international, political and economic agendas. Thus, the relationship which has developed between church, nation, state and society over the centuries has been embellished by various myths that serve national political goals. The task of this thesis has been to offer a reinterpretation of the role of the church in Bulgaria's history based not on nationalistic bias, political machination, or national myth, but on verifiable archival, literary and oral evidence.

From its inception the Bulgarian church was imbued with nationalist tendencies as it struggled to disassociate itself and the Bulgarian kingdom from foreign interference. Even so, it has been demonstrated that after the conquest of Bulgaria in 1396 and the dissolution of the Bulgarian Church, Eastern Orthodox Christians were not distinguished by ethnicity or nationality under the Ottoman *millet* system. The church became a political tool, separating along ethnic lines in the nineteenth century, when the leaders of the national revival saw the restoration of the Bulgarian Church as a necessary precondition for national emancipation. In the process toward independence Bulgarian Orthodoxy was dressed in national garb: Bulgaria's cultural, linguistic and ecclesiastical distinctions were emphasised while Christian canon was disregarded in order to link the national church struggle to the secular political goals of the insurgents. This resulted in the Bulgarian Orthodox Church being described as an attribute of Bulgarian nationality and an instrument of national state politics.[2]

The connection between the BOC and the establishment of the nation-state can be seen to have negatively effected its development. The influence of national revival romanticism gave birth to the view that Bulgaria survived through centuries of Ottoman slavery, oppression and enforced conversion solely because of the bravery of the BOC. This interpretation of history instilled hatred towards the ruling Ottoman and Greek authorities, but it does not stand up to historical scrutiny. Archival evidence, Ottoman and Bulgarian, demonstrates that the prolonged period of Islamic rule in Bulgaria was strict but generally tolerant toward the Christian population. Regional ecclesiastical struggles for tax alleviation, the introduction of Bulgarian clergy, Slavonic worship and separate Bulgarian ecclesiastical institutions were all pivotal in the process of national awakening during the later Ottoman period. To this degree it is fair to assert that the church was instrumental in awakening Bulgarian self-consciousness and accelerating the national independence movement. But the pressure for political autonomy and independence owed as much to secular enlightenment influence, the decline of the Ottoman empire, foreign intrigue, and nineteenth century nationalism.

However, in the campaign of the separatist movement for a sovereign Bulgarian state religion and the church became political instruments that were used in order to attain their national goal. This represented not continuity but an elemental break with both Orthodoxy's Byzantine legacy and the non-ethnic character of the Ottoman *millet* system. The national movement therefore defined Bulgarian national characteristics by transforming millet thinking and emphasising the cultural, linguistic and ecclesiastical difference between Bulgarians on the one hand and both Muslim Ottomans and Christian Greeks on the other. The idea of Bulgaria's distinct national roots and unique cultural features, highlighted by Paisii of Hilendar and Yuri Venelin, thus marginalised Muslims and other Orthodox Christians and justified the desire to pursue a singular national and religious identity.

The nineteenth century national idea transformed Balkan history, firstly by transforming the traditional *millet* into the concept of nation, and secondly by placing the people (the nation) at the political centre. Nevertheless, the connection between national identity and religious affiliation in Bulgaria cannot be claimed to have been the result of this nineteenth century phenomenon. This was already established earlier during the ninth century when Tsar Boris' political acumen, his craving for international acceptance, national autonomy and socio-ethnic unity persuaded him to introduce Christianity to Bulgaria. Rather than accepting Latin or Byzantine autocracy, however, he established an autocephalous church within a strongly independent nation, and inaugurated the link between church and nation. This gave rise to the so-called *continuity theory* that played an important part in the ideology of Bulgarian socialism. Socialist historians attempted to portray a direct correlation between twentieth century political and ecclesiastical structures and those of Bulgaria's medieval kingdoms. In support of this theory they elaborated another, the so-called *catastrophe theory* that painted the era of Ottoman domination as one of unmitigated disaster for the Bulgarian people. The communist authorities used the results from Volume Four of the *History of Bulgaria* to promote socialist initiatives and introduce discriminatory policies against Bulgaria's Muslim population. Thus the re-embellishment of a nineteenth century interpretation of Bulgarian church history created the foundation for the contemporary national self-understanding about the Bulgarian nation's continuity and identity.

The BOC remains an important instrument of state, as witnessed by the latest Religious Act (2002/3), in which the church has once again been granted a privileged and protected position in society. However, throughout Bulgarian history the granting of this position has expressed itself as an unequal partnership between church and state, the church being politically subservient to the state, despite being at the same time the repository of Bulgarian historical identity. In order to accommodate this situation, the Holy Synod seeks to bolster its legitimacy and acceptance by invoking history to justify its case before the Bulgarian people: "The history of the Bulgarian Orthodox Church is the history of Bulgarian culture."[3] But as this research has shown, this claim expresses only a partial truth, a mixture of history, myth and deliberate falsification.

For contemporary Bulgarian society the BOC is growing increasingly marginal to their everyday life of the people – its main point of reference before society is its national nomenclature. The church has become what it claims to be, a historical national monument. It is however a monolith that has little to do with practical life. This thesis has shown that the Bulgarian people believe the BOC has failed to provide pastoral guidance through the intricacies of modern life. We must conclude therefore that the BOC needs to re-assess its future role in society, particularly as Bulgaria heads towards European integration, either as an instrument of state or as a pastor to the nation. The church must stop looking back and move forward into the twenty-first century and discover once again its greatest strength, contextualised ministry in service to the people. A return to November 1939 is suggested, when the church leadership sought means to reconcile and strengthen relations with society through the introduction of practical social programmes to help families, support the sick and old and to develop education. This task is today being fulfilled by foreign missions agencies and by the laity of the Orthodox Church who refuse to condemn, but do not condone the inactivity of their leadership. Today the Bulgarian Orthodox Church must decide whether to remain a historical monument or reaffirm its true mission to serve contemporary Bulgaria as a living church, answering the needs of modern Bulgarian society.

APPENDIX ONE

Firman issued by Sultan Selim III (1789-1807) protecting the rights of Rila Monastery, issued 7 Dhu-al-Hijjah 1215 (1801)

(Translated from the original held in the archives of Rila Monastery in 2003)

To my learned, worthy and renowned judge in Dupnitsa. May Almighty Allah reveal to you the glory of his power.

From the text of this my royal decree, adorned with the proper Sultan's seal, you will learn that I have received from the Greek Patriarch and the Holy Synod, which met in session in my glorious city of Constantinople, the authority relative to Rila Monastery now added to my Royal Empire.

It states, as in the provision of the old law, which was and is in force, that no one can confront without imperial authorisation, or raise a hand against the church or monastery, which is under the Orthodox supervision of the Metropolitan, who is subordinate to the Greek Patriarchate. It also states that no one from my civil or military authority has the right to use force or cruelty within the Christian church or monastery without my explicit permission.

Proclaim this before everyone; make every effort to intervene and to settle divisions and violent disturbances. In line with the old laws regarding the church and monastery, no one from my authority, no influential person, may raise taxes within the monastery estates that they call St. Ivan Rilski which lies in the Rila mountains, which is in your jurisdiction. I reiterate this as this Christians are constantly moaning about this before my throne.

Finally, as I have notified you, tell also my citizens, military authorities and bureaucratic departments to report details of illegal acts and atrocities which occur within the precinct of the monastery.

Let this be favourably received and referred to for verification within the government and episcopal departments whose records are preserved within my imperial treasury. It is thereby established that no one may confront without my imperial permission, or may lay hands on the church and monastery, which from ancient times has found itself under the unique authority of the Metropolitan. No one from my civil or military authority has the right to use force or violence in the church and monastery.

In the presence of everyone and everything I announce my Imperial Royal Firman, which from this day is included in my acts and should be followed exactly according to its contents and my wishes.

You are obliged not to violate the rights and privileges bestowed upon the Metropolitan, and to the church and monastery, which are in his eparchy, and more, you are not to violate the rights and privileges which are preserved in my imperial treasury according to the regulations and instructions in this Imperial Royal berat.

You are also obliged not to let anyone from my civil or military authority enter Rila monastery, or any other church or monastery, for their own material benefit, or on the pretext that facing resistance they committed violence within the monastery.

As you know, so you will act!

This Firman is issued in my glorious city of Constantinople, according to the holy tradition and filled with faith and heart felt respect for the Imperial Royal position marked by my monogram and seal.

7 Dhu-al-Hijjah 1215

Firman issued by Sultan Abdulaziz (1861-1876) announcing the establishment of the Bulgarian Exarchate, issued 12 March 1870

Translated from the original text of the document available in
S. Protic, *The Aspirations of Bulgaria*
(London: Simpkin Marshall, Hamilton, Kent & Co., 1915), pp. 245-249

It has been my imperial desire that all faithful peoples and subjects dwelling in my empire should enjoy to the full extent such order and security as are necessary for the professing of their religions, as also in their social relations, that they should live in peace, in order that they may by doing so aid us to the utmost of their ability in our incessant efforts for the furtherance of our empire and of civilisation.

But inasmuch as there have of late arisen – contrary to our imperial wish – certain misunderstandings and misinterpretations as to how far the Bulgarian metropolitans, bishops, priests and churches be dependent upon the Patriarchate – which have greatly grieved us – it has been found necessary to institute an investigation into the causes which have led up to the said misunderstandings and misinterpretations and to submit them to a thorough examination. The results of this investigation are embodied in the following articles, which have been adopted and approved as being the definite solution to the controversy.

ARTICLE I

A separate ecclesiastic district shall be established under the official name of 'the Bulgarian Exarchate', the same will include certain districts over and above the metropolitanates and bishoprics to be mentioned hereafter. The administration of the spiritual and religious matters in these districts is entirely vested in the Exarchate.

ARTICLE II

The chief Metropolitan of these districts shall bear the title of 'Exarch'. He shall be the canonical president of the Bulgarian Holy Synod.

ARTICLE III

The internal spiritual administration of the Exarchate will be established by a supplementary law, which must be in accordance with the fundamental canon and religious regulations of the Orthodox Church and which must be previously subjected for the approval of my imperial government.

This supplementary law precludes the possibility of any interference, either direct or indirect, on the part of the Patriarchate, with religious matters, or with the election of bishops and exarchs. As soon as the Exarch is elected the Bulgarian Synod will inform the Patriarchate of the fact, and the Patriarch, on his part, shall immediately grant his approval in accordance with religious law.

ARTICLE IV

The Exarch, having been appointed through our sublime Firman will mention the name of the Patriarch in the prayers in accordance with the rubric of the church; but previous to his election the person considered worthy of the office of Exarch must be personally presented to my government.

ARTICLE V

In matters pertaining to his jurisdiction, the Exarch will have the right to negotiate directly with the local authorities and, if need be, even with our Sublime Porte. His approval must be sought before investiture and may be granted to such persons in holy orders as come under his jurisdiction.

ARTICLE VI

All matters concerning the Orthodox faith and necessitating mutual consultation must be referred by the Bulgarian Holy Synod to the Vasselenski Patriarchate and Synod; and these shall be bound to render assistance without delay and to answer without hesitation such questions as may be put to them.

ARTICLE VII

The Bulgarian Holy Synod shall receive Holy Oil from the Patriarch of Constantinople.

ARTICLE VIII

Such bishops, archbishops, and metropolitans as are subject to the Vesselenski Patriarchate shall be at liberty to approach the Bulgarian Exarchate, in the same manner as the Bulgarian also be permitted to sojourn to the capitals of the vilayets and other centres of administration; but they must not convoke synods outside the limits of their own diocese, not officiate without the permission of the bishop of the diocese in which they happen to be.

ARTICLE IX

Even as the metoch of Jerusalem, which is situated in the Phanar, is dependent upon the Patriarch of Jerusalem, so the Bulgarian metoch and church situated in the same suburb shall belong to the Bulgarian Exarchate. And whenever the Exarch requires to come to Constantinople, he shall be allowed to reside in his metoch.

ARTICLE X

The jurisdiction of the Bulgarian Exarchate shall extend over the eparchies of Sofia, Vratsa, Tulcea, Vidin, Nis, Pirot, Kustendil, Samakov, Veles, Plovdiv and Sozopol, with the exception of about twelve villages on the shores of the Black Sea, between Varna and Constanta, which are inhabited by non-Bulgarians. The following towns will also be outside Bulgarian Exarchak jurisdiction: Varna, Mesembria, Plovdiv and Stanimaka, together with the villages of Kuklen, Voden and Panaggia, Novo-Selo, Leskov, Batchovo, Belasitsa and the monasteries of St. Anargirius, St. Paraskeva and St. George. The monastery of St. Panaggia and the interior of Plovdiv shall belong to the Exarchate, but such inhabitants of the eparchy who do not wish to be under the Exarchate shall be free. The details of this matter shall be arranged between the Patriarchate and the Exarchate in accordance with canon and ecclesiastic law.

If the population of any other place besides those enumerated above, professing the Orthodox faith, should wish to unanimously, or at least two-thirds of them wish to be subject to the Bulgarian Exarchate, their desire ought to be granted

ARTICLE XI

Such monasteries as are situated in the Exarchate and which are, by canon law subject to the control of the Patriarchate shall continue to be governed as they have been hitherto.

APPENDIX THREE

The Constitution of the Principality of Bulgaria, issued 16 April 1879

Accessed from http://www.ncf.ca/bg-ottowa/Tirnovoconstitution.html
on 12 August 2002

SECTION IX – Religion

Article 37. The state religion of the principality of Bulgaria is the Eastern Orthodox confession.

Article 38. The prince of Bulgaria and his descendants are restricted to the exclusive profession of the Orthodox religion, but the first prince of Bulgaria may, exceptionally, profess his original religion.

Article 39. The principality of Bulgaria, from an ecclesiastical point of view, forms an inseparable part of the jurisdiction of the Bulgarian Church, which is subject to the Holy Synod, the highest spiritual authority in the Bulgarian Church, wherever that may exist. By the same authority, the principality remains united with the ecumenical Eastern Church in matters regarding dogma and faith.

Article 40. Christians of other than Orthodox faith, and those professing any other religion whatever, whether Bulgarian born subjects or naturalised, as well as foreigners permanently or temporarily domiciled in Bulgaria, have full liberty to profess their religion so long as the performance of their rites does not violate existing laws.

Article 41. No one can, under the pretext of religious scruples, exempt himself from conformity with the general laws, which are binding on all in common.

Article 42. The ecclesiastical affairs of non-Orthodox Christians, and of non-Christians generally, are managed by their own ecclesiastical administration, subject however, to the ultimate superintendence of the competent minister, according to the special laws to be promulgated in his regard.

Appendix Four

Questions and results (March-June 2003)

7,203 questionnaires were returned for analysis. The first question presents a percentage breakdown of Christian affiliation, further questions relate solely to those who considered themselves Orthodox. However, it should be noted that 8% of those stopped classed themselves Muslim:

To which Christian church/denomination are you personally affiliated?

Orthodox	86.0%
Unsure	13.4%
Catholic	0.5%
Protestant	0.1%

Would you describe yourself as deeply religious?

Deeply religious	9.0%
Slightly religious	48.0%
Not really religious	30.0%
Completely unreligious	11.0%
Unsure	2.0%

When you face difficult personal problems, where do look for help/support?

Spouse	55.8%
Friends	35.2%
Family	33.0%
Myself	24.9%
Never have problems	3.7%
God	3.2%
Clairvoyant	0.9%
Priest/Orthodox Church	0.7%

Do you consider yourself an active member of the Orthodox Church?

Active membership	0.5%
Non-active membership	2.5%
Consider themselves to be Orthodox but not members of the Church	97.0%

What has most influenced your attitude towards religion?

Family	60.0%
Friends	25.0%
Media	5.5%
Not influenced	5.0%
School	2.0%
University	1.5%
Church	1.0%

APPENDIX FIVE

Chronological Timeline: Sultans, Bulgarian Exarchs, Ecumenical Patriarchs, Bulgarian Monarchs, Presidents and Prime Ministers.
From the Fall of Turnovo (1393) to the Present Day (2005)

Sultans	Ecumenical Patriarchs	Bulgarian Patriarchs, Exarchs & Important Historical Events	*Bulgarian Monarchs* *Bulgarian Presidents* Bulgarian Prime Ministers
1389-1401 Bayezit I	1389-1390 Antony IV 1390-1391 Macarius 1391-1397 Antony IV	1393 Patriarch Evtimi (Bulgarian Church dissolved)	
	1397 Callistus II 1397-1410 Matthew I 1410-1416 Euthymius II		
1413-1421 Mehmet I	1416-1439 Joseph II		
1421-1444 Murat II	1440-1443 Metrophanes II 1443-1450 Gregory III		
1444-1446 Mehmet II	1450-1453 Athanasius II		
1446-1451 Murat II	1453-1456 Gennadius II 1456-1457 Isidore II 1458 Gennadius II 1462-1463 Gennadius II	1453 Fall of Constantinople	
1451-1481 Mehmet II	1463-1464 Sophronius I 1464-1466 Joseph I 1466 Marcus II 1466 Symeon I 1466-1471 Dionysius I 1471-1474 Symeon I 1475-1476 Raphael I 1476-1481 Maximus III 1481-1486 Symeon I 1486-1488 Nephon II 1489-1491 Dionysius I 1491-1497 Maximus IV 1497-1498 Nephon II 1498-1502 Joachim I	1466 Rila Monastery rebuilt after fire	
1481-1512 Bayezit II	1503-1504 Pachomius I 1504 Joachim I 1504-1513 Pqchomius I		
	1513-1522 Theoleptus I		
	1522-1545 Jeremias I 1546 Joannicus I 1546-1555 Dionysius II 1555-1565 Joseph II		

Sultans	Ecumenical Patriarchs	Bulgarian Patriarchs, Exarchs & Important Historical Events	*Bulgarian Monarchs* *Bulgarian Presidents* Bulgarian Prime Ministers
1566-1574 Selim II	1565-1572 Metrophanes III		
1574-1595 Murat III	1572-1579 Jeremias II		
	1579-1580 Metrophanes III		
	1580-1584 Jeremias II		
	1584-1585 Pachomius II		
	1585-1586 Theoleptus II		
1595-1603 Mehmet III	1596 Matthew II		
	1596 Gabriel I		
	1597 Theophanes I		
	1598-1602 Matthew II	1598 Turnovo peasant	
	1602-1603 Neophytus II	revolt	
1603-1617 Ahmed I	1603 Matthew II		
	1603-1607 Raphael II		
	1607-1612 Neophytus II		
	1612 Cyril I		
1617-1618 Mustafa I	1612-1620 Timotheus		
1618-1622 Osman II	1620-1623 Cyril I		
	1623 Gregory IV		
	1623 Anthimus		
1623-1640 Murat IV	1623-1634 Cyril I		
	1634 Athanasius III		
	1634-1635 Cyril I		
	1635-1636 Cyril II		
	1636-1637 Neophytus III		
1640-1648 Ibrahim	1637 Cyril I		
	1638-1639 Cyril II		
	1639-1644 Parthenius I		
	1644-1646 Parthenius II		
	1646-1648 Joannicius II		
	1648-1651 Parthenius II		
1648-1687 Mehmet IV	1651-1652 Joannicius II		
	1652 Cyril III		
	1652-1653 Paisius I		
	1654 Cyril III		
	1654-1655 Paisius I		
	1656-1657 Parthenius III		
	1657 Gabriel II		
	1657-1662 Parthenius IV		
	1662-1665 Dionysius III		
	1665-1667 Parthenius IV		
	1667 Clement		
	1668-1671 Methodius III		

Sultans	Ecumenical Patriarchs	Bulgarian Patriarchs, Exarchs & Important Historical Events	*Bulgarian Monarchs* *Bulgarian Presidents* Bulgarian Prime Ministers
	1671-1673 Dionysius IV		
	1673-1674 Gerasimus II		
	1676-1679 Dionysius IV		
	1679 Athanasius IV		
	1679-1682 James		
	1685 Parthenius III		
	1685-1686 James	1686 Veliko Turnovo peasant revolt	
1687-1691 Suleyman II			
	1688 Callinicus II	1688 Chiprovets peasant revolt	
	1688 Neophytus IV		
	1689-1693 Callinicus II		
1691-1695 Ahmed II			
	1693-1694 Dionysius IV		
	1694 Callinicus II		
1695-1703 Mustafa II	1702-1707 Gabriel III		
	1707 Neophytus V		
1703-1730 Ahmed III	1707-1709 Cyprianus I		
	1709-1711 Athanasius V		
	1711-1713 Cyril IV		
	1713-1714 Cyprianus I		
	1714-1716 Cosmas III		
	1716-1726 Jeremias III		
	1726-1732 Paisius II		
	1732-1733 Jeremias III		
	1733-1734 Seraphim I		
	1734-1740 Neophytus VI		
1730-1754 Mahmud I	1740-1743 Paisius II		
	1743-1744 Neophytus VI		
	1748-1751 Cyril V		
	1752-1757 Cyril V		
1754-1757 Osman III		1753 Rila Monastery rebuilt after 2nd fire	
1757-1774 Mustafa III	1757 Callinicus III		
	1757-1761 Seraphim II	1762 Paisii	
	1761-1763 Joannicius III	Hilendarski's *Slavo Bulgarian History*	
	1763-1768 Samuel I	published	
		1765 Sofroni	
	1768-1769 Meletius II	Vrachanski meets	
	1769-1773 Theodosius II	Paisii for the 1st time	
1774-1789 Abdulhamit I	1773-1774 Samuel I		
	1774-1780 Sophoronius II		
	1780-1785 Gabriel IV		
	1785-1789 Procopius I		
1789-1807 Selim III	1789-1794 Neophytus VII		
	1794-1797 Gerasimus III		

Sultans	Ecumenical Patriarchs	Bulgarian Patriarchs, Exarchs & Important Historical Events	*Bulgarian Monarchs* *Bulgarian Presidents* Bulgarian Prime Ministers
	1797-1798 Gregory V		
	1798-1801 Neophytus VII		
	1801-1806 Callinicus IV		
1807-1808 Mustafa IV	1806-1808 Gregory V	1806 Sofroni's autobiography	
	1808-1809 Callinicus IV	published	
1808-1839 Mahmud II	1809-1813 Jeremias IV		
	1813-1818 Cyril VI	1815 1st Hellenic-Bulgarian school opens in Svishtov	
	1821-1822 Eugenius II		
	1822-1824 Anthimos III		
	1824-1826 Chrysanthos I	1824 1st recorded Bulgarian request for a Bulgarian bishop	
	1826-1830 Agathangelos I		
	1830-1834 Constantios I		
	1834-1835 Constantios II		
	1835-1840 Gregory VI	1835 1st Bulgarian secular school opens in Gabrovo	
1839-1861 Abdulmecid I			
	1840-1841 Anthimos IV	1839 Hatt-i Sherif	
	1841-1842 Anthimos V		
	1842-1845 Germanos IV	1844 1st mandate to the Porte for recognition of separate Bulgarian church	
	1845 Meletios III		
	1845-1848 Anthimos VI		
	1848-1852 Anthimos IV		
	1852-1853 Germanos IV	1849 Bulgarians recognised as a distinct people by Sultan's firman	
	1853-1855 Anthimos VI	1853-56 Crimean War	
	1855-1860 Cyril VII	1856 Hatt-i Humayun	
1861-1876 Abdulaziz	1860-1863 Joachim II		
	1863-1866 Sophronios III	1863 Danube vilayet created	
		1866-68 Cretan Uprising	
		1870 Bulgarian Exarchate established	
		Exarch	
	1873-1878 Joachim II	1872 Ilarion	
1876 Murat V		1872-1877 Antim I	
1876-1909 Abdulhamit II	1878-1884 Joachim III	1876 April Uprising 1877-1915 Josef	

Sultans	Ecumenical Patriarchs	Bulgarian Patriarchs, Exarchs & Important Historical Events	*Bulgarian Monarchs* / *Bulgarian Presidents* / Bulgarian Prime Ministers
		1878 Bulgarian national independence	*1879-1886 Alexander I*
		1879 1st National Constitution	1879 Todor Burmov
			1879-1880 Archbishop Kliment
			1880 Dragan Tsankov
			1880-1881 Petko Karavelov
			1881 Johann Ernrot
			1882-1883 Leonid Sobolev
			1883-1884 Dragan Tsankov
	1884-1887 Joachim IV		1884-1886 Petko Karavelov
		1885 Bulgarian National Unification	1886 Archbishop Kliment
			1886 Petko Karavelov
			1886-1887 Vasil Radoslavov
	1887-1891 Dionysios V		*1887-1918 Ferdinand*
			1887 Konstantin Stoilov
	1891-1894 Neophytos VIII		1887-1894 Stefan Stambolov
	1895-1897 Anthimos VII		1894-1899 Konstantin Stoilov
	1897-1901 Constantine V		
			1899 Dimitur Grekov
			1899-1901 Todor Ivanchov
	1901-1912 Joachim III		1901 Racho Petrov
			1901-1902 Petko Karavelov
			1902-1903 Stoyan Danev
		1903 Ilinden Uprising	1903-1906 Racho Petrov
			1906-1907 Dimitur Petkov
			1907 Dimitur Stanchov
		1908 Young Turk revolution	1907-1908 Petur Gudev
1909-1918 Mehmet V		1908 Bulgaria declares full independence	1908-1911 Alexandur Malinov
	1913-1918 Germanos V	1912-13 Balkan Wars	1911-1913 Ivan Geshov
			1913 Stoyan Danev
		1914-18 1st World War	1913-1918 Vasil Radoslavov
		Chairman of Holy Synod	
		1915-1918 Parfeni	
1918-1922 Mehmet VI			*1918-1943 Boris III*
		1918 Radomir rebellion	1918 Alexandur Malinov

Sultans	Ecumenical Patriarchs	Bulgarian Patriarchs, Exarchs & Important Historical Events	*Bulgarian Monarchs* / *Bulgarian Presidents* / Bulgarian Prime Ministers
		1918-1921 Vasili	1918-1919 Teodor Reodorov
			1919-1923 Alexandur
	1921-1923 Meletios IV	1921-1927 Maxim	Stamboliski
1922-1924 Abdulmecid II			
	1923-1924 Gregory VII		1923-1926 Alexandur
	1924-1925 Constantine VI		Tsankov
	1925-1929 Basil III		
		1928-1930 Kliment	1926-1931 Andrei Lyapchev
	1929-1935 Photius II		
		1930-1944 Neofit	
			1931 Alexandur Malinov
			1931-1934 Nikola Mushanov
			1934-1935 Kimon Georgiev
			1935 Petur Zlatev
			1935 Andrei Toshev
	1936-1946 Benjamin I		1935-1940 Georgi
		1939-45 2nd World War	Kyoseivanov
			1940-1943 Bogdan Filov
		1941 German invasion of Balkans	
			1943-1946 Simeon II
			1943 Petur Gabrovski
			1943-1944 Dobri Bozhilov
		1944-1945 Stefan	1944 Ivan Bagrianov
			1944 Konstantin Muraviev
		1945 Soviet Army enters Bulgaria	1944-1946 Kimon Georgiev
		Exarch	
	1946-1948 Maximos V	1945-1948 Stefan	
			1946-1947 Vasil Kolarov
			1946-1949 Georgi Dimitrov
		Chairman of Holy Synod	*1947-1950 Mincho Neychev*
	1948-1972 Athenagoras	1948 Mihail	
		1949-1951 Paisii	1949-1950 Vasil Kolarov
			1950-1958 Georgi Damyanov
			1950-1956 Vulko
		1951-1953 Kiril	Chervenkov
		Patriarch	
		1953-1971 Kiril	
			1956-1962 Anton Yugov
			1958-1964 Dimitur Vurbanov

Ecumenical Patriarchs	Bulgarian Patriarchs, Exarchs & Important Historical Events	*Bulgarian Monarchs* *Bulgarian Presidents* Bulgarian Prime Ministers
1972-1991 Demetrios I	1971- Maxim	1962-1971 Todor Zhivkov *1964-1971 Georgi Girovski* *1971-1989 Todor Zhivkov* 1971-1981 Stanko Todorov
		1981-1986 Grisha Filipov 1986-1990 Georgi Atanasov
1991- Bartholomew I		*1989-1990 Petur Mladenov* 1990 *Andrei Lukanov* *1990 Stanko Georgiev* *1990 Nikolai Todorov* *1990-1997 Zhelyu Zhelev* 1990-1991 Dimitur Popov 1991-1992 Filip Dimitrov 1992-1994 Lyuben Berov 1994-1995 Reneta Indzhova 1995-1997 Zhan Videnov *1997-2002 Petur Stoyanov* 1997 Stefan Sofiyanski 1997-2001 Ivan Kostov 2001-2005 Simeon Saxocoburg *2002- Georgi Purvanov* 2005- Sergei Stanishev

NOTES

CHAPTER 1: THE BULGARIAN CHURCH: AN HISTORICAL ANALYSIS OF THE CRITICAL MOMENTS IN THE FORMATION OF BULGARIAN ORTHODOX IDENTITY (865-1396)

1. See I. Duichev (1972), R. Poptodorov (1971) and S. Runciman (1930).

2. This was the first time that a Byzantine emperor had lost his life in battle since the death of Valens at the hands of the Goths in 378.

3. The proto-Bulgars were a Central Asian tribe based originally in the Greater Volga region.

4. G. Moravcsik, *Byzantinoturcica*, II(1958)296.

5. R. Browning, *Byzantium and Bulgaria: A Comparative Study Across the Early Medieval Frontier* (London, 1975), p. 140.

6. Theophanes, 'Chronographia', *Greek Sources for Bulgarian History* (Sofia, 1954), this records that over ten thousand prisoners were deported from the city of Adrianople alone.

7. Metropolitan Simeon, 'Theofilact of Ohrid's epistolae', *Сб БАН*, XXVII (Sofia, 1931).

8. Annales Fuldenses, *MGH-Scriptores*, III, pp. 367-368.

9. V. Giuselev, *Prince Boris I* (Sofia, 1969), p. 38.

10. Annales Bertiniani, *MGH-Scriptores*, I, p. 448.

11. V. N. Zlatarski, *History of the Medieval Bulgarian State*, Vol. I (Sofia, 1937), p. 22.

12. Pope Nicholas I, 'Letter to Hincemar, Archbishop of Rheims', *MGH-Epistolae Karolini Aevi*, IV, p. 601.

13. Theophanes, IV, pp. 162-163.

14. 'Boyar' – Bulgarian aristocracy: Annales Bertiniani, I, p. 448.

15. J. V. A. Fine, *The Early Medieval Balkans* (Ann Arbor, 1983), p. 119.

16. *Epistulae et Amphilochia*, B. Laourdas and L. G. Westerink (eds.), Vol. I, p. 20 (Leipzig, 1983).

17. Pope Nicholas I, 'Responsa ad Consulta Bulgarorum', E. Perels (ed.), *Epistolae Karolini Aevi*, VI (Munich: MGH, 1925), p. 599.

18. Cyril and Methodius – the creators of the Glagolitic and Slavonic alphabets (see pp. 20-27).

19. Pope Nicholas I, p. 599.

20. L. Simeonova, *Diplomacy of the Letter and the Cross: Photius, Bulgaria and the Papacy, 860s-880s* (Amsterdam, 1998), pp. 197-200.

21. Pope Nicholas I, p. 603.

22. 'Fragmenta Registri Iohannis VIII. Papae', *MGH-Epistolae*, VII, p. 278.

23. The introduction of indigenous clergy is dealt with in detail in Section 1.3.2 'The Slavonic Mission in Bulgaria'.

24. R. Browning, *Byzantium and Bulgaria* (London, 1975), p. 154.

25. A. Milev, 'Vita St. Clementis', *The Greek Biography of Kliment Ohridski* (Sofia, 1966); M. Kusseff, 'Vita St. Naoum', *The Slavonic and East European Review*, XXIX(1950-51)142.

26. D. Obolensky, *The Byzantine Commonwealth: Eastern Europe 500-1453* (London, 1971), p. 72.

27. *Constantine Porphyrogenitus De Administrando Imperio*, G. Moravcsik, ed. (Budapest, 1949), pp. 124-126.

28. M. Kantor, *Medieval Slavic Lives of Saints and Princes* (Ann Arbor, 1983), pp. 65-66.

29. G. Cankova-Petkova, 'Contribution au sujet de la conversion des Bulgares au christianisme', *Byzantino-Bulgarica*, IV(1973)21-39

30. *Epistulae et Amphilochia*, ibid., Vol. I, Ep. 2, p. 41.

31. G. Ostrogorsky, *History of the Byzantine State* (New Brunswick, 1969), p. 226.

32. I. Duichev, 'Au lendemain de la conversion du people bulgare (L'epitre de Photius)', *Medioevo Bizantino-Slavo*, Vol. I (Rome, 1965), pp. 107-109.

33. V. Giuzelev, 'Photius' Constantinople Model of Christian Leadership', *Slavische Sprachen*, 9(1985)30.

34. From Pope Nicholas I, *Epistolae*, in E. Perels, ed., *Papst Nikolaus und Anastasius Bibliothecarius* (Berlin, 1929), pp. 171-172.

35. F. Dvornik, *The Photian Schism: History and Legend* (Cambridge, 1948), pp. 104-109.

36. *Anastasii Bibliothecarii Historia de vitis Romanorum Pontificum*, cap. 608, J. P. Migne (ed.), Patrologiae cursus completus (Paris, 1844), pp. 1373-1374.

37. *Photii Epistulae et Amphilochia*, Vol. I, Ep. 1, p. 53.

38. The Photian Schism was an extension of the dispute over Bulgaria. As Rome and Constantinople vied for control the dispute took on a theological dimension arguing over variant practices: celibacy versus marriage, *azymes* against *artos*, and over the insertion of the *filioque* clause in the Nicene Creed. Pope Nicholas then disputed Photius' election and excommunicated the Patriarch.

39. *Anastasii Bibliothecarii Historia de vitis Romanorum Pontificum*, cap. 609, ibid., pp. 1373-1374.

40. Pope John VIII, 'Epistolae passim collectae', No. 9, *MGH-Epistolae*, VII, p. 327.

41. 'Anastasii Bibliothecarii Epistolae sive praefaciones', *MGH-Epistolae*, VII, p. 413.

42. *Anastasii Bibliothecarii Praefation in Synodum Octavum*, J. P. Migne (ed.), Patrologiae cursus completus (Paris, 1844).

43. L. Simeonova, p. 268.

44. An English translation of the Vitae of the brothers is available in, I. Duichev, *Kiril and Methodius: Founders of Slavonic Writing; A Collection of Sources and Critical Studies* (Boulder, 1985).

45. P. Devos and P. Meyvaert, 'Trois enigmas Cyrillo-Methodiennes de la Legende Italique resolues grace a un document inedit', *Annalecta Bollandiana*, 73(1955)375-461

46. Theophylact's *vitae* available in I. Duichev (1985), pp. 93-126.

47. *Vita Constantini*, XIV, p. 2-4.

48. *Vita Methodii*, IV, p. 8.

49. A. Schmemann, *The Historical Road of Eastern Orthodoxy* (London, 1963), pp. 257-258.

50. D. Obolensky, *Six Byzantine Portraits* (Oxford, 1988), pp. 8-33.

51. R. Fletcher, *The Conversion of Europe: From Paganism to Christianity 371-1386* (London, 1997), p. 364.

52. E. Georgiev, *Bulgaria's Contribution to Slavonic and European Cultural Life in the Middle Ages* (Sofia, 1981), p. 14.

53. E. Georgiev, pp. 18-20.

54. Pope John Paul II, *Encyclical Epistle Slavorum Apostoli of His Holiness John Paul II* (London, 1985).

55. *Vita Methodii*, I, p. 163.

56. A. N. Tachiaos, 'The Cult of Saint Methodius in the Byzantino-Slavonic World', in *Christianity Among the Slavs: The Heritage of Saints Cyril and Methodius* (Rome, 1988), pp. 131-142.

57. A problem for the Orthodox Church in the sense that Bogomilism was a popular heterodox religious and social movement which challenged the authority of the established Church.

58. Theophanes, *Chronographia*, C. de Boor, ed. (Hildesheim, 1963), p. 422.

59. D. P. Hupchick, *The Balkans: From Constantinople to Communism* (New York, 2004), p. 52.

60. The letter of Theophylact Lecapenus to Tsar Petur appears in I. Duichev, 'L'epistola sui Bogomil del patriarca constantinopolitano Teofilatto', *Melanges E. Tisserant* (Rome, 1964), pp. 88-91.

61. The discourse of Cosmas *Against the Bogomils* can be found in Y. Stoyanov, *The Hidden Tradition in Europe* (New York, 1994).

62. R. C. Zaehner, *Zurvan: A Zoroastrian Dilemma* (Oxford, 1955), appendix.

63. Y. Stoyanov. *The Hidden Tradition in Europe* (London, 1994), p. 113.

64. Y. Stoyanov, pp. 132-133.

65. This attempt to halt the advance of Bogomilism was contemporaneous with the pope's suppression of the Albigensian heresy in Southern France.

66. J. and B. Hamilton, *Christian Dualist Heresies* (Manchester, 1998), pp. 114-134.

CHAPTER 2: RELIGIO-HISTORIAL CONTEXT PRIOR
TO THE BULGARIAN NATIONAL REVIVAL

1. G. Chavrokov, *Centres of Bulgarian Literacy IX-XVIII* (Sofia, 1987), p. 137.

2. O. Todorova, *The Orthodox Church and the Bulgarian Nation through the 15th – third quarter of the 18th century*) (Sofia, 1987), pp. 43-46

3. P. Nikov, *Revival of the Bulgarian Nation* (Sofia, 1929); P. Petrov, *The Fateful Centuries of the Bulgarian Nation* (Sofia, 1975); C. J. Jirecek, *Geschichte der Bulgaren* (Prague, 1876), pp. 448-478.

4. For example Snegarov (1958) and Gandev (1972).

5. M. Kiel, *Art and Society of Bulgaria in the Turkish Period* (Assen, 1985), p. 53.

6. A. Popovic, *L'Islam balkanique. Les Musulmans du sud-est europeen dans la periode post-ottomane* (Berlin, 1986), p. 3.

7. Sheikh al-Islam Ali effendi (1703-1712), НБКМ Ор. отд., ОII 432, p. 170.

8. Sheikh al-Islam Duri-zadi sahid Mehmed effendi (1785-1798), НБКМ Ор. отд., ОII 360, p. 149.

9. Snegarov 1958 and Gandev 1972.

10. The Jizie registers assessed the Ottoman Empire's population according to religious affiliation for the purpose of legal status and tax appropriation.

11. H. Inalcik and D. Quataert, *An Economic and Social History of the Ottoman Empire, 1300-1914* (Cambridge, 1994), p. 25.

12. BOA, *Mevkufat Kalemi*, No. 2873, f.108.

13. P. Petrov, *The Fateful Centuries of the Bulgarian Nation* (Sofia, 1975), p. 178.

14. S. Andreev, *The History of Ore Mining and Metalwork in Bulgaria through the 15-19th Centuries* (Sofia, 1993), pp. 81-84.

15. E. Radushev, 'Christians and Muslims in the Western Rhodopes through the 15-18th Century', in. *Religion and the Church in Bulgaria*, ed. by G. Bakalov (Sofia, 1999), p. 355.

16. BOA, *MAD*, No. 525, f.19.

17. BOA, *TD* 3.

18. BOA, *Mevkufat Kalemi*, No. 2873, f.108.

19. H. W. Lowry, 'Changes in the Fifteenth Century Ottoman Peasant Taxation', in *Continuity and Change in Late Byzantine and Early Ottoman Society* (Birmingham, 1986), p. 31.

20. M. Mazower, *The Balkans* (London, 2000), p. 52.

21. H. Inalcik, 'Ottoman Methods of Conquest', *Studia Islamica*, II, 1954, p. 116.

22. S. Tahirov, *The Unification* (Sofia, 1981), pp. 69-80.

23. B. Braude and B. Lewis, *Christians and Jews in the Ottoman Empire: The Functioning of a Plural Society* (London, 1982), p. 2.

24. B. Angelov, *In the Old Bulgarian, Russian and Serbian Literature* (Sofia: 1967), pp. 268-279.

25. B. Angelov and M. Genov, *Ancient Bulgarian Literature (IX-XVIII)* (Sofia, 1922), pp. 565-574.

26. S. Gerlach, *The Diary of a Journey to the Ottoman Porte in Tsarigrad* (Sofia, 1976), p. 264.

27. G. Chavrokov, p. 160.

28. I. Ivanov, *Bulgarian Antiquities in Macedonia* (Sofia, 1931), pp. 597-600.

29. I initially read of these archives in D. Ihchiev's *Turkish Documents in Rila* Monastery (Sofia, 1910). During March 2003 I was able to visit Rila Monastery and investigate these archives personally; See appendix one for a translation of the *firman* protecting the rights of Rila (1801).

30. M. Kiel (1985), p. 160.

31. P. Nikov, *Vladislav Gramatik* (Sofia, 1928), pp. 165-187.

32. BOA, *MAD* 525, f.19.

33. M. Todorova, *Balkan Identities: Nation and Memory* (London, 2004), p. 131.

34. S. Zakhariev, *A Geographical-Historical-Statistical Account of the Tartarmarket kaza* (Vienna, 1870).

35. I. Todorov, 'The Chronicle of Metodi Draginov', *Old Bulgarian Literature* 16(1984)60-62.

36. C. J. Jirecek, pp. 448-478.

37. Ducas, *Decline and Fall of Byzantium to the Ottoman Turks* (Detroit, 1975), p. 148.

38. F. Babinger, *Mehmed der Eroberer und seine Zeit* (Munich, 1953), pp. 212-213.

39. Vizier – a minister of state.

40. H. A. R. Gibb and H. Bowen, *Islamic Society and the West. A Study of the Impact of Western Civilisation on Moslem Culture in the Near East*, Vol. I (London, 1957), pp. 207-261.

41. 'Roman' does not refer to Rome or the Latin Church, rather it comes from the Arabic/Turkish *rum* and applied to the Orthodox Christian subjects of the Ottoman empire.

42. M. MacDermott, *A History of Bulgaria 1393-1885* (London, 1962), pp. 51-52.

43. Cathcart to Bulwer, 20 July 1860, *Great Britain, Parliamentary Papers* (London, 1861) vol. 67.

44. E. Durham, *The Burden of the Balkans* (London, 1905), pp. 143-4.

45. T. H. Papadopoullos, *Studies and Documents Relating to the History of the Greek Church and People under Turkish Domination* (Brussels, 1952), pp. 143-45.

46. B. Tsvetkova, 'Some Forms of Resistance Against the Turkish Feudal System', in V. Traikov (1962), p. 221.

47. B. Tsvetkova, *The Haidouks in Bulgarian Lands Through the 15-18th Centuries* (Sofia, 1971), p. 54.

48. B. Tsvetkova (1971), pp. 26-27.

49. B. Tsvetkova, in Traikov (1962), pp. 237-239.

50. Roman Catholic involvement in Bulgaria mentioned in, *Speculum Veritatis inter orientalem* (Vienna, 1725) and *Concilis et Orthodoxorum Patrum* (Cologne, 1560).

51. N. Chernokozhev, 'The Book of the Bulgarians' in *Paisii Hilendarski. A Slavo-Bulgarian History. A Facsimile of the Original Zograph Manuscript Draft (1762)*, ed. by B. Atanasov (Sofia: St. Kliment Ohridski University Press, 2000) p. ii.

52. M. Drinov, 'Father Paisii, His Times, His History and His Students', *Periodical of the Bulgarian Literary Society*, No. 4 (Braila, 1871) p. 115ff.

53. N. Stanev, 'Paisii and the Bulgarian Writers', *Collective Memories of Prof. Petur Nikov* (Sofia, 1940), pp. 411-417.

54. B. Atanasov, *Paisii Hilendarski. A Slavo-Bulgarian History. A Facsimile of the Original Zograph Manuscript Draft (1762)* (Sofia: St. Kliment Ohridski University Press, 2000) p. 155.

55. A Cyrillic printing press was available as early as 1761 in Tyrnau, Hungary. However, this was controlled by the Uniate movement.

56. The National Revival is the period covering the second part of the 18th century – from the completion of Paisii's *Slavo-Bulgarian History* in 1762 until the liberation of Bulgaria from Turkish rule after the Russo-Turkish War of 1877-78.

57. Ed. B. Atanasov (2000), p. 234.

58. K. Topolov, 'The Great Man from Mount Athos and his work to the Benefit of the Bulgarian People' in. B. Atanasov (2000) p. 269.

59. Ed. B. Atanasov (2000), p. 157.

60. Ed. B. Atanasov (2000), pp. 151-52.

61. Ed. B. Atanasov, pp. 155-56.

62. Ed. B. Atanasov, p. 156.

63. Ed. B. Atanasov, p. 156.

64. Ed. B. Atanasov, p. 156.

65. Ed. B. Atanasov, p. 156.

66. Ed. B. Atanasov, p. 157.

67. Ed. B. Atanasov, p. 156.

68. Ed. B. Atanasov, p. 166

69. Ed. B. Atanasov, pp. 202-03.

70. Ed. B. Atanasov, p. 216.

71. Ed. B. Atanasov, pp. 209-10.

72. Ed. B. Atanasov, p. 225.

73. Ed. B. Atanasov, p. 241.

74. Ed. B. Atanasov, p. 155.

75. Ed. B. Atanasov, p. 241.

76. Ed. B. Atanasov, pp. 155,157.

77. Ed. B. Atanasov, p. 241.

78. H. Radevski, *The Third of March* (Sofia, 1938).

79. M. MacDermott, *History of Bulgaria 1393-1885* (London, 1982), p. 92. This is the first known copy of Paisii's *Slavo-Bulgarian History*.

80. M. MacDermott (1982), pp. 97,103-104.

81. S. Vrachanski, *Autobiography of Sofroni Vrachanski* (Sofia, 1914), p. 36.

82. R. J. Crampton, *A Concise History of Bulgaria* (Cambridge, 1997), p. 53.

83. I. Pastukhov, Bulgarian History (Sofia, 1943), vol. II, p. 566.

84. I. Pastukhov, p. 573.

85. Pasvanoglu's province consisted of over 200 Bulgarian villages reaching from Vidin into Southern Bulgaria.

86. L. S. Stavrianos, *The Balkans since 1453* (New York, 1958), p. 218.

87. A. Neale, *Travels through some parts of Germany, Poland, Moldavia and Turkey* (London, 1818), p. 266.

88. M. MacDermott (1982), p. 100.

89. S. Vrachanski, p. 3.

90. N. Genchev, The Bulgarian National Revival Period (Sofia, 1977), p. 36.

91. N. Genchev (1977), pp. 40-41.

CHAPTER 3: THE JOURNEY TOWARDS CULTURAL AUTONOMY

1. M. V. Pundeff, 'Bulgarian Nationalism', in *Nationalism in Eastern Europe*, ed. by Peter F. Sugar and Ivo J. Lederer (Seattle, 1969), pp. 93-105.

2. L. S. Stavrianos, *The Balkans since 1453* (New York, 1958), p. 219.

3. See, D. Quataert, *The Ottoman Empire, 1700-1922* (Cambridge, 2000), pp. 64-68 and R. H. Davison, *Reforms in the Ottoman Empire, 1856-1876* (Princeton, 1963), pp. 3-60.

4. E. Engelhardt, *La Turquie et la Tanzimat* (Paris, 1882), vol. 1, p. 142.

5. A. H. Midhat, *The Life of Midhat Pasha* (London, 1903), p. 33.

6. Russia's influence grew after the 1774 Treaty of Kuchuk Kainardji was agreed between Russia and Turkey granting St. Petersburg an unprecedented role as spiritual protector of the Ottoman Empire's Orthodox subjects.

7. R. H. Davison, p. 133.

8. By the time Selim assumed the throne in 1794 the once exclusive Janissary corps had degenerated into a force dedicated to self-aggrandizement opposing the proposed reform programme.

9. R. J. Crampton, *A Concise History of Bulgaria* (Cambridge, 1997), p. 60

10. Cell Schools – kilino uchilishte (килийно училище).

11. N. Genchev, *The Bulgarian National Revival* (Sofia, 1977), p. 55.

12. P. Mitev, *The Bulgarian National Revival* (Sofia, 1999), p. 55.

13. P. Mitev (1999), p. 56.

14. P. Mitev (1999), p. 58.

15. M. MacDermott (1982), p. 119.

16. M. V. Pundeff, p. 105.

17. P. Mitev (1999), p. 59.

18. This model is named after the British educationalists Joseph Lancaster (1778-1838) and Andrew Bell (1753-1832).

19. M. V. Pundeff, p. 106.

20. In the second half of the 18th century a series of wars took place between Russia and Turkey. The Bulgarians took part hoping that liberation would ensue. Although Russian troops entered Bulgarian territory on these occasions the Bulgars gained nothing and indeed suffered terribly from Turkish reprisals when Russian troops withdrew until the 1877-78 War of Liberation: Russo-Turkish Wars 1768-74, 1787-91, 1806-12, 1828-29, 1877-78.

21. Y. Venelin, *The Moscow Gazette* (translated from a photocopy of the newspaper cutting dated Moscow, 1828).

22. Y. Venelin, *The Ancient and Present Day Bulgarians in Their Political, National, Historical and Religious Relations with the Russians* (Lvov, 1829).

23. E. Georgiev, 'Bulgaristics – The Fundamental Discipline of Slavistics', *The Basis of Slavistics and Bulgaristics* (Sofia, 1979), pp. 78-93.

24. P. J. Safarik, *Geschichte der slavischen Sprache und Literatur nach allen Mundarten* (Ofen, 1826).

25. V. D. Konobiev, *The National Freedom Movement in Bulgaria, 1829-1830* (Sofia, 1972), pp. 180-271.

26. Y. I. Venelin, *Critical Researches on the History of the Bulgarians, by Y. I. Venelin. From the Arrival of the Bulgarians on the Thracian Peninsula to 968, to the Subjection of Bulgaria by the Russian Grand Prince Svyatoslav* (Moscow, 1849).

27. K. Mechev, 'Yuri Ivanovich Venelin and the Question of the National Affiliation of Cyril and Methodius', *BHR* (2:72-83, 1978).

28. D. P. Hupchick, *The Pen and the Sword: Studies in Bulgarian History* (New York, 1988), p. 142.

29. Modern scholarship is quite dismissive of Venelin's academic work, suggesting that he was the victim of romantic enthusiasm.

30. N. A. Popov, *A Brief Account of a Decade of Activities (1858-1868) of the Slavic Charitable Committee in Moscow* (Moscow, 1871), p. 2.

31. N. A. Popov, p. 2   .

32. These centres known in Bulgaria as *chitalishta* (читалища) have no adequate English translation. A combination of the German 'Kulturheime' and the English 'Community Centre' capture the essence of the establishments.

33. From the Statutes of the Moscow Slavonic Charitable Committee (Moscow, 1877), p. 1.

34. A. Andreev, 'The Russian Orthodox Church in the 17th Century – Reform and Schism', *BHR* (3:14-31, 1995).

35. The concept of Moscow as the 'Third Rome' was first articulated by the Russian monk Filofei in a letter to Tsar Ivan III soon after the fall of Constantinople in 1453: "Pious Tsar! Listen and remember that all Christian Kingdoms have now merged into one, your [tsardom]. Two Romes have fallen, the third stands firm and there will not be a fourth." (B. Dmytryshyn, *Medieval Russia: A Source Book, 850-1700* (Fort Worth, TX, 1991), pp. 259-261.

36. M. Glenny, *The Balkans 1804-1999: Nationalism, War and the Great Powers* (London, 1999), p. 129.

37. *ГАРФ*, f.1750, op. 1, a.e.67, l.61.

38. *ГАРФ*, f.1750, op. 1, a.e.31, l.1-7.

39. S. Nikitin, *The Slavonic Committee in Russia in 1858-1876* (Moscow, 1960), p. 121.

40. *ГАРФ*, f.730, op. 1, a.e.1003, 1004, 1006, l.1-3.

41. A. Andreev, 'The Moscow Slavonic Charitable Committee', in G. Bakalov, ed. (1999), p. 140.

42. S. Nikitin, pp. 58-60.

43. S. Nikitin, pp. 58-60.

44. S. Nikitin, pp. 58-60.

45. E. Z. Karal, *Islahat Fermani devri, 1861-1876* (Ankara, 1956), p. 153.

46. Sanie – a leading position within Ottoman administrative hierarchy.

47. A. H. Midhat, p. 32.

48. R. H. Davison, p. 145.

49. Henry C. Barkley was so impressed with Midhat Pasha's Bulgarian road building campaign that he devotes a whole chapter to it in: *Bulgaria before the War during Seven Years' Experience of European Turkey and its Inhabitants* (London, 1877).

50. A. H. Midhat, pp. 38-40.

51. *Tuna*, 3 March 1865, No. 1.

52. *Tuna*, 17 March 1865, No. 3.

53. *Tuna*, 10 March 1865, No. 2.

54. *Tuna*, 21 July 1865, No. 21.

55. *Tuna*, 27 November 1865, No. 35.

56. D. Tsonkov, *The Development of Elementary Education in Bulgaria from 1878 to 1928* (Sofia, 1928), p. 12.

57. *Tuna Vilayeti Salnamesi* (Tuna Vilayet Year Book), Vol. 7, pp. 121-122.

58. F. Outendirck, *La Turquie a l'exposition universelle de 1867* (Paris, 1867), p. 213.

59. F. Kanitz, *Donau-Bulgarien und der Balkan. Historisch-geographisch-ethnographische Reisestudien aus den Jahren 1860-1878* (Leipzig, 1875), pp. 295-319.

60. M. Glenny, p. 96

61. S. J. Shaw, *History of the Ottoman Empire and Modern* (Cambridge, 1977), p. 117.

62. I. Testa, *Recueil des traits de la Porte ottomane avec les puissances etrangeres* (Paris, 1864), p. 459.

CHAPTER 4: THE STRUGGLE FOR BULGARIAN ECCLESIASTICAL INDEPENDENCE

1. Many Bulgarians paid the Church twice that which they were required to pay in state taxes. *БИА НБКМ*, f.40, ed.3, l.80-81.

2. The first bishops of Vratsa were Seraphim (1782-1794), the Bulgarian Sofroni (1794-1804), and Antim (1804-1813).

3. *БИА НБКМ*, f.40, ed.3, l.84-85.

4. *БИА НБКМ*, f.40, ed.7, l.44.

5. *БИА НБКМ*, f.40, ed.7, l.25.

6. Letter of Georgi Mihalov (Pleven) to Dimitraki Hadjitoshev (Vratsa), 6 March 1824, *БИА НБКМ*, f.40, ed.2, l.47.

7. Letter from Ilarion Kritski (Turnovo) to Dimitraki Hadjitoshev (Vratsa), 12 September 1824, *БИА НБКМ*, f.40, ed.2, l.21.

8. *БИА НБКМ*, f.40, ed.2, l.56.

9. H. Semerdjiev, *Samokov and the Surrounding Region. A Contribution to its Past from the Turkish Conquest to the Liberation* (Sofia, 1913), p. 13.

10. H. Semerdjiev, p. 20.

11. Z. Markova, *The Bulgarian National Church Movement to the Crimean War* (Sofia, 1976), p. 100.

12. *Сб НУНК*, XV, 1898, p. 313.

13. M. Arnaudov, *Neofit Hilendarski Bozveli, 1785-1848* (Sofia, 1971), pp. 462-466.

14. *Сб НУНК*, XIII, 1896, p. 360.

15. M. Arnaudov, pp. 512-586.

16. P. Mitev, *The Bulgarian National Revival* (Sofia, 1999), p. 78.

17. 'Hambar' – the centre for Bulgarian crafts in which thousands of Bulgarians worked.

18. See section 4.1.2 'Foreign involvement in the Bulgarian Church dispute'.

19. The Bulgarian people remained part of the general Orthodox millet. However, the firman recognised that the Constantinople Church was solely the property of the Bulgarian people. The church would be administered by a twenty strong council who had the authority to appoint priests. This governing council was the first new and specifically Bulgarian organisation to receive official recognition in the Ottoman empire since 1393.

20. P. Mitev, p. 80.

21. *Сб НУНК*, XIX, 1903, pp. 323-364.

22. S. Damyanov, 'French-Russian Contradictions in the Balkans and the activities of the Polish Emigrants', *BHR*, 1 (1974), 36.

23. *AMAE*, CP, t.283, f.55-59.

24. M. Handelsman, *Adam Czartoryski* (Warsaw, 1949), p. 153.

25. Lazarists: Also known as Vincentians, founded by St. Vincent de Paul in 1617 and officially approved by the Catholic Church in 1626, a.k.a. 'the congregation of secular clergymen'.

26. K. Sarova, 'Les Bulgares dans la politique balkanique de l'emigration polonaise (1842-1843)', *BHR*, 2 (1974), pp. 34-52.

27. *AMAE*, CP, t.300 (1848-1849), f.248.

28. *AMAE*, CP, t.300 (1848-1849), f.294-295.

29. *AMAE*, CP, t.299 (1848), f.254-255.

30. *ANF*, f.19, 6237a.

31. E. Druzhinina, *Kucuk Kaynarca Treaty, 1774* (Moscow, 1955), pp. 349-360.

32. V. Teplov, *Russian Representation in Constantinople, 1496-1891: Historical Articles* (St. Petersburg, 1891), p. 59

33. Article 1. There shall be forever peace, amity and alliance between His Majesty the Emperor of all the Russia's and His Majesty the Emperor of the Ottomans, their empires and their subjects, as well by land as by sea. This alliance having solely for its object the common defence of their dominions against all attack, their Majesties engage to come to an unreserved understanding with each other upon all the matters which concern their respective tranquillity and safety, and to afford to each other mutually for this purpose substantial aid, and the most efficacious assistance, in *The Great Powers and the Near East, 1774-1923*, ed. by M. S. Anderson (London: E. Arnold, 1970), pp. 42-43.

34. Z. Markova (1976), p. 182.

35. *АВПР*, ф. ГА, V-A, d.515 (1845), l.64-67.

36. *АВПР*, ф. Посолъство в Константинополе (The Embassy in Constantinople), d.589 (1846), l.7-10.

37. *AMAE*, CP, t.295, f.246-248.

38. V. Paskaleva, *Russia and the Bulgarian Church Question* (Sofia, 1965), p. 523.

39. P. Mitev, p. 81.

40. P. Mitev, p. 82.

41. T. A. Meininger, *Ignatiev and the Establishment of the Bulgarian Exarchate 1864-1872* (Madison, 1970), p. 22.

42. P. Mitev, p. 83.

43. P. Voeikov, 'The Records of Count N. P. Ignat'eva, 1864-1874', *Journal of the Ministry of Foreign Affairs*, 1 (1914) pp. 103-104.

44. P. Voeikov, p. 161.

45. Kiril, Patriarch of Bulgaria, *Count N. P. Ignatiev and the Bulgarian Church Question: Examination and Documentation* (Sofia: 1958), pp. 211-212.

46. Kiril, Patriarch of Bulgaria (1958), pp. 213.

47. L. S. Stavrianos, 'L'Institution de l'Exarcat bulgare: Son influence sur les relations interbalkaniques', *Les Balkans*, XI (1939) 61.

48. Kiril, Patriarch of Bulgaria (1958), p. 219.

49. Kiril, Patriarch of Bulgaria (1958), p. 206.

50. D. N. Dontas, *Greece and the Great Powers, 1863-1875* (Thessalonica, 1966), p. 71.

51. M. G. Popruzhenko and T. Panchev (eds.), *From the Archive of Naiden Gerov* (Sofia: 1931), p. 411.

52. From an untitled column by the Russian correspondent of the *Levant Herald*, attached to the diplomatic dispatch of Morris to Seward, 10 October 1866. USNA, *Despatches from United States Ministers to Turkey, 1818-1906*, R.20.

53. P. Voeikov, pp. 101-102.

54. Kiril, Patriarch of Bulgaria (1958), pp. 229-230.

55. Kiril, Patriarch of Bulgaria (1958), p. 241.

56. Kiril, Patriarch of Bulgaria (1958), pp. 241-242.

57. Kiril, Patriarch of Bulgaria (1958), pp. 246-247.

58. S. Radev, *La Macedoine et la renaissance bulgare au XIX siecle* (Sofia, 1918), p. 222.

59. S. Radev (1918), pp. 245-247.

60. The 'moderate' faction was generally made up of older Bulgar statesmen who worked within Ottoman administration. They promoted gradual and evolutionary solutions to Bulgaria's problems. They did not want to break from the Ottoman Empire or the Patriarchate and desired to maintain relations with the Russians. The 'extremists' on the other hand consisted of younger men with modern university educations who felt alienated from society for socio-political and nationalistic reasons. They favoured revolutionary action, advocating a free Bulgarian Church for all Bulgarians, even if it provoked schism. They were not particularly concerned about Russian considerations.

61. Kiril, Metropolitan of Plovdiv (Plovdiv, 1956), pp. 195-201.

62. Kiril, Patriarch of Bulgaria (1962), pp. 257-258.

63. L. S. Stavrianos, 'L'Institution de l'Exarcat bulgare: Son influence sur les relations interbalkaniques', *Les Balkans*, XI (1939) 63.

64. Kiril, Patriarch of Bulgaria (1962), pp. 258-260.

65. Kiril, Patriarch of Bulgaria (1962), p. 263.

66. Kiril, Patriarch of Bulgaria (1962), p. 269.

67. P. Voeikov, p. 160.

68. Kiril, Patriarch of Bulgaria (1962), p. 286.

69. M. G. Popruzhenko and T. Panchev (eds.), p. 533.

70. See appendix two for a translation of the *firman* announcing the establishment of the Bulgarian Exarchate (1870).

71. Preliminary Statement from the mixed conference, *ЦА*, 3, 1931, pp. 125-132.

72. *ЦДИА*, f.111, op. 1, a.e.66.

73. *Македония*, No. 48, 9 May 1870.

74. *Македония*, No. 55, 4 June 1870; No. 57, 10 June 1870; No. 64, 8 July 1870.

75. *Право*, No. 28, 7 September 1870.

76. *Право*, No. 43, 21 December 1870.

77. Materials on the Church Dispute, *Сб НУ*, 24, 1908, 107-108.

78. *НА БАН*, f.8k (N. Mihailovski to N. Zlatarski, 18 May 1870).

79. Materials on the Church Dispute, *Сб НУ*, 24, 1908, 113-114.

80. *ЦА*, 3, p. 181.

81. Z. Markova, *The Bulgarian Exarchate 1870-1879* (Sofia, 1989), p. 40.

82. The Constantinople Council on the Bulgarian question proclaimed:

> We reject and condemn racial division, that is, racial differences, national quarrels and disagreements in the Church of Christ, as being contrary to the teaching of the Gospel and the holy canons of our blessed fathers, on which the holy Church is established and which adorn human society and lead it to divine piety.

In accordance with the holy canons, we proclaim that those who accept such division according to race and who dare to base on it hitherto unheard of racial assemblies are foreign to the One, Holy, Catholic and Apostolic Church and are real schismatics.

In T. I. Filippov, *Contemporary Church Questions* (St. Petersburg, 1882), pp. 185-186.

83. Kiril, Patriarch of Bulgaria, p. 489.

84. H. Gandev, *The April Uprising* (Sofia, 1976), p. 66.

85. C. and B. Jelavich, *The Establishment of the Balkan National States, 1804-1920* (Seattle, 1977), p. 135.

86. M. MacDermott, *History of Bulgaria 1393-1885* (London, 1982), pp. 202-203.

87. M. MacDermott, p. 203.

88. This is exemplified clearly in I. Vazov's *Under the Yoke* (Sofia: Foreign Language Press, 1960). One of Bulgaria's most acclaimed author's, this work of fiction is read almost as a work of history rather than of fiction based on historical events.

89. T. Koev, *An Overview of the Bulgarian Orthodox Church*; available from http://www.bok.at/en/geschichte.htm: accessed 18 May 2004.

90. *Право*, No. 28, 21 September, 1872.

91. O. Mazhdrakova-Chavdarova, 'Deacon Ignatius (Vasil Levski) in Plovdiv, 1863-1864', *ИПр* 3(1997).

92. *БИА НБКМ*, II А 6957.

93. *АЦИАИ*, Letters of the Exarch, 1874-1875, l.389-390.

94. *АЦИАИ*, Reports of the Mixed Council, 1875-1878, l.83.

95. *АЦИАИ*, l.98.

96. *ОДА-Русе*, f.43k, op. 1, a.e.6, l.70-71.

97. *НА БАН*, f.54k, a.e. 364, l.94-95.

98. *AMAE CP*, Turquie-Roustchouk, t.2, l.306-309.

99. *АЦИАИ*, l.170.

100. *БИА НБКМ*, II А 6091.

101. M. MacDermott. (1982), p. 276.

102. J. A. MacGahan, *Daily News*, 29 August, 1876.

103. E. Schuyler, *Daily News*, 29 August, 1876.

104. W. E. Gladstone, *Bulgarian Horrors and the Question of the East* (London, 1876)

105. *АЦИАИ*, l.269-270.

106. The Enquiry Commission for Investigation of the Outrages Committed to Suppress the April Uprising in 1876, *Изв. НБКМ*, 14 (20), 1978, l.663-664.

107. *АЦИАИ*, l.262.

108. M. Balabanov, *Pages from the Politics of the National Revival* (Sofia, 1904), p. 73.

109. Letter from Antim I to the Russian Synod (11 August, 1876), *БИА НБКМ*, f.16, a.e.4, l.109-112.

110. *АЦИАИ*, l.294.

111. *АЦИАИ*, Reports of the Holy Synod 1877, l.17-20.

112. *БИА НБКМ*, II А 3039.

113. Text of the letter can be found in *The Liberation of Bulgaria from the Turkish Yoke: Documents*, Vol. II (Moscow, 1964), pp. 564-568.

114. W. N. Medlicott, *A Diplomatic History of the Near Eastern Settlement, 1878-1880* (London, 1938), pp. 39-57.

115. I. Ormandzhiev, *The New and Most Recent History of the Bulgarian Nation* (Sofia, 1945), p. 410.

CHAPTER 5: DEVELOPING RELATIONSHIPS THE CHURCH, STATE CONSOLIDATION, NATIONAL UNIFICATION AND WAR (1878-1945)

1. H. Temelski, 'Exarch Josef as a Politician and Diplomat', *Rodina* 3(1996)32.

2. *The Constitution of the Principality of Bulgaria* (16 April 1879), Section 9, Article 39; see Appendix Three for a translation of Section IX in the first constitution dealing with religion.

3. The map of San Stefano 'Greater Bulgaria' followed the borders of the Bulgarian Exarchate's territory. The Church therefore became central to the rationale behind the State's territorial claims.

4. P. Petkov, 'The Development of the Attitude Between the Bulgarian Orthodox Church and the State Authorities (1878-1896)', in G. Bakalov, ed. (1999), p. 193.

5. H. Temelski, p. 32.

6. *АЦИАИ*, Records of the Exarchate 1883-1886, l.3.

7. Sofia was designated the new capital of Bulgaria, replacing Turnovo, as it symbolised the centre of 'Greater Bulgaria' where developments in Thrace and Macedonia could be more effectively influenced.

8. H. Temelski, 'The Bulgarian Exarchate – Defender of the Bulgarian National Spirit in Macedonia and Odrinska Thrace', in G. Bakalov, ed. (1999), p. 224.

9. *АЦИАИ*, Records of the Exarchate 1883-1886, l.27-28.

10. *Bulgarian Exarch Josef I, Diary* (Sofia, 1992), pp. 103-104 (1 April 1881).

11. *НА БАН*, f.54k, a.e.228, l.233.

12. During the National Revival period from 1830-70s a significant part of Bulgaria's intelligentsia and business elite (the people who now made up the present state administration) had been hostile towards the spiritual, educational and legal jurisdiction of the Church authorities. The present situation done nothing to ally their fears.

13. *The Constitution*, ibid., Section 9, Articles 39, 40, 60, 86, 132.

14. *ДВ*, №95, 23 December, 1880.

15. *ДВ*, №103, 8 September, 1882, Art. 94, 96.

16. *ДВ*, №137, 20 December, 1883.

17. *Official Reports of Proceedings in the National Assembly* (Sofia, 1879), №1, pp. 200-202; №2, pp. 207-219.

18. *НА БАН*, f.54k. a.e.250, l.8-9.

19. *Official Reports of Proceedings in the 2nd National Assembly* (Sofia, 1881), l.37, 7.8

20. D. Kalakandjieva, *The Bulgarian Orthodox Church and National Democracy* (Silistra, 2002), p. 29.

21. *ЦДА*, f.166, op. 1, a.e.58, l.21.

22. C. E. Black, *The Establishment of Constitutional Government in Bulgaria* (Princeton, NJ, 1943), p. 75.

23. C. E. Black, p. 181.

24. C. E. Black, p. 210.

25. *ГСУ БФ*, 6(1939)134-138.

26. All ranks in the Bulgarian Army upwards of lieutenant were held by Russians.

27. C. E. Black, p. 238.

28. P. Nikov, 'Relationships Between the Bulgarian State and the Bulgarian Church,' *Records of the Historical Society*, XII (Sofia, 1932), pp. 302-305.

29. *НБКМ БИА*, f.290, a.e.168, 1.1-2.

30. *Селянин* (BG newspaper, *Peasant*), V, August 1886, p. 4.

31. P. Kisimov, Open letter to D. Petkova, chief editor of the newspaper *Свобода*, October 1886.

32. *Свобода*, No. 109, 13 December 1887, p. 3.

33. *Независимост*, No. 3, 12 March 1886, p. 4.

34. *Свобода*, No. 411, 22 November 1890, p. 2.

35. *Свобода*, No. 234, 10 May 1889, p. 1.

36. Z. Stoyanov, *It Wasn't the Time. Response to the Brochure "Misunderstanding between the Bulgarian and Russian Governments"* (Ruse, 1886), p. 50.

37. Canon 13 from the Synod of Antioch states: "Let no bishop dare to go from one province to another and ordain anyone... anything performed by him is invalid."

38. *Almanac of the Bulgarian Constitution* (Plovdiv, 1911), p. 175.

39. *Almanac of the Bulgarian Constitution* (1911), p. 177.

40. P. Petkov, p. 197.

41. *The Constitution*, ibid., Section 8: "The Bulgarian Prince and his offspring cannot follow another religious confession except for Orthodoxy. Only the first elected Bulgarian Prince may belong to another faith."

42. *АЦИАИ*, Records of the Holy Synod 1886-1890, No. 17, 17 December 1888, 1.97-100.

43. *Новини*, No. 19-22, 24-27 November 1892.

44. Exarch Josef I of Bulgaria, *Diary* (Sofia, 1992), p. 318.

45. G. Todorov, *Bulgaria, Orthodoxy, History* (Sofia, 2003), p. 94.

46. G. Todorov (2003), p. 94.

47. G. Todorov (2003), p. 97.

48. G. Todorov (2003), p. 98.

49. *Dr. Konstantin Stoilov's Diary*, Part II (Sofia, 1892), pp. 148-149.

50. *ДА*-Turnovo, f.74k, op. 1, a.e.51, 1.77.

51. The diary of Konstantin Stoilov is interesting as it records that the Austrian and British governments attempted to stop the baptism of Prince Boris into the Orthodox faith. It is even suggested that they tried to bribe Exarch Josef and Metropolitan Gregory with the aim of forcing them to acknowledge the Pope. In *Dr. Konstantin Stoilov's Diary*, Part II (Sofia, 1892), pp. 246-269.

52. I. Dimitrov, *The Prince, the Constitution and the People* (Sofia, 1972), p. 205

53. Article 194 of the Constitution of Eastern Rumelia stated, "Eastern Rumelia contributes a share in meeting the expenses of the Empire."

54. See for example Georgi Pashev's book, *От Цариград до Белово* (*From Constantinople to Belovo*) (Sofia, 1965), pp. 138-280, which refers to the Porte's opposition to the building of a major railway line in Rumelia which would have been vital to the development of the economy.

55. *НА БАН*, Archive of M. Grekov, No. 2374, p. 55.

56. *A Collection of Russian Treaties with Other States, 1856-1917* (Moscow. 1952), pp. 228-233.

57. With Macedonia and Thrace returned under Ottoman power the BCRC decided to concentrate their unification activities on Eastern Rumelia.

58. E. Corti, *Alexander von Battenburg* (London, 1954), p. 164.

59. G. C. Logio, *Bulgaria: Past and Present* (Manchester, 1936), p. 331.

60. A. F. Golowine, *Furst Alexander I von Bulgarien* (Vienna, 1896), p. 279.

61. S. Tatishchev, *From the History of Russian Diplomacy* (St. Petersburg, 1890), p. 430.

62. K. Krachounov, *Diplomatic History of the Unification of Bulgaria* (Sofia, 1919), pp. 45-46.

63. E. Corti, *Alexander von Battenburg* (Vienna, 1920), pp. 165-168.

64. M. Lalkov, *Bulgaria after the Liberation (1871-1912)* (Sofia, 2001), p. 116.

65. H. Temelski, 'Exarch Josef I as a Politician and Diplomat', *Rodina* 3 (1996) 28-31.

66. *АЦИАИ*, No. 10978, p. 17 (Confidential Letter No. 41, 5 April 1912, from Exarch Josef I to Prime Minister Stambulov).

67. *ЦДА*, f.176, op. 2, a.e.1071, l.20-22.

68. H. N. Brailsford, *Macedonia: Its Races and their Future* (London, 1906), p. 102.

69. H. Temelski (1999), p. 228.

70. *ЦДА*, f.176, op. 2, a.e.154, l.33.

71. Known as such from their journal *La Jeune Turquie*.

72. J. McCarthy, *The Ottoman Turks* (London, 1997), pp. 315-318; S. Pavlowitch, *The Balkans 1804-1945* (London, 1999), pp. 167-170.

73. E. Skatula, *Valka na Balkane: Valecne tazeni Bulharska, Srbska, Recka a Cerne Hory proti Turecku* (Prague, 1913), p. 394.

74. According to *Armies of the Balkan States*, from the War Office in London, 1915, the Bulgarians were spending over £2,500,000 annually on building their army.

75. A. Rossos, *Russia and the Balkans: Inter-Balkan Rivalry and Russian Foreign Policy, 1908-1914* (Toronto, 1981), pp. 45-46.

76. Details of the alliance treaties are in E. C. Helmreich, *The Diplomacy of the Balkan Wars, 1912-1913* (Cambridge, 1938). It is interesting to note that Bulgaria agreed to meet all of Montenegro's war expenses.

77. A. Zlateva, 'Organisation and Activities of the Military Clergy at the time of the Struggle for National Unity', in G. Bakalov, ed. (1999), p. 234.

78. *Мир*, No. 3717, 18 November, 1912.

79. Mr. Young to Sir H. Bax-Ironside, Public Records Office, Great Britain, Unpublished Documents, Foreign Office 371/1782.

80. E. Skatula, p. 446.

81. H. R. Madol, *Ferdinand of Bulgaria: The Dream of Byzantium* (London, 1933), pp. 170-176.

82. Metropolitan Josef of Turnovo, *Memorandum No. 6849* (23 October 1915).

83. See the report of British Vice-Consul C. A. Grieg writing from Monastir, Public Records Office, Great Britain, Unpublished Documents, Foreign Office 371/1830.

84. H. Temelski (1999), p. 231.

85. S. Constant, *Foxy Ferdinand: 1861-1948, Tsar of Bulgaria* (London, 1979), p. 290.

86. A. Palmer, *The Gardeners of Salonika* (London, 1965), p. 57.

87. *ЦДА*, f.791, op. 1, a.e.30, l.19.

88. *ЦВА*, f.40, op. 2, a.e.1006, l.237.

89. A. Zlateva (1999), p. 235.

90. P. Petkov, *The United States and Bulgaria in World War I* (New York, 1991), p. 50.

91. J. D. Bell, *Peasants in Power: Alexander Stamboliski and the Bulgarian Agrarian National Union, 1899-1923* (Princeton, 1977), p. 135.

92. *ЦДА*, f.791, op. 1, a.e.65, l.78-81.

93. S. Eldurov, 'The Spiritual Mobilisation of the Bulgarian Orthodox Church (1939-1944)', in G. Bakalov, ed. (1999), p. 250.

94. S. Eldurov (1999), p. 251.

95. S. Eldurov (1999), p. 252.

96. *ЦДА,* f.791, op. 1, a.e.65, l.3.

97. The reports of both commissions were published in *Църковен вестник* during Nov. 1939 – July 1940.

98. *ЦДА,* f.791, op. 1, a.e.65, l.40.

99. *Църковен вестник,* No. 11, 8 March 1940, p. 129-130.

100. *ЦДА,* f.791, op. 1, a.e.65, l.65-74.

101. D. Cohen, *The Survival* (Sofia, 1995), p. 181.

102. *ЦДА,* f.791, op. 1, a.e.66, l.175.

103. *ЦДА,* f.791, op. 1, a.e.67, l.30-38.

104. *ЦИАИ,* f.2, op. 1, a.e.67, l.33.

105. *Църковен вестник,* No. 19, May 1941, p. 211.

106. J. Belchovski, *The Historical Foundation for the Autocephaly of the Macedonian Orthodox Church* (Skopje, 1990), pp. 137-140.

107. E. Kofos, *Nationalism and Communism in Macedonia* (Thessalonica, 1964), pp. 95-112.

108. *АМВнР,* op. 9, d.3, pr.48, l.100-102.

109. *ЦДА,* f.791, op. 1, a.e.67, l.352.

110. *ЦИАИ,* f.2, op. 1, a.e.67, l.3-4.

111. T. Todorov, *The Fragility of Goodness* (Princeton, 1999), p. 9.

112. D. Cohen, *The Survival* (Sofia, 1995), p. 42.

113. On 23 February 1943 an agreement was reached between A. Belev and Theodor Dannecker according to which the Bulgarians would deport Jews and Gypsies from Macedonia and Thrace (Decree No. 127, 2 March 1943).

114. Statement No. 3603, 26 June 1944 from the Holy Synod to Ivan Bagryanov.

CHAPTER 6: THE CHURCH AND THE COMMUNIST REGIME

1. S. Georgiev – Politsa, P. S. Kiselkov – Tryavna, D. G. Rublev – Kustendil, N. Tasev – Kazanluk, E. P. Vitoshki – Sofia, V. V. Vulkov – Gorna Dubnik (died 9 September 1944); P. P. Ivanov – Novoselsko (12 September 1944); N. V. Georgiev – Chirpan (27 September 1944); R. Raev – Gorna Oryahovo, H. N. Stoimenov – Kustendil, D. Vulkov – Panagurishte (October 1944); S. T. Marinov – Trun (1 October 1944); G. Atanasov – Pazardjik, P. Davidov – Razlog, I. A. Ivanov – Lovech, S. K. Krivoshiev – Sevlievo, S. M. Tafrov – Plovdiv (6 October 1944); I. K. Popov – Mudrets (10 October 1944); I. Kabakchiev – Pleven (14 October 1944); A. I. Stamenov – Gorna Malina (18 October 1944); G. Velichkov – Sofia (24 October 1944); N. P. Milenkov – Podgore (January 1945); K. G. Dudevski – Sopot (20 January 1945); A.V. Andonov – Haskovo, S. Hristov – Nova Zagora (February 1945); T. P. Hristov – Gorno Oryahovo (15 February 1945); B. Delev – Batak (21 February 1945); P. Kiselov – Dryanovsko (24 February 1945); I. N. Yotov – Gorna Dubnik (March 1945); M. M. Danov – Vidin (4 March 1945); I. Angelov – Lovech (10 March 1945); N. T. Kaladjiev – Chirpan (14 March 1945); K. M. Dimitrov – Radomir (16 March 1945); V. Dochev - Shumen, D. I. Petrov – Kustendil, I. N. Tsankov - Popovsko (23 March 1945); L. R. Yurokov – Panagurishte (30 March 1945); A. Kamberov – Novoselsko (April 1945); A. Yanev – Elhovo (10 April 1945); I. Todorov – Stara Zagora, B. Vulkanov – Stara Zagora (14 April 1945); P. Vulkanov – Pleven (16 April 1945); I. V. Drenovski – Bresnitsa (9 September 1945); A. Martinov – Novoselsko (6 October 1945); V. Vulkov – Pleven (9 November 1945): From a Report on the deaths of Orthodox clergy by the Communist regime – presented to the Senate Legislation Committee – Subcommittee for Domestic Security, 29 August 1965

2. *ЦПА*, f.1, op. 6, a.e.3472, l.83.

3. The BOC had been without an Exarch since the death of Exarch Josef in 1915. The schism was proclaimed by the Constantinople Patriarchate in September 1872.

4. *ЦДА*, f.791k, op. 1, a.e.29, Report of the Holy Synod, No. 11 from 20 April 1918

5. Metropolitan Stefan of Sofia, 'The Spirit is not Extinguished', Radio Sofia, broadcast 19 September 1944.

6. *Църковен вестник*, No. 16-19, 1944.

7. *ЦДА*, f.791k, op. 2, a.e.40, Letter addressed to Prime Minister Kimon Georgiev on behalf of the Holy Synod.

8. *Statutes of the Holy Synod*, No. 22, 17 October 1944.

9. *ЦПА*, f.1, op. 7, a.e.180.

10. *Reports of the Holy Synod*, No. 5, 21 January 1945.

11. ПС, No. 5 from 21 January 1945.

12. ПС, No. 6 from 22 January 1945.

13. АЦИАИ, f.2, op. 4.

14. ПС, No. 15 from 27 March 1945.

15. *ЦПА*, f.1, op. 7, a.e.67.

16. *ЦПА*, f.1, op. 7, a.e.117.

17. *ЦПА*, f.1, op. 7, a.e.164.

18. *ЦПА*, f.1, op. 7, a.e.346.

19. *ЦПА*, f.1, op. 7, a.e.401.

20. *ПС*, No. 34 from 19 July 1945.

21. *ЦПА*, f.1, op. 7, a.e.564 (personal letter from Exarch Stefan to G. Dimitrov, 7 August 1945).

22. *ЦДА*, f.509, op. 1, a.e.25, l.135-136.

23. *ЦДА*, op.cit., l.138.

24. *ЦДА*, f.509, op. 1, a.e.29, l.91.

25. *ЦДА*, f.509, op. 1, a.e.25, l.143.

26. *ЦДА*, op.cit., l.144.

27. *ЦДА*, f.509, op. 1, a.e.19, l.1-2.

28. *ЦДА*, op.cit., l.6-7.

29. *ЦДА*, op.cit., l.52-53.

30. *ЦДА*, op.cit., l.120.

31. *ЦДА*, f.147b, op. 3, a.e.917, l.32-33.

32. *ЦДА*, f.507, op. 1, a.e.20, l.37-43.

33. *АМВнР*, op. 1, d.60, a.e.715, l.2-7.

34. *ЦДА*, f.1b, op. 6, a.e.1067, l.6-11.

35. *ЦДА*, f.509, op. 1, a.e.30, l.14.

36. *ЦДА*, f.28, op. 1, a.e.27 (Memorandum No. 396 issued on 6 October 1944).

37. *АЦИАИ*, f.2.

38. *ЦДА*, f.28, op. 1, a.e.45 (Edict No. 235 issued on 1 October 1945).

39. *ПС*, No. 1 from 21 March 1946.

40. *ЦДА*, f.791k, op. 1, a.e.130.

41. *ЦДА*, f.791k, op. 1, a.e.130.

42. *ЦПА*, f.146, op. 5, a.e.1133.

43. *ЦДА*, f.28, op. 1, a.e.27.

44. *ПС*, No. 29 from 25 September 1946.

45. G. Dimitrov, *Съчинение* (*Works*), Vol. 12 (Sofia, 1954), pp. 186-190.

46. G. Dimitrov, p. 186.

47. G. Dimitrov, p. 187.

48. G. Dimitrov, p. 188.

49. G. Dimitrov, p. 189.

50. *ЦПА*, f.1, op. 7, a.e.164.

51. *ЦДА*, f.28, op. 1, a.e.28.

52. *ПС*, No. 37 from 21 October 1946.

53. *Report of the Holy Synod of the BOC on the commencement of the new Constitution as related to the Church* (Sofia, 1946), pp. 1-3.

54. Op.cit., p. 7.

55. Op.cit., p. 8.

56. D. Kalkandjieva, *The Bulgarian Orthodox Church and National Democracy* (Silistra, 2002), p. 184.

57. *ЦДА*, f.791k, op. 1, a.e.176, Letter from the Director of Religious Affairs to the Holy Synod, 2 December 1948.

58. *ЦДА*, op.cit., 14 December 1948.

59. *АЦИАИ*, f.2.

60. *ЦПА*, f.146, op. 6, a.e.582.

61. *ЦДА*, f.1318k, op. 1, a.e.2344.

62. *Църковен вестник*, No. 29-30 from 21 September 1948.

63. *ЦПА*, f.146, op. 5, a.e.1129, Report dated 16 April 1945.

64. *ЦПА*, f.147, op. 3, a.e.917.

65. *ЦПА*, f.146, op. 5, a.e.1129.

66. *ЦПА*, f.1, op. 7, a.e.988.

67. *ЦПА*, f.147, op. 2, a.e.1022.

68. *ЦПА*, f.146, op. 6, a.e.94.

69. *РЦХИДНИ*, f.17, op. 132, r.8, 1.30.

70. Metropolitan Krutitski was in charge of foreign contacts with the Russian Orthodox Church.

71. *РЦХИДНИ*, f.17, op. 132, r.8, 1.99.

72. *РЦХИДНИ*, f.17, op. 132, r.8, 1.107.

73. *ЦПА*, f.1, op. 6, a.e.94.

74. *ЦПА*, f.146, op. 5, a.e.607.

75. *ЦДА*, f.165, op. 3, a.e.128.

76. S. T. Raikin, *Rebel With a Just Cause* (Sofia, 2001), p. 271.

77. *ЦДА*, f.165, op. 1, a.e.4.

78. *ЦПА*, f.147, op. 3, a.e.917.

79. *ПС*, No. 48 from 16 Dec 1946.

80. *ЦДА*, f.28, op. 1, a.e.31.

81. *ЦПА*, f.146, op. 4, a.e.802.

82. *ЦПА*, f.1, op. 6, a.e.539.

83. *ЦПА*, f.165, op. 4, a.e.819.

84. *Proceedings of the Third People's Church Congress* (Sofia, 1953), pp. 47-50.

85. Collectivism: The principle of ownership of the means of production by the State or the people.

86. *АМВнР*, f.13, op. 1, a.e.154, 1.56.

87. In 1997 a document was released from the communist archive labelled "*Decision 'A' No. 145 of the Politburo of the BCP*," dated 8 March 1971, which stated that Maxim had been chosen to lead the BOC and that, "Comrade Mihail Kuchukov will do the preparatory work to insure the election of Metropolitan Maxim."

88. *Catastrophe theory* discussed in detail in Chapter Two.

89. M. Todorova, 'Historiography of the Countries of Eastern Europe: Bulgaria', *American Historical Review*, 97(1992)1105.

90. *ИПр*, May 1968.

91. *History of Bulgaria*, Vol. I (1979, Sofia), p. 21.

92. *History of Bulgaria*, Vol. IV (1983, Sofia), pp. 54-61.

93. Op.cit., pp. 240-251.

94. S. Georgieva, 'Some of the Main Consequences of the Ottoman Conquest of Bulgarian Lands' in *Collection of Lectures from the Master's Post-Graduate Qualification*, IV(1979)213-238.

95. A. Zhelyazkova, 'Social Aspects of the Process of Islamization in the Balkan Possessions of the Ottoman Empire', *Etudes Balkaniques* 3(1985)107-122.

96. Although the government promulgated its atheistic policies upon Bulgaria society it still required to use the Church to affect the prominently Christian orientated population.

97. Възродителен процес (The Process of National Rebirth – commonly known as the Muslim name-changing campaign).

98. V. Dimitrov, 'In Search of a Homogeneous Nation: The Assimilation of Bulgaria's Turkish Minority, 1984-1985', *Journal on Ethnopolitics and Minority Issues in Europe*, December 2000, p. 2.

99. A. Eminov, *Turkish and other Muslim Minorities of Bulgaria* (London, 1997), p. 71.

100. V. Stoyanov, *The Turkish Population in Bulgaria and Official Minority Policy* (Sofia, 1993), p. 204.

101. S. Trifinov, '*The Muslim in the Politics of the Bulgarian State*' (Sofia, 1993), pp. 212-213.

102. K. Karpat, *The Turks of Bulgaria* (Istanbul, 1990).

103. H. Hoppe, 'Bulgarien und seine Turken. Zur Minderheitenpolitik Sofias', *Osteuropa-Archiv* (Stuttgart), A467-A489.

104. P. Petrov, *More Traces of Violence* (Sofia, 1987), pp. 150-151.

105. G. Yankov, *Aspects of the Development of the Bulgarian Nation* (Sofia, 1989), pp. 5-10.

106. Interview with D. Kalkandjieva, 18 March 2005.

107. T. Bringa, *Being Muslim the Bosnian Way: Identity and Community in a Central Bosnian Village* (Princeton, 1995), p. 19.

108. V. Georgiev and S. Trifonov, *The Conversion of the Bulgarian Muslims, 1912-1913*.

109. See Mary Neuburger's argument that the BOC did not enter into the renaming process, in *The Orient Within: Muslim Minorities and the Negation of Nationhood in Modern Bulgaria* (New York, 2004), p. 149.

CHAPTER 7: POST-GLASNOST, CONTEMPORARY BULGARIA AND THE ORTHODOX CHURCH (1989-2005)

1. 15 February 1990.

2. Bulgaria signed the accession treaty with the EU on 25 April 2005. If the EU invokes the safeguard clause accession will be delayed by one year.

3. S. Raikin, 'The Predicaments of the Bulgarian Orthodox Church Today,' in *Occasional Papers on Religion in Eastern Europe* (Vol.XII, No. 1, February 1992) p. 21.

4. I. Katsarki, 'The Bulgarian Orthodox and the Imperative of Modernisation', in G. Bakalov, ed. (1999), p. 23.

5. The 1992 census showed that 85.7% of the population identified themselves with Orthodoxy.

6. Between March-June 2003 thirty-five Bulgarian research assistants, in ten centres (Sofia, Plovdiv, Veliko Turnovo, Varna, Burgas, Stara Zagora, Sliven, Shumen, Blagoevgrad, Ruse) asked 7,203 people these questions.

7. These group discussions took the form of an introductory overview of the situation followed by an open session of debate directed by a chairperson. The groups involved where: Students Associations in Turnovo, Varna and Sofia (23,24,27 March 2003); Meeting with artists and actors (Sofia, 13 July 2003); Orthodox Lay conference (Shumen, 3 September 2003).

8. The National Church Council did not convene until July 1997.

9. M. Kumanov and T. Nikolova, *Political Parties, Movements and Organisations in Bulgaria and their Leaders* (Sofia, 1999), p. 51.

10. S. Raikin, 'The Schism in the BOC, 1992-1997,' in J. D. Bell, *Bulgaria in Transition* (Boulder, 1998), p. 211.

11. R. Poptodorov, 'Съспендирането на устава на Българската православна църнва и деформаците в неиното устройство и управление' ('The Suspension of the Statutes of the BOC and the Deformation of its Structure and Government'), *Отечество* (*Fatherland*) No. 3, 1990, pp. 18-20.

12. *Демокрация*, 22 March 1991.

13. *Православен пастир*, Vol. 1, May 1992, p. 1.

14. The statement is recorded in the Synodal Journal as No. 1234-A, 19 March 1992. Stefan of Veliko Turnovo who was in his nineties had retired from ministry and was suffering from acute Alzheimer's. His name was added to the statement without his knowledge or approval.

15. *Дума*, 6 June 1992.

16. 'Fighting in God's Church,' *Земеделско знаме* 5 June 1992.

17. 'Maxim's People Attack and Seize the Seminary,' *Демокрация* 16 September 1992.

18. Metodi Spasov to the Commercial Bank, Council of Ministers, Department of Ecclesiastical Matters, No. 96, 3 June 1992.

19. K. Kunev quoted in J. Broun, 'The Schism in the Bulgarian Orthodox Church, Part 2', *Religion, State and Society* (Vol. 23, No. 3:264, 2000).

20. The Constitutional Court of the Republic of Bulgaria. Decision No, 11/1992 from 11 June 1992.

21. *Address of the Prelates Council of the BOC to our clergy, monks and Orthodox Christians*, circular letter issued by the Council of Prelates on 22 July 1992.

22. 'The Provisional Church Council takes action against Maxim, Neofit, Natanial and Kiril', *Демокрация* 25 July 1992.

23. *24 Часа*, 18 December 1993.

24. *Демокрация* 24 November 1993.

25. J. Broun, 'The Schism in the Bulgarian Orthodox Church, Part 2,' *Religion, State and Society* (Vol. 28, No. 3:268 2000).

26. *Църковен вестник*, 4 July 1994.

27. *Църковен вестник*, 11 July 1994.

28. *24 Часа*, 18 December 1995.

29. Article 37(2) "Freedom of conscience and religion may not be detrimental to national security, public order, public health or morality, or to the rights and freedoms of other citizens."

30. *Дума*, 2 July 1996; *24 Часа*, 2 July 1996; *Труд*, 5 July 1996.

31. *Стандарт*, 5 July 1996.

32. *Patriarchal and Synodal Appeal to all Clergy and Orthodox Christians in the Diocese of the Bulgarian Orthodox Church*, Records of the Holy Synod, No. 686, 12 July 1996.

33. Anathema – not only excommunicated but cursed for their denunciation of Christian doctrine.

34. K. Connolly, *Europhile*, 18 January 1997.

35. *Труд*, 20 August 1996.

36. *Демокрация*, 12 January 1997.

37. 'Patriarch Maxim offended by Stoyanov', *Дума*, 24 January 1997.

38. *Труд*, 21 January 1998.

39. Personal interview, 13 January 2003.

40. *Дума*, 10 March 1997.

41. *Glaube in der Zweiten Welt*, No. 6, 1997, p. 4.

42. *Демокрация*, 22 May 1997.

43. *Демокрация*, 12 June 1997.

44. *Дума*, 25 June 1997.

45. *Reports from the Fourth Church National Council*, Sofia 2-4 July 1997.

46. M. Zlateva, 'The Ecumenical Council awaited by Christian Orthodox Bulgarians for 44 years deliberated only two days', *Face to Face* (Bulgarian Helsinki Committee, 1997), p. 6.

47. *Declaration of the Holy Synod*, 19 December 1997.

48. 'Sofia: le President Bulgare demande la demission du patriarche Maxime', *Service Orthodoxe de Presse* (225:8-9, February 1998).

49. I. Bell, 'Bulgariens Kirche und die Politik', *Glaube in der Zweiten Welt*, No. 7/8, 1998, p. 23.

50. J. Broun, 'The Schism in the Bulgarian Orthodox Church, Part 3,' *Religion, State and Society* (Vol. 30, No. 4:376, 2002).

51. I. Bell, p. 24.

52. *Църковен вестник*, 1 September 1998.

53. *Демокрация*, 19 September 1998.

54. Personal interview, 23 April 2003.

55. 'Bulgarie', *Service Orthodoxe de Presse* (236:15-16, March 1999).

56. Ibid. (257:9, April 2001).

57. S. Carshaw, 'Bulgarians set to vote for their ousted king as prime minister', *The Independent*, 16 June 200.1

58. S. Raikin, Letter to Dr. Philip Walters of Keston Institute, 30 September 2000.

59. Personal interview with informant within BOC archive department, 25 August 2003.

60. D. Whitaker, 'On the trail of the shy abbot', *Observer*, 18 February 2001

61. *Дневник*, 13 August 2002.

62. Personal interview with a priest, from the schismatic branch of the BOC, who wished to remain anonymous, 10 June 2003.

63. Tolerance Foundation, *Annual Report of the Bulgarian Tolerance Foundation on the State of Religious Human Rights in Bulgaria*, Sofia, September 2004.

64. *Law on Religions*, Article 10(1). The stipulation of the Canonical Orthodox Church in this Article therefore is fully supportive of Patriarch Maxim and his Synod, although it does not mention Maxim by name.

65. *Law on Religions*, Article 11(2).

66. *Constitution of the Republic of Bulgaria*, ДВ, No. 56 from 13 July 1991.

67. *Persons and Family Act – Amendments and Introduction of Article 133A*, ДВ, 3 February 1994. (Eastern Orthodox, Islam, Judaism).

68. *Bulgarian Law on Religions: Problematic Law Out of Step with OSCE Commitments*, a report prepared by the staff of the OSCE, 108th Congress, 1st Session, Washington, DC, 2003.

69. Op.cit., p. 1.

70. Op.cit., p. 2.

71. European Law Centre, *Statement on the Anti-Constitutionalism of the Religions Act* (unpublished statement registered at Sofia City Court, Case No. 4606/2000).

72. Bulgarian Ministry of Education and Science, *Proposal for Introduction of Religious Education into Bulgarian Schools* (Sofia, 1993).

73. Bulgarian Ministry of Education and Science, *The Elaborated Proposal for Introduction of Religious Education into Bulgarian Schools* (Sofia, 1997).

74. Universal Declaration of Human Rights, created 6 July 1994, edited 27 January 1997.

75. Ministry Commission, *Curricula for Continuing Education in Teaching Religion at School.* (Sofia, 1998).

76. Ministry of Education and Science, *Religion: Educational Textbook* (Sofia, 2003).

77. Z. Dragova, 'Religions as a school subject will be experimentally introduced in Bulgarian schools from the 1998/99 academic year onward', *Face to Face* (Sofia: Bulgarian Helsinki Committee, 1997), p. 2-3.

78. D. Tomova, 'Religion in Bulgarian Schools – For Orthodox Christians Only', *Face to Face* (Sofia: Bulgarian Helsinki Committee, 1997), p. 6.

79. *Survey on the Social, Ethnic, and Cultural Features in Religious Education of School Children*, carried out in March-April 1996.

80. *Radio Free Europe* (2000) 58, 22 March.

81. Information on the Pokrov Foundation is available from www.pokrovfoundation.org.

82. P. Sivov, 'Under the Protecting Veil of the Mother of God: New Hope for a Country in a Social Havoc,' *Мирна*, March 2000, p. 2.

83. P. Sivov (2000), p. 5.

84. 'Message from the Pokrov Foundation', *Мирна*, March, 1997, p. 1.

CHAPTER 8: NATION, NATIONALISM AND THE BULGARIAN ORTHODOX CHURCH

1. S. Raikin, 'Nationalism and the Bulgarian Orthodox Church', in P. Ramet (ed.), *Religion and Nationalism in Soviet and East European Politics* (Durham, 1984), p. 371.

2. P. Kuzmic, 'Christian Mission in Europe', *Themelios*, 18(1992)23.

3. Letter from Patriarch Maxim and the Holy Synod addressed to Mr. Stanko Todorov, Chairman of the National Assembly of the People's Republic of Bulgaria (18 December 1989).

4. S. Raikin (1984), p. 201.

5. P. Nikov, *Revival of the Bulgarian Nation* (Sofia, 1929), p. 41.

6. P. Ramet, 'Autocephaly and National Identity in Church-State Relations in Eastern Christianity', *Eastern Christianity and Politics in the 20th Century* (Durham, 1988), p. 6.

7. J. G. von Herder, *Auch eine Philosophie der Geschichte der Bildung der Menschheit* (Riga, 1774).

8. M. Velikonja, 'Historical Roots of Slovenian Christoslavic Mythology', *Religion in Eastern Europe*, 19(1999)17.

9. E. Lemberg, *Nationalismus* (Hamburg, 1964), p. 52.

10. R. E. Park and E. W. Burgess, *Introduction to the Science of Sociology* (Chicago, 1924), p. 931.

11. E. Hobsbawn, *Nations and Nationalism Since 1780: Programme, Myth, Reality* (Cambridge, 1992), pp. 9-11.

12. F. Meinecke, *Weltburgertum und Nationalstaat: Studien zur Genesis des deutschen Nationalstaates* (Munich, 1919), pp. 2-3.

13. T. Schieder, *Nationalismus und Nationalstaat* (Gottingen, 1991), p. 87.

14. G. Florovsky, *Christianity and Culture* (Belmont, 1974), p. 132.

15. For the full text of the Edict of Milan in English see: http://gbgm-umc.org/umw/bible/milan.stm

16. D. J. Geanakoplos, 'Religion and Nationalism in the Byzantine Empire and After: Conformity and Pluralism', *GOTR*, 22(1977)98-116.

17. D. J. Geanakoplos, p. 100.

18. B. J. Groen, 'Eastern Orthodoxy in the Balkans, Nationalism and Reconciliation', *Exchange*, Vol. 27, No. 2(1998)126.

19. See J. Meyendorff, *The Orthodox Church: Its Past and its Role in the World Today* (Crestwood, 1996), pp. 131-132; T. Ware, *The Orthodox Church* (Harmondsworth, 1993), pp. 173-174.

20. A. Schmemann, *The Historical Road of Eastern Orthodoxy* (London, 1963), p. 281.

21. M. Mpegzos, 'Ethnikismos: ho echthros tou ethnous', *Kath' Hodon*, 1(1992)18-26.

22. The Greek Helsinki Committee, *Ratsismos, antisemitismos, xenophobia kai misallodoxia sten hellenike koine gnome*, sent to various newspapers in June 1995.

23. See Chapter Two for a detailed analysis of Paisii Hilendarski.

24. I. Kepov and V. Kepova, *Brief Instruction for the Teaching of History in Junior High Schools* (Sofia, 1932), p. 6.

25. See Chapter Three for information on the development of Bulgaria's educational system.

26. S. Dimitrova, 'Bulgarian Historical Education and Perspectives of the National Identity', *Balkanistic Forum* (Blagoevgrad, 1999), p. 57.

27. P. M. Kitromilides, 'Imagined Communities' and the Origins of the National Question in the Balkans', *European History Quarterly*, 19(1989)149-192.

28. P. M. Kitromilides (1989), p. 149.

29. P. M. Kitromilides (1989), p. 178.

30. P. M. Kitromilides (1989), p. 177f.

31. D. J. Geanakopolos, *Byzantium. Church, Society, and Civilisation Seen through Contemporary Eyes* (Chicago, 1984), p. 136.

32. P. M. Kitromilides (1989), p. 178.

33. L. S. Stavrianos, *The Balkans Since 1453* (New York, 1958), p. 371.

34. S. Radev, *The Construction of Contemporary Bulgaria* (Sofia, 1911), p. 69.

35. I. Ormandzhiev and M. Velkova, *General and Bulgarian History for III Grade of the National Junior High School. Approved from 1937 to 1941* (Sofia, 1941), p. 123.

36. N. Stanev, *The Most Recent History of Bulgaria 1878-1941* (Sofia, 1943), p. 294.

37. N. Stanev, p. 295.

38. P. Enev, 'Nationalism, Internationalism and Education', *School Review*, 5-6(1938)607.

39. I. Kepov and V. Kepova, *Universal and Bulgarian History for III Grade of Junior High Schools* (Sofia, 1940), p. 115.

40. B. Bozhikov, *Bulgarian History for VII Grade of High School* (Sofia, 1946), p. 434.

41. Census statistics between 1965 and 1992 provide no information on national minorities, they simply provide a population figure of Bulgarian inhabitants.

42. S. Trifinov, 'The Muslim in the Politics of the Bulgarian State', *Pages from Bulgarian History* (Sofia, 1993), pp. 212-213.

43. *Нова Светлина*, 5 April 1990.

44. I. Ilchev and D. Perry, 'Bulgarian Ethnic Groups: Politics and Prospects', *RFE/RL Research Report*, Vol. II, No. 12, pp. 35-41.

45. G. Rohrmoser, *Religion und Politik in der Krise der Moderne* (Graz, 1989), p. 161

46. P. Mojzes, *Religious Liberty in Eastern Europe and the USSR before and after the Great Transformation* (Boulder, 1992), p. 383.

47. *Law on Religions*, December 2002.

48. S. Filitov, 'The Russian Tradition of Spiritual Tyranny and the New Law on Religion', *The 1997 Law on the Freedom of Conscience: The International Norms and the Russian Tradition* (Moscow, 1998), pp. 4-7.

49. H. Grymala-Moszczynska, 'Established Religion vs. New Religions: Social Perceptions and Legal Consequences', *Journal of Ecumenical Studies*, 33(1996)69-73.

50. M. Ley, 'Historische und theoretische Uberlegungen zum Nationalismus', *Das Ende des Nationalismus* (Vienna, 1996), p. 18.

51. I. Merdjanova, p. 23.

52. I. Pavlov, 'The Imperial Revanchism and the Freedom of Conscience', *The 1997 Law on the Freedom of Conscience: The International Norms and the Russian Tradition* (Moscow, 1998), pp. 48-51.

53. P. Hammond, *With Liberty for All. Freedom of Religion in the United States* (Louisville, 1998), p. xi.

54. P. Mikat, *Geschichte – Recht – Religion – Politik*, Vol. 2 (Munich, 1994), p. 838.

55. Bulgarian Ministry of Education, *Instructions for the Organisation of Teaching history in the General Education of Schools* (Sofia, 1993), p. 1.

56. Personal Interview with Father Boyan Stanimirov, 2 September 2003.

57. F. Dostoyevsky, *The Brothers Karamazov* (New York: Modern Library, 1960), pp. 61-63.

58. D. Martin, *A General Theory of Secularization* (Oxford, 1978), p. 96.

59. I. Merdjanova, *Religion, Nationalism, and civil Society in Eastern Europe* (Lampeter, 2002), p. 43.

60. E. Gellner, *Nations and Nationalism* (Oxford: Blackwell, 1983); A. D. Smith, *The Ethnic Origins of Nations* (Oxford: Blackwell, 1986); A. Hastings, *The Construction of Nationhood. Ethnicity, Religion and Nationalism* (Cambridge: CUP, 1997).

61. E. Gellner (1983), p. 49.

62. E. Gellner (1983), p. 7.

63. B. Anderson, *Imagined Communities. Reflections on the Origin and Spread of Nationalism* (London, 1991).

64. P. James, *Nation Formation. Towards a Theory of Abstract Community* (London, 1996), p. 192.

65. P. James, p. 122.

66. H. Kohn, *The Idea of Nationalism. A Study in its Origins and Background* (New York, 1961).

67. H. Kohn, p. 339.

68. A. D. Smith, *The Ethnic Origins of Nations* (Oxford, 1986), pp. 134-144.

69. A. D. Smith, *National Identity* (London, 1991), p. 41.

70. A. D. Smith (1986), p. 192f.

71. A. D. Smith (1991), p. 62.

72. Amnesty International, *Bulgaria: Imprisonment of Ethnic Turks* (Lasa, 1956), pp. 4-5; G. S. Nikolaev, *'Forced Assimilation of the Turks'*, Борба, 9 March 1985, p. 192.

CHAPTER 9: CONCLUSIONS

1. James R. Payton, 'Religion and the Historiography of Eastern Europe', *Religion in Eastern Europe*; available from http://www.georgefox.edu/academics/undergrad/departments/soc-swk/ree/payton_rat01_01.html ; accessed 30/01/2003.

2. S. Tsankov, 'The Bulgarian Orthodox Church from the Liberation to the Present Day', *ГСУ-БФ* (Sofia 1938/39), XVI, p. 8.

3. *Църковен вестник*, November 1981, pp. 2-7.

BIBLIOGRAPHY

ARCHIVAL SOURCES

АВПР (Russian Federation Archive of Foreign Politics)
АМВнР (Archive of the Bulgarian Ministry of Foreign Affairs)
Архив на Рила манастир (Rila Monastery Archive)
АЦИАИ (Bulgarian Church History Archive and Archival Institute)
БИА НБКМ (Bulgarian Historical Archive of the National Library "Sts. Cyril and Methodius)
ГАРФ (Gosudarstven Russian Federation Archive)
ГСУ БФ (Annual of Sofia University "St. Kliment Ohridski," Theological Faculty)
ДА-Пловдив (State Archive- Plovdiv)
ДВ (State Gazette)
ИАНГ (The Archive of Naiden Gerov)
НА БАН (Academic Archive of the Bulgarian Academy of Sciences)
НБКМ Ор. отд. (National Library "Sts. Cyril and Methodius", Oriental Department)
ОДА (Regional State Archive)
РЦХИДНИ (Russian Centre for Preservation and Study Documenting Modern History)
Сб БАН (Collection of the Bulgarian Academy of Sciences)
Сб НУНК (Сб НУ) (Bulgarian Collection for National Folklore, Science and Literature)
ЦА (Bulgarian Church Archive)
ЦВА (Bulgarian Central Military Archive)
ЦДА (Bulgarian Central State Archive)
ЦДИА (Bulgarian Central State Historical Archive)
ЦИАИ (Bulgarian Central Historical Archival Institute)
ЦПА (Bulgarian Central Party Archives)
AMAE CP (Archives du Ministere des Affaires Etrangeres, Correspondance Politique)
ANF (Archives Nationales de France)
BOA (Basbakanlik Ottoman Archive)

NEWSPAPERS AND PERIODICALS

Демокрация (Democracy)
Дневник (Journal)
Дума (Word)

Земеделско знаме (Agrarian Standard)
Македония (Macedonia)
Мир (Peace)

Мирна (Peaceful)

Свобода (Freedom)
Селянин (Villager/Peasant)
Православен пастир (Orthodox Pastor)
Стандарт (Standard)
Труд (Labour)
Църковен вестник (Church Paper)
Туна (Tuna)

Независимост (Independence)   *24 Часа* (24 Hours)
Нова Светлина (New Light)
Новини (News)
Право (Right)

INTERVIEWS
Groups
Student Association in Turnovo (23 June 2003)
Student Association in Varna (24 June 2003)
Student Association in Sofia (27 June 2003)
Meeting with artists and actors in Sofia (13 July 2003)
Meeting with philosophy graduates in Bankya (12 August 2003)
Orthodox Lay conference in Shumen (3 September 2003)

Individuals
Dimitrina Merdjanova, interviewed by author, 13 January 2003
Maria Dimitrova, interviewed by author, 23 April 2003
Anonymous priest from the schismatic branch of the BOC, interviewed by author, 10 June 2003
Father Boyan Stanimirov, interviewed by author, 2 September 2003
Anonymous former Church employee who held a position within the BOC archive department, interviewed by author, 25 August 2003.

PRIMARY BULGARIAN AND RUSSIAN LANGUAGE SOURCES
Books
Andreev, S. *Историята на рударството и металургията в българските земи през XV-XIXв.* (The History of Ore Mining and Metalwork in Bulgaria through the 15-19th Centuries). Sofia: National Library "Sts. Kiril and Metodii", 1993.

Angelov, B. and Genov, M. 'Стара българска литература (IX-XVIIIв.)', (Ancient Bulgarian Literature (IX-XVIII)), *История на българската литература* (History of Bulgarian Literature), Book 2. 1922.

Angelov, B. *Из старата българска, руска и сърбска литература,* (In the Old Bulgarian, Russian and Serbian Literature). Sofia: BAN, 1967.

Angelov, D. *Богомилството в българия* (The Bogomils in Bulgaria). Sofia: Sofia Press, 1980.

Arnaudov, M. *Неофит Хилендарски Бозвели, 1785-1848. живот, дело, епоха* (Neofit Hilendarski Bozveli, 1785-1848. His Life, Work, Era). Sofia: Nauka i Izkustvo, 1971.

Atanasov, B., ed. *Paisii Hilendarski. A Slavo-Bulgarian History. A Facsimile of the Original Zograph Manuscript Draft (1762).* Sofia: St. Kliment Ohridski University Press, 2000.

Bakalov, G., ed. *Религия и църква в българия: Социални и културни измерения в православието и неговата специфика в българските земи,* (Religion and

Church in Bulgaria: Social and Cultural Dimensions in Orthodoxy and its Specifics in Bulgaria). Sofia: Gutenburg, 1999.

Balabanov, M. D. *Страница отъ политическото ни възраждане* (Pages from the Politics of the National Revival). Sofia: Bulgarian Library, 1904.

———. *Гаврил Кръстович: Народен деец, книжовник, съдия, управител* (Gavril Krustovich: National Worker, Author, Judge, Governor). Sofia: Pechatnitsa "Den", 1914.

Belchovski, J. *Исторически основи за автокефалноста на македонската православна църква* (The Historical Foundation for the Autocephaly of the Macedonian Orthodox Church). Skopje: J. Belchovski, 1990.

Bozhikov, B. *Българска история за VII клас на гимназите* (Bulgarian History for VII Grade of High School). Sofia: BAN, 1946.

Bulgarian Ministry of Education and Science. *Указание за организиране на учебната работа по история в общообразователните училища за учебната 1992/93* (Instructions for the Organisation of Teaching History in the General Education of Schools). Sofia: Bulgarian Ministry of Education, 1993.

———. *Предложение за интродукцията на религиозен училища в българска учебната* (Proposal for the Introduction of Religious Education into Bulgarian Schools). Sofia: Bulgarian Ministry of Education, 1993.

———. *Прекалената предложение за интродукцията на религиозен училища в българска учебната* (The Elaborated Proposal for the Introduction of Religious Education into Bulgarian Schools). Sofia: Bulgarian Ministry of Education, 1997.

———. Curricula for Continuing Education in Teaching Religion at School. *Sofia: Bulgarian Ministry of Education, 1998.*

———. *Religion: Educational Textbook.* Sofia: Bulgarian Ministry of Education, 2003.

Burmov, T. S. *Българо-гърцката църковна разприя* (The Bulgarian-Greek Church Dispute). Sofia: Izdava sv. Sinod na bulgarskata tsurkva, 1902.

Chavrokov, G. Средищи на Български грамотност IX-XVIII век (Centres of Bulgarian Literacy IX-XVIII). Sofia: Nauka i izkustvo, 1987.

Cohen, D. *Оцеляаването* (The Survival). Sofia: Shalom, 1995.

Dimitrov, G. *Съчинение* (Works). Sofia: BCP, 1954.

Dimitrov, I. *Князът, конституция и народът* (The Prince, the Constitution and the People). Sofia: OF, 1972.

Dinekov, P. *София през XIX век до освобождението на България* (Sofia through the XIX century to the Liberation of Bulgaria). Sofia: Nauka i izkustvo, 1971.

Drinov, M. *Исторически преглед на българската църква от самото и начало и до днес* (Historical Survey of the Bulgarian Church from its Beginning to Today). Vienna, 1869.

Druzhinina, E. *Кючук-Кайнарджиски мир, 1774 года* (Kucuk Kaynarca Treaty, 1774). Moscow: Izd-vo Akademi nauk, 1955.

Dryanovski, B., ed. *Борбите на българите от варненска и преславска епархия за църковга независимост 1840-1879* (The Struggle of the Bulgarians from the Varna and Preslav Eparchies for Church Independence 1840-1879). Varna: Spavena, 2002.

Duichev, I. *Българско средновековие* (Bulgarian Middle Ages). Sofia: Nauka i izkustvo, 1972.

Eldurov, S. *България и ватикана 1944-1989: Дипломатически, църковни и други взаимоотношения* (Bulgaria and Vatican 1944-1989: Diplomatic, Ecclesiastic and other Interrelationships). Sofia: Logos, 2002.

Filippov, T. I. *Современнъ церковя вопросъ* (Contemporary Church Questions). St. Petersburg: Obshchestvenaya pol'za, 1882.

Gandev, H. *Българската народност през XV век. Демографско и етнографско изследване* (The Bulgarian Nation through the 15th Century. Demographic and Ethnographic Research). Sofia: Nauka i izkustvo, 1972.

_____. *Априлското въстание* (The April Uprising). Sofia: Nauka i izkustvo, 1976.

Genchev, N. *Възрожденският Пловдив* (The Plovdiv National Revival). Plovdiv: Khristo G. Danov, 1981.

Georgiev, E. *Основи на славистиката и българистиката* (The Basis of Slavistics and Bulgaristics). Sofia: Nauka i Izkustvo, 1979.

_____. *Bulgaria's Contribution to Slavonic and European Cultural Life in the Middle Ages.* Sofia: Sofia Press, 1981.

Georgiev, V. and Trifinov, S. *Покръстването на българите мохамедани, 1912-1913* (The Conversion of the Bulgarian Muslims, 1912-1913). Sofia: Prof. Marin Drinov, 1995.

Gerlach, S. *Дневник на едно пътуване до Османската порта в Цариград* (The Diary of a Journey to the Ottoman Porte in Constantinople) [Bulgarian translation of Gerlach's 1674 diary]. Sofia: Otechestveni, 1976.

Giuselev, V. *Княз Борис I* (Prince Boris I). Sofia: Nauka i izkustvo, 1969.

Hristov, H. *Страници из Българската история* (Pages in Bulgarian History). Sofia: Nauka i Izkustvo, 1989.

Ihchiev, D. *Търски документи на Рилския манастиръ* (Turkish Documents in Rila Monastery). Sofia: Sofia University, 1910.

Ivanov, I. *Български старини из македония* (Bulgarian Antiquities in Macedonia). Sofia: Durzhavna Pechatnitsa, 1931.

Kalkandjieva, D. *Българската православна църква и "народната демокрация" (1944-1953)* (The Bulgarian Orthodox Church and "National Democracy"). Silistra: Demos, 2002.

Kepov, I. and Kepova, V. *Кратко упътване в обучението по история в прогимназиите* (Brief Instruction for the Teaching of History in Junior High Schools). Sofia: G. Danov, 1932.

_____. *Обща и българска история за III клас на прогимназиите* (Universal and Bulgarian History for III Grade of Junior High Schools). Sofia: G. Danov, 1940.

Kiril, Metropolitan of Plovdiv. *Екзарх Антим 1816-1888* (Exarch Antim 1816-1888). Sofia: Sinadalno knigoizdatelstvo, 1956.

_____. *Католическата пропаганда сред Българите през втората половина на XIXвек.* (Catholic Propaganda in Bulgaria during the Second Half of the 19th Century). Sofia: Sinadalno knigoizdatelstvo, 1958.

Kiril, Patriarch of Bulgaria. *Граф Н.П. Игнатиев и българският църковен въпрос: Изследване и документи* (Count N. P. Ignatiev and the Bulgarian Church Question: Research and Documentation). Sofia: Sinadalno izdatelstvo, 1962.

Krachounov, K. *История дипломатиката на обединениета българия* (Diplomatic History of the Unification of Bulgaria). Sofia: Den, 1919.

Kumanov, M. and Nikolova, T. *Политически партий, организаций и движение в българия и техните лидери* (Political Parties, Organisations and Movements in Bulgaria and their Leaders). Sofia: Ariadna, 1999.

Lalkov, M. *България след Освобождението* (Bulgaria After the Liberation (1878-1912)). Sofia: Polis, 2001.

Markova, Z. *Българското църковно-национално движение до кримската война* (The Bulgarian National Church Movement to the Crimean War). Sofia: BAN, 1976.

_____. *Българката екзархия, 1870-1879* (The Bulgarian Exarchate, 1870-1879). Sofia: BAN, 1989.

Milarov, S. *Василий Евстатиевич Априлов, мощният подвижник на новото образование в България. Опис на живота му и на деятелността му* (Vasil Evstatievich Aprilov, The Powerful Achievements of New Education in Bulgaria. An Account of his Life and his Work). Odessa, 1888.

Milev, A. *Гръцките житие на Климент Охридски* (The Greek Biography of Kliment Ohridski). Sofia: BAN, 1966.

Mitev, P. *Българското възраждане* (The Bulgarian National Revival). Sofia: Polis, 1999.

Mitev, Y. *Съединението на България 1885* (The Unification of Bulgaria 1885). Sofia: Sofia Press, 1982.

Nikitin, S. *Славянские комитетъ в Русси в 1858-1876* (The Slavonic Committee in Russia in 1858-1876). Moscow: Moscow University, 1960.

Nikov, P. *Изследвани в исторически средството но българия и във история на българска народна църквата* (Studies in the Historical Resources of Bulgaria and in the History of the Bulgarian National Church). Sofia: Pechatnitsa "Den", 1920.

_____. 'Владислав Граматик – пренасяне мощите на Св. Иван Рилски от Търново в Рилския манастир' (The Carrying of the Relics of St. Ivan Rilski from Turnovo to Rila Monastery), *Българска историйчески библиотека* (Bulgarian Historical Library), II, pp. 165-187. 1928.

_____. *Възраждане на българския народ: Църковно-национални борби и постижение* (Revival of the Bulgarian Nation: The Church National Struggle and Achievement). Sofia: Izdanie Strashimir Slavchev, 1929.

Ormandzhiev, I. *Нова и най-нова история на български народ* (New and Most-Recent History of the Bulgarian Nation). Sofia: Nauka i Izkustvo, 1945.

Ormandzhiev, I. and Velkova, M. *Обща и българска история за III клас на народните одобрен за 1937 и 1941 години* (General and Bulgarian History for III Grade of the National Junior High School, Approved from 1937 to 1941). Sofia: 1941.

Pantev, A. *Българският април 1876 в Англия и САЩ* (The Bulgarian April 1876 in Britain and USA). Sofia: Marin Drinov, 2003.

Paskaleva, V. *Русия и българската църква въпрос* (Russia and the Bulgarian Church Question). Sofia: BAN, 1965.

Pastukhov, I. *Българска история* (Bulgarian History). Sofia: Hemus, 1943.

Pavlov, I. 'Имперский реваншизм и свобода совестъ' (The Imperial Revanshism and the Freedom of Conscience), *Закон о свобода совестъ 1997 года: международныи нормъ и русский традиций* (The 1997 Law on the Freedom of Conscience: The International Norms and the Russian Traditions). Moscow: Moscow Obshtestvenny Nauchny Fond, 1998.

Penev, B. *Паиси Хилендарски* (Paisii Hilendarski). Sofia:, Papers on Bulgarian Literature, 1918.

Petrov, P. *Съдбоносни векове за българската народност.* (The Fateful Centuries of the Bulgarian Nation). Sofia: Izdatelstvo Nauka i izkustvo, 1975.

_____. *По следите на насилието. Документи и материали за налагане на исляма* (More Traces of Violence. Documents and Materials Regarding the Imposition of Islam). Sofia: BAN, 1987.

Popov, N. A. *Краткий отчет о десятилетней деятелъности (1858-1868) Славянското благотворителъного комитета в Москва* (A Brief Account of a Decade of Activities (1858-1868) of the Slavic Charitable Committee in Moscow). Moscow, 1871.

Popruzhenko, M. G. and Panchev, T., eds. *Из архивата на Найден Геров, 1857-1870* (From the Archive of Naiden Gerov). Sofia: Durzhavna pechatnitsa, 1931.

Radev, S. *Строителите на съвременна българия* (The Construction of Contemporary Bulgaria). Sofia: Pechatnitsa P. Glushkov, 1911.

_____. *Македония и българското възраждане.* Sofia: Ministry of National Education, 1943.

Radevski, H. *Третата Марта* (The Third of March). Sofia: Durzhavna pechatnitsa, 1938.

Raikin, S. T. *Политически проблеми пред българската общественост в чужбина: Проблеми на българската православна църква* (Political Problems before the Bulgarian Public Abroad: Problems of the Bulgarian Orthodox Church). Sofia: D. Yakov, 1993.

Sabev, O. *Османски училища в българските земи XV-XVIII век* (Ottoman Schools in Bulgarian Lands XV-XVIII centuries). Sofia: Lubomadrie-Chronika, 2001.

Semerdjiev, H. *Самоков и околноста му: принос към миналото им от турското завоевание до освобождението* (Samokov and the Surrounding

Region: A Contribution to its Past from the Turkish Conquest to the Liberation). Sofia: Den, 1913.

Snegarov, I. *Търското владичесто пречка за културно развитие на българския народ и другите балкански народи* (Turkish Rule an Obstacle to the Cultural Development of the Bulgarian Nation and the other Balkan Nations). Sofia: BAN, 1958.

Stanev, N. *Най-нова история на българия 1878-1941* (The Most Recent History of Bulgaria 1878-1941). Sofia: Ivan Vazov, 1943.

Staneva, K. *Гласове на възраждането* (Voices of the National Revival). Sofia: Polis, 2001.

Stoilov, K. *Дневник* (Diary). Sofia: Kliment Ohridski University, 1996.

Stoyanov, P. *Църкви и изповедание в народна република българия* (Churches and Religions in the People's Republic of Bulgaria). Sofia: Sofia Synodal Press, 1975.

Stoyanov, V. *Търското население в българия и официалната малцинствена политика (1878-1944)* (The Turkish Population in Bulgaria and Official Minority Policy). Sofia: LIK, 1993.

Stoyanov, Z. *Не му беше времето. Отговор но брошурата "Недоразуменията между българското и руското правителство"* (It Wasn't the Time. Response to the Brochure "Misunderstanding between the Bulgarian and Russian Governments"). Ruse, 1886.

Subev, T. *Априлското въстание и българското православно църква* (The April Uprising and the Bulgarian Orthodox Church). Sofia: Sofia Synodal Press, 1977.

Tahirov, S. *Обединението* (The Unification). Sofia: Izdatelstvo na Otechestveniya, 1981.

Tatishchev, S. *Из история на русский дипломация* (From the History of Russian Diplomacy). St. Petersburg: A. S. Suvorin, 1890.

Todorov, G. *България, Православсето, историята* (Bulgaria, Orthodoxy, History). Sofia: Foundation 'St. Prince Boris', 2003.

Todorova, O. *Православна църква и българският народ през XV- третата четвърт на XVIII век.* (The Orthodox Church and the Bulgarian Nation through the 15th – third quarter of the 18th century). Sofia/1987/88. Ph.D. Thesis, unpublished.

Traikov, V. Паисий Хилендарски. Литературни извори за епохата, живота и дейността му. - Паисий Хилендарски и неговата епоха (1762-1962). Сборник от изследвания по случай 200-годишнината от "История славянобългарска" (Paisii Hilendarski. Literary Sources during His Time, Life and Activity – Paisii Hilendarski and His Epoch (1762-1962). A Research Collection for the 200th Anniversary of His Slavo-Bulgarian History). Sofia: Sofia University Press, 1962.

Tsonkov, D. *Развитие на основното образвание във българия от 1878 до 1928* (The Development of Elementary Education in Bulgaria from 1878 to 1928). Sofia: Educational Textbook No.VII, 1928.

Tsvetkova, B. *Хайдуцвото в българските земи през 15-18 век* (The Haidouks in Bulgarian Lands through the 15-18th Centuries). Sofia: Nauka i Izkustvo, 1971.

Velchev, V. *Паисий Хилендарски, баща на българското просвещение* (Paisii of Hilendar, Father of the Bulgarian Enlightenment). Sofia: Narodna prosveta, 1981.

Venelin, Y. *Древніе и нынъшніе Болгаре въ политическомъ, народописномъ, историческомъ и религіозномъ ихъ отношеніи къ Россіянамъ. Историкокритическія изысканія* (The Ancient and Present Day Bulgarians in their Political, Ethnographic and Religious Relationship to the Russians: A Historical-Critical Research). Lvov: Lvov University, 1829.

Vrachanski, S. *Автобиография на Софроний Врачански* (Autobiography of Sofroni Vrachanski). Sofia: Sofia Synodal Press, 1914.

Yankov, G. *Проблеми на развитието на българската народност и нация* (Aspects of the Development of the Bulgarian Nation). Sofia: Sofia Press, 1989.

Yovkov, M. *Павликяни и павликянски селища в българските земи, XV-XVIII век.* (The Paulicians and the Paulician Towns and Villages in Bulgaria, XV-XVIII Centuries). Sofia: Kliment Ohridski University Press, 1991.

Zakhariev, S. *Географски-историко-статистическо описание на Татарпазарджишката кааза* (A Geographical-Historical-Statistical Account of the Tartarpazardjik Region). Vienna, 1870 (from a photo-copied edition dated 1973 in the National Library of Bulgaria).

Zlatarski, V. N. *История на средновековната българска държава* (A History of the Medieval Bulgarian State). Sofia: Kliment Ohridski University Press, 1937.

Articles

Dimitrova, S. 'Bulgarian Historical Education and Perspectives of the National Identity', *Balkanistic Forum*. Blagoevgrad: Neofit Rilski University, 1999.

Drinov, M. 'Отец паисий. Неговото време, неговата история и учениците му', (Father Paisii. His time, His History and His Teaching), *Braila*, No. 4(1871): 19.

Enev, P. 'Национализъм, интернационализъм и възпитание' ('Nationalism, Internationalism and Education'), *Училищен преглед* (School Review), 5-6(1938): 605-620.

Filitov, S. 'Российския традиции духовноъ тирании и новъ закон о религии', (The Russian Tradition of Spiritual Tyranny and the New Law on Religion), *Закон о свободе съвести 1997 года: Международня нормъ и Российския традиции*, (The 1997 Law on the Freedom of Conscience: The International Norms and the Russian Tradition). Moscow: Moscow Obshtestvenny Nauchny Fond, 1998.

Georgieva, S. 'Някой главни последици от османското завоевоние на българските земи' (Some of the Main Consequences of the Ottoman Conquest of Bulgarian Lands) in *Сборник от лекции за следдипломна квалификация на учителите*, (Collection of Lectures from the Master's Post-Graduate Qualification), IV(1979): 213-238.

Mazhdrakova-Chavdarova, O. 'Дякон Игнатий (Васил Левски) в Пловдив' (Deacon Ignatius (Vasil Levski) in Plovdiv, 1863-1864), *ИПр* 3(1997).

Mechev, K. 'Юри Иванович Венелин и въпросът на националното присъединяване га Кирил и Методи'(Yuri Ivanovich Venelin and the Question of the National Affiliation of Cyril and Methodius), *BHR*, 2(1978): 72-83.

Nikolaev, G. S. 'Усилен асимилация на турчините'(Forced Assimilation of the Turks), *Борба*, 9 March 1985.

Poptodorov, R. 'Православно-християнската вяра и българската народна църква като фактори за запазването на българския народ, за формирането на националното му съзнание и за културното му развитие през време на петвековно османско робство' ('The Christian-Orthodox Faith and the Bulgarian National Church as a Factor in the Preservation of the Bulgarian Nation, in the Forming of its National Awareness and its Cultural Development through the Period of the Five Century Ottoman Bondage'), *Годишник на духовната академия* (Annual of the Ecclesiastical Academy), XX(1970): 65-261.

Snegarov, I. 'Взаимоотношение българскои и русскои православник църквей и после провоглашения (1872 год.)' (Interrelations between the Bulgarian and Russian Orthodox Churches after the Instigation of Schism (1872)), *Годишник на духовната Акадамия "Св.Климент Охридски"* (Annual of the Ecclesiastical Academy "St. Kliment Okhridski"), II (1951-52): 206.

Svetkova, B. 'Проблеми от историята на европейския югоизток през периода на османското проникване' (Problems from the History of South-Eastern Europe during the period of Ottoman Penetration), *Исторически преглед* (Historical Review), 6(1974): 78-93.

Temelski, H. 'Екзарх Йосиф както полотик и дипломат' (Exarch Josef as a Politician and Diplomat), *Rodina* 3(1996): 32.

Todorov, I. 'Летописнят разказ на поп Методи Драгинов' ('The Chronicle of Father Metodi Draginov'), *Старобългарски литература* (Old Bulgarian Literature), 16(1984): 60-77.

Trifinov, S. 'Мюсюлманите в политиката на българската държавна' ('The Muslim in the Politics of the Bulgarian State'), in M. Isusov, *Страници от българската история* (Pages from Bulgarian History). Sofia: Prof. Marin Drinov, 1993.

Tsankov, S. 'Българската православна църква от Освобождението до настояще време'('The Bulgarian Orthodox Church from the Liberation to the Present Time'), *ГСУ БФ*, VI, XVI, (Sofia, 1938/9)

Voeikov, P. 'Запски графа Н.П.Игнатиев, 1864-1874' (The records of Count N. P. Ignatiev, 1864-1874), *Известия Министерства Иностранух дел.* (Journal of the Ministry of Foreign Affairs), Vol. I (1914).

SECONDARY SOURCES
Books

Alp, I. *Bulgarian Atrocities*. Lefkosa: K. Rustem & Bro., 1988.

Amnesty International. *Bulgaria: Imprisonment of Ethnic Turks*. Lasa: Amal International, 1956.

Anderson, B. *Imagined Communities. Reflections on the Origin and Spread of Nationalism*. London: Verso, 1991.

Anderson, M. S. *The Great Powers and the Near East, 1774-1923*. London: E. Arnold, 1970.

Babinger, F. *Mehmed der Eroberer und seine Zeit* (Mehmed the Conqueror and his Time). Translated by R. Manheim. Princeton: Princeton University Press, 1978.

Barkley, H. C. *Bulgaria before the War during Seven Years Experience of European Turkey and its Inhabitants*. London: Murray, 1877.

Barros, J. *The League of Nations and the Great Powers: The Greek-Bulgarian Incident*. Oxford: Clarendon Press, 1970.

Bell, J. D. *Peasants in Power: Alexander Stamboliski and the Bulgarian Agrarian National Union, 1899-1923*. Princeton: Princeton University Press, 1977.

_____. *Bulgaria in Transition: Politics, Economics, Society, and Culture after Communism*. Boulder, CO: Westview, 1998.

Black, C. E. *The Establishment of Constitutional Government in Bulgaria*. Princeton: Princeton University Press, 1943.

Brailsford, H. N. *Macedonia: Its Races and their Future*. London: Methuen, 1906.

Braude, B. and Lewis, B. *Christians and Jews in the Ottoman Empire: The Functioning of a Plural Society*. London: Holmes & Meier, 1982.

Bringa, T. *Being Muslim the Bosnian Way: Identity and Community in a Central Bosnian Village*. Princeton: Princeton University Press, 1995.

Brown, J. F. *Bulgaria Under Communist Rule*. London: Pall Mall, 1970.

Browning, R. *Byzantium and Bulgaria: A Comparative Study Across the Early Medieval Frontier*. London: Temple Smith, 1975.

Burchard, Bishop of Worms. *Loci communes congesti cum ex Decretorum libri, turn Concilis et Orthodoxum Patrum decretis*. Cologne: Apud Ionnem Birckmannum iuoiorem, 1560.

Castellan, G. *History of the Balkans: From Muhammed the Conqueror to Stalin*. Boulder, CO: East European Monographs, 1992.

Clarke, J. F. *Bible Societies, American Missionaries and the National Revival of Bulgaria*. New York: Arno Press, 1971.

_____. 'Protestantism and the Bulgarian Church Question n 1861' in *Essays in the History of Modern Europe*, ed. D. C. McKay. New York: Harper, 1936. 79-97.

Coleman, J. and Tomka, M. *Religion and Nationalism*. London: SCM Press, 1995.

Constant, S. *Foxy Ferdinand: 1861-1948, Tsar of Bulgaria*. London: Sidgwick & Jackson, 1979.

Corti, E. *Alexander von Battenburg*. London: Cassell, 1954.

Crampton, R. J. *A Concise History of Bulgaria*. Cambridge: Cambridge University Press, 1997.

_____. *The Balkans Since the Second World War*. London: Longman, 2002.

Daskalov, R. *The Making of a Nation in the Balkans: Historiography of the Balkan Revival*. Budapest: Central European University Press, 2004.

Davison, R. H. *Reforms in the Ottoman Empire, 1856-1876*. Princeton: Princeton University Press, 1963.

De Boor, C. *Theophanes the Confessor: Chronographia*. Liepzig: Teubner, 1885.

Dimitrov, V. *The Uneven Transition*. London: Routledge, 2001.

Dmytryshyn, B. *Medieval Russia: A Source Book, 850-1700*. Fort Worth: Harcourt Brace Jovanovich, 1991.

Donchev, A. *Time of Parting*. New York: William Morrow, 1968.

Dontas, D. N. *Greece and the Great Powers*. Thessalonica: Institute for Balkan Studies, 1966.

Dostoyevsky, F. *The Brothers Karamazov*. New York: Modern Library, 1960.

Ducas. *Decline and Fall of Byzantium to the Ottoman Turks*. Translated by H. Magoulias. Detroit: Wayne State University Press, 1975.

Duichev, I. *Melanges Eugene Tisserant*. Rome: Vatican City, 1964.

_____. *Kiril and Methodius: Founders of Slavonic Writing; A Collection of Sources and Critical Studies*. Boulder, CO: East European Monographs, 1985.

Durham, E. *The Burden of the Balkans*. London: Nelson, 1905.

Durman, K. *Lost Illusions: Russian Policies Towards Bulgaria in 1877-1887*. Uppsala: Uppsala University Press, 1988.

Dvornik, F. *The Photian Schism: History and Legend*. Cambridge: Cambridge University Press, 1948.

Eminov, A. *Turkish and other Muslim Minorities in Bulgaria*. London: Hurst, 1997.

Engelhardt, E. *La Turquie et la Tanzimat*. Paris: A. Cotillon, 1882.

Fine, J. V. A. *The Early Medieval Balkans: A Critical Study from the Sixth to the Late Twelfth Century*. Ann Arbor: University of Michigan Press, 1983.

Fischer-Galati, S. and Kiraly, B. K. *Essays on War and Society in East Central Europe, 1740-1920*. Boulder, CO: East European Monographs, 1988.

Fletcher, R. *The Conversion of Europe: From Paganism to Christianity 371-1386*. London: Harper Collins, 1997.

Florovsky, G. *Christianity and Culture*. Belmont, MA: Nordland, 1974.

Geanakoplos, D. J. *Byzantium. Church, Society, and Civilisation Seen through Contemporary Eyes*. Chicago: University of Chicago Press, 1984.

Genchev, N. *The Bulgarian National Revival Period*. Sofia: Sofia University Press, 1977.

Giatzidis, A. *Civil Society in Post-Communist Bulgaria*. Ph.D. Thesis, University of Sheffield, 2000.

Gibb, H. A. R. and Bowen, H. *Islamic Society and the West. A Study of the Impact of Western Civilisation on Moslem Culture in the Near East*, Vol. I. London: OUP, 1957.

Gill, J. *Byzantium and the Papacy, 1198-1400.* New Brunswick, NJ: Rutgers University Press, 1979.

Gladstone, W. E. *Bulgarian Horrors and the Question of the East.* London: J. Murray, 1876.

Glenny, M. *The Balkans 1804-1999: Nationalism, War and the Great Powers.* London: Granta, 1999.

Golovin, A. F. *Furst Alexander I von Bulgarien, 1879-1886.* Vienna: Carl Fromme, 1896.

Hall, D. and Danta, D. *Reconstructuring the Balkans: A Geography of the New Southeast Europe.* Chichester: John Wiley, 1996.

Hall, R. C. *The Balkan Wars 1912-1913: Prelude to the First World War.* London: Routledge, 2000.

Hamilton, J. and Hamilton, B. *Christian Dualist Heresies in the Byzantine World c.650-c.1405.* Manchester: Manchester University Press, 1998.

Hammond, P. *With Liberty for All. Freedom of Religion in the United States.* Louisville, Kentucky: Westminster John Knox Press, 1998.

Handelsman, M. *Adam Czartoryski.* Warsaw: Naukowego Warsawskiego, 1949.

Held, J. *Populism in Eastern Europe: Racism, Nationalism and Society.* Boulder, CO: East European Monographs, 1996.

Helmreich, E. C. *The Diplomacy of the Balkan Wars, 1912-1913.* Cambridge, MA: Harvard University Press, 1938.

Hobsbawn, E. *Nations and Nationalism Since 1780: Programme, Myth, Reality.* Cambridge: Cambridge University Press, 1992.

Hristov, H. *Bulgaria 1300 Years.* Sofia: Sofia Press, 1980.

Hupchick, D. P. *The Bulgarians in the 17th Century: Slavic Orthodox Society and Culture Under Ottoman Rule.* Jefferson, NC: McFarland, 1993.

———. *The Balkans: From Constantinople to Communism.* New York: Palgrave Macmillan, 2004.

Inalcik, H. and Quataert, D., eds. *An Economic and Social History of the Ottoman Empire, 1300-1914.* Cambridge: Cambridge University Press, 1994.

James, P. *Nation Formation. Towards a Theory of Abstract Community.* London: SAGE, 1996.

Jelavich, C. and B. *The Establishment of the Balkan National States, 1804-1920.* Seattle: University of Washington Press, 1977.

Jirecek, C. J. *Geschichte der Bulgaren.* Prague: F. Tempsky, 1876.

John Paul II, Pope. Encyclical Epistle Slavorum Apostoli of His Holiness John Paul II: In Commemoration of the Eleventh Centenary of the Evangelising Work of Sts. Cyril and Methodius. London: Catholic Truth Society, 1985.

Kanitz, F. *Donau-Bulgarien und der Balkan: Historisch-geographisch-ethnographische Reistudien.* Leipzig: H. Fries, 1875.

Kantor, M. *The Medieval Slavic Lives of Saints and Princes.* Ann Arbor: University of Michigan, 1983.

Karal, E. Z. *Osmanli Tarihi: Islahat Fermani devri 1861-1876.* Ankara: Turk Tarih Kurumu Basimevi, 1956.

Karpat, K. *The Turks of Bulgaria: The History, Culture and Political Fate of a Minority.* Istanbul: Isis, 1990.

Kiel, M. *Art and Society of Bulgaria in the Turkish Period. A Sketch of the Economic, Juridical and Artistic Preconditions of Bulgarian Post-Byzantine Art and its Place in the Development of the Art of the Christian Balkans, 1360/70-1700. A New Interpretation.* Assen/Maastricht: Van Gorcum, 1985.

Kiraly, B. K. *Tolerance and Movements of Religious Dissent in Eastern Europe.* Boulder, CO: East European Monographs, 1975.

Kofos, E. *Nationalism and Communism in Macedonia.* Thessalonica: Institute for Balkan Studies, 1964.

Kohn, H. *The Idea of Nationalism. A Study in its Origins and Background.* New York: Macmillan, 1961.

Konobiev, V. D. *The National Freedom Movement in Bulgaria, 1829-1830.* Sofia: Sofia Press, 1972.

Kostadinova, T. *Bulgaria 1879-1946: The Challenge of Choice.* Boulder, CO: East European Monographs, 1995.

Lang, D. M. *The Bulgarians from Pagan Times to the Ottoman Conquest.* London: Thames & Hudson, 1976.

Laourdas, B. and Westernik, L. G. *Epistulae et Amphilochia Photii Patriarchae Constantinopolitani,* Vol. 1. Leipzig: Teubner, 1983.

Lemberg, E. *Nationalismus. Band 2: Soziologie und politische Padagogik.* Hamburg: Rowohlt, 1964.

Logio, G. C. *Bulgaria: Past and Present.* Manchester: Sherratt & Hughes, 1936.

MacDermott, M. *The Apostle of Freedom: A Portrait of Vasil Levsky Against a Background of Nineteenth Century Bulgaria.* Sofia: Sofia University Press, 1979.

_____. *History of Bulgaria 1393-1885.* London: Jessica Kingsley, 1982.

McCarthy, J. *The Ottoman Turks: An Introductory History to 1923.* London: Longman, 1997.

Madol, H. R. *Ferdinand of Bulgaria: The Dream of Byzantium.* London: Hunt & Blackett, 1933.

Mahon, M. *The Politics of Nationalism Under Communism in Bulgaria: Myths, Memories and Minorities.* Unpublished Ph.D. thesis, SSEES/2000/01.

Mardin, S. *The Genesis of Young Ottoman Thought: A Study in the Modernization of Turkish Political Ideas.* Princeton: Princeton University Press, 1962.

Marriott, J. A. R. *The Eastern Question: A Study in European Diplomacy.* Oxford: Clarendon Press, 1940.

Martin, D. *A General Theory of Secularization.* Oxford: Blackwell, 1978.

Mazower, M. *The Balkans.* London: Weidenfeld & Nicolson, 2000.

Medlicott, W. N. *The Congress of Berlin and After: A Diplomatic History of the Near Eastern Settlement, 1878-1880.* London: Methuen, 1938.

Meinecke, F. *Weltburgertum und Nationalstaat: Studien zur Genesis des deutschen Nationalstaates.* Munich: Oldenbourg, 1919.

Meininger, T. A. *Ignatiev and the Establishment of the Bulgarian Exarchate 1864-1872: A Study in Personal Diplomacy.* Madison: University of Wisconsin, 1970.

Memisoglu, H. *Bulgarian Oppression in Historical Perspective.* Ankara: Devran Matbaasi Necatibey Cad., 1989.

Merdjanova, I. *Religion, Nationalism, and Civil Society in Eastern Europe: The Postcommunist Palimpsest.* Lampeter: Edwin Mellen Press, 2002.

Meyendorff, J. *The Orthodox Church: Its Past and its Role in the World Today.* Crestwood, NY: St. Vladimir's Seminary Press, 1996.

Midhat, A. H. *The Life of Midhat Pasha: A Record of his Services, Political Reforms, Banishment, and Judicial Murder Derived from Private Documents and Reminiscences.* London: J. Murray, 1903.

Migne, J. P. *Patrologiae cursus completes.* Paris: Apud Garnieri Fratres, 1844.

Mikat, P. *Geschichte – Recht – Religion – Politik*, Vol. 2. Munich: Paderborn, 1994.

Mojzes, P. B. *A History of the Congregational and Methodist Churches in Bulgaria and Yugoslavia.* Unpublished Ph.D. dissertation, Dept. of Theology, Boston University, 1965.

_____. *Religious Liberty in Eastern Europe and the USSR before and after the Great Transformation.* Boulder, CO: East European Monographs, 1992.

Moravcsik, G. *Constantine Porphyrogenitus De Adminisitrando Imperio.* Budapest: Pazmany Peter Tudomanyegyetemi Gorog Filologial Intezet, 1949.

Neale, A. *Travels through some parts of Germany, Poland, Moldova and Turkey.* London: Longman, Hurst, Rees, Orme and Brown, 1818.

Nestrova, T. *American Missionaries among the Bulgarians (1858-1912).* Boulder, CO: East European Monographs, 1987.

Neuburger, M. *The Orient Within: Muslim Minorities and the Negotiation of Nationhood in Modern Bulgaria.* Ithaca, NY: Cornell University Press, 2004.

Nicoloff, A. *The Bulgarian Resurgence.* Cleveland: A. Nicoloff, 1987.

Obolensky, D. *The Bogomils: A Study in Balkan Neo-Manichaeism.* Cambridge: Cambridge University Press, 1948.

_____. *The Byzantine Commonwealth: Eastern Europe 500-1453.* London: Phoenix Press, 1971.

_____. *Six Byzantine Portraits.* Oxford: Clarendon Press, 1988.

_____. *Byzantium and the Slavs.* Crestwood, NY: St. Vladimir's Seminary Press, 1994.

Ostrogorsky, G. *History of the Byzantine State.* New Brunswick, NJ: Rutgers University Press, 1969.

Outendirck, F. *La Turquie a propos l'Exposition Universalle de 1867.* Paris: Ad. Laine & J. Havard, 1867.

Palmer, A. *The Gardeners of Salonika.* London: Deutsch, 1965.

Papadakis, A. 'The Historical Tradition of Church-State Relations under Orthodox', in P. Ramet, *Eastern Christianity and Politics in the 20th Century.* Durham, 1988. 37-58.

Papadopoullos, T. H. *Studies and Documents Relating to the History of the Greek Church and People under Turkish Domination.* Brussels: De Meester, 1952.

Park, R. E. and Burgess, E. W. *Introduction to the Science of Sociology.* Chicago: University of Chicago Press, 1924.

Pavlowitch, S. K. *A History of the Balkans 1804-1945.* London: Longman, 1999.

Peichich, C. *Speculum veritatus inter orientalem.* Vienna: Societatis Albrizianae, 1725.

Perels, E. *Epistolae Karolini aevi.* Munich: Monumenta Germaniae Historica, 1975.

Petkov, P. M. *United States and Bulgaria in World War I.* Boulder, CO: East European Monographs, 1991.

Popov, K. *Cultural Policy in Bulgaria.* Paris: UNESCO, 1970.

Popovic, A. *L'Islam balkanique: les musulmans du sud-est Européen dans la période post-ottomane.* Berlin: Osteuropa-Institut, 1986.

Pundeff, M. 'Church-State Relations in Bulgaria under Communism', *Religion and Atheism in the USSR*, ed. B. Bociurkiw. 328-350.

Quataert, D. *The Ottoman Empire, 1700-1922.* Cambridge: Cambridge University Press, 2000.

Raikin, S. 'Decapitation of the Orthodox Church in Post-Communism: Bulgaria.' Unpublished manuscript: Stroudsburg, PA, August 1997.

_____. *Rebel with a Just Cause: A Political Journey against the Winds of the 20th Century.* Sofia: Pensoft, 2001.

Ramet, S. P. *Religion and Nationalism in Soviet and East European Politics.* Durham: Duke University Press, 1984.

_____. *Eastern Christianity and Politics in the 20th Century.* Durham: Duke University Press, 1988.

_____. *Nihil Obstat: Religion, Politics and Social Changes in East-Central Europe and Russia.* Durham: Duke University Press, 1988.

_____. *Social Currents in Eastern Europe: The Sources and Meaning of the Great Transition.* Durham: Duke University Press, 1991.

Riggs, C. T. *History of Mehmed the Conqueror by Kritobulos.* Princeton: Princeton University Press, 1954.

Riis, C. *Religion, Politics, and Historiography in Bulgaria.* Boulder, CO: East European Monographs, 2002.

Rohrmoser, G. *Religion und Politik in der Krise der Moderne.* Graz: Styria, 1989.

Rossos, A. *Russia and the Balkans: Inter-Balkan Rivalries and Russian Foreign Policy, 1908-1914.* Toronto: University of Toronto Press, 1981.

Runciman, S. *A History of the First Bulgarian Empire.* London: G. Bell & Sons, 1930.

Saab, A. P. *Reluctant Icon: Gladstone, Bulgaria and the Working Class, 1856-1878.* London: Harvard University Press, 1991.

Safarik, P. J. *Geschichte der Slavischen Sprache und Literatur nach allen Mundarten.* Ofen: Schriften University, 1826.

Samuelson, J. *Bulgaria Past and Present: Historical, Political and Descriptive.* London: Trubner, 1888.

Schenker, A. M. *The Dawn of Slavic: An Introduction to Slavic Philology.* New Haven: Yale University Press, 1995.

Schieder, T. *Nationalismus und Nationalstaat: Studien zum nationalen Problem im modernen Europa.* Gottingen: Vandenhoech and Ruprecht, 1991.

Schmemann, A. *The Historical Road of Eastern Orthodoxy.* London: Harvill Press, 1963.

Shannon, R. *Gladstone and the Bulgarian Agitation, 1826.* London: Harvester Press, 1975.

Shaw, S. J. *History of the Ottoman Empire and Modern Turkey. Vol. II. Reform, Revolution and Republic: The Rise of Modern Turkey, 1808-1975.* Cambridge: Cambridge University Press, 1977.

Simeonova, L. *Diplomacy of the Letter and the Cross: Photius, Bulgaria and the Papacy, 860s-880s.* Amsterdam: A. M. Hakkert, 1998.

Simsir, B. N. *The Turks of Bulgaria (1878-1985).* London: K. Rustem & Brother, 1988.

Skatula, E. *Valka na Balkane: Valecne tazeni Bulharska, Srbska, Recka a Cerne Hory proti Turecku.* Prague, 1913.

Skendi, S. *Balkan Cultural Studies.* Boulder, CO: East European Monographs, 1980.

Smith, A. D. *The Ethnic Origins of Nations.* Oxford: Blackwell, 1986.

_____. *National Identity.* London: Penguin, 1991.

Stavrianos, L. S. *The Balkans since 1453.* New York: Holt, Rinehart & Winston, 1958.

_____. *Balkan Federation: A History of the Movement toward Balkan Unity in Modern Times.* Hamden: Archon Books, 1964.

Stoyanov, Y. *The Hidden Tradition in Europe: The Secret History of Medieval Christian Heresy.* New York: Arkana, 1994.

Sugar, P. F. and Lederer, I. J., eds. *Nationalism in Eastern Europe.* Seattle: University of Washington Press, 1969.

Sullivan, R. E. *Christian Missionary Activity in the Early Middle Ages.* Aldershot: Variorum, 1994.

Tachiaos, A. N. 'The Cult of Saint Methodius in the Byzantino-Slavonic World', in *Christianity Among the Slavs: The Heritage of Saints Cyril and Methodius,* eds. E. G. Farrugia, R. F. Taft, G. K. Piovesana. Rome: Pontifical Oriental Institute, 1988.

Testa, I. *Recueil des traits de la porte ottomane avec les puissances estranges.* Paris: Amyot, 1864.

Theophanes. 'Chronographia', *Гръцки извори за български история (Greek Sources for Bulgarian History.* Sofia: BAN, 1954.

Thompson, E. P. *Beyond the Frontier: The Politics of a Failed Mission, Bulgaria 1944.* Woodbridge: Merlin Press, 1997.

Todorov, N. *The Balkan City 1400-1900.* Seattle: University of Washington Press, 1983.

_____. *Society, the City and Industry in the Balkans, 15th-19th Centuries.* Aldershot: Ashgate, 1988.

338   The Bulgarian Orthodox Church

Todorov, T. *The Fragility of Goodness: Why Bulgaria's Jews Survived the Holocaust*. Princeton: Princeton University Press, 1999.
Todorova, M. *Balkan Identities: Nation and Memory*. London: C. Hurst & Co., 2004.
Tsvetkov, P. *A History of the Balkans*. San Francisco: California University Press, 1993.
Undzhiev, I. N. *Vassil Levsky: The Great Bulgarian Patriot and Revolutionary Democrat*. Sofia: State Printing House, 1953.
Varga, I. 'Orthodoxy, Modernity and Post-Communism', *Religions Sans Frontieres*, ed. R. Ciprian. 144-149.
Vasiliev, A. A. *History of the Byzantine Empire 324-1453*, Vol. 1. Madison: University of Wisconsin Press, 1952.
Vazov, I. *Under the Yoke*. Sofia: Foreign Language Press, 1960.
von Mach, R. *The Bulgarian Exarchate: Its History and the Extent of its Authority in Turkey*. London: T. Fisher Unwin, 1907.
Ware, T. *The Orthodox Church*. Harmondsworth: Penguin, 1993.
Zaehner, R. C. *Zurvan: A Zoroastrian Dilemma*. Oxford: Clarendon Press, 1955.

Articles
Angelov, B. 'The Russian Orthodox Church in the 17th Century – Reform and Schism', *BHR*, 3(1995): 14-31.
Broun, J. 'The Schism in the Bulgarian Orthodox Church', *Religion, State and Society* 21/2(1993): 207-220.
_____. 'The Schism in the Bulgarian Orthodox Church, Part 2: Under the Socialist Government, 1993-97', *Religion, State and Society* 28/3(2000): 263-289.
_____. 'The Schism in the Bulgarian Orthodox Church, Part 3: Under the Second Union of Democratic Forces Government, 1997-2001', *Religion, State and Society* 30/4(2002): 365-394.
_____. 'The Bulgarian Orthodox Church: the Continuing Schism and the Religious, Social and Political Environment', *Religion, State and Society* 32/3(2004): 209-245,
Cankova-Petkova, G. 'Contribution au sujet de la conversion des Bulgares au christianisme', *Byzantino-Bulgarica* IV(1973): 21-39.
Cohen, E. and Kanev, K. 'Religious Freedom in Bulgaria', *Journal of Ecumenical Studies* 36(Winter-Spring 1999): 243-264.
Devos, P. and Meyvaert, P. 'Trois enigmas Cyrillo-Methodiennes de la Legende Italique resolues grace a un dicument inedit', *Annalecta Bollandiana* 73(1955): 375-461.
Duichev, I. 'Au lendemain de la conversion du people bulgare (L'epitre de Photius)', *Medioevo Bizantino-Slavo* (Rome: Vatican City), I(1965): 107-109.
Geanakoplos, D. J. 'Religion and Nationalism in the Byzantine Empire and After: Conformity and Pluralism', *The Greek Orthodox Theological Review* 22(1977):98-116.
Giuselev, V. 'Photius' Constantinople Model of Christian Leadership', *Slavische Sprachen* 9(1985).

Groen, J. 'Eastern Orthodoxy in the Balkan, Nationalism and Reconciliation', *Exchange: Journal of Missiological and Ecumenical Research* 27/2(1998): 121-140.

Inalcik, H. 'Ottoman Methods of Conquest', *Studia Islamica* II(1954): 103-129.

Kalkandjieva, D. 'The Abolition of the Bulgarian Schism (22 February 1945)', (unpublished article). Sofia, 2000.

Kiel. M. 'Nevrokop', *Encyclopaedia of Islam*, Vol. 8. Leiden: Brill, 1995. 9-11.

Kitromilides, P. M. 'Imagined Communities' and the Origins of the National Question in the Balkans, *European History Quarterly* 19(1989): 149-192.

Kusseff, M. 'Vita St. Naoum', *The Slavonic and East European Review* XXIX(1950-51): 142.

Kuzmic, P. 'Christian Mission in Europe', *Themelios* 18(1992): 23.

Ley, M. 'Historische und theoretische Überlegungen zum Nationalismus', *Das Ende des Nationalismus*. Vienna: WUV, 1996.

Lowry, H. W. 'Changes in the Fifteenth-Century Ottoman Peasant Taxation: The Case Study of Radilofo', *Continuity and Change in Late Byzantine and Early Ottoman Society*. Centre for Byzantine Studies: University of Birmingham, 1986.

Merdjanova, I. 'In Search of Identity: Nationalism and Religion in Eastern Europe', *Religion, State and Society* 28/3(2000): 233-262.

Mpegzos, M. 'Ethnikismos: ho echthros tou ethnous', *Kath' Hodon* 1(1992): 18-26.

Neuburger, M. 'The Russo-Turkish War and the 'Eastern Jewish Question': Encounters Between Victims and Victors in Ottoman Bulgaria', *East European Jewish Affairs* 26(Winter 1996): 53-66.

Nitzova, P. 'Islam in Bulgaria: A Historical Re-appraisal', *Religion, State and Society* 22/1(1994): 97-102.

Pantazopoulos, N. 'Church and Law in the Balkan Peninsula during the Ottoman Rule', *Institute for Balkan Studies* 92(1967).

Popov, S. 'Perestroika Without Christ? An Eastern Orthodox Perspective', *Religion in Eastern Europe* 11(1991): 8-17.

Raikin, S. T. 'The Communists and the Bulgarian Orthodox Church, 1944-48, the Rise and Fall of Exarch Stefan', *Religion in Communist Lands* 12(1984): 281-292.

_____. 'Successes and Failures of Atheism in Bulgaria (2 parts)', *RCDA* 27(Spring 1988): 55-58, 27(Summer 1988): 88-92.

_____. 'The Predicaments of the Bulgarian Orthodox Church Today', *Religion in Eastern Europe* 12(1992): 18-31.

_____. 'Schism in the Bulgarian Orthodox Church', *Religion in Eastern Europe* 13(1993): 19-25, 1993.

Sarieva, I. 'Some Problems of the Religious History of Bulgaria and Former Yugoslavia', *Religion, State and Society* 15(1995): 1-23.

Sarova, K. 'Les Bulgares dans la politique balkanique de l'émigration polonaise (1842-1843)', *BHR* 2(1974): 34-52.

Stoikov, V. 'The Religious and Social Importance of the Works of St. Sofrony of Vraca', *Journal of the Moscow Patriarchate* 11(1989): 56-59.

Sugareff, V. K. 'The Constitution of the Bulgarian Revolutionary Central Committee', *Journal of Modern History* IV (December 1932): 572-580.

Summer, B. H. 'Ignatyev at Constantinople, 1864-1874', *Slavonic and East European Review* XI(January 1933).

Todorova, M. 'Historiography of the Countries of Eastern Europe: Bulgaria', *American Historical Review* 97(1992): 1105-1117.

Trubetskoi, G. 'La Politique russe en Orient: Le Schisme bulgare, 1854-1872', *Revue d'histoire diplomatique* XXI(1907): 162-67.

Velikonja, M. 'Historical Roots of Slovenian Christoslavic Mythology', *Religion in Eastern Europe* 19(1999): 15-32.

Walters, P. 'Overcoming the Old, Greeting the New', *Religion, State and Society* 25/1(1997): 11-101.

Witte, J. and Mojzes, P. 'Pluralism, Proselytism and Nationalism in Eastern Europe', *Journal of Ecumenical Studies* 36(Winter-Spring 1999): 1-268.

Wolff, R. E. 'The Second Bulgarian Empire. Its Origin and History to 1204', *Speculum* XXIV/2(1949): 167-206.

Zhelyazkova, A. 'Social Aspects of the Process of Islamization in the Balkan Possessions of the Ottoman Empire', *Etudes Balkaniques* 3(1985): 107-122.